My Life with
Jacqueline Kennedy

MY LIFE WITH

JACQUELINE
KENNEDY

by

MARY BARELLI GALLAGHER

edited by

Frances Spatz Leighton

DAVID McKAY COMPANY, INC.   New York

My Life with Jacqueline Kennedy

Fourth printing, October, 1969

Library of Congress Catalog Card Number: 77-97224

MANUFACTURED IN THE UNITED STATES OF AMERICA

VAN REES PRESS • NEW YORK

In loving memory of
my parents
Mr. and Mrs. Peter Barelli
whose unselfish love
always inspired and guided me

And with my deepest gratitude
to those
whose personal sacrifices and contributions
played a major part
in making my career possible:
My husband, Raymond
Our sons, Christopher and Gregory
My mother-in-law, Mrs. Ann Gallagher

I acknowledge
with sincerest thanks and appreciation
the kind help I received
in writing this book
from my
Editorial Assistant,
Frances Spatz Leighton

Contents

Illustrations between pages 182 and 183.

PART ONE

ONE FOOT IN CAMELOT

1 ∾ "THE MOST WELL-KEPT SECRET"

*S*OME WOMEN ARE BORN TO BE QUEEN—OR
its equivalent. Jacqueline Bouvier Kennedy Onassis is such a
woman. Born to cause excitement wherever she goes, to
attract all eyes. Always at the very center—and yet aloof
from it.

Born to exact homage, to be a law unto herself, to be
obeyed, sought after.

Born to have power, to be envied, followed, copied,
watched—and to be worshipped.

That is the woman called Jacqueline—the woman who has
become a living legend.

Once in a generation does a woman possess such magnetism that the world is spellbound by her, seeing only what
she wants it to see. And even when the spell is broken, people
still wonder; they still ask what actually happened, what is
Jackie Kennedy really like? What was real, and what was
the dream?

I can tell you that not everything was as it seemed.

I know, because for eight incredible years I lived in Jackie's
world as her Personal Secretary, before, during, and after
John F. Kennedy entered the White House.

She remarried, and a nation awakened to find that Camelot
is no more—in my mind Camelot was where she lived with a
modern King Arthur, the place where dreams came true.

To me, Mrs. Kennedy was always "Jackie" when we were
speaking in private. I never called her "Mrs. Kennedy," except
when speaking of her to others. And Jackie would call me

"Mary," or "Sweet Mary" if she were especially pleased with me or in a very light-hearted mood.

First Families are a part of history. I have been a part of history in my relationship with this First Family. Long after I am gone, historians will be using my recollections to understand more fully the man who was the 35th President and his life and times. I think he would want it that way.

As for my own presence in the White House, there was a curtain of silence. It was one of the many things that made even my friends and neighbors wonder, "Just what *does* Mary do?" They knew I had the White House phone in my kitchen. They saw it there. They knew a chauffeur-driven limousine with White House license plates drove up to the house every morning and that someone held the door open while I got in. I merely told them I was Mrs. Kennedy's secretary.

Jackie did not wish it known that she had a personal secretary, and I went right along with it so as not to distress her. It seemed that she wanted the public to feel that it was having direct contact with her—the wife of the President.

So I kept out of the public eye.

In fact, when William Manchester, doing research for his much-publicized book *Death of a President,* was introduced to me on April 2, 1964, by JFK's secretary Evelyn Lincoln, Manchester shook my hand with disbelief. "You are the most well-kept secret of the whole Administration!" he said. And I understood his amazement.

As a matter of fact, I was the only member of her professional staff to be with her in the living quarters. And how I remember those days in the Treaty Room, when the table was piled so high with Jackie's mail and folders of things to do that she would come in and hold her head at the sight of it. I was never safe from dictation. Even at night, Jackie would call me at home, saying, "Oh, Mary, I just have a few things I wanted to get off my mind," and I would start writing in shorthand.

It is very amusing that in the book of Pierre Salinger (the President's Press Secretary) he says Jackie was "an inveterate memoranda writer" and wrote them "all in longhand." Not by a long shot.

The funniest thing that I can remember about her dictation happened the day that I finally found myself with some time off. I had decided to run off to the swimming pool of my neighborhood club in Alexandria, Virginia, near my home, and was looking forward to a day of just lolling beside the water, vegetating.

For once I felt safe. Jackie was out of Washington and surely wouldn't need me. Still, just from habit, I did take a tiny notebook off the telephone stand at home and a pencil. I had hardly sunk into a chaise lounge beside the pool when the lifeguard hurried over to say I was wanted on the phone.

It was Jackie with a few thoughts, and I reached for my notebook automatically. A half-hour later, I was still standing in a pretzel shape there, while the manager watched amazed. My head held the phone box open, and with my left leg I was barely able to remain standing. My right knee became the desk for my notebook. With my left hand, I held the receiver of the phone as I wrote furiously away!

I didn't break Jackie's train of thought. It was my pride that I never asked anything over a second time. I got it down. I checked later. Soon I was signaling the lifeguard wildly for more paper. He gave me pool schedules. I turned them over.

I should have won an award just for maintaining my position without losing balance. After I was through, the worried manager said, "Mrs. Gallagher, we can provide you a little office if you are going to have much work to do here. Let me show you."

"No, thanks, Mr. Saunders," I said, "I doubt that I'll be spending much time here. It wouldn't be worth your trouble." Jackie would always be that way! Or so I thought.

I was sure that I knew Jackie. I was sure that, regardless of where Jackie was, she would always be calling in with something on her mind. And, somehow, as I envisioned the years ahead, even after her husband's assassination, I always thought that her life and activities would revolve around her role as a Kennedy and the First Lady.

When the headlines broke out about Jackie's marriage to Onassis, I must admit that I wasn't different from the rest of the world. Even with my inside view, it came as a complete shock to me. In fact, I couldn't make myself believe it and waited twenty-four hours for continuing reports and news stories to confirm it.

If you wonder whether I ever saw Aristotle Onassis at the White House, the answer is yes, just once—I'll eventually get to that—but I attached not too much significance to it.

I had never thought that Jackie would remarry. I fully believed that she would remain tied to the Kennedy name for the rest of her life, devoting herself completely to the perpetuation of the President's name and the Kennedy Library and all the works of a cultural nature connected with it.

2 ∾ INTO THE KENNEDY WORLD

I REALLY SHOULD TELL HOW I HAPPENED TO get caught up in the Kennedy world in the first place. It's a most amusing story, looking back—a sort of name game.

In 1944, when I was a wide-eyed girl just out of high school, I was proud to be chosen for a job interview because I was top of my class in shorthand and typing. The name of the man who hired me for my first job at the Hollingsworth and Whitney Paper Company was—John *H.* Kennedy.

How could I know that for the next twenty years I would never be without a *Kennedy* in my life?

For 8½ years, I remained with this top paper company, rising to become secretary to two men—the Vice President in

Charge of Sales, J. B. Cowie, and his assistant, L. B. Abbiati.

I left because of another Kennedy, John F. Kennedy.

The man who brought this about was P. Kenneth O'Donnell, a former salesman who had left the company to work for the Senatorial candidate, John F. Kennedy. The year was 1952. It was November, in fact, when Kenny O'Donnell returned to see Mr. Abbiati. I was especially curious about his visit because three months before, when Kenny left, he had asked me to go along to work for him.

My curiosity about that visit built up until that Friday when we were leaving the office. I said, "Mr. Abbiati, aren't you going to do anything to help Kenny get his old job back?" I had assumed *that* was what Kenny was back for.

Mr. Abbiati looked at me strangely and seemed reluctant to discuss the matter, so I dropped it.

I was just about to leave then when he suddenly said, "Kenny's visit had nothing at all to do about his job—actually he was asking about your going to Washington to work for Senator Kennedy."

I laughed, thinking he was kidding me, but he said, "I'm not joking. Kenny left it to me to decide whether or not I should mention it to you. The only reason I'm telling you, now, is because I know your mother and father will never allow you to go."

He was right in that we were a close-knit Italian family, but I was thrilled at the opportunity.

"I'm glad you did tell me," I said. "Thanks. I'll ask my parents and see how they take it." How strange—if I hadn't asked Mr. Abbiati about Kenny, my whole life would have been different—no John F. Kennedy, no White House.

My parents were proud. If Washington was calling, maybe I'd better answer the call.

The girls at the office were as excited as I, and on the day of my scheduled interview with the man they considered the most glamorous bachelor in Washington, they were almost as nervous.

I was to report to the Senator's Bowdoin Street apartment

there in Boston. As I climbed the flight of stairs and knocked on the door, I could feel my knees tremble a bit, but soon I was in the living room answering the girl at the desk, who asked my name.

"Miss Barelli," I said. "I have an appointment with Senator Kennedy."

"Oh yes," she acknowledged, "the Senator's expecting you."

Now my knees were trembling even more. Every chair was filled. There wasn't a bare spot to be found anywhere—newspapers literally covered chairs, table, and every inch of the floor from one end of the room to the other. The secretary was busily clipping away, so I stood and waited. Fortunately, it was for only a minute or two.

Then the door to the next room opened, and before I knew it, I was being warmly greeted by the magnetic, smiling man who had emerged in his stocking feet and rolled-up shirt sleeves. I was amazed to see that it was the Senator himself. His hand outstretched, he shook mine tightly, and he almost shouted, "Oh hi, there. How are you? Come on in."

Whether it was his handshake, his strong voice, or his extremely informal appearance, I really don't know—but my knees suddenly steadied as I followed him into his bedroom.

He closed the door. Pointing to one of the twin beds, he offered me a seat as he sat on the other.

I was glad my parents couldn't see all this informality. The new Senator asked several questions about my experience, but he seemed particularly interested in my aptitude for the Italian language. We all spoke Italian at home.

The interview lasted about ten or fifteen minutes. And as I left, he thanked me for coming and said "I'll have Kenny call you in a few days."

Regardless of the outcome, I thought, at least I had met our newly elected Senator from Massachusetts, who with his natural easygoing manner was so full of warmth and spirit.

Before the week was out, however, I received word that I was hired, and that I "should arrange to be in Washington on January 3rd."

I can see most vividly that final day when I, a secretary who had never ventured from home, said goodbye to my boss, Mr. Cowie—half wondering if I was being rash venturing into the world of politics.

His words now suddenly brought tears to my eyes. "Now, Mary, I'll let you go, but you'll just have to promise that if after three days or three months or three years, you find you don't like Washington, you'll come right back here. Promise?"

Dignified as he was, I could not resist embracing him with a warm hug and a little kiss.

The first thing I noticed when I reported to work on Capitol Hill was that Senator Kennedy occupied a suite of rooms in the Old Senate Office Building—Room #362—located directly across the hall from Vice President Richard M. Nixon—in Room 361.

Initially, Senator Kennedy's staff had consisted of only four secretaries, including my roommate Lois Strode, who was in charge of veterans and military service cases.

I remember our great pride as we "Original Four"—Evelyn, Jean, Lois, and I—were officially sworn in to carry on our new duties.

That was a very interesting situation. Evelyn Lincoln had arrived about a week before. The whole staff was new, except for Ted "T.J." Reardon, his administrative assistant, who had been with the Senator during his years as a Representative from Massachusetts.

It was decided at the outset that Mrs. Lincoln, who had past experience on the Hill, would be his personal secretary. Jean McGonigle, who had campaigned in Boston, was chosen to be receptionist. I handled immigration matters.

Ted Sorensen was hired to be the Senator's legislative assistant, and before long, Lee White had also joined the staff to help on legislative matters. From time to time, the Senator added other aides and secretaries.

As the Senator's popularity increased, he was more and more in demand for speeches around the country, as well as in his home state. For these excursions, it was the responsibility of Muggsy O'Leary—his chauffeur and right hand man—to get the Senator to the airport on time. O'Leary was the Senator's jovial, cigar-chomping, well-padded sidekick. He would leave the car waiting out front and come up to the office.

"Is the boss ready?" he'd ask. Very seldom would the boss be ready. The Senator was almost always oblivious to the time, taking care of last-minute details in his office, or just talking in leisurely fashion on the telephone. Sometimes it was almost too much for everyone's nerves, waiting to see whether Muggsy could make the deadline to the airport. He would stand in the doorway, calmly chewing his cigar, while the rest of us in the office fidgeted.

But when JFK was ready, he was ready. He'd come out of his office and say, "All right there, Muggsy . . . All set?"—as if it were Muggsy who was holding up the works! Off they'd rush, leaving us all to wonder if it could be done—getting him there on time. Eventually Muggsy would return and say, "We had one minute to go," or "We had two minutes," and then there was one day when he came back and said, "They held the plane!"

Along with learning how to handle constituents' problems, we were to master as well the knack of using the Senator's language and style in answering his mail. We each had responsibility to carry through correspondence with any one individual from start to finish, in the Senator's style.

I seemed to have a magic touch with immigration cases, but there was one case that absolutely defied me. It was the case of Toy Lin Chen. The Senator wanted very much to help him. The poor man would be deported unless a private bill to give him permanent status in the United States could be passed through Congress.

Month after month, the Senator and I worked over his case, keeping Toy Lin Chen in the country on temporary extensions. But each time the case came up before the full committee, there was always something more they asked for.

I wanted so much to succeed in this case because JFK had carried it over with him from his days in the House of Representatives. Even though Toy Lin Chen had meanwhile moved from Massachusetts to New Hampshire, the Senator continued to fight for him.

To learn the ins and outs of immigration, I sought help everywhere—from Betty Bryden of Senator Saltonstall's office, from Mrs. Rae Pittarelli of the Visa Office of the Department of State. Eventually, I came to earn the title bestowed on me, "The Immigration Expert."

I was also chosen to be in charge of incoming calls. For some reason, the Senator decided, after testing us all for a "friendly sounding voice," that it should be my voice to be heard on the phone first.

But I was staggered at another assignment. One day Evelyn Lincoln went from desk to desk with the Senator's signature, asking each of us to "copy this."

I copied it as the others had, and she disappeared into the inner office. When she came out, she walked directly to my desk and happily announced, "The Senator thinks you've come closest to copying his signature and would like for you to start signing all of his official outgoing mail. The personal letters he'll continue to do himself."

Since the Senator strongly preferred that his signature look "authentic," I practiced for hours until finally I reached the point where I found it difficult to distinguish *his* "John Kennedy" from my own.

It is interesting that John Fitzgerald Kennedy did not sign his middle initial, except rarely, during his Senate years, though on letters typed by his secretaries, we did use it.

Even in the White House, the President was not consistent in signing his middle initial. Before and during the White House years, some notes sent to me personally were signed with or without the "F.", or simply "Jack."

Sometimes he would stop at my desk at the end of the day and watch for a few minutes as I swiftly wrote his name on one letter after another.

He always had a word of encouragement. "You're doing a great job there, Mary," or, even more heartening, "Terrific!" Or, perhaps, a smile that showed his amused approval at this bit of forgery. One afternoon I said, "Wouldn't it be funny if you were to slip a *check* in here by mistake?" He laughed and walked away. It was clear he thought I would never have to worry about that!

The joke was really on both of us. We didn't imagine that I would eventually become a part of his financial affairs and that I would indeed be signing checks with *my* name, to be paid out of *his* account.

It was amusing to us all that our very wealthy Senator never had enough money in his pockets. Stories among the campaign aides increased every day about the way the Senator was always finding his pockets empty and borrowing some quick, spending money. The men around him would pay for the newspapers, for hamburgers, or for the milk shakes that he dearly loved and be reimbursed later—if they thought of it —from Petty Cash without bothering him. After becoming President, he even borrowed a $5 bill from a Secret Service Agent, before going into church one day, to put into the collection plate.

The Senator had many idiosyncrasies. One was that the door to the outer office must be kept open at all times, to give an available feeling to his constituents. But since he drew everyone like a magnet, the girls in the building were forever peering in the door as they walked by, hoping to catch a glimpse of the man they considered the most vital, most attractive bachelor in Washington.

Even older and very married girls could fall apart over him. One particular afternoon a group of ladies from Massachusetts came into the office and asked if they might see him for a minute or two.

They couldn't have been more thrilled when they were told that he would soon be with them.

Half sitting on the edge of their seats, they chatted gaily as they waited in eager anticipation. Before the Senator came out of his private office, however, the spokeswoman for the group, who was just too bubbly to sit still, practically danced her way over to my desk, starting with general conversation, then reciting her little spiel apparently intended for the Senator. I had the feeling that she must have felt it wise to have this little "rehearsal."

Then the Senator came bounding from his office and approached her directly, offering his outstretched hand and his usual greeting: "Oh, hello there. How are you? So nice to see you."

Now that it was her turn to speak, she was completely spellbound. Clutching his hand, she simply stared into his face—and though her lips were moving, she was absolutely without the voice to carry out her mission.

The Senator understood her predicament, and with his usual aplomb, he skillfully turned his conversation to the rest of the waiting group, and they managed to get their message across. The Senator sorted it all out and showed sincere interest. The ladies departed, leaving no doubt in anyone's mind that this had been a very great moment for all—including the Senator. He was smiling to himself as he went back to his office.

There was only one exception to the "open door policy." That was whenever a favorite singer would come to the offices to visit. Then, the Senator would order the outer door closed and "force" his guest to give a command performance. Everyone stopped work and gathered round to listen. Once when his good friend Morton Downey sang "Danny Boy," there wasn't a dry eye in the office.

Whenever he could, the Senator would get each singer to put his all into JFK's very favorite—"Bill Bailey, Won't You Please Come Home?" That song seemed to match his own exuberance for life. Its peppy rhythm would bring a broad grin as he listened to it.

Another Kennedy talent was his ever-present wit. You could get away with anything if you could turn it into a witticism, somehow.

His own humor was sometimes sophisticated, but could be very earthy, as when he would say, "As the cow said to the farmer, 'Thank you for a warm hand on a cold morning.'"

Once, when he was in a particularly jocular mood, he kept a few members of his staff in his private office entertaining them with his stories—Ted Reardon, Ted Sorensen, and a few others. They had a friendly argument over whether a particular story could be repeated in mixed company, and the Senator laughingly told the men, "Let's test it out on the most naive girl in the office." But at the last minute someone prevailed on him not to tell it, so none of the girls ever heard what *that* story was!

3 ∽ THE SEASON FOR WEDDINGS

*A*S I RECALL, THE FIRST TIME I SAW JACQUE-line Bouvier, she came into the office, looking very young, with tousled, dark short hair. She appeared poised and walked past the girls with friendly greetings.

Availing herself of the open-door policy, she simply walked into the Senator's private office unannounced, and he must have been expecting her, because she did not come out immediately.

Years later, I was to read the memoirs of John H. Davis, Jackie's cousin, in which he told of having lunch with Jackie during the time she was dating Jack Kennedy. I was very much amused to learn that Jackie hesitated to take him too seriously because of his "outlandish ambition." Kennedy had confided to Jackie that he "intended to become President."

The Senator did not talk about his romantic activities, yet

everyone in the office was caught off guard when we read the announcement that it was Jacqueline Bouvier who had captured our bachelor boss.

She had not been the only glamorous girl to pass through that door.

I remember Audrey Hepburn—and I remember how the whole office was so impressed when she walked in. She was as graceful as a swan and carried a long, slim, red umbrella.

Up to that point, a few of us had been aware that the boss liked to go to movies with various girls and that his personal secretary would have to call to make the dates for him—so busy was he. But, somehow, he had managed to find the time to call Jackie himself, as I later learned from Evelyn.

However, in those days that she dated the Senator, her column in the Washington *Times-Herald* was peppered with her sense of humor. Jackie, "The Inquiring Photographer," roamed the city getting comments to her clever and amusing questions.

She was always coming up with something different—one day asking children why Santa's reindeer don't come down the chimney and getting the answer, "They're too fat"; another day, asking pets what they were doing at the veterinarian's and reporting everything from treatments for gout to psychological problems.

Her column, we at the office felt, had a prominent place in her romance with the Senator. Biographers always write of the famous dinner arranged by her friends the Charles Bartletts in June of 1951 at which she was supposed to have met Jack Kennedy as a Congressman. But their romance did not become serious until after she interviewed him as a Senator. She asked him what he thought about Senate Pages, photographed him, and repeated the procedure with his colleague across the hall, Vice President Richard Nixon.

Her column quoted Senator Kennedy as saying, "I've often thought that the country might be better off if we Senators and Pages traded jobs. If such legislation is ever enacted, I'll be glad to hand over the reins to Jerry Hoobler, whom I've often mistaken for a Senator."

Jackie then quoted the Page as telling how Senator Kennedy was always being mistaken for a tourist or Page because of his youthful appearance. "The other day," said Jerry Hoobler, "he wanted to use the special phones, but the cops told him, 'Sorry, Mister, these are reserved for Senators.'"

The story appeared in the *Times-Herald* of April 21, 1953, at which time romance might have been uppermost in her mind because her sister, Lee, had been married just three days before to Michael Canfield.

Within two months of this interview, Jackie's engagement to the Senator was being announced in the same newspaper, on June 25th.

The story making the rounds on Capitol Hill was that at the Bartlett dinner "the young Congressman leaned across the asparagus and asked the pretty girl for a date."

Jackie was the daughter of John Vernou Bouvier III, a New York stockbroker, who had been divorced from her mother when Jackie was quite young. He had not remarried.

It was surprising how many parallels there were between the Senator and Jackie's father. Both had back trouble. Her father had suffered a slipped disk, too.

Both were considerably older. Jack Bouvier had been 14 years older than Jackie's mother, and Jackie was 12 years younger than the Senator. Both were known for their charm and eligibility.

They were also both interested in politics—but from completely different viewpoints. Jackie's father was an out-and-out Republican, who liked the Senator in spite of his political party.

He also liked him in spite of the Senator's father, Joseph P. Kennedy, who had been chosen by President Roosevelt to head the Securities and Exchange Commission. Jack Bouvier felt that many of his problems on Wall Street stemmed from the elder Kennedy's policies.

Later I was to learn that Jackie had considerably held up her engagement announcement a few weeks until after *The*

16 ౸

Saturday Evening Post could run its article on "The Senate's Gay Young Bachelor."

The Senator himself, as I recall, was not too pleased when he saw a copy of the magazine. He grasped it in his hand and frowned. The title, in itself, infuriated him because this was not the image he was trying to project.

Sure, he was a bachelor and, sure, he dated quite a few girls, but that was secondary. He was—and wanted it known that he was—a serious, hard-working Senator from Massachusetts, albeit the junior Senator, who was striving for more important recognition.

I do believe that it was Jacqueline's wit, as much as anything, that set her apart from the crowd of girls who would gladly have married Jack Kennedy. Jacqueline has a freshness of expression and a sort of let-the-chips-fall-where-they-may attitude that can be devastating or funny, depending on which side of the joke you are on.

Busy as he was, the Senator was nice even to the girls in the office. When he would go to "Merrywood," sometimes without Jackie—it was her mother's home—he would invite all of his staff to come along on weekends, and we would swim in the pool.

At this particular time, he was not swimming himself, because of his back problems that had begun with his PT-109 experience during the war. But he thoroughly enjoyed watching others swim as he sat at the edge of the pool, dangling his feet in the water.

One Sunday, as he sat at the shallow end, I was unaware that he was watching as I tried to get up my courage to dive off the high board. It was a particularly high board. I had almost made up my mind to take the plunge when he suddenly called out loudly, "Okay there now, Mary. Let's see you do it!"

That was all I had to hear!

Now that I knew he was watching, my knees started shaking —and, if I had thought I could turn around without falling, I would have crawled back. But, under the circumstances, it seemed the only thing left to do was to close my eyes, hold my nose and—jump!

With a loud splash, the water gurgled in my ears as I hit bottom and sprang up to the surface, only to be met face to face—eyeball to eyeball—by the most tremendous St. Bernard dog I had ever seen!

Everybody, it seemed, had swimming pool privileges around the Senator.

I met Ethel and Robert Kennedy when they were very young marrieds with just two children. In fact, as a single girl, I learned a little bit about married life through them.

What I mean is that during my first two years in Washington, when I worked for the Senator, I—along with my roommate, Lois—was asked on a few occasions to baby-sit for their children Kathleen and Joe—then very young tots. This would happen when the nurse had the night off and Bobby and Ethel wanted to see a movie or had to attend a party. At the time, Bobby and Ethel were living on O Street in Georgetown, and my roommate and I were living at 2500 Q Street.

To reciprocate, Bobby and Ethel invited us to their home for small party get-togethers with friends, including among others, their long-time friend, Dave Hackett.

These were gay, informal affairs, even though the butler lent a most incongruous note with his formal appearance as he graciously passed around drinks from a constantly replenished tray.

My first Old Fashioned at the Bobby Kennedys', incidentally, quickly taught me that one had to be "steady on deck" handling the tumblers they were served in. They were huge and required *both* hands to insure a steady grip.

If one had the slightest inclination to reach for, and manipulate, a tasty snack along with the drink, it just couldn't be done. So not too much food was consumed, as long as one was drinking.

At the end of one such party, Lois and I gallantly stepped

18 ੬ఞ

forward when Ethel asked for volunteers to prepare the after-midnight breakfast-feast. Ethel was most appreciative and, with much glee, showed us the kitchen, throwing open doors to the refrigerator and cabinets.

There were a dozen or so guests to be fed and, between the two of us, we made record time in preparing and serving our first meal in "bulk" form. I can still recall the happy, wide-eyed, grateful expression, mixed with disbelief, that came over Ethel's face when our mission was accomplished.

In the days before her marriage to the Senator, Jackie appeared to be carefree and gay, with a ready smile. I would have guessed she was an extrovert. But, as I got to know her in her Georgetown home, I discovered that her manner was really rather reserved and introverted—living more within herself than enjoying having people around her.

By the time she got to the White House, it was as though she had developed an "aloof" air, with everyone having to come to her.

That wonderful summer of 1953, was suddenly the season for weddings.

First came Eunice Kennedy's wedding in May to Sargent Shriver, to which all of us in the office received invitations. After the beautiful ceremony at St. Patrick's Cathedral in New York, the reception followed at the Waldorf-Astoria. The dominant song was "April in Portugal," and, to this day, I never hear it without thinking of Eunice. That was the first time I ever drank pink champagne—it flowed beautifully, from several magnificent fountains!

Eunice was the Kennedy sister we saw most often. She would come bounding into the office, always with some message or other for the Senator, asking that we get so-and-so on the line for her, and so on. When her business was over with, she'd flash out as fast as she'd flashed in. By nature, she was quick and fast-talking, and like her brother, she had a solution to every problem.

Since the Kennedys were noted for their wealth, it always surprised me to see Eunice with her hair flying and, like her brother, totally unconcerned about clothes—sometimes with runs in her stockings or run-down heels. But her quick visits always seemed to have an exhilarating effect on the office.

In September, the Senator's own spectacular wedding to Jacqueline Bouvier took place at Newport, Rhode Island. I was there, caught in the crush of guests and cameras and reporters and spectators. I was afraid the bridal car would be overturned. Poor Jacqueline, I thought, that's what comes of capturing the most sought-after bachelor.

The Senator had extended personal invitations to everyone in the office to attend his wedding to Jackie on the 12th of September. None of us would have dreamed of missing it, even if we had to travel by donkey cart. As it was, a couple of girls from the office and I were lucky enough to manage a ride to the church that morning with Larry O'Brien and his wife. He had been one of the Senator's campaign managers.

Driving wasn't easy. At St. Mary's Church, there were mobs of people, inside and out. For a few minutes, I didn't know whether I was coming to a County Fair or to a wedding.

I felt quite lucky to have a seat right on the aisle for a close view of Jackie and her bridal party as they passed by. Jackie was on the arm of her stepfather, Hugh D. Auchincloss, but my eyes like everyone else's, were on Jackie.

Her father, Jack Bouvier, had come to Newport and was at a hotel, I later learned, waiting for the big moment. But he had been too ill to participate in his daughter's wedding.

Jackie walked with head held high, and there were admiring gasps, even in this sophisticated assemblage. Her gown was spectacular: of eggshell silk taffeta, with an off-the-shoulder neckline and little cap sleeves. A very wide skirt fell from a tightly fitted waist, and there were circles of ruffles, row on row, on the huge bouffant skirt.

Archbishop Cushing officiated at the ceremony. There was a dramatic moment when the Senator's brother, Bobby, searched frantically for the ring; finally he found it and all was well.

After the ceremony it was bedlam as the bride and groom emerged. People were yelling their congratulations and refused to move, so the newlyweds couldn't get to their car. I was on the steps trapped behind them in the crowd, feeling apprehensive for their safety. Finally the police had to help.

Several hundred cars took the guests to Hammersmith Farm, the Auchincloss estate, for the reception.

The house itself was a tremendous manor set back from the road with a long entrance drive. A battery of attendants were on hand to take the cars and drive them down to the pastures in quick rotation.

The lawn was in bloom with colorful umbrellas, like giant flowers, rising above circular lawn tables. But the wind was causing a little havoc, tumbling over a few of the "flowers," soon righted by the vast staff of servants who were everywhere.

The bridal couple seemed in a gay mood as we went through the receiving line. Jackie gave me a warm greeting as we shook hands and, as for the boss, we girls had a kiss on the cheek for him.

The orchestra played as the guests danced under a canopy. I have a photograph of Jackie and the Senator as they danced the first dance.

When the Senator danced with his mother, it was hard to believe that this slim, youthful woman was actually his mother.

It was fascinating to see for the first time all the people who had been just names to me. The Ambassador, Joseph P. Kennedy, who had been only a voice on the phone; the Senator's kid brother Ted; and all the sisters—but of course we had already had glimpses of them in the office.

I met Jackie's attractive, dark-haired mother, Mrs. Hugh D. Auchincloss, Jackie's sister Lee, her stepbrother, Yusha, and stepsister, Nina, as well as her half-sister and half-brother, Janet and Jamie, 9 and 6.

The women guests were using Jackie's bedroom to powder their noses, and I had never seen a more beautiful bedroom. It was unbelievably large, with a most fantastic feature—the huge white bear rug on the floor. I sighed, wondering how she could leave such a pretty room behind.

Jackie stood at the top of the curved staircase to toss her bridal bouquet.

Before she and the Senator took off for their honeymoon, the Senator wanted to share his good fortune and told us to spend a few days with our families in Boston before returning to Washington.

When the Senator returned from his honeymoon, one of the first things he did was to change his insurance beneficiary to his bride. Evelyn Lincoln and I were the witnesses.

After their marriage Jackie seldom came up to the Hill or visited her husband's office. I remember once, on her way to listen to the Senator give a speech, she poked her head into the doorway to smile and wave—then she was gone again.

As time went on, we sometimes remarked how strange it was, in contrast, that Ethel faithfully visited the Hill during Senate Rackets Committee hearings when Bobby served as legal counsel. We would run into her, bright and eager, as she drove up with several children around her, arriving promptly at 9 A.M. as though she herself were one of the chief counselors!

But Jackie did something else that had quite an impact on the office. As a surprise for the Senator—and, as it turned out, to the rest of us—she had the tremendous sailfish that he had caught during their honeymoon at Acapulco mounted and delivered to his office. It was startling, upon entering his office, to find it there, with its fierce-looking sword. Later it hung in the room opposite the President's office at the White House in what was called "The Fish Room" since FDR days.

Soon after the wedding, we heard that Jackie had decided to take a course in American history at Georgetown University. The no-longer-bachelor Senator maintained a busy schedule in the interest of his constituents and was placed on three committees—Labor and Public Welfare, Government Operations, and the Select Committee on Small Business.

Not too long after his marriage, we noticed the Senator coming into the office on crutches. He tried to appear his normal self with a cheerful "Good morning" as he walked into his office, but as the day wore on, he could not hide the grimaces of pain caused by the pressure on his spine.

No matter how he felt, he kept the crutches out of sight when constituents arrived, walking out to greet them as though there was nothing at all bothering him. I have a picture of him ten months after the wedding, standing on his crutches when he came from the Senate floor to meet my sister, Louise, who had arrived from Boston to visit with me. The Senator was always kind to my family and went out of his way to see them.

We all felt sorry for the Senator as he tried to keep his life as normal as possible and admired him for his courage. On his desk was the coconut shell memento of World War II—the very one that contained his SOS message, carved by him and delivered by a native after his PT-boat 109 was struck by the Japanese. His back had been injured but, in spite of it, he had rescued several of his crew, including one injured man whom he towed to shore, swimming three miles with the man's lifejacket belt clenched between his teeth. But this was not the beginning of the Senator's back trouble. It had actually begun at Harvard when he suffered a ruptured disk while playing football.

The Senator and Jackie were living those first two years of marriage in a rented house, belonging to Blair Childs, on Dent Place, N.W. It was a typical narrow and quaint Georgetown house, adequate for two. I saw the house once when they gave a cocktail party there to which the office staff was invited. Jackie was friendly, making the rounds of the room, staying with each group for several minutes to become acquainted. I recall she commented on the pink dress I was wearing—liking the color and the bustle effect in the back.

It was still the season for weddings and, in spite of his back, the Senator managed to attend his sister Pat's wedding in New York to Peter Lawford, the movie star.

But during the ensuing months, it became quite obvious that his back was getting progressively worse and that something would have to be done about it. He held out until the fall after Congress had adjourned and then entered the New York Hospital for corrective surgery. This was in October, 1954. Unfortunately, infection set in after the operation, and he hovered between life and death for days. Sometimes the doctors themselves didn't expect him to live through the night. Each time, he hung on. Jackie was with him, spending most of her time right by his side.

We, at the office, found ourselves suffering every moment with him, awaiting every new bulletin with extreme anxiety.

It was a great triumph when he was well enough two months later to be flown to Palm Beach—still on a stretcher—for Christmas.

This, however, was not the last of his back operations. Once more he returned to New York for further surgery, and it was not until the end of February that he again left the hospital. This time the operation was successful, and as he lay on his back, he kept himself busy reading stacks of material sent to him from the office.

Upon his release from the hospital, books were sent to him from the Library of Congress to Palm Beach where he was recuperating.

Here is where his book *Profiles in Courage* was born—the book for which he won the Pulitzer Prize. Jackie once told how that book happened to be written. She said the idea had come from reading the life of Edmund Ross a year or so before the operation. He was impressed with the fact that Ross had risked his political life to do what he felt was right in casting the vote that kept President Andrew Johnson from being impeached, and Jackie said he would "try to find similar anecdotes about other men who risked their political careers."

All of us were touched, during these months of operations and convalescence, that one of our most faithful visitors at the office was a Republican—a very prominent Republican. He was our neighbor from across the hall—Vice President Nixon. He never failed to stop by every day for a few minutes, asking about "my friend, Jack"—and remarking on several occasions, "He's one of the finest men I know."

I thought of that a few years later in 1960, when Kennedy was running for the Presidency against his neighbor across the hall and both of them were hurling every insult and barbed comment they could.

The one I liked best was when Kennedy said, "Mr. Nixon has, in the last seven days, called me an economic ignoramus, a Pied Piper, and all the rest. I've just confined myself to calling him a Republican. But he says that is getting low."

The series of weddings went on. The following November, 1954, my roommate, Lois, announced that she was getting married. I remember when she said goodbye, she rubbed my shoulder and said, "I'm passing the same good luck on to you."

She must have, as a month later, I, too, became engaged.

Like my career, it happened as if by fate, rather than any planning on my part. It had been my office friends Katie Griffin and Eleanor Elhajj who forced me to go with them to the Statler Hotel on August 31, 1954, at the time of the National Convention of the American Legion. I wanted to stay in my nice cool apartment, it was so hot, but they insisted we should look up some friends among the Massachusetts Legionnaires.

Somewhere in the crowded hotel lobby, a man asked to borrow my pencil to fill in a coupon for a car raffle. As he tells it now, "I only wanted to borrow a pencil. I didn't expect to end up with the whole girl."

What I remember most about that evening is that I had never laughed so much in my life and that he—his name was Ray Gallagher—was nice enough to take all of us home.

As a return favor, I promised to translate a letter he mentioned getting from an Italian who had been his shoeshine boy in Italy during the war. Surprisingly, there really *was* an

Italian shoeshine boy, and the correspondence goes on with him today, many years and many CARE packages later.

Ray and I were married in April, 1955. I have a lovely 3-page letter handwritten from Jackie to my mother, sent two weeks before my wedding. It told how she and the Senator might or might not make it to the wedding, because "Jack" was still recuperating at Palm Beach. The Senator had even mentioned it to Jackie in the hospital.

That is one of the disarming things about Jacqueline—her sudden acts of kindness, such as this letter to my mother, taking her into her confidence and mentioning how a bad back could be so unpredictable. He had done something silly, bending over to pull out a drawer, and that did it—the back was crippled up again. Up to that point, she said, Jack had been feeling wonderful and walking on the beach over two miles a day. So that had set him back again. He wanted so much to get around on his own two feet and get rid of those "foolish" crutches. Jackie said that if she came up early by herself to get their New York apartment ready, she would come to the wedding in Boston by herself and report all about it to her husband.

Her words of praise for me—how much Jack thought of me—also warmed my mother's heart—and mine.

Jackie did not make it, but a message signed Jack and Jackie arrived at the reception on the day of the wedding.

Among our most treasured possessions today is their wedding gift—an extremely lovely sterling silver serving tray, which we continue to use and cherish deeply.

By the time Ray and I had returned in May from our honeymoon of touring the New England states, the Senator was back in the office after his recuperation period in Palm Beach. In all, he had been away from the office approximately eight months. It was great seeing him there, back to normal.

The open-door policy was stronger than ever now, with so many people coming from everywhere to shake the Senator's hand and welcome him. They didn't realize that he wasn't completely free of the back pressure and that he wore underneath his clothing a special corset-like support. His smile was as ready as ever.

The Senator and Jackie were delighted now to be moving into their first *owned* home. They bought "Hickory Hill," an old historic estate that dated from the Civil War. It was not too far from Washington—just across the Potomac in McLean, Virginia, near "Merrywood," the estate of Jackie's mother and stepfather.

As I approached my first wedding anniversary, I was also approaching the birth of my first child. The girls were getting a little nervous about my billowing figure, but I told them stubbornly that I was not leaving the office until I had cleared up once and for all the one case that had lingered with me from the first day I had come there. This, of course, was that of our old friend, Toy Lin Chen.

Again, it was to come up on the Senate floor—and, this time, I was to represent Senator Kennedy personally at the Judiciary Committee hearing. That preceding weekend, I had spent every minute boning up, preparing myself for any questions the Committee could throw at me—I was ready. The Senator was not about to give up, and neither was I—baby or no baby.

Within twenty-four hours after I had appeared to testify, I had the very great privilege of relaying the exciting news on the telephone to Toy Lin Chen that the Committee had, indeed, acted favorably on his bill, ensuring its final passage by the House of Representatives. We were so excited, Toy Lin Chen and I, that we both cried as we talked. And, when I hung up, the girls in the office were also wiping their eyes.

When the bill came up on the Senate floor, I held my breath—and that afternoon, the Senator stopped by the office to see me. Bounding in and coming directly toward me, he boomed his warmest "Congratulations!" And with his broadest smile, exclaimed, "How did you *ever* do it?"

I was in my final week at the office, just two weeks before the blessed event; and I was busy training my replacement, Helen Lempart of Chicopee, Massachusetts.

Consternation was running high among the girls around me. "If you don't get out of here soon," they bellowed, "we'll have an emergency in the Senate, for sure!"

It was at this particular moment that the Senator returned from the Senate floor, and stopped to inquire how I was feeling. As he stood by my desk, I replied, "Oh, just fine, thank you, Senator. As a matter of fact, I couldn't be feeling better."

He smiled, confidently. "That's great! Then you'll be around for a while longer."

"Well, no, not really," I hurriedly corrected him. "I'm leaving this coming Friday."

He seemed rather perplexed and annoyed as he retorted, "But you just said you felt fine!" He seemed to think that if you felt at all well, it was your duty to carry on.

"Yes," I said, "I know, but you must remember, Senator, first things first."

And now, grinning broadly as though he understood the situation, he was willing to concede that perhaps having a baby was different from having a bad back. He agreed, though still rather reluctantly. "Oh, yes. Yes, I guess you're right."

One of the last things I did before going to the hospital was to send the Senator a letter from home, telling him how much I had enjoyed the years of working for him.

Soon after I got back home from the hospital with my baby son, he unexpectedly wrote me a note and with his typical touch of personal warmth added: "We miss you."

His Pulitzer Prize-winning book, *Profiles in Courage*, arrived shortly after, inscribed with ". . . from her old friend and 'boss.' "

About a month later, when Ray and I carried Christopher into the office for his first "showing," we also brought this much-treasured book to ask the Senator to add just a short inscription to mark our "happy event." Most obligingly, he wrote a line to Christopher, expressing great hope for his future.

But the most thoughtful surprise came in still another note from the office, this one from Evelyn Lincoln. She said that when she had taken the Senator a gift received from Toy Lin

Chen, JFK had said he thought it should go "to Mary."
Evelyn was delighted to be sending it to me.

Accompanying the note was a royal-blue velvet-lined case
containing six sterling silver dessert spoons of exquisite Oriental design.

4 ~ MOTHER AND DAUGHTER

OVER THE NEXT SEVERAL MONTHS, I KEPT
getting calls from the office, asking if I couldn't return. My
answer was always the same. I willingly volunteered that if the
Senator had anything that I might handle for him from home,
I would be more than happy to do so.

The calls stopped, and I thought that was the last of it,
but rather late in the fall of the same year, 1956, I received a
phone call from the Senator's mother-in-law, Mrs. Hugh D.
Auchincloss.

She began the conversation with "Jack suggested I call you."

She needed a personal secretary who could work at "Merrywood" for "about one day a week."

This seemed ideal. Deep inside, I still harbored the hope of
being able to do something, directly or indirectly, for the Senator, whom I so admired. And it would keep me from getting
rusty until that time. Besides, it was somehow "family." Even
if I couldn't be hearing the Senator's great quips or hear him
laugh, it would at least provide a little change from the diaper-
formula routine.

My mother-in-law, Ann Gallagher, agreed to come over and
care for Christopher in my absence.

"Merrywood" was perhaps the loveliest estate I had yet
seen. I felt privileged each time just to be driving my little

red Hudson Jet beyond the entrance gates over the little bridge through the woods and up the circular driveway to the house, where I would be greeted by one or more of the huge, friendly dogs.

When I worked for her mother, it was, in a way, a preview of what life would be like with Jacqueline—a feeling of great wealth, a certain slow pace, and of children cared for by governesses or nannies. A feeling of living a little apart—a little remote.

A butler would answer the doorbell, take my coat, and announce: "Mrs. Auchincloss is ready for you." Or, more often than not, Mrs. Auchincloss herself would be waiting at the top of the curved staircase as I entered. She would call down cheerfully, "Good morning . . . how are you?" and invite me to join her upstairs.

Mrs. Auchincloss was the epitome of the graceful, cultured woman. Her poise, her walk, and her overall manner could have graced any royal house of Europe. She was dark-haired with quiet brown eyes—rather slim. She was of average height, but carried herself so well that she seemed taller.

In the daytime, when I saw her, she always wore only the most conservative colors—grays, browns, and beiges—but the materials were of the finest texture. Her shoes were of the softest leathers with comfortable, medium heels.

Her attitude toward me was so gentle and relaxed that I felt more like a daughter when I arrived at her home than a secretary.

She was a charming person in every respect, and always as meticulously neat—never a hair out of place—as her beautiful home was immaculate and elegantly furnished.

Occasionally, I arrived just as Mr. Auchincloss was leaving for his downtown office, and he, too, never failed to impress me with his very pleasant and courtly manner.

Hugh D. Auchincloss was considerably taller than his wife and had light hair. Somehow his glasses added to his distinguished look as well as his rather heavyset figure. His name was well known in Washington circles because it came first in the firm of Auchincloss, Parker and Redpath—a stockbrokerage.

Now and then, little Janet, about ten or eleven, Jackie's half-sister, named after her mother, would greet me with a polite curtsey. After her formal greeting, she would be sent off to play. Her little brother, Jamie, about three years younger, was seldom in sight, either.

My workday with Mrs. Auchincloss usually began at around 10 A.M., when we would settle down in the little study off the master bedroom—a cozy nook with prettily framed photos of the family all about.

She would sit at her desk and in well-organized fashion proceed with the correspondence, invitations, bills, and miscellaneous matters. She generally finished dictating in an hour or so, and I would go up to the third floor to a desk and typewriter beside a window in a huge sitting room and work for the remainder of the day.

It was a comfortable room for quiet times. There were many family albums and scrapbooks, which rested on a large, round, center table.

It was here, in fact, that I first saw pictures of Jackie and heard of the man to whom she had previously been engaged in New York—the stockbroker, John Husted. It rather surprised me at the time, because I had never heard any mention of it around the office or elsewhere for that matter.

In this palatial home there was a place for everything, and everything was always in its proper place. Even the general atmosphere—silent, cloistered, and peaceful—was most conducive to concentrating and getting my job done.

I often marveled at how the entire household seemed to be run under such masterful control that there was never a servant to be seen, nor a sound to be heard, as the daily chores were being tended to. Not even music.

On the days I reported to "Merrywood" I can't recall seeing Jackie there. But often her name would crop up in conversation between her mother and me.

Jackie had gone through much sadness, I knew. She had lost her first baby in a miscarriage in 1955. She had decorated the nursery at "Hickory Hill," anticipating another baby. During that pregnancy, she had gone with the Senator to the 1956 Democratic National Convention in Chicago, at which time he had narrowly missed out on the Vice Presidential nomination—losing to Senator Estes Kefauver from Tennessee.

Her husband had stayed at a hotel with Torbert MacDonald, while she had stayed with her sister-in-law, Eunice; and Jackie would see him only when he stopped in for a few minutes en route elsewhere.

But the night when things came to a head, and it seemed that he had a chance for the Vice Presidency, Jackie had gone with him to dinner and then to his headquarters.

The excitement of this hectic time apparently proved too much for her, and for the second time she lost her baby. After this tragedy, she did not return to "Hickory Hill," which had such sad memories. They moved back to Georgetown, to a house at 2808 P Street, N.W., rented from Joe Pyne.

Early in 1957, when I was pregnant with my second child, Jackie called me. "I understand you're going out to Mummy's one day a week. Do you suppose you might do the same thing for me?"

I was very happy when my doctor gave me permission to work the "double shift." I now went to "Mummy's" one day or so a week, and at the beginning, one or two days to Jackie's.

The P Street house was similar to the first home they had lived in on Dent Place, tall and narrow and quaint. My office was located in a second-floor study facing the street.

I remember those early days in 1957 at P Street. I would be met at the door by Provi—Providencia Paredes, Jackie's maid—in her neat white uniform. Provi came from the Dominican Republic and spoke with a Spanish accent. She was young and attractive and totally dedicated to Jackie. Jackie was in New York, awaiting the birth of her baby, but I well knew where my work was—all the morning's mail and bills were waiting for me on the desk.

At noontime, when Provi carried in my lunch tray, she would invariably remind me, "Eat it all up now, Mees Gallaga, you know you have the baby to feed, too."

The baby turned out to be Gregory—named by my husband for a fresco of Gregory the Great that he had been greatly impressed with at St. Peter's in Rome. Chistopher, our firstborn, had also been given a name Ray had chosen—a tribute to St. Christopher for the fact that Ray had come through his many World War II travels safely.

Gregory was born May 13, 1957, just six months before the birth of Caroline in November.

Two months before Gregory was born, I got a foretaste of what my future would include. Typical of every family's home, no matter how wealthy, it involved finances. You might say, it was the future President's toothache that got me involved in his finances and brought about a stronger alliance between us. On St. Patrick's Day, he was scheduled to march in the parade.

As I made my way to the study upstairs, I was surprised, on passing his bedroom door, to find him home with a swollen face, propped up in bed. He was surrounded by papers and writing away. After I had been working for several hours at my desk, he entered, barefoot and pajama-clad, wanting to know, "How are you coming along?" At the same time, he caught sight of the stack of envelopes that held the many outgoing checks ready for Jackie's signature.

Immediately, he began asking questions—and with one fell swoop, he scattered the neat pile over the desk for more careful study.

Surprised and irked at the numerous expenditures, he then ordered in a stern, angry tone, "From now on, Mary, please see to it that I get a complete list of all the checks written and exactly what they're for."

That was just the beginning. Jackie's finances would haunt my nights and days from then on, all through the White House years and even after. But, at the time, I thought it was just a passing fancy and that the Senator would soon tire of looking at household and personal accounts.

On occasion Mrs. Auchincloss also confided in me. She once asked if I would approach Jackie about her manner of dress. That happened about several days after she and Jackie had gone to an Embassy tea. Mrs. Auchincloss was rather distressed over the short dress that her daughter had worn. She said that when Jackie bent over for something, you could see her garters at the top of her hose. "Could you just mention to her that you think she should start wearing her dresses a little longer?"

Much as I would have loved to oblige Mrs. Auchincloss, I never could muster up enough courage to tell Jackie. Nor would I have ever considered mentioning to Jackie that her mother had been critical in any way.

Jackie stayed at her mother's summer house at Newport now and then. She called her stepfather "Uncle Hughie."

After I had been working for Mrs. Auchincloss for a few years, she met me at the door one morning to tell me "Hughdie would like to see you in the study."

My mind quickly raced back to the past week, remembering the checks I had made out and left to be signed by Mrs. Auchincloss. I wondered if I might have done something wrong. He quickly put my mind at ease as soon as I sat down in the library. His first words were, "My wife may never forgive me for this . . ." and he went on to offer me a job as his secretary.

It was a very tempting offer, and he could see that I was interested.

I thought about it long and hard, but I could not turn my back on Jackie. The 1960 campaign had begun, and I felt she needed me more than ever; I knew that the Senator would expect me to stay and help his wife.

I still felt my first loyalty was to him.

5 ∽ THE HOUSE ON N STREET

*T*HE SENATOR WAS SO DELIGHTED WHEN Jackie presented him with a baby daughter on November 27, the day before Thanskgiving, 1957, that he in turn presented her with a new house—bigger and better than the little house on P Street. It was located in Georgetown at 3307 N Street, N.W. From here he was eventually to run for the Presidency.

And in the eleventh day of Caroline's life, a new person entered her life and mine, who would become world famous —Nurse Maud Shaw. Miss Shaw had come from England to take care of Caroline, and she was everything an English Nanny is supposed to be. Proper and very British, with an accent to match. "Touch wood," I remember, was a favorite expression of hers when she wanted something to happen and not be spoiled by bad luck.

Up and down the stairs she went in the new house, happily ministering to Caroline's needs.

And there were many steps to climb!

It was a three-story, red brick house with living room, library, dining room, and kitchen on the first floor, guestroom on the mezzanine, and a master bedroom and study on the second floor.

This study, directly off the master bedroom, also served as a dressing room for the Senator and contained a handsome highboy of neatly arranged clothing, as well as a closet full of fine tailored suits. Here my "office" was also located, at the desk by the window overlooking the back patio.

The red and white custom-upholstered bed beside my desk

was used, for the most part, by Jackie as she tended to the day's mail and dictated to me.

Senator Kennedy usually breakfasted alone from a tray in the downstairs library and browsed through the morning papers.

When Caroline learned to walk, she often joined him, tottering along on her own two little feet, chatting away and sharing his toast.

When he was ready to leave, he would call up the stairs a loud "Bye, Jackie," and briskly head for his car. From my window, I always watched him go. I used to wish that Jackie would eat breakfast downstairs with the Senator, or at least come down to see him off at the door.

Aside from entertaining in the evenings, her days were strangely lonely. She seldom called up friends or had them over to visit.

She was constantly fixing up one room or another. At times, it was an all-consuming passion. It seemed to me there were just two things that John F. Kennedy wanted—a comfortable, familiar, *unchanging* place to read in peace and quiet, and second, no money worries. Strangely enough, these remained elusive. Jackie was never satisfied with furnishings where they were, either at Georgetown or in the White House. I remember one day at Georgetown, when she was changing things around, that he was furiously hunting for a comfortable nook. It wasn't to be found—and he finally hollered out in disgust, "Dammit it, Jackie, why is it that the rooms in this house are never completely livable all at the same time?"

In the study alone, the wallpaper was changed no less than three times in just a matter of months—including an expensive watercolor pattern that I'd been told was imported from England.

Downstairs, the adjoining living room and library looked very serene in soft, muted tones of beige and off-white. The sofas were so soft and comfortable that you sank and sank as you sat down. But the most elegant feature was a fur rug draped casually over one of the sofas.

On the walls were paintings from Jackie's own collection, together with one that the Senator had painted himself while recuperating from his back operation. (Jackie had bought him a set of paints.)

It was too bad that Jackie's father could not have lived a few months longer to see his granddaughter, Caroline. She was born three months after his death and was given the middle name of Bouvier, for him.

When her father died in the summer of 1957, it was a great tragedy for Jackie. He had worshipped her and she him.

Sometime after her father died, Jackie wanted me to type in duplicate, with a copy for sending to her sister, Lee, in London, many letters her father had written her when she was away at school. I could tell they were letters she would treasure forever.

Little by little, I had gotten to know about Jackie's childhood. After the divorce of her mother and John Vernou Bouvier III, in 1938, Jackie, then only 9, and her sister, Lee, just 5, began to shuttle back and forth between parents during vacations and holidays. She had a horse named "Danseuse," which her father kept for her at the Bouvier estate at East Hampton, L.I., and started winning prizes for horsemanship at the age of eight. I learned that she had gone in the summer of 1948 on a tour of Europe with several girl friends and that she had fallen in love with France. In 1949 she went again for a year's study at the Sorbonne.

An important part of her history concerned her talent in fashion. In 1951, she had competed against 1,000 contestants and won *Vogue* magazine's Prix de Paris contest, for her judgment on high fashions and her writing about people she wished she had known—Oscar Wilde and Charles Baudelaire being two of them. Her prize was to have been a year on the staff of *Vogue*, six months in Paris, and six months in New York. But, as I learned, she was talked out of accepting it. This may have been the reason she then took a newspaper job at the Washington *Times-Herald*. It was the Auchincloss's friend Arthur Krock, of *The New York Times,* who helped her get the job, for which she earned a beginner's wage of $42.50 a week. The highlight of her newspaper career was her trip to London in May, 1953, to report on Queen Elizabeth II's Coronation.

The difference in attitude toward clothes between Jackie and her husband would be hard to exaggerate. At the office, we used to kid among ourselves, "Which is the Senator and which is the administrative assistant?"

Ted Reardon was always meticulously dressed and well groomed, while the Senator was tousle-headed and wore whatever his hand fell on. Those were the days he would sometimes ask me to take some Scotch tape and get the lint off his suit jacket.

It was after the Senator married that his general appearance took on a more "cared-after" look, and later, during his Presidency, he gained the title of "America's Best Dressed Man of the Year." By this time, clothes had become important to the President as well as to Jackie.

Perhaps one thing I noticed as much as anything was that there were never any sounds of laughter, or gaiety, nor any background music from either radio or stereo played in any of the rooms. Never, in fact, have I ever remembered hearing Jackie herself as much as *hum* a little tune as she went about her daily business, or indulge in a really hearty laugh. Perhaps one explanation for this could be attributed to her rather "reserved" personality.

In trying to understand why Jackie's way of living contrasted so greatly with that of the average American housewife and mother, I find I can only explain it in one way. And that is, that she was born and groomed to a queenly role.

Neither Jackie nor her sister were brought up to do household chores. It was the cook who was up early each morning to prepare the breakfast for the husband of the house before he went off to his office, and for the children. And it was also the cook who had the responsibility of ordering groceries and preparing the meals.

It was the maids who looked after the general cleaning of the rooms, making the beds, tending to the laundry, ironing, etc. It was the butler-valet who looked after her husband's clothing and saw to it that his bags were packed for trips. It was the nanny who devoted herself completely to the children and cared for them during times of sickness. It was the chauffeur who drove her and members of her family for their daily appointments. And when it came to sending someone out on errands, it was Muggsy whom the Senator depended on to shop for him if the need arose. He bellowed once at him because some shirts had cost too much—$3.50 apiece.

Concerning the campaign stories about the lunch baskets that Jackie was supposed to have prepared and delivered daily to her husband in his Senate office, actually except for a few rare occasions when she did deliver them herself, it was Muggsy who delivered the lunch. And it was always the cook who prepared the food and packed the basket—Tania, Paula, and finally Pearl, as the parade of cooks came and went.

Jackie's days, in other words, were for the most part spent without the normal physical strain endured by the average woman. In short, Jackie was the "director" over those who actually carried out her housewifely and motherly chores and responsibilities.

By evening, well rested and relaxed after her daily nap, Jacqueline was fresh and fit for her husband and guests, if any. I imagine, too, that it was during these evening hours that sounds of music would fill the rooms from time to time.

Even Jackie's writing of her daily diary—so that she could remember everything—was given an assist by her husband's secretary, Evelyn Lincoln.

At Jackie's suggestion, I sent a diary (similar to her own) over to Evelyn so that she could list JFK's activities of the day so Jackie wouldn't have to do it. At the end of the year, Evelyn would send it back, filled.

As the campaign year of 1960 approached, I began to spend

more time with Jackie and, of course, less time with her mother. My responsibilities had now increased to the point where I had acquired a new role. I was busy handling servant problems—forever soothing hurt feelings of the household help from the kitchen to the parlor. Considerable friction of personalities existed. There was a fast turnover of the cooks, in particular. I'm afraid we kept Mrs. Pauwels of the Eugenia Pauwels Employment Service in Washington rather busy. Jackie would not become concerned until a servant was actually quitting, and she would simply ask, "Mary, would you call Mrs. Pauwels and see how soon we could have another cook?"

I breathed a sigh of relief when we finally hit upon a cook who could handle and please everyone—Pearl Nelson. Hired just a few months prior to the election, Pearl took all the extra activity in amazing stride. The President-elect took a special liking to her style of cooking. She adjusted remarkably to the Kennedys' scattered meal shifts, the extras who suddenly appeared on the scene for lunch or dinner. The Senator gave her the highest marks for the way she fixed his favorite Fish Chowder and Baked Seafood Casserole. Occasionally, they would be sent to his office or on his travels when the craving struck him. Pearl always kept some in the freezer, to be ready.

Whenever the Kennedy admirers, during the campaign, wrote and asked for a recipe, I would send out one or the other of these. I typed them in batches so many times that I had them memorized. To be on the safe side in sharing them now, I am carefully referring to my recipe file:

FISH CHOWDER

2 pounds haddock	1 bay leaf crumbled
2 ounces diced salt pork	1 teaspoon salt
2 onions sliced	freshly ground pepper
4 large potatoes diced	1 quart milk
1 cup chopped celery	2 tablespoons butter

Simmer haddock in 2 cups water for 15 minutes. Drain. Reserve broth. Remove bones from fish. Sauté diced pork until crisp, remove and set aside. Sauté onion in pork fat until golden brown. Add fish, potatoes, celery, bay leaf, salt, and pepper. Pour in fish broth, plus enough boiling water to make 3 cups liquid. Simmer 30 minutes. Add milk and butter. Simmer 5 minutes. Serve sprinkled with diced pork. Serves 6.

BAKED SEAFOOD CASSEROLE

1 pound crab meat and lobster meat combined
1 pound cooked and deveined shrimp
1 cup mayonnaise
½ cup chopped green peppers
¼ cup minced onion
1½ cups finely chopped celery
½ teaspoon salt
1 tablespoon Worcestershire sauce
2 cups crushed potato chips
  paprika

Mix ingredients all together as though making a seafood salad, fill baking pan, and completely cover with crushed potato chips. Sprinkle with paprika and bake at 400 degrees from 20 to 25 minutes. Serves 12.

The Senator was fond of a rather spicy hot fruit dessert that went with them.

HOT FRUIT DESSERT

3 small cans apricots
3 small cans pineapple pieces
3 small cans peaches
3 No. 2 cans pitted Bing cherries
3 oranges
3 lemons
½ cup light brown sugar

Grate rind of oranges and lemons into sugar. Spread fruits, layer by layer, including oranges and lemons, sliced very thin, in baking dish. Sprinkle each layer with brown-sugar mixture and a generous sprinkling of nutmeg. Heat all until very hot, and serve topped with some sour cream.

Jackie's food tastes were completely different. She loved French food, which was part of her background, just as seafood was the President's. She enjoyed foods with savory sauces or cooked in wine. For desserts, her preference leaned to such things as chocolate soufflé, meringue tarts filled with berries, or fruit topped with whipped cream.

For small dinner parties or private receptions—as when Lee was married to the Polish Prince, Stanislas Radziwill—fine French food was served. Small tables were set up in the dining room, and Jackie would usually employ the services of her favorite caterers, Avignone Frères.

Even with catering service, Jackie's house assumed the air of a Democratic Headquarters. With the growing influx of visitors, guests, and campaign aids, she felt the need for more help.

It was back to Mrs. Pauwels again!

Another maid, Consuelo Quiroz, originally from Peru, arrived to cope with the mounting household chores and give a helping hand to Provi, whose time was now devoted exclusively to Jackie and her clothes.

Few people knew that Jack Kennedy was allergic to animal fur. I found that out when Jackie asked, "How would you like to have a dog for the boys?"

She explained that she had a Golden Retriever "Tippy" which I understood she was keeping at "Merrywood." She assured me that he was an ideal dog for children. I assumed he was a puppy and readily accepted her offer. But later in the day, when it came time to put him in the car for the trip home, I couldn't have been more surprised. I wondered what my husband's reaction would be when he saw me coming up the steps with a large Golden Retriever, charging at him from the end of a leash!

I soon found that my fears were completely unwarranted. Ray and the boys took to Tippy in no time at all. He was, indeed, a beautiful dog with his big brown eyes, long reddish-brown hair, and a tail that wagged forcefully with every pat on his head.

We had to watch closely, however, his exuberant reactions to the children's affection, as he would playfully topple little Gregory, who was about half his size, like a ten-pin. Yet, mutual admiration persisted.

So good-natured was Tippy that often as he lay on the floor, Gregory would use him as a footstool for a better look out of the windows. Tippy never objected, pretending not to notice—but, then, as we observed, his long tail would immediately go into action, flapping happily away.

When he died, everyone grieved, and eventually Ray put up a little marker in the back yard to show that Tippy had lived there.

6 ∾ WIFE OF THE CANDIDATE

I WILL NEVER FORGET THE 1960 CAMPAIGN. It was like living in a hurricane to be around 3307 N Street after the Senator announced his Presidential candidacy in January. People coming and going whom I could barely glance at. Phones ringing. The private numbers had to be changed several times. Only around Jacqueline was there serenity and a sense of regal aloofness from the grubby details of politics.

I was so busy with Jackie's work four and five days a week, that I no longer had time to give Mrs. Auchincloss. She was most understanding and said, "Jackie comes first now."

People were both cruel and kind. The kind ones sent letters requesting Jackie's photograph or the favorite Kennedy Fish Chowder recipe, or campaign buttons and literature. Or they sent congratulatory messages because Jackie was expecting a child.

The cruel ones showed jealousy of the fashion-plate Jacqueline—criticizing or berating her, suggesting what she should or should not wear. A few insulting letters enclosed haircombs, expressing the wish that Jackie change her hairstyle to one they thought more suitable for the wife of a Presidential candidate.

I tried to shield Jackie from the unfavorable mail, but the candidate himself was not unaware of it—obviously, he was getting a bit of the same in his office. One day he said to me, "Oh, Mary, how is the mail running on Jackie's hair?" I said, "Heavy."

In due time, Jackie's answer came out in the form of a campaign letter, in which she was quoted as saying, "All the talk over what I wear and how I fix my hair has me amused, but it also puzzles me. What does my hairdo have to do with my husband's ability to be President?"

This type of impertinent letter, of course, was simply handled with routine acknowledgment. Those of a friendly, strictly personal nature I brought to Jackie's attention and she would dictate appropriate replies. Eventually, in accordance with Jackie's wishes, I learned to copy her signature and relieved her of the burden of signing her increasing mail.

It was Capitol Hill all over again.

Jackie did not relish politics. She did not get a thrill, as the Senator did, in hearing a crowd outside his window cheering him. Nor was she like her husband, who took a moment or two from the day to step outside the front door to offer a smile or quick wave to everyone.

The birth of her second child was expected sometime early in December. But even before the doctor had placed restrictions upon her activity, Jackie was a reluctant campaigner. She did not take to politics as the other Kennedy women did —the candidate's mother, sisters, and sisters-in-law. At one point, her own mother came to her rescue and gave one of the teas for her at "Merrywood."

I seldom saw the other Kennedy women in the N Street house during this time. They would hit the campaign trail on their own, or appear with the candidate where and whenever he needed them. But since JFK did want Jackie to help as much as possible, she did hold several Press Teas, as she called them, in the living room of the N Street House. It did appear to me that Jackie prepared for these brief political soirées with the attitude of being inconvenienced, rather than whole-heartedly, considering the ultimate goal that she could help reach. I looked at Jackie and thought how thrilled I would be if it were my husband who was running for the Presidency.

In line with Jackie's practice of handling things herself when observers were around, I did not participate. I worked at my desk upstairs. On one occasion, she did ask that I "pour" for her. I did, until it was time for the picture-taking. Jackie entered the dining room and I was immediately dismissed as she took her place in the chair and started to pour. The flashbulbs were popping when I made my way back up to the second floor.

The eager watchers on the sidewalks and the hordes of press photographers saw another Kennedy more than they saw Jackie. She was Caroline, just a little tot, but she turned out to be her father's secret weapon. Her little jaunts to and from the house with her nanny, or, waving to her daddy when he was leaving, were all happily recorded.

Inside, I spent many hours sending a lovely picture that showed her with her mother and father to every corner of the nation. And it brought forth a great response from those who received it.

Little Caroline had heard so much about people volunteering to help her daddy that, though only 3 years old, she, too, undertook to help. Each morning, before she went off with Miss Shaw for her walk, she would come in and volunteer— "I can help."

Each day, I gave her a little pile of unopened mail and a letter-opener. She was very proud to be "working" on her mommy's campaign mail.

Everyone in the family, it seemed, was excited and enthusiastic, except one. Finally, one afternoon, almost as if she were thinking out loud, Jackie remarked with apparent resignation, "If Jack didn't run for President, he'd be like a tiger in a cage."

Even Lee's husband, the Polish Prince Stanislas Radziwill, was off campaigning for Kennedy among the Polish-speaking Americans, and Jackie was delighted to have her sister, Lee, to herself for a few days. Later, as a thank-you gift, the President gave the Prince a special framed map, marking every city in which "Stash" had campaigned.

Jackie was happiest when her sister was around because Lee was the one person with whom she could relax and pour out her feelings. They were like schoolgirls together, sharing confidences and telling how some frustrating or dense person "drove me up the wall—screaming and knocking everything over." Or, how someone had "a knack for being interested in and remembering the dullest details."

Mrs. Auchincloss was concerned that Lee was too thin, and Lee tried to eat more when her mother was around—"trying to stuff," as she put it.

Frankly, I had the same concern about Jackie, feeling that she was dieting too much during her pregnancy. I had not been able to ignore completely her concern with her figure during these particular months. She seemed to be eating very little.

On one occasion, as I walked past her, she observed, "Oh, Mary, I just hate you for being so thin!"

Lee's campaign activities with her husband the Prince had been suddenly curtailed by the premature birth of her second child, Anna Christina, born August 18, 1960. The baby had to stay on at the hospital because she weighed only two-and-one-half pounds.

Lee recuperated sufficiently to travel by September, and she wanted to have Miss O'Malley, the Kennedys' masseuse, go to London with her; Miss O'Malley gave the most relaxing rubdowns. Jackie was determined to help her, and suddenly I felt I was back on Capitol Hill as I tackled the "immigration" problem.

"How soon will Miss O'Malley need this passport?" I asked Lee.

She casually answered, "Oh, tomorrow."

Though I could hardly offer any promise, I wasted no time in getting Mrs. Pittarelli on the line. For the better part of the day, we negotiated back and forth. By the end of the day, she came through—as I had always known her to do— with the clear, crisp message, "We're all set, Mary. Have Miss O'Malley come by in the morning. We'll have the passport ready for her."

Jackie and Lee, of course, gasped with delight at what they now considered a little miracle.

About that time, my mountain of work made me cancel a trip to Europe that Ray and I had made reservations for a year in advance. Jackie needed me more and more, and I hadn't the heart to let her down. I still have the letter from the United States Lines, showing how ten days before we were to leave, we gave up our reservations. I didn't even let Jackie know about it.

I felt emotionally involved in whether our idol, John Fitzgerald Kennedy, would be able to rise victorious over our "old neighbor" Richard Milhous Nixon. It was nip-and-tuck all the way.

I saw Ted Kennedy's wife, Joan, for the first time at the Kennedys' Georgetown house before we went to the White House, and I can still recall her sheer beauty. When she saw me working in the study for Jackie, she asked exactly what I did as secretary to a Senator's wife. She was apparently contemplating her own role at such time as Teddy might also become a Senator. When I explained my duties, she said she'd have to start thinking about that side of her life, too.

Tending to her more personal affairs in Georgetown or the White House, Jackie never seemed to lack the ambition, energy, strength, and enthusiasm for coping with the endless details.

One of the most time-consuming of these involved the planning of her wardrobe, ordering clothes, standing through fittings, or dictating endless letters that gave her clothing "scouts" enough to do for weeks at a time! The scouts, whom she leaned on more and more at the White House, were, for the most part, friends and professionals who kept on the look-out for gowns or fabrics in the various collections that they knew Jackie would like.

Among Jackie's clothing scouts abroad, she had Letizia Mowinckel in Paris and Princess Irene Galitzine in Rome. Among the several in New York there was Mrs. Tackaberry McAdoo, whom she called Molly. Lee used some of the same scouts abroad, and once I was amused when Jackie warned Mrs. Mowinckel not to show anything to Lee until she—Jackie—had first chance to pick what she wanted.

Jackie herself also kept track of what the couturiers in Paris and London were featuring and would get in touch with her scouts to order the items she liked without anyone's knowing they were for her. She would sometimes fall in love with the material a famous designer had used and order something in the same fabric to be made for her by another designer.

All this took time and energy. And this energy was evident in the fall of 1960 as she prepared for her post-natal period. One morning, quite by surprise, she asked as I arrived upstairs, "Mary, what are your measurements?"

I quoted the three basics and Jackie exclaimed excitedly, "Fantastic!" She asked if I would please go into the dressing room and try on some muslin samples she had just received from New York.

In their raw state, I must say, the muslins really didn't look like much of anything. But I tried one on and came out for the first "modeling," only to have Jackie's keen eye confirm my uncertainty in this new experience. At first glance, she said, "Mary, you've got the top on backwards—the buttons belong in the back—have Provi help you."

My second appearance went over much better and, as I stood there, she and Provi applied a few pins around the arms and shoulders. Finally, with fittings out of the way, Jackie proceeded to dictate her letter to the dressmaker, describing the alterations she wanted made.

If I had been taken by surprise by her opening question about my measurements, I was even more surprised when she wrote to the dressmaker that the muslins had been fitted to her sister Lee.

Eventually, I would no longer be surprised when Jackie used other people's names in letters. Usually, it was to hide the fact that she was the one who wanted something. Frequently, she would say, "Jack wants ..." or, "my sister advises against ..." or, "so-and-so won't let me ..."

During the campaign, Jackie's clothes drew the attention of busybodies who chose to be concerned with what she spent on her wardrobe. I remember when the story broke that Jackie was spending $30,000 a year for her clothes, she retorted, "I would have to wear sable underwear to spend that much."

At that time, it was not my responsibility to keep strict accounts. However, at the end of 1961, her first year in the White House, I was amazed to see how close those estimates had been. Actually, Jackie's clothing expenditures for 1961 amounted to just over $40,000.

The wife of the Republican candidate, Mrs. Richard Nixon, had spoken of her own "plain Republican cloth coat."

Jackie had said that she, too, wore things straight off the rack and was buying them at $29 and $39 a dress. As I recall, these were maternity dresses, which she had ordered in several shades of the same styles.

Around the house, we did not talk much about what the Republican side of the campaign was doing. I never heard Jackie mention Pat Nixon or refer to her in any way.

It was during the campaign that the curtain of silence about my status was fully lowered. I arrived at the Georgetown house one morning to find several representatives from *Life* magazine waiting in the study.

Jackie called me into the bedroom and whispered that pictures would be taken, and would I cooperate by sitting at the desk. I drew the clear inference that the pictures would be of her alone, but I took my place at the desk as instructed.

When the October 10, 1960 issue of *Life* arrived I saw that the photos and story depicted the various roles of the wives of the Presidential candidates, Mrs. Kennedy and Mrs. Nixon. To the general public, I noticed, it appeared that Jackie carried the major burden of coping with the voluminous mail she received. My picture did not appear—and my name had been eliminated as well. The caption said: "Reading the 225 daily letters, Jackie answers each with help of a part-time secretary. 'I could use one full time these days,' she says."

At this point, incidentally, my days at 3307 N Street couldn't possibly have been more full-time. The volume of mail had become so great that I was carrying it home with me for reading and sorting in the evening hours—with Ray volunteering his help as well. I was working six and seven days a week, and nights.

Turning the page from where my picture might have been, I saw that Jackie's "image" was carried one step further.

There was no mention of Miss Shaw, the live-in nurse. The full-page photo shows Jackie alone, leaning over Caroline's crib. Its caption proclaimed, "Tucking her daughter in for an afternoon nap, Jackie, who does not have a nurse for Caroline . . ."

If this was politics, I thought, I might just as well get used to it.

Maud Shaw and I continued to learn that the way to stay on the good side of Jackie was to stay on the side *away* from the cameras. We both made every effort. I could manage, but it didn't always work for Miss Shaw, who had to scramble after the children, cameras or no cameras. And her mistress would be annoyed.

"What does she expect me to do," Miss Shaw would grumble to me, "just leave the children there and hide?"

Among my souvenirs of the campaign days are several of

50 ह•

the original photos taken by *Life* magazine, showing, of course, both Jackie and me at the N Street house, which the reporter Gail Cameron later sent me.

In the final weeks of the '60 campaign, the pressure of work kept me too busy to shop for a winter coat, which I needed desperately. I remembered that Jackie had a blue, double-breasted mohair coat that she no longer wanted. In fact, I had already sent it out to Encore, a New York clothing resale house, where, in accordance with Jackie's instructions, I usually shipped her clothing—to be resold under my name and home address. As the various items were sold, Encore's check would come to me, and I would deposit it in my personal bank account. At the same time, I would write out a check for the same amount to be deposited in Jackie's account.

The blue coat was perfect for me, and since we wore the same size and were the same height, I asked Jackie if she would mind if I asked Encore to return that particular garment—listed at $65. I said I'd be happy to pay her for it. Jackie agreed, and when the coat was returned, I handed her the check. She told me to deposit it in her bank account.

This was so typical of Jackie—sometimes bequeathing heaps of garments with a wave of her hand, but at other times being very businesslike. Provi and Miss Shaw and I would all benefit from the generous moods when she would suddenly tackle her closets, quickly judging and separating the items she would keep from those she felt she no longer liked or needed. From the racks would fall a large collection of suits, dresses, coats, blouses, slacks, and other paraphernalia, which would then be sorted into two heaps—the one for resale, the other for us.

Usually, Jackie would simply let us riffle through to choose what we felt we could use. One time at N Street, when she reached for a pretty red chiffon evening dress on its hanger, she did not toss it onto the heap.

She looked at it, and she looked at me. "You may not ever have any need for this, Mary," she said, "but it's just your color." She generously handed it to me, and she was right—it was just my color. And she was right again—I still have no use for it. It was a maternity dress!

7 ∾ FIRST LADY-ELECT

On TUESDAY, NOVEMBER 8, 1960, THE voters acclaimed their choice for President. John Fitzgerald Kennedy.

After the Senator's victory, the mail was being delivered in such huge sacks that volunteers from the neighborhood, who had given their services to the candidate, continued to help by working on the mail in their own Georgetown homes— Nan McEvoy, Hortense Burton, and Mary Russell, especially. I also remember Mrs. Thomas Braden, who had arranged Jackie's schedules for campaign teas and appearances.

Meanwhile, in the mail I was handling every morning, I would send neatly categorized stacks of letters and appropriate replies to Pierrette Spiegler in Senator Kennedy's office, and she would run the replies through her Robotype machines. Without her help, these letters might have been delayed for weeks.

The first big change for Jackie after the election was the arrival of the Secret Service Agents at the Georgetown house. At first Jackie seemed to regard them as a nuisance. But when they, along with local police, were able to quiet the noisy crowds that appeared at all hours, she suddenly changed her attitude.

Prior to the arrival of the Secret Service, there had been no control over the people who congregated outdoors, nor over the noises, cheers, and calls for Jack and Jackie which, sometimes, carried right on through the night.

Once posted outdoors, the agents quelled the disturbances beneath the bedroom window, to Jackie's relief. The next morning she happily conceded, "How great to get a good night's sleep!"

This was my first experience with the Secret Service, too. I can vividly recall how greatly impressed I had been with the first few agents who had quietly entered the study that morning after the election to introduce themselves: James Jeffries, Lynn Meredith, and a Mr. Bouch.

With notebooks in hand, they immediately jotted down telephone numbers of people who were important to the Kennedys.

Further protection was also provided by the police after the election. Captain Kennedy, of Precinct 7 in Georgetown, arranged adequate shifts to cover both the front of the Kennedy home and the rear. As the new aura of excitement continued to rise and permeate the entire block of N Street, even a neighbor across the street—a Miss Montgomery—was gaining fame by feeding the cold and hungry reporters who kept their vigil outside our door.

The newsmen were grateful—for the coffee and for the two extra telephone lines she let them have installed in her house. They later gave Miss Montgomery a plaque for her home, for all future sightseers to read:

In the cold winter of 1960-61 this house had an important role in history. From it was flashed to the world news of pre-inaugural announcements by President John F. Kennedy.

Presented by

The grateful newsmen who were given warm haven here by Miss Helen Montgomery and her father Charles Montgomery

During the ensuing weeks, President-elect Kennedy spent more and more time at home, conducting business with members of his staff. Aware of his presence behind the closed doors, the crowds became thicker and thicker—hopefully awaiting the chance to catch some sight of him or of Jackie as they left or entered the house. Standing or sitting in vantage points across the street, their unfaltering attention focused for hours and hours on the big, red brick house. Some remained from morning until night.

Jackie regally ignored crowds unless nudged by her husband. President-elect Kennedy loved people. At certain intervals during these busy days, he took at least a few minutes to appear on the front doorstep, if only to offer a broad smile, a wave of appreciation, or a few words. He was met with wild cheers and screams.

On one particular afternoon, I watched from the second-floor bedroom window as he crisply demonstrated an even more kind and warm gesture. Almost as if drawn to them by magnetism, he crossed over to the other side of the street, grasping the eagerly outstretched hands, one after the other, until he completed the long front line.

As I continued to watch the various reactions—clutching at hearts by girls, broad smiles by men—I could sense the joy that he brought to them all out there.

I called Jackie's attention to this touching sight, expecting her to hurry over to the window so she could witness it. Instead, she simply sighed, "Oh, Mary . . ." and she continued with her own business.

Only once do I remember Jackie's losing her indifference. That was when the President-elect called up the stairs to tell her that a very important visitor was with him—President Truman. Jackie was embarrassed. She was in her robe and could not go downstairs at that minute. Instead, she came from her bedroom and stood at the top of the stairs, leaning over the banister to offer a "Hello, Mr. President."

I caught a glimpse of Harry Truman, myself, and was thrilled to see him, but it was only a glance. I was back at my typewriter in seconds.

During this time, I was sharing the guestroom-study for weeks with Pierre Salinger, the President-elect's press secretary. He would grab anything on my desk to make his notes

54 ॐ

as he answered phones and made calls and consulted with the President-elect. In his whole book he doesn't mention me, though he tells about all the other key secretaries. At the White House we ate at the same mess, and he almost fell over me now and then as he scurried through the halls.

In all that hubbub, I remember the name of Governor Terry Sanford of North Carolina kept coming up. And arrangements for meetings with Clark Clifford. And the names Chester Bowles, Dean Acheson, Robert A. Lovett, Bill White, and Bill Lawrence.

And there was a breakfast meeting Pierre was setting up that included Senator Smathers and a meeting later with Adam Clayton Powell. And in the midst of a million and one things, Pierre suddenly had to find out from Jack Kennedy for a reporter "What Christmas Means to Me."

One of Jackie's concerns was hiring her social secretary for the White House. She was considering Letitia "Tish" Baldrige, who had been at Tiffany's in New York and before that was social secretary to Clare Booth Luce at the American Embassy in Rome.

As far back as July, 1960, we had contacted Tish about this. Jackie had wanted to tell her to stand by for a possible job, depending on the election.

One morning, Jackie handed the phone back to me after she had talked to Tish for a while.

Now that the election was over, Tish wanted to make the official announcement to the press of her appointment and was calling to get it cleared by Mrs. Kennedy. With Tish dictating on one hand and Jackie commenting on the other, I was the girl in the middle until the release was finished and became just one more piece of business in a busy day.

As the pace quickened, it became necessary for the President-elect to have Evelyn Lincoln, his personal secretary, come out to the house each day. The mezzanine guestroom was quickly converted into another office with the installation of extra telephone lines.

Selfishly speaking, I couldn't have been more delighted with

Evelyn's presence at the house. I had been crowding many of the President-elect's quick messages into my own schedule while trying to keep abreast of Jackie's affairs, and I was afraid that the snowballing effect might soon overwhelm me.

Now I could find a work corner of this new office at such times as my own nook in the study was taken over by the President-elect or any of his aides. It was a convenient arrangement, especially since Evelyn and I could manage our tasks in complete and perfect harmony.

Our most constant and cheerful little visitor during these otherwise hectic days was little Caroline.

I recall once Caroline came in demanding, "Mary, please draw me some birds." Busy as I was, I took a few minutes to sketch some birds as I remembered doing it from grade school. I was no artist like her mother, but Caroline seemed perfectly content with my version.

Always when I least expected it, she bounced into the room with all kinds of happy chatter, using the most persuasive tactics to get us to "draw some pictures" for her, or allow her to use the typewriter, which interested her even more.

After a few sessions, however, the typewriter was thrown out of commission, which meant a call for a repair man. Since we were limited to two typewriters, we simply couldn't risk any further hazards, so we cut short Caroline's secretarial career, much to her disappointment.

Maud Shaw, well aware of the demands on our time, fully realized the need for rescuing us from her little charge after a certain length of time. With a quick clap of her hands, she would come to fetch Caroline, announcing that it was either "time for our walk," "time for lunch," or "time for a nap." Reluctantly, Caroline would go.

There was but one person whose every handclap and call for Caroline caused her to bound forth in the most excited, exhilarated way—her daddy. His loud, sharp claps, accompanied by his usual call of "Buttons, where's Buttons?" would have Caroline scampering in the direction of his voice with incredible, almost uncontrollable, speed.

On many occasions, her starting and finishing line would be from the third-floor nursery down to the foot of the first-floor staircase. I found myself holding my breath until she reached that last step safely and was caught in her father's arms.

It was like a private game between them—but it reflected the general feeling of enthusiasm within the entire household whenever the President-elect was around. We all felt good.

With her mother, Caroline was more subdued. But then, I seldom saw her around her mother when Jackie was working. She would be off somewhere with Miss Shaw or playing upstairs in her bedroom. Usually, when Jackie was having breakfast, Miss Shaw would bring her in for a little visit with "Mommy." Jackie would say, "Where are you going today with Miss Shaw?" or "What are you and Miss Shaw up to today?"

Then Miss Shaw with her little charge would leave the house with a few happy words from George Thomas as he let them out the front door.

George was the Kennedys' butler-valet, who would continue to work for the President-elect after he was in the White House as full-time valet. He was rather short, rotund, and happy-go-lucky.

These were the happy days. The President-elect was forever popping in to tell Jackie that he would like her to see this group or that, or asking her to go downstairs with him to meet some visitor. Jackie hardly ever hurried her preparations, whether it was for a simple greeting downstairs or an evening out.

She often kept JFK waiting for her. As he paced impatiently, she would simply continue with her last-minute touch-ups. No matter how impatient JFK became, the strongest thing he would say was, "For God's sake, Jackie." I was to become familiar with the phrase.

Another characteristic of Jackie was that she would leave little notes for her husband whenever she had something on her mind. Not trusting her own memory and fearing that she might forget something before he got home, she would jot it down and leave it in a strategic place. One place that she could be sure he would find it was in his own bathroom. I did not make a practice of reading her notes, but I couldn't avoid seeing one, because I happened to be using the same bathroom.

Referring to her second attempt at getting rid of a pest who was haunting their N Street house, she wanted JFK to know she had just issued the unwelcome visitor his Second Farewell Address! This, to me, was Jackie's wit at her finest.

Jackie always prepared a season ahead for her wardrobe. Now, though pregnant, she was getting ready for her move to the White House in January. Despite the work of closing the house and taking inventory, she was looking ahead to her spring wardrobe.

Soon after election, she dictated a long letter to Oleg Cassini in New York, outlining her specific needs with her usual precision—types of ensembles, fabrics, colors. She requested that Cassini send her some sketches, but her preference was for materials used by Balenciaga and Givenchy. She was so meticulous about the fabric used that she was willing to wait for the sketches until Cassini had seen the new materials.

Furthermore, the arrangement was that if she liked his sketches, she would let it be known that he had done her spring wardrobe. Jackie refused to have her clothes dull or dreary.

She made it clear that she would make just one major concession in her role as First Lady. She would have to be suitably covered up, not décolleté.

My mind was occupied with the million and one other details surrounding us. For example, Caroline's third birthday party on November 27 was coming up and Jackie wanted to be ready in advance.

Jackie handed me her written list of the names of Caroline's little friends and relatives, asking that I "pick up about one-and-a-half dozen invitations—the regular kind that can be bought at the stationer's." She wanted them all written out and mailed a week ahead.

A simple task, indeed, yet certainly most time-consuming, considering the many pressing matters at hand requiring immediate attention. Other arrangements still remained—refreshments, decorations, individual favors—I remember jotting down "balloons, lots of balloons!"

All the calls had to be sandwiched in between the numerous calls being made on my phone—placed or received—by the President-elect, Mrs. Kennedy, Mrs. Lincoln, or me.

Thank heaven for Parties Unlimited of Georgetown, who came to my rescue with a promise of a "real live clown!"

But not everything was on that happy note of balloons and clowns and birthday favors.

The President-elect had occasion sometimes to be distressed at what was going on. He was not at all happy about an interview the social-secretary-to-be had given. It was November 23 when he came running out of his office at the Georgetown home.

In the past, it had not been the least bit unusual for the President-elect to shout out from time to time on matters that might have instantly changed his normally happy and pleasant mood to one of anger.

But this time, on this particular morning, he suddenly darted from the study to the guestroom clutching the newspaper he had just been reading and waving it into the air with some pretty strong words, reflecting his displeasure at the article purporting to quote Tish Baldrige, Mrs. Kennedy's newly appointed social secretary.

He told Mrs. Lincoln to see about putting a stop to this.

I looked at the three local papers to see what the fuss was about. Tish had indeed made news, "speaking in a flip way" among friends in the press, as she later commented in her book, *Diamonds and Diplomats*. She would be in charge of everything, as she put it, "everything from calling cards to laundresses," including all things concerned with "the comfort of the President and his wife."

The other part of her job, she was quoted as saying, was to be on duty every night attending to the social affairs.

Her interview appeared in four columns in the *Evening Star*, five in the Washington *Post*, and two in the Washington *Daily News*.

The various papers reported on November 23, 1960:

That Jackie planned to display contemporary American paintings in the White House and that "I'm sure it could be arranged even if it means makeshift arrangements like hanging them in front of other paintings." (Washington *Daily News*)

That she was going to scrape paint off the dining-room wall paneling to see what lay under the green paint the reporter said she didn't like—"I'll get my little knife out the first day and see what it looks like." (*Daily News*)

That she had called Mrs. Eisenhower's secretary, Mary Jane McCaffree, and was going to see her and "She's going to be a great help, I know." (Betty Beale in the *Evening Star*)

That she thought Mrs. Kennedy would hold regular press conferences. "I think she will. There will be so much news to impart that that will be the most efficient way to handle it." (*Evening Star*)

That Mrs. Kennedy planned to move in a lot of her own things, such as some 18th-century furniture, and porcelains, as well as "knicknacks" to make the family White House quarters "homey. She has a distinct flair for decorating." (*Evening Star*)

That Jackie would wear *American clothes*, and "I don't think she feels she can play favorites among designers." (*Evening Star*)

She was also quoted as having described receptions given by women's clubs, "those great vast hordes of women," amending it to "I mean those large groups of very interesting ladies." (Carol Le Varn, Washington *Daily News*)

Her answer to the press ladies' question about whether Mrs.

60 ॐ

Eisenhower had invited Mrs. Kennedy to see the living quarters was, according to Betty Beale, "The invitation has not been extended yet—but we hope it will be."

In fact, the Washington *Daily News* headline of the story was: "JACKIE ISN'T DISTURBED ABOUT MISSING INVITATION."

Tish later reported that Mrs. Kennedy said there would be no more Social Office press conferences.

8 ～ JOHN-JOHN

EVEN BEFORE JACKIE WENT TO THE HOSPITAL to have John, Jr., gifts from the public were pouring in for the expected baby. Almost every item was lovingly hand-made. There were knitted or crocheted bootees, crib blankets, coverlets, complete outfits of baby caps, rompers, and bootees in various pastel colors.

But strangely enough, they were mostly blue—as if willing the Kennedys to have a boy.

The packages would arrive at the Georgetown house and be heaped, unopened, on the couch beside my desk, giving an untidy post-office look to the room. This bothered Jackie. So, after I had removed the gift cards and addresses for thank-you notes, Jackie would order me to clear them out. "Put them in your car when you go, just get rid of them," she would say to me, leaving it to my discretion what to do with them.

I took them home, and Ray helped me open and sort them. Then I would bring the cards and addresses back to the office for acknowledgment.

Since these were gifts that I knew would be appreciated by charitable organizations, I made various anonymous donations, which I thought would be the way Jackie would want it all handled.

But a few I saved—for memory—and now and then I open the chest and look at them and remember.

Pink bootees and blue bootees and white bootees—some crocheted, some knitted, and even a pair in blue-and-white checked gingham, delicately handsewn. Crocheted bibs with dainty pink and blue flowers embroidered on them and edged with blue ribbon. A white full-length cape and hood set, knitted in intricate design and tied at the neck. A carriage cover, crocheted in white and interlaced in a diamond effect with pink and blue yarn, to play it safe. And, most quaint of all, a crib quilt appliquéed with various colorful animals doing tricks or studying their ABCs.

I, too, had frantically knitted something that would be ready for Jackie when she brought the baby home from the hospital. But so sure was I that it would be a girl, I made my little creation in pink—a little cardigan sweater with two rabbits on a seesaw across the front. Needless to say, when Jackie gave birth to a boy, I decided not to disturb the sea of blue with my pink present.

In November, 1960, millions of families were preparing for their traditional Thanksgiving Day festivities, but I found myself too busy to make a move toward shopping for even one sweet potato. With the sweeping tide of events, I simply resigned myself to the inevitable sacrifices, reporting to Georgetown Thanksgiving Day.

By late afternoon of that day, the President-elect and Mrs. Kennedy returned from Middleburg, Virginia, where they had gone to look over some houses. It was Jackie's hope that they would be able to get away from the White House on weekends and have a place to ride her horses.

As I left them in the study, I wished them a happy holiday and told them I'd see them in the morning, not realizing what the morning would bring.

At 2:30 A.M., I was suddenly awakened by the blaring phone in Ray's office. As I ran down the strairs all I could think of was an emergency in my family in Boston. I gripped the receiver to my ear, and to my complete surprise, I heard the voice of Jeff, the Secret Service Agent James Jeffries.

His message was brief, as he informed me of Mrs. Kennedy's quick trip to the hospital where, around midnight, she gave birth by Caesarian to a baby boy. I was startled and very much concerned. This was three weeks premature. But I was greatly relieved by his assurance, "They're both doing just fine."

My next thought instantly flashed to the Kennedy family nurse, Louella Hennessey. I knew Jackie would be looking for her the very first thing. I reminded Jeff, but it was unnecessary. From various phone numbers I'd given him to tuck into his little notebook just a few days ago, he was already about to call Louella. Considering that he was assigned to Mrs. Kennedy just a little over two weeks, I was impressed by his efficiency and thoughtfulness in calling me.

It required no imagination to guess what *this* day would be like when I arrived at Georgetown. And it was almost 5:30 A.M. around the clock again before I returned to my pillow after the long day of endless calls and telegrams. Such was the identification of the nation with Jacqueline—everyone shared in the joy of the birth.

The President-elect received the news of his son's birth while aboard the family plane, the *Caroline*, en route to Palm Beach, Florida. He immediately arranged for a turn-about flight back to Washington and went directly to Georgetown Hospital to visit with Jackie and have a peek at his son through the nursery window. His pictures on the front pages of the morning papers clearly showed his surprise, anxiety, and happiness over the sudden birth of the baby, John F. Kennedy, Jr.

Though Jackie was scheduled to remain in the hospital for some ten to twelve days, she felt well enough after the first few days to think about her personal affairs, and she asked for me. I took along whatever required her attention, but kept these items strictly to the minimum.

To avoid the press, I made my way as inconspicuously as possible to the hospital's third floor, where I found the Secret

Service Agents stationed in a little room directly across the hall from Mrs. Kennedy's.

This was my first meeting with Louella Hennessey. She was an ageless New Englander, never without a smile, and her eyes crinkled with laughter. Spotless from head to toe, she always smelled of the nicest colognes.

She immediately captured my heart. "No wonder Jackie wants her around at a time like this," I thought. "Just looking at her and knowing she was there would make any sick person feel better."

Most people have the mistaken impression that Miss Hennessey was the nurse for the Kennedys' newborn babies. She wasn't. She was the nurse for the new mothers, and was known for her ability to jolly them into doing what they should.

Finding Jackie looking so well and in such good spirits, I couldn't help feeling that Miss Hennessey had a lot to do with it.

Miss Hennessey took care of all the Kennedy mothers— Jackie, Ethel, Eunice, Pat, and Jean. And she always maintained that Ethel was the strongest female of the Kennedy clan —the one who would spring back and be on her feet quicker than any of them after a birth.

Jackie planned to leave for Palm Beach as soon as she was released from the hospital. Preparations were already in the works for the trip, for the Christmas holidays, for the Inaugural activities in January, and for the move from Georgetown to the White House by the 20th.

Between hospital visits and the pace of work at Georgetown, the momentum of my ride on the proverbial merry-go-round sped up. I began to lose a lot more weight from my already too-lean, size 10, frame.

It was only my continued loyalty to the Kennedys that kept me going. Even so, I wondered at times whether or not I'd have sufficient strength to get Jackie through her move to the White House.

The President-elect visited twice daily with his wife and new son. Emerging from his bedroom for the visits to the hospital, he always appeared in a fresh set of clothing, looking so handsome.

Invariably, he paused long enough by the guestroom office to pass a cheerful comment or some quick witticism to me and Evelyn, usually ending up with a rapid fire of more instructions to her. He would leave us shaking our heads with amazement at the number of important thoughts he accumulated during just the short process of getting himself dressed.

While Jackie rested in the hospital after John-John's birth, Caroline was the star. She usually accompanied her father on his daily visits to the hospital and, on Sunday, attended church services with him as well.

Her press coverage became almost equal to her father's. The faces she made at cameramen behind her daddy's back, and the toys she dragged along the ground were becoming familiar to everyone.

Just before the President-elect took Caroline to Palm Beach on December 2, I brought my boys in to say goodbye to her. Ray, too, decided the occasion would be a good opportunity to congratulate the President-elect on his recent victory at the polls, as well as on the birth of his new son. In the hope of getting a picture or two for the boys' albums, we took along our camera with colored film.

We chose bright red shirts for the boys and, upon arriving at Georgetown, we found Caroline completely dressed in red, too. The red-carpeted stairway in the front hall was to be the setting of our picture. But first, there was the problem of getting Caroline to sit quietly between Chris and Greg. She was in an exceptionally jubilant mood, running the length of the stairs from top to bottom and up again.

Thanks to Muggsy O'Leary, who was conveniently on hand at the moment, she did consent to sit for the quick "look at the birdie." Then, it was up and down the stairs again!

Shortly afterward, there was the loud familiar call for "Buttons" and, with it, the swiftest ascent that Caroline could muster as she headed directly for her father's bedroom. Together they emerged with hands clasped to join us in the guestroom.

JFK expressed his thanks to Ray for his good wishes and seemed equally pleased by the outstretched hands of Chris and Greg, who followed with their little handshakes as well.

Concluding our visit, Ray asked permission of the President-elect for one quick picture. He not only agreed, but observing that Ray had positioned himself with camera in hand, he thoughtfully asked, "Ray, wouldn't you like to get into the picture, too?"

"But who will take the picture?" Ray responded with obvious pleasure.

"Oh, I'm sure we can find *someone*," JFK vouched and, in the next breath, emitted a loud call for Provi.

"But I never took a picture," wailed Provi.

"Well," the President-elect said, thrusting the camera in her hands, "now's as good a time as any for you to learn. Just push the button."

It was an order.

Ray showed her the button and again we quickly took our places. But now, there was another kind of hold-up. Caroline, who was standing directly in front of her daddy, turned to him, wanting to be picked up. Because of his back problem, he gently urged her instead to turn around again and face the camera.

But she remained adamant and, finally her father, laughing, gave Provi the signal to go ahead and snap the picture, anyway, with Caroline's back turned to the camera.

How could we have known the very great favor Provi had actually done for us? Our "family photo" with the President-elect and Caroline now remains the one and only such picture.

The President-elect continued to carry a full-time schedule at the house, causing not only the usual excitement among those outdoors who waited to see him come and go, but creating an overload of visitors and activities inside, as well.

Besides meeting daily with members of his staff, he inter-

66 ॐ

viewed prominent people who were being considered for his Cabinet.

Formal announcements of his appointments were made to the press from the front doorsteps of the house—moments considered a great privilege to witness. The first such appointment I peered out upon was the President-elect announcing his selection of Governor Abraham Ribicoff of Connecticut to head the Department of Health, Education and Welfare, on December 1st.

After the President-elect took Caroline to Palm Beach, he was soon back, and I knew he was working on more appointments. In fact, I recall that Sargent Shriver brought Robert McNamara in through the back door, so that the reporters out front would not see them. He was scouting McNamara for Secretary of Defense.

About this time, I also caught a glimpse of Dean Rusk, who was being considered, along with Senator William Fulbright, for Secretary of State.

As it turned out, it was Dean Rusk, rather than McNamara, whose appointment was announced first—from Palm Beach, where the President had gone again, this time to take Jackie and the new baby. I saw by the papers that in Palm Beach the future President, following the same practice he had started in Georgetown, made his announcements from his father's home—Adlai Stevenson as U.S. Ambassador to the United Nations and Chester Bowles as Assistant Secretary of State.

It wasn't until JFK got back to N Street on the 13th that McNamara was formally appointed as Secretary of Defense. In rapid succession, he was filling other Cabinet posts—Governor Orville Freeman of Minnesota as Secretary of Agriculture, Arthur Goldberg as Secretary of Labor, and Douglas Dillon as Secretary of the Treasury.

But the surprise appointment was that of the President-elect's younger brother, Bobby, as Attorney General. There hadn't been any particular talk of it around the house, at least not where I was. I was completely wrapped up in Jackie's world, and she was not talking about politics and appointments during the hours when I was there. Except for one.

The appointment that Jackie showed interest in was that of the White House Chief of Protocol—Angier Biddle Duke, of whom she approved. But instead of going on the record herself, she asked Tish Baldrige how *she* liked Duke. Obviously, both were happy with this appointment.

At times, though I was racing against the clock myself, I couldn't resist offering Evelyn a helping hand. As in the old days in the Senate, no matter how much work she had before her, her answer was always the same: "No thanks, Mary, you're sweet to ask, but I think I can manage."

And manage she did.

Still, on a few occasions, I was asked to pinch-hit by the President-elect himself. Once when I was in the study—and apparently more readily accessible than his valet, George Thomas—the President-elect made the most startling of all his quick requests: "Oh, Mary," he called out from the bedroom, "would you run me a bath, please?"

Restraining my consternation, I dropped what I was doing, calling back, "How do you like it? Hot? Cold? Lukewarm?"

I needn't have asked at all. He was so preoccupied with more important decisions, he did not even answer.

Soon, he was in and out—apparently satisfied with what I regarded to be a happy-medium temperature. Passing me on his way back to the bedroom after his bath, his tall, manly physique suddenly took on the most innocent, boyish appearance as he clutched rather haphazardly at the large, loose towel around him.

This was just one of the many incidents that made me feel a member of the family. It emphasized the President-elect's down-to-earth behavior which would be a part of him in the White House as well.

I remember how concerned he was when my mother died. She, like his own mother, was a devout Catholic, with the responsibilities of a large family. And she started each day of her life by attending 7 A.M. Mass. That is, until she was stricken with gall bladder infection at the age of 72 and was hospitalized for the first time—then Communion came to her.

She had been a remarkable woman. She had come to this country from Italy in 1907, married my father, who had preceded her here by a few months, and settled in Hyde Park, Massachusetts. They remained in the same house for the rest of their lives, where their twelve children were born—all at home. I was the youngest.

She carried on her daily chores without the luxury of modern conveniences—she never wanted them. From her black coal-wood stove in the kitchen came the home-made *pasta*, huge loaves of Italian bread, and pizza—the likes of which I will never taste again!

When she scrubbed her sheets white on her old-fashioned washboard—we never could persuade her to use the washing machine—she would send chills up my spine as her strong voice rent the air with "O Sole Mio," "Santa Lucia," and "Sorrento."

Put quite simply, my mother's health was her greatest wealth; her family her greatest happiness; and morning Mass her only diversion. She never saw a movie, never went to the beach, or ever took a trip. She was completely satisfied staying at home, saying, "Everything I want is right here."

It was the morning of Friday, December 9th, that Jackie was discharged from the hospital, and the President-elect eagerly set out for his final trip there. He returned shortly with his wife and new son. I stood at the top of the long stairway as they entered the front door and, for a terrible moment, wondered to myself how Mrs. Kennedy would manage the climb.

The thought no sooner flashed through my mind, however, than the two Secret Service Agents quickly formed a "chair" for Jackie by firmly grasping each other's hands in a cross-locked position, just as we used to do in grade school, and with amazing ease they carried her right to the top.

What I remember most about that important last day at N Street was Jackie's inspection trip to the White House. Time was limited as, at noon, she was to meet with Mrs. Eisenhower at the White House for a tour of the rooms there, and a few short hours later, to board the plane for Palm Beach.

The whole household was now racing furiously against the clock on last-minute details as time itself continued to race unmercifully before us.

Finally, the fond farewells and good wishes went right along with the President-elect and his family as they made their scheduled departure—not to return until mid-January, and never to live in the house again except for Inauguration week.

Later, of course, Jackie set herself to the task of having the White House completely redecorated to her own meticulous tastes.

Gone was all the darkness, the wild array of potted palms, and everything else that contributed to what she considered the "dreary" appearance of the rooms as she had found them.

But, apparently, the memory of the tour still lingered when, about a year and a half later, she quipped to a friend how it had almost sent her "back to the hospital with a crying jag."

9 ∾ PALM BEACH

WITH THE NEW YEAR CAME A SUMMONS from Mrs. Kennedy in Palm Beach, asking that I please make arrangements to join her there for a few weeks. I left on New Year's Day and returned to Washington with her two and a half weeks later.

On the plane, I thought how nice it would be to get some sun on the Florida beach while helping Jackie get ready for the Inauguration—as a reward for all the extra hours I had put in. Then, I would go back to part-time work somewhere— maybe with her mother, Mrs. Auchincloss, again. Or, with Jackie's stepfather, Hugh Auchincloss, who had offered me a job. I wasn't worried too much about it. I had had a wonderful experience with Jacqueline and felt that I had helped in the election.

Except for the very modest earnings I was receiving as a "part-time" employee, Jackie had been good to me. She had sent lovely Christmas gifts—a beautiful pin, which had arrived at the Georgetown house for me, and a beautiful poinsettia which had been delivered to my house in Alexandria on Christmas morning, and which bore a tag, "With the deep appreciation of 'All The Kennedys.' " The pin had been accompanied by a card saying, "Merry Christmas, Mary, and lots of love, Jackie."

Yet, for all the joy that these two lovely gifts had brought to me at Christmas, there had been still another which I had received from Jackie a few weeks earlier, which had made me proudest of all—an autographed photo of her, the President-elect, and Caroline—such as we had used during the campaign —bearing by far the most significant and meaningful message:

"For Mary—what would we ever do without you!—Jackie."

A room was reserved for me at the Palm Beach Towers Hotel. As I set out for the Ambassador's house that first morning, I stopped at the Press Office on the first floor of the hotel to inquire about directions and transportation for getting out there. Sue Mortensen and Chris Camp, Pierre Salinger's secretaries, were typing away and, from the back of the room, a loud clatter also resounded from the Teletype machines.

The busy atmosphere left me with a feeling of intrusion. Yet, this seemed the logical spot for me to obtain the information I was seeking. So I remained waiting for the opportunity to speak.

At one side of the room, I noticed another woman also

standing and assumed that she, too, was waiting for one of the girls to stop typing long enough to answer a question. But I was obviously wrong.

When I finally broke the noisy spell of typewriters and Teletypes with the brief explanation of my visit, the woman, standing quietly by, heard me and broke into the most spontaneous reaction.

Smiling, she rushed toward me and rather excitedly asked. "What did you say your name is? Are you down here to work for Mrs. Kennedy?" That's as far as she was able to get.

Like a match set to a firecracker, her questions suddenly ignited the Press Office girls.

"Don't answer that! You don't have to answer any of her questions," they exclaimed, almost in unison, while Sue Mortensen actually leaped from her seat, grabbed me by the arm, and rushed me out of the room—leaving her all-important duties behind.

She led me to her parked car outside and personally chauffeured me to the Ambassador's house, explaining as we drove along that the woman asking all the questions was a news reporter—Helen Thomas of United Press—and that my being in Palm Beach to help Mrs. Kennedy was to remain quiet. I was to be incognito!

It seemed strange to be entering the Ambassador's rather palatial home for the first time. But, it didn't seem strange for long. The first person who greeted me was Caroline, saying, "Hello, Mary, do you want to come upstairs and see my baby brother?" I said, "Sure, you lead the way."

I followed her up the stairs to the nursery and found John nestled in his little crib, watched over by the new nurse, Mrs. Phillips, who had been hired just for him. She was about the same age as Miss Shaw and had flown to Palm Beach with the Kennedys from Washington.

The Ambassador's home was absolutely lovely in every way, with my desk set up in the living room just a few steps down the hall from Jackie's bedroom, so that I would be readily accessible for her work.

Through a window of the huge room, I looked out on a beautiful view of the beach and ocean. As time went on, I longed even more for the opportunity to enjoy that beach, even for a few minutes.

I never made it.

My living room office was in direct line with the entrance to the outdoor swimming pool, and I watched members of the family, as well as officials, meeting with the President-elect, talking animatedly, as they meandered or relaxed around the pool.

It was here that I first met and shook hands with many persons who eventually came to hold some high office in the Kennedy Administration. Most of the faces seem to have blurred together. There were so many of them, and I was so busy in Jackie's bedroom or at my desk. But I vividly remember looking up from my typewriter and being shocked to see the Vice President-elect—Lyndon B. Johnson—right there suddenly in front of me, his hand outstretched. I stood up, and we shook hands. "I'm Lyndon Johnson," he said.

Dressed in swimming trunks, he was on his way to the pool. I was left with a strong impression of how tall he was and how rugged. Yet, how gracious it was of him to have taken this minute to come over and introduce himself.

Important visitors were always coming and going. Someone pointed out Senator Paul Douglas of Illinois and Congressman Mendel Rivers of South Carolina.

A few were names that were not familiar to me. There was Chris Dunphy, a local friend, with whom the President-elect went for a game of golf. And another one I remember was Carroll Rosenbloom, owner of the Baltimore Colts, who had won Caroline's heart by bringing her a toy whale that she could float in the bathtub.

Lem (K. LeMoyne) Billings was another, and I was to see much more of him at the White House. He was one of the President's oldest friends. They had gone to school together at Choate.

Meetings were forever convening or breaking up for swimming or golf. Once JFK accidentally hit a Secret Serviceman with his ball, fortunately not injuring him too badly, and the President-elect told his mother, "Eisenhower didn't do much as a President, but at least he didn't do *that!*" Whenever the President-elect could, he would grab a few minutes to go into the "Bull Pen"—a walled area—to sunbathe in the altogether. He was not content, however, with just the healthy tan he had developed. Another development bothered him.

I remember his bit of humor that started one particular day off with a hearty laugh for Evelyn Lincoln and me, when he made his startling discovery. As our President-to-be looked into a mirror while we sat admiring him for a moment, like his private fan club, he suddenly became displeased with himself.

He slapped at his jowls and said, "If I don't lose some of this weight before the Inauguration, we'll just have to call the whole thing off!"

Another amusing episode almost brought to a halt the press conference the President-elect was holding out on the patio. Caroline suddenly appeared and took the spotlight right away from him. No wonder. She was dramatically dressed in her nightclothes with her pajama bottoms rolled up and clomping along in her mother's high-heel shoes!

This, however, didn't disturb her daddy, who laughed along with everyone else while the photographers had a field day.

The gay moments for me were very limited as I sat almost glued to my typewriter.

But then, I wasn't the only one who was busy. The whole household was a beehive of constant activity.

There was Evelyn, of course, who shuttled back and forth to D.C. with the President-elect.

There was Bonnie Williams, a most attractive girl, who it seemed to me, should have been modeling clothes on Fifth Avenue, but here she sat in a little room on the second floor, tending to her secretarial duties for the Ambassador and Mrs. Kennedy.

There was, of course, the Ambassador, whom I met again

74 &

my first day there. I found him to be gracious and sociable at all times. The first day, when I was working away in his study on the first floor, he came in to fix himself a cool drink from the bar. He offered me a Coke, then sat for a little while talking to his niece, Ann Gargan, who had come in with him. They seemed to enjoy each other's company very much and to have a great rapport.

It took a few days before Ann herself began any conversation with me. And when she did, her first question was, "How long have you been with Jackie?" From then on, it seemed, I qualified for *her* sociability.

There was Evelyn Jones in full charge of the housekeeping details, who was on her feet from one end of the day to the other.

There was the family cook, Matilda, who labored endlessly over meals for the family and guests.

And, of course, Miss Shaw had sole responsibility for taking care of Caroline and making her feel important so that she would not feel the new baby was displacing her in any way.

The atmosphere was so pleasant and exciting that for the first week I hardly minded the pace I was expected to set from day to day.

I was fascinated by Rose Kennedy, the President-elect's mother. Her figure was fantastically good, even in a bathing suit, and she seemed so vibrant and interested in everything her children and grandchildren did.

She dressed in colorful slack outfits when she was taking off for the golf course, making a beautiful picture in her soft pastels. She was quite a sportswoman, I was told, playing a good game of golf, ice skating, and swimming. She was so different from Jackie, who spent much of her time closeted in her bedroom, even having meals served there. I sensed that this seemed rather strange to the senior Mrs. Kennedy—that her daughter-in-law should stay secluded and not participate more—and I suspected that the two women did not understand each other too well.

The climax came one particular morning when Mrs. Rose

Kennedy stopped by my desk. "Do you know if Jackie is getting out of bed today?" she asked. When I responded that I couldn't be sure, she added, "Well, you might remind her that we're having some important guests for lunch. It would be nice if she would join us."

I immediately went in to relay the message to Jackie, but she took it gaily. She imitated her mother-in-law's manner of speech and sing-songed, "You might remind her we're having important guests for lunch . . ."

The luncheon guests arrived and departed without any sight of Jackie. In my own opinion, things were never the same between Jackie and her mother-in-law after that. Though the Kennedys never washed their family linen in public and kept things normal and polite on the surface, I felt that the relationship was strained from then on.

But to her credit, Mrs. Rose Kennedy always included Jackie in the family notes and reminders of religious days and anniversaries that she would mail to each Kennedy wife. She even sent reminders to Jackie concerning memorial Masses for Jackie's own father.

Jackie's usual practice with these, as well as other personal notes and letters from family, relatives, and close friends, was to hand them to me to be tucked away in a special "SAVE" file in my office.

I had heard that Jackie had been ordered to take it easy because of the effects of John-John's birth but I didn't know what Rose Kennedy might have been told.

It was not too surprising that Jackie refused to participate in the luncheon. While she was in Palm Beach, Jackie left her bedroom only for specific appointments that involved her alone. Once she was interviewed for *Time* magazine.

Another time, close to the end of our stay there, the fitters arrived from New York with Jackie's Inaugural gown—Miss Frankau of Bergdorf Goodman and her assistant—and again Jackie came out of seclusion. The gown was tried on and adjusted to her.

This was one time, I thought, that she would come out of

her quiet, subdued, mood and be bubbly and thrilled. It was, after all, a historic gown. But she went through the fittings in the most casual, unanimated way, it seemed.

I had just been looking on as the pins were being tucked here and there and had felt excited. She looked just lovely standing there in the gown, which she had designed herself. It was deceptively simple-looking, but elegant. I knew how complicated the pattern was.

It was composed of several parts. There was the silk crepe floor-length white gown on which the bodice had been painstakingly embroidered with silver thread. Then, over the sleeveless bodice, came the white sheer chiffon overblouse—also sleeveless. Over both, there was the white floor-length cape of the same crepe material as the dress. It stood high at the neck with a little mandarin collar.

But in spite of all the trouble that Bergdorf Goodman had gone through in bringing Jackie's idea to reality, executing it beautifully, and bringing it down to Palm Beach to be fitted, Jackie said she was more interested in Oleg Cassini.

At this point Cassini was doing some designing for her. Yet, she was holding tight the reins on Cassini, too, telling Pam that his sketches should come directly to her, so that all releases could be cleared.

Yes, it may have seemed quiet outside Jackie's door at Palm Beach, but inside there was plenty of activity. It is interesting how many things occupied Jackie's time in those history-packed days.

She wanted me to send back some pens she had ordered from Cartier, the New York jeweler, but to let them know that she was keeping one.

She wanted three copies of a picture the UPI photographer Stan Trettick had taken of her and the President-elect the day after the election, in which she was wearing a raincoat.

She wanted a picture the New York *Herald Tribune* had used of the President with Caroline's rag doll.

She wanted to arrange for hiring a stable manager for the house they had rented in Middleburg, if his price wasn't too exorbitant, and if it didn't seem that she was stealing him away from his current job.

And there were dozens of other things.

She was borrowing one of her mother's horses while getting her Middleburg friend, Paul Fout, to find a gentle horse for her husband. She told him that her mother was willing to lend them Happy Son to see if Jack wanted to ride, before they bought another horse.

She wanted me to tell George, the butler, back in Georgetown, to make up a package of each kind of liquor—but mostly Dom Pérignon champagne—and get it to the White House so that when she got there, she could set up a little bar.

Oleg Cassini was working on Jackie's Gala gown, and I recall she wanted him to bring down to Washington some shoes that Mr. Mario (her shoe designer at Eugenia of Florence) was making for her. Mr. Mario was kept busy, too. Besides these particular shoes, she wanted him to make up about 4 pairs to begin with—in preparation for next summer.

She wanted three more trunks from Burdine's—things to be packed were really piling up fast.

Jackie's hat for the Inauguration ceremony was on her mind. "Miss Marita" at Bergdorf Goodman's was to make two "domed" hats—they would later be called *pillboxes*.

Evidently Jackie was not quite sure what hat she was wearing for the Swearing-In ceremony. She was playing it safe, arranging for several. As I told Marita on the phone, "Mrs. Kennedy says one must be black velvet, the other deep red velvet. She must have them because she will wear them for the Inaugural—one or the other. Also, send the beige jersey hats, too, as planned." They were to be ready for the 18th or 19th, because, as I mentioned, she had to have them, even if they were only basted. They were fashioned, incidentally, after a white felt hat Marita had loaned her in the fall.

I recall Jackie told Pierre Salinger to call Oleg Cassini to tell him not to speak to any newspapers and magazines who called him for comments at any time in the future, and not to release any more sketches of her clothes but just to say, "No comment."

On another occasion, I sent a sharp letter to a would-be benefactor in the field of fashion, who had been reported in *Women's Wear Daily* as supplying one of her gowns, a sketch of which accompanied the article. My letter said:

"Mrs. Kennedy has asked me to write you about a sketch which appeared in Women's Wear Daily. She has not received this dress, nor does she wish it. If you have sent it to her house in Washington, she will have it returned to you. She is surprised that you would do this."

One afternoon Jackie asked me to call Colette, her favorite Palm Beach hairdresser, to see if she could give lessons in hairdressing to Miss O'Malley. Miss O'Malley, the masseuse for the Kennedys, "massage-hopped" from one room to the next here in Palm Beach, and was due to return to Washington with us at Inauguration time to spend the next few weeks at the White House. It seemed now that her busy fingers would become even busier!

When I had gone to work for Jackie, and she had first asked for an appointment with a masseuse, I had been surprised. At the time, I thought only sportsmen or those exerting extreme physical effort required an occasional massage.

But I made the appointment without questioning it, and my education was soon broadened even further. In fact, I soon came to learn that daily massages were not the least bit unusual in the everyday lives of the Kennedy family.

The pre-Inauguration project that amazed me most was Jackie's negotiations through her social secretary, Tish Baldrige, to borrow from Tiffany, the famous New York jewelry store, the diamond pin and pendant diamond earrings that she wore at the Inaugural Ball. (Tish had worked at Tiffany before becoming Jackie's social secretary.)

"Tell Tish," Jackie ordered, "that if it gets in the newspapers, I won't do any more business with Tiffany. If it doesn't, we'll buy all State presents there."

The amusing thing is that JFK found out about Jackie's

plan to borrow jewelry from Tiffany and had forbidden her to do so. But Jackie got around it.

As I explained to Tish, at Jackie's request, if Tiffany would back up Jackie's story that she had borrowed the pin from her mother-in-law, she still would wear it and the earrings. But I was to caution Tish to be very tactful.

Jackie also told me to arrange for painters to start repainting the rooms of the rented Middleburg house, Glen Ora, in colors she liked better.

When my long days at Ambassador Kennedy's home with Mrs. Kennedy were completed, I returned to the Palm Beach Towers to pick up right where I left off. I averaged 5 or 6 hours' sleep. The typewriter and desk installed in my room were getting more use than the bed.

We were nearing the end of our stay, and now I could hardly wait to get back home to Alexandria to rest up from this "rest"!

It was about at this point that Pierre Salinger was making a list of official appointments to the White House Staff for the President and Mrs. Kennedy. He asked Jackie, as he was seated near my desk, "Will you be keeping Mary Gallagher" to which she replied quickly, "Oh, yes, Pierre. Mary knows everything."

At this point, I hadn't been hired for the White House. Mrs. Kennedy had never asked me whether I wanted to go to the White House, and I had not expected to go. Now, as she questioned me directly, there was only one answer. I thanked her for her consideration, but pointed out that Chris and Greg must now come first, and working at the White House would keep me from my family more than I would like.

As a one-year stint, I had devoted myself night and day to the campaign, but eight years looming ahead were a different matter.

I made it clear to Jackie that I would certainly understand her hiring someone else to take my place, explaining, "I'm sure you'll be needing a full-time secretary once you're in the White House," and that, "I would be willing to just bow out gracefully," at this time.

But she wouldn't hear of it.

Jackie said she readily understood, of course, my wanting time for the children, but still, she "couldn't do without me." She suggested that perhaps we could work out something on a "part-time basis"—adding, "You just make your own schedule."

This, then, seemed a bit more acceptable, and I agreed to three days a week—Mondays, Wednesdays, Fridays. That, apparently, suited her just fine.

"Good," she said, "and that way, I won't feel completely tied down to dictating every day, either."

She seemed very relieved to have the matter settled and instructed me to contact Tish Baldrige—who was already at the White House, arranging office space—to tell her to take steps for putting me on the White House payroll.

10 ∽ INAUGURATION

*T*HE SNOW HAD FALLEN WITHOUT LET-UP THE day after our arrival in Washington aboard the *Caroline*. There was every indication that it would continue on throughout the night—that Gala night, January 19.

My car was parked in the garage behind the house on N Street, but by shortly after noon, transportation became impossible. So it was the combination of this and the jam-packed moments of the day that led Jackie to suggest that I sleep over.

What a day it was! Jackie's bedroom and sitting room became a battlefield of beauty with the troops charging in all directions. I was running from the guestroom like Paul Revere with messages. Provi was chasing around like a sergeant, trying to keep everything organized. The dressmakers were making the final adjustments on the Gala gown, the Inaugural gown, the swearing-in costume. Everything had to be assembled, accessories with ensembles.

And poor Jean Louis, the handsome, dark-haired hairdresser, was nervously waiting for Jackie to settle down for her new hairdo. I remember how Jackie had given the instruction from Palm Beach on how he should avoid the press. "Come in the back door. Don't say anything to anyone."

Meanwhile, the snow was falling, falling, falling—and everyone inside was getting more uneasy by the minute.

The Commander in Chief had done the only sensible thing. He had escaped to Bill Walton's house down the street and was using his friend's house as his headquarters to be away from all the commotion at home.

Jean Louis was lucky, too. He had left the house early, promising that he would return eventually for Jackie's final combing.

Evelyn Lincoln and I were both planning to attend the Gala at the Armory that night. We didn't want to miss the Kennedy brother-in-law, Peter Lawford, and Frank Sinatra, who was to be the master of ceremonies.

Evelyn had gone to the beauty parlor earlier that snowy afternoon, but I didn't have time. I was still working on a guide list that Jackie wanted to leave for the new owners of her house. Her words echoed in my mind. "It would be nice if they could have a list of everyone they will be needing after they move in here. You know, like the electrician, the gardener, the caterers, the grocery stores, the florist, the bookshops . . ."

Also, I was going in and out, taking last-minute instructions of what Jackie would be needing at the White House—what would be stored and what would be taken with her.

Evelyn returned to the house early that evening. She was upset and told me that it had taken her almost four hours to come from the beauty shop. Muggsy had been driving and had gone to Jean Louis's shop, where Evelyn was getting her hair done, and was bringing Jean Louis back. But the hairdresser had given up midway and walked back to his shop, leaving it to Muggsy and Evelyn to go it alone.

There was no point now in Evelyn's even trying to get home again to dress for the Gala that night, so she decided to sleep over, too. We both laughed when the President-elect appeared in the doorway of the guestroom and asked if we were going to the Gala. We told him, "If we could, we would!"

By now, I didn't envy them the jammed schedule that lay before him and Jackie—first a dinner with the Philip Grahams, of the Washington *Post*. From there to the traditional pre-Inaugural concert at Constitution Hall, and finally, the Gala at the Armory.

Jackie had put on her Gala gown, and there were only minutes left before leaving the house. However, there seemed to be some question between her and the President-elect as to whether or not she would wear jewelry with her gown—a lovely set of emerald necklace and earrings.

The discussion finally led to the President-elect's calling me over to ask my opinion on the matter. He had Jackie show me the effect both with and without the jewelry. With no hesitation, I favored *with*. He quickly asked, "Why?"

"Well," I said, "because I think it adds just the right touch of color against all the white." I had no idea as to whose side I was on, nor could I understand, either, why there should have been any question about it at all. Jackie stood silent throughout this little ordeal—apparently annoyed that her husband was questioning her judgment. It soon became apparent that I had agreed with the President-elect. Jackie yielded to his wishes and wore it.

In all the excitement and confusion of the evening, I was also pressed into getting Caroline ready for bed. This I thoroughly enjoyed, as it made me feel so at home. Miss Shaw was not on hand, and I took it on automatically, without a second thought.

"My word, Mary," Jackie exclaimed, "now you're even baby-sitting!" She looked radiant and lovely.

After saying goodnight to Caroline, she and the President-elect headed out into the snowy night for the first round of the Inaugural festivities.

With all the strength I had left in me, I made my way upstairs to run a good hot bath, hoping to relieve some of the tension, and retired to the bedroom, knowing that tomorrow would be another whirlwind day.

Miss O'Malley, the masseuse, came upstairs shortly after I did and saw how exhausted I was.

"What you need is a good massage—you've just been going for days and weeks without stopping," she said.

The next thing I knew, with a jar of cream at her fingertips, she began working on me from the very tips of my toes. Very soon, I neither heard nor felt anything more. Her soothing fingers had put me to sleep before I was able to say "Thank you," or "Goodnight." I have never forgotten, and perhaps never will, the feeling of that one treatment!

I awoke to see all outdoors transformed into glistening white. Inauguration Day!

Excitement reached its highest peak that morning. The phones rang incessantly, and throughout the entire household, every pair of hands moved swiftly. The President-elect rehearsed his Inaugural speech behind closed doors in the downstairs library. Provi was with Jackie, seeing to it that she had her breakfast and that her clothes were neatly laid out for the swearing-in ceremony at the Capitol. I manned the phones.

I saw Jackie when she was finally dressed. Her outfit was captivating—a fawn-colored wool cloth coat with a little stand-up sable collar and muff to match. Her pillbox, after all the fuss about getting the red and the black ones from Marita on time, matched the color of the coat. To combat the snows, Jackie wore elegant dark high-heeled, fur-trimmed boots.

Provi packed the Inaugural gown ready to be transported—

she would accompany it herself to the White House—for the new First Lady to wear that evening.

At noon, time was running out as the President-elect, ready with hat in hand, stood in the front hall, anxious to leave. But Jackie wasn't quite ready. She was in the front living room, looking into a compact mirror and touching up her make-up.

With an air of impatience, the President-elect called in to her, "Please hurry," and seemed even more fidgety as the next minute or two passed.

As I stood there to bid them both farewell and good luck, he turned to me and asked if I thought he should wear his hat, popping it off and on his head to allow for my quick judgment.

"You look handsome either way," I told him. "Just carry it in your hand, if you want to, but please get started—those people out there are getting pretty anxious."

Before I knew it, he began rattling off one last quick message—and, for the first time, I was without my notebook in hand. I never expected this—and at such a historical moment!

Asking that I call his office to arrange appointments for the following week, he spun off three names in one-two-three order. The first one was rather tricky and I knew I'd better jot them all down somewhere.

Muggsy O'Leary was standing close by, and from his breast pocket I grabbed a protruding envelope, scribbling the first name as "George McBundy" (instead of McGeorge Bundy, which I later learned was a common mistake made by others, too). The second name was Chester Bowles, and the third was Dean Rusk.

I recall that I was simply amazed at his clear thinking at a time like this, but I also wished, for his sake and mine, that they would hurry on their way.

Jackie was still touching up her nose; the President-elect took a few steps, leaned his head in the doorway, and saw what she was doing. "Come on, Jackie," he said more insistently. "For God's sake, let's go."

She could hear his impatience, and wordlessly, came out to join him.

The President-elect was frowning one moment but smiling the next as the door opened and they stepped out together.

They were off to start a new life. There was no turning back now. Soon they would be "Mr. President" and "First Lady," never to be ordinary citizens again.

There would be the swearing-in ceremony on Capitol Hill and the parade that followed it—and the White House to sleep in this night—and the next—and the next.

It was a secret, but I was one of the few to know that the new President would sleep in the Lincoln Room and his lady in the Queen's Room.

After the door had closed behind them, I turned toward the stairs. They looked like a mountain. The climb up to my office seemed an eternity. I wondered if I could make it. Were these the same stairs I had dashed up and down a thousand times during these last weeks with no effort at all?

I had to make that one phone call—his last request. Somehow, I did.

I slumped into a chair. That was it. I couldn't move.

The room swam around me, and the voices I heard seemed muted—the voices of Provi and of Tish. Tish had arrived to pick up Provi with Jackie's Inaugural gown to drive to the White House. Their words seemed far off, but I could sense their concern over my condition. Tish reached for the phone.

Vaguely, I recall being driven home by a White House chauffeur. That was all I remember. I slept right through the rest of the day—to be deprived of witnessing those historic moments when John F. Kennedy became the 35th President of the United States.

Vaguely, I recall a hand shaking me and a voice saying, "Wake up, wake up." Vaguely, I recall getting dressed to go to the Inaugural Ball with our best friends, Mary and Peter Kosak.

My husband tells me I "looked lovely" in my "Jackie" dress. I wouldn't know. I was there, all right, but I was practically a stretcher case—and I did wear a gown that Jackie had given me.

It was flesh-pink satin (with matching long gloves and clutch bag) in Empire style, the one in which Jackie had been photographed for an article appearing in *Time* magazine during the campaign, alongside a photograph of Pat Nixon, also in a long gown.

It fitted me beautifully but, for fear of recognition by the press—which I had realized Jackie would want me to avoid—I had asked Mrs. Odette Lehmann, Jackie's dressmaker at the time, to alter the bodice slightly.

Vaguely, I recall arriving at the Armory and crowds of people and music and voices, but what the Ball was really like—how it looked and what happened—that part of history will have to come from someone else.

PART TWO

THE GOLDEN YEAR

11 ∽ *INTO THE WHITE HOUSE*

*M*EMORIES, MEMORIES.

I leaf through my diaries that remind me of the White House I knew—the White House of the Kennedy years. Back, back, I go, to Camelot.

I am sitting at home now, in comfort in my Kennedy rocker, upholstered for me by White House upholsterer Larry Arata, who was kept busy with furniture for the 132 rooms of the White House.

Can all these things have happened in 3 short years—1961, 1962, 1963? I see across the room the painting sent to Jackie after she visited Ravello, Italy, in 1962, showing the town and the steps to the sea. And then I glance at the other Kennedy memorabilia scattered about or hung on the walls—the albums of photos, a framed invitation, autographed books, and etchings. So many things.

I read over my diary entries, and it is like remembering something that happened earlier today. Tomorrow I will surely hurry to the White House; JFK will catch me in the hall and say, "How are you doing with the bills?" Jackie will want me to call "Mummy" on the phone and say she can't make it. Caroline will come through my office dragging her Raggedy Ann doll.

I see their names.

Monday, June 12, 1961: Saw Pres. land in helicopter (w/ crutches), returning from Fla. weekend.
Caroline spent time with me in Monroe Room—requested

my bringing Tom Kitten to W. H. so she could see him.
Ernie Barcella sent over copy of article for proof-reading
(one in a series of 3 on the First Lady's "First Ladies").

I sigh, thinking how short these lines are for the stories
they tell. You could write a book about the President and his
health—and Dr. Janet Travell, one of his White House
doctors, did. She also had the White House carpenters make
a special writing board for me to put on an armchair when I
worked on Jackie's financial accounts at home. "Your back is
very important. It will make you sit up straight, yet be relaxed
while you're working." How right she was!

What a mixture I see of items of my "two families"—notations on my two boys, Chris and Greg, mixed in with news of
Caroline and John-John, as I leaf back and forth through
the years.

"Chris lost his first tooth" (August 10, 1962), and "Chris
and Greg were extended invitations for lunch with Caroline
by Miss Shaw. I am sure they'll love that." (March 4, 1961)
I also see that Caroline "thoroughly enjoyed playing with
Chris and Greg and shared a spot at their dinner table."

> June 15, 1961: Mrs. K. to return from European trip at mid-
> night.
> Chris no better. During night, carried 103° temperature
> and rash broke out all over body. At 2:30, we saw Dr.
> Broocks—diagnosis: measles!

Dr. Edward Broocks, pediatrician for Caroline and John-John,
was pediatrician for Chris and Greg too.
The next day we welcomed Jackie home.

> Saw Mrs. K. 10:00 A.M. She met me with very sweet "Hi
> Mary" and gentle embrace. She remarked how well I looked,
> and thought I had gained some weight!
> Came home to find Chris feeling much better!
> Mrs. K. brought me cigarettes from Greece.
> Provi brought me some dress material, white with gold design
> of Acropolis on it.

Provi also brought back blue drinking mugs for Chris and Greg.

S. S. Jeffries brought me Arpège from France.

Here's an entry right after "JBK"—we used "JFK" and "JBK" a lot to speak of the President and First Lady—left for India:

March 9, 1962: Called Dr. Donnally [my doctor].
Four medicines—stay in bed.

I really was exhausted that time. No wonder. Here is the item a few days earlier, March 2:

Worked 'til 9:00 P.M. Slept over at White House.
Saw Bobby and Ethel.

In fact, it got so busy that by 1963, almost all entries started with capital letters, "BUSY DAY." A few days earlier Jackie decided soon after the beginning of the year that she had had enough.

January 11, 1963: at W.H.—BUSY DAY! Jackie says, "I have done enough as 1st Lady, I am taking the veil!" Memo to Tish—advising JBK wants schedule cut down this year. Would like to spend more time with husband and children...

January 17, 1963: 9:15/JBK/Jean Paul appointment—Hair 1:00—A. G. (Attorney Gen.)—1st Court Case...JBK wants to be present opening.
3:15—Anne Lincoln: "Provi is called "The Mexican Princess"...We'll have to think of a good title for YOU!"

I smile as I see January 17, 1963; after "BUSY DAY" there is the notation, "Finally got to bathroom at 4:30 P.M.!"

I wish I could bring it all back (no time for bathroom and all). But in a way, I do bring it back when I turn these diary pages or look through the newspaper clippings I saved to show to my children some day when they are old enough and curious about their mother's day-to-day life with figures of history.

I notice in the old news photos and even in some of my album photos how often the President is toying with that front button on his coat. Even back on Capitol Hill, he was holding that button any time he seemed to need a little security. To me it was his "comfort button."

I had seen the White House before. I had even been in it. The first time was in my Senate days on the Hill. Lucy Torres, one of the girls in the office, knew one of President Eisenhower's secretaries and took me along for a visit one noontime.

We saw the President's Oval Office, looked out on the Rose Garden, and saw where the reporters wait for the President in the West Wing Reception Room. It was all very impressive, even though some reporters were dozing in the deep comfortable chairs. We didn't get to see "Ike"—he wasn't there.

Then there was a second time, when my sister, Louise, came to spend a few days with me. I booked our places on the "VIP Tour" at 8 o'clock in the morning, which gets to see more of the public rooms than the average tourist sees. I remember most the red-carpeted hall and foyer, extending up the grand staircase. I recall how the guard told about the little Eisenhower grandchildren—David and his sisters—romping up and down the red carpets. I never dreamed that someday I would see Presidential children romping on the same rug and a President and First Lady descend the same staircase.

Nor did I have time to think about it as I approached the White House on that first strange morning, my first day at work—January 23, 1961.

How snowy-white everything looked—the grounds and the building. I hadn't remembered how big the building looked close up. The guard challenged me. Nobody, it seems, was expecting me. I had no pass. I had nothing but my name to offer. In my arms, I carried such a bundle of folders and loose papers that anyone would have had the right to be suspicious!

Somehow I got in and reported to the East Wing of the White House. I went directly to Tish Baldrige's office, on the second floor, assuming she would have appropriate office space ready for me. None was set up at all. Instead, I was greeted with her instruction: "Oh, my dear, just grab yourself a chair somewhere." She was very busy at the moment.

I walked along the corridor, past the First Lady's Correspondence Section and the offices of the President's Military Aides. All the offices were occupied except one small room, next to Tish. It had a desk, chair, typewriter, and telephone, so I got to work with Jackie's personal bills, writing countless checks accumulated from the past weeks in Florida.

On Tuesday, in accordance with the agreement reached with Jackie, I remained at home, operating from my office there, and on Wednesday I reported to the White House again. Tish called me into her office first to "discuss something" with me.

She talked on for several minutes, and I wondered what she was getting at. I soon got the gist of it—that she was assuming authority over Mrs. Kennedy's personal affairs, as well as her own social affairs.

"Mrs. Kennedy can't be having so many secretaries with titles," she explained. "Social Secretary, Press Secretary, *and* Personal Secretary!" And she added, "But we can still give you some kind of title, like Assistant Secretary to the Social Secretariat."

She explained that I would be "doing exactly the same" as I had been doing for Mrs. Kennedy, adding, "Then, if you should have some extra time, you could help out here in the Correspondence Section." She elaborated, "You see, I can't have you as my secretary because I've brought Anne Lincoln down from New York."

"Tish," I broke in, "I'm not here looking for any titles. . . . I'm here strictly for *Mrs. Kennedy*, on the basis that we both agreed to in Florida. I think the best thing for me is to talk it over with her and get it straightened out."

95

"Oh, but we've already discussed it," she exclaimed, "and it's just that Mrs. Kennedy can't have a personal secretary. Mamie Eisenhower never had one!"

"I know that," I said, "but Mrs. Kennedy is *not* Mrs. Eisenhower."

Later, a little research brought out that Mrs. Truman and Mrs. Roosevelt both had had personal secretaries.

On Friday, I reported in with the decision that my working relationship with Mrs. Kennedy had again come to an end. I picked up the remainder of my work and headed over to the Mansion, the main part of the White House, to give Jackie the final word.

She was in her own room, the Queen's Room, breakfasting from a bed-tray, and greeted me with a pleasant "Good morning, Mary." Placing the folders at the foot of her bed, I simply announced, "Well, Jackie, it's all been very nice. I've enjoyed the past years with you, but, now, my job seems to be finished, so I'll just quietly say goodbye."

With a shocked expression, she cried out, "What are you saying? What's happened? You can't do this."

I filled her in on Wednesday morning's incident and explained that, under the circumstances, I felt the best thing was just for me to leave.

"Oh, but I *need* you, Mary," she said, "you can't leave me." She seemed most sincere, and I found I could not ignore her words. I agreed to reconsider only on the one condition that I could continue to serve in the same capacity as I always had, as her personal secretary.

"Yes, yes," she interjected. "Go back and tell Tish that I said to fix you an office over there—a nice, big one—and I don't mean in the Correspondence Section, either. Then, early next week, I'll walk over to see how things are set up."

As in the past, my devotion to Jackie overcame any qualms I felt, and I was willing, at least, to give the matter one more try. I was sorry that she was not giving me the official recognition at the White House, that both her social secretary and her press secretary had.

I questioned her about it, then added, "It's rather embarrassing, Jackie, especially since I can't offer any explanation to my family and friends, who know I've been working for you over the past few years." I prepared to leave the room, and Jackie, responding to my feelings, asked, "Would you prefer that I call Tish about your office?"

"Yes, Jackie," I said, "I'd appreciate that very much." She reached for the phone as I left.

By Monday morning, Tish had fixed up a "nice, big office" for me, adjoining the little room I'd been using during the past week. This one was previously used by Robert Montgomery, who served as television adviser to President Eisenhower.

I tried hard to absorb myself completely in my work, but the loud voices of the next office and the distance between me and Jackie remained too great for me to carry out the job.

I naturally expected adjustments by all of us during this first week in our new surroundings. Yet, adding to the misgivings I'd experienced so far was the phone call I received from Jackie one morning. She sounded most annoyed. "Mary, where is my address book? I can't seem to find it, and I need it. Do you have it there? I must have it right now!"

This was the first time that she had spoken in such sharp and impatient tones. I gently reminded her that I was still working with the book, adding all the up-to-date information she had asked me in Florida to insert.

"Now, Jackie," I continued, "if you're *asking* me for it, I'll be more than happy to bring it over to you."

Her voice was soft and her response apologetic. "Oh, yes, Mary, that's right. I completely forgot. I didn't mean to sound so harsh. We just have to blame it on the tensions of this first week here. Everything is so confusing!"

By the middle of the week, Jackie came over to the East Wing to see how things were set up. When she and Tish entered my office, Tish proudly announced, "And in here, we have Mary Gallagher."

She seemed pleased to show Mrs. Kennedy that the order

she was given about an office for me had been carried out to the fullest. Jackie and I exchanged a little smile.

"Gosh, Mary, you look like the real executive in this big office!" she said. And they went off to the next rooms.

But it soon became obvious that it had taken just this little trip to the East Wing for Jackie to realize that I was farther away than she, herself, preferred.

Within the next twenty-four hours she instructed me to "go through everything you have to do and whatever belongs to me personally, you hang on to. Everything else, just stack it up, turn it over to Tish, and ask her to handle it.

"Gosh," she continued, "you'd need a pair of roller skates for getting back and forth. We'll fix you an office right up here next to my bedroom like we used to have in Georgetown."

Suddenly I had another new office—the Monroe Room just a few steps across the hall from Jackie's bedroom—the Queen's Room.

12 ∽ THE FIRST LADY'S TYPICAL DAY

I LOVED THAT FIRST OFFICE I HAD IN THE White House proper—the Mansion, as we called it. It was in the elegant and historic Monroe Room in which three Presidents had made momentous decisions—Lincoln, concerning the Civil War, McKinley, the Spanish-American War, and Franklin D. Roosevelt, World War II. It was a serene island, in the living quarters of the Presidential family on the second floor.

For the first three months Jackie used the Queen's Room

for her bedroom, while the President used the Lincoln Room.

I smiled to myself as I thought many times in the days and months to come, "This is like Georgetown extended." All around me in the great house was activity and planning.

At the White House, my first call in the morning would be to the telephone operator to report in, and the next phone call was to the kitchen. Within minutes, I would be served coffee and toast or sweet roll on a silver service at my desk.

Jackie breakfasted from a bed-tray, while looking over the morning papers. I could usually expect Provi's voice on the phone between 9:30 and 10:30 saying, " 'The Lady' ees finished. She ees asking for you."

At times, the tray and newspapers would still be on the bed when I went in. If Jackie wanted to start right in with the morning's dictation, I'd simply take the tray and put it on the carpet by the door.

Provi, wearing her white uniform and shoes, would soon come in to remove it and carry it to the kitchen.

Jackie and I always exchanged a pleasant "Good morning." Occasionally, upon noticing what I was wearing or how I looked in general, she would add some cheerful remark.

"Oh, Mary, how do you stay so nice and thin?" Or, as on a St. Pat's Day morning: "Gosh, Mary, how nice you look with your bit o' green!" For the most part, just her happy smile said more than any little word could!

As I sat in the tufted chair by her bed, I'd invariably marvel to myself how wonderful she looked. She really needed no make-up; and I rather enjoyed seeing her without it—young and fresh as a child. She needed no curlers. Her hair, already brushed, fell loosely around her face, accentuating the youthful, carefree appearance.

Caroline would come in before school for her "Good morning" kiss, after she had walked her daddy to his office. She would have had her breakfast with her nurse.

John-John's visit would be next—either in the arms of his Nanny or Miss Shaw, or—when he had accomplished the great feat of walking—he'd storm in on his own!

If his mother's breakfast tray was still on the bed, he'd put his little legs to work and climb right up on it for his "treat"—sharing her toast and honey. It reminded me of Caroline at that age when, in Georgetown, she would slip downstairs to the library, indulging in the same pleasure with her daddy.

But there was a difference between then and now. I found myself watching nervously, worrying about his mother's elegant bedspreads. I'd fidget—would he drip that honey on them?

Propped up against the pillows, Jackie would reach rather methodically into the straw basket of mail that I'd carried in, tackling one folder at a time. They came from every direction of the White House—East Wing, West Wing, Curator's Office and, of course, my own separate folder of personal mail and messages.

Her dictation was sure and fluent, and covered a vast variety of details. They centered mainly on the ordering of her clothes, cosmetics, jewelry, and household items. There were details of running or decorating the White House, as well as the weekend house in Middleburg, the acceptance of gifts or the polite rejection of them. Some were dealings with various art galleries and art scouts, who were looking for things for her personal art collection. Others concerned paintings that were being offered for loan, as gifts, or were being purchased for the White House. And some were decisions about press interviews and requests that she pose for pictures (usually denied).

Even to the photographer Toni Frissell, one of the most famous child photographers, the answer was no. She wrote her a "Dear Toni" letter, thanking her for wanting to photograph her with the baby, but declining, saying that she would love to have Miss Frissell do something for her later on.

It was interesting to see that Jackie saw herself as a wife first and as a First Lady second. The White House switchboard was instructed to stop leaving messages for the "First Lady" and to call her "Mrs. Kennedy" on their notes.

And as wife, she remembered that JFK liked the jams and jellies made by Evelyn Jones, the head housekeeper at the

Ambassador's Palm Beach residence, who had a little side business in jellies up at Cape Cod.

We ordered those jams and then relayed a message to Evelyn Lincoln to have the President send Mrs. Jones a "short thank-you letter."

Jackie may not have been interested in current politics, but she was fascinated by history. Anything of a historical nature simply gripped her. I'll never forget how delighted she was that first year in the White House when the great philanthropist, Henry du Pont, brought her a facsimile of the first letter that had ever been sent from the White House.

Accepting it ecstatically, she said she was "absolutely thrilled" with it. She was, too. She placed it on an easel in the President's reception room outside his office, so that those who were waiting for an appointment would be able to see it. Commenting on the gift, Jackie said, "It is such a strange feeling to be in the White House now and looking at the first letter written from it so many years ago."

The amusing thing was that some of the current things *she* was sending from the White House at that moment were also being looked at and saved. And that was causing problems. The items in question were small checks she signed to cover daily purchases.

Many people who received these checks were not cashing them in, preferring instead to hold on to them as "souvenirs"! The same situation prevailed with those sent out by the President.

The result was bookkeeping chaos.

But the Kennedys quickly solved these problems in a manner that soon became quite familiar to me. In the future, it was to be my signature that would appear on all the checks being sent out for Jackie—with a brand-new bank account established in the name of "Mary B. Gallagher—Special." It was set up at the Riggs National Bank of D.C., the same bank Lincoln had used a century before. An initial deposit was made in the amount of $10,000, and it was kept at this level through monthly deposits.

I would write and sign the checks and keep a very strict account of them all.

Result: No more "souvenir holders"!

I was also signing Jackie's outgoing letters, just as I used to sign her husband's name on his mail when I worked in his Senate office. I had practiced copying her signature and trained myself at her direction so that she would be relieved of signing all but the most personal or diplomatic letters.

Finally, there was the matter of the code used at the White House on Mrs. Kennedy's personal mail. Anything that was to receive her personal attention was marked: "Mary B. Gallagher—Special."

Jackie instructed those who would be writing to her on a personal basis to apply this notation at the bottom left-hand corner of envelopes addressed to her.

From the first days, Jackie chose this as the way of ensuring that mail directed to her by members of the family, close relatives, and friends did not fall in with the piles of general mail automatically forwarded to Tish at her Social Office or the Correspondence Section in the East Wing.

From the White House Mail Room, her letters were immediately directed to me, via the Ushers' Office, and I, in turn, would bring them to Jackie's attention.

Items of a personal nature for Jackie were usually ordered in my name. At the same time, I would automatically instruct the sender of such items to use the special code notation on their outside mailing wrapper.

Jackie was not in the habit of lolling on the phone; she did not have long, drawn-out conversations. If something specific was on her mind, she would pick up the phone herself and ask the White House operator to "get So-and-So" on the line.

On incoming calls, the operators were well aware of relatives and the few close friends Jackie wanted put through directly. The rest of the calls were routed through the Social Office or through me.

At times when Jackie was not in the mood for accepting a

call, she would ask me to take it, and I would give her the message.

Or if she were away, I would act in her behalf. For example, when the President's mother called to say she was coming to attend a dance being given by Bobby Kennedy and would like to stay at the White House, I told her that Jackie was in Virginia but that I was sure she would be happy to hear it.

Someone had told me that Pat Nixon was a good friend of Jackie's. Yet, in my years with her, it was a name that never cropped up.

As for inter-office calls, Jackie liked even these to be brief and to the point. If she were dictating and the phone rang, she would allow what she considered an adequate length of time for me to get the message. If the caller showed signs of continuing longer than Jackie liked, she would signal to me and whisper, "Make it fast."

Usually, I could sense whether Jackie's patience was running out and would do something about shortening the conversation. But, on a particular afternoon, as Jackie stood by my desk, waiting to give me one of her own instructions, a female member of the staff simply would not be hurried. When I finally hung up, Jackie asked, "What was that all about?"

I started to tell her but, as soon as she heard who the caller was, she commented, "Oh, her. She just repeats and repeats herself all the time," and she lost interest in what the call was all about.

Our morning work sessions would normally last until around lunchtime. Once in a while, we would both have a bite while we worked, but usually, I would go to the White House Staff Mess while Jackie would join the children for lunch.

Afterwards, she would take a nap, putting a nightgown on. Provi would even change the sheets because, as she put it, "Mees Kennedy likes nice fresh sheets." And indeed Provi would have the bed freshly made up again, looking fit for a queen, at that!

The President, too, was a confirmed "napper," and he would come in from his luncheon midday swims in the White

House pool, have lunch, and try to get in an hour or so each day before heading back to his office in the West Wing.

Whether or not *his* bed was given the nap treatment of "fresh sheets," I couldn't say.

After her nap, Jackie would dress in slacks and a loose-fitting blouse or pullover for our afternoon work sessions. She particularly liked turtleneck pullovers with long sleeves made of lightweight jersey, which we bought in great quantity from a store called Jax-Manhattan, Inc., in New York. In the winter, her slacks would be gray or brown, but in the summer, she would blossom out in the colors of the garden—pinks and other bright colors.

The afternoon sessions would normally run for an hour or so. And, as a rule, I'd be sufficiently caught up with the day's affairs by 4 o'clock and head for home in time to prepare dinner for Ray and the children. But, then, whenever necessary, I'd stay a few extra hours and arrange dinner with a quick phone call to my mother-in-law, who would automatically take over.

I'd carry Mrs. Kennedy's bookkeeping accounts in my briefcase, and after dinner immediately settle down to the homework it entailed. The "black book," as we referred to it, never left me. If anyone got curious, asking what I had in the briefcase, I'd simply refer to it as "my little pet baby"—and they'd settle for that.

When the Kennedys needed a figure or a bill, they would call me at home, and I'd have the answer without delay. So it was imperative that I have it with me at all times!

One of the first things I learned at the White House was that the financial affairs of the Kennedys were handled at the office of the old patriarch himself, Joseph P. Kennedy.

His whole family referred to him as "the Ambassador" (dating from the days he had been American Ambassador to the Court of St. James's) and so did the rest of us around him. He took an acute interest in the affairs of his sons and daughters and they, in turn, made it a point of pride to show that they could handle their money properly.

His headquarters, then located at 200 Park Avenue, New York, was highly active in handling the accounts for all the Kennedys. The man there with whom I dealt the most was Tom Walsh, in charge of handling the President's and Mrs. Kennedy's personal financial affairs. I was frequently on the phone with him concerning some arrangement for Jackie; or, at times, on a quick summons he would make a flying trip to the White House to help solve some problem at our end. He was efficient, reliable, and always full of good humor.

Not long after we had taken our first strides toward coping with Jackie's finances, he sent me the most humorous cartoon —so significant of the moment! It depicted a rather distressed housewife, crouched on a couch by a desk in the den, as she begged sympathy from an irate husband who stood hovering over her clutching a handful of bills. From her lips came the words: "I'll bet Jack wouldn't yell at Jacqueline if she were overdrawn!"

Tom and I could laugh—we could see the funny side of this story. But, unfortunately, for the President it was no laughing matter. It was, actually, a situation that continued to cause him more and more concern as time went on.

It was very quiet upstairs during the daytime hours when I was with Jackie. As at Georgetown, members of the Kennedy clan, Ethel, Eunice, Pat, and Jean, appeared very rarely. I saw Ethel only a few times, and the others certainly no more. As for the brothers, I can't recall having seen Teddy upstairs in the White House, and Bobby only infrequently. From what I had heard, Bobby was careful to be like the other Cabinet members, making appointments through Evelyn Lincoln to see the President at his office.

As a matter of fact, stories were told around the White House of how adamant Bobby was that people show proper respect in referring to his brother as the President. Once, a State Department official was telling Bobby something about what "your brother" did.

Bobby snapped back with, "You mean the President, don't you?"

But that was in line with how all the Kennedys felt about their family's titles. One day, my husband was having lunch at the New York Athletic Club with a group of Kennedy associates. The conversation got around to Joseph P. Kennedy and, in his casual way, Ray referred to him as Joe Kennedy. He was quickly corrected by one of the Kennedy corporation men, who said firmly, "We always call him the Ambassador." Ray was somewhat taken aback; Joseph Kennedy had not been Ambassador for over twenty years, and Ray didn't realize that he was still being called by that title. "I'm very sorry," he said.

I was surprised when Pam Turnure, who was only 23 and had no newspaper experience, was named Press Secretary to the First Lady soon after the election.

Inasmuch as the management of Jackie's press relations during the campaign-election period had been handled by Gladys Uhl of the Democratic National Committee, it had been my assumption that Gladys would become Jackie's press secretary at the White House.

However, while we were still in Georgetown, Jackie received a note one afternoon from Pamela Turnure, then the receptionist in her husband's Senate office, asking about "working with the press." Pam felt that she could learn the duties gradually.

Jackie simply dictated a note at the time to Tish Baldrige, suggesting that she contact both Gladys Uhl and Pam Turnure and "interview" them.

How these "interviews" went, I had no way of knowing. But in the end, Pam was appointed to the position of Mrs. Kennedy's Press Secretary.

It was to the Monroe Room that Tom Walsh came down from New York on Tuesday morning, March 21, 1961, to help me set up my new ledger system for keeping strict account of where Jackie's heaviest expenses were incurred.

After dinner, I posted figures to ledger until 10 P.M., including every check written over the past 2½ months. This, as it turned out, was the very beginning of the mammoth book-keeping system for which I was to be responsible to the President over the ensuing years, along with my regular secretarial duties for Jackie.

Though my schedule at the White House—Monday, Wednesday, and Friday—was considered part-time, this extra-curricular activity "with the books" had soon begun to fill the alternating days at home, and eventually, the better part of my weekends, too. My weeks, as a whole, amounted to a full-time job, almost from the beginning, even though I did not personally appear at the White House each and every day of the week.

On this particular ledger-night at the White House, Tom Walsh and I had been working on and off since 10:30 in the morning and would be back at it again early the next morning. So a lovely guestroom on the third floor had been readied for me.

Much to my chagrin, once the White House doorman, Mr. Jones, had led me to it, I suddenly realized that I was without a nightgown. I thanked him for showing me to the room and, as he turned to leave, I asked him whether Provi was still on hand.

"No, ma'am," he answered, "Provi's been gone since five o'clock." "Oh," I said, "are any of the other maids still on duty?"

"No, ma'am," he answered again, "since Mrs. Kennedy's not here tonight, they've all gone home. Is there something I can do for you?"

"Oh, no, Mr. Jones," I stammered, "that's quite all right— I can manage. I just thought one of the girls might still be around."

"No, ma'am," he repeated, "I'm sorry. Goodnight, ma'am."

I had heard of people sleeping "between the sheets" before, but the thought of my chalking up this little experience at the White House was beyond expectations!

However, after a relaxing bath, I ventured between the cool, crisp sheets *au naturel* for one of the most restful night's sleep I had ever known!

This, then, was my first historic experience of "sleeping over" at the White House. And to play it safe, from then on, an overnight case, packed and readily available, was in my office closet.

13 ∽ OUTSIDE THE QUEEN'S ROOM

*M*Y OFFICE IN THE MONROE ROOM OPPOSITE the Queen's Room was convenient to Jackie. It also allowed me to meet visitors and dignitaries I might otherwise never have seen.

For one, Peter Lawford, an in-law of the Kennedys, had always been a favorite of mine from his *Thin Man* series on TV. Though I had had brief glimpses of him at the Ambassador's house in Florida, I was pretty excited over his first trip to the White House, when he came into my office in the Monroe Room. I obtained his autograph on a small, white, gold-engraved "White House" card. Thereafter his visits became more frequent, and I was able to accept his presence with a little less excitement. He was just a member of the family. One morning, as he passed me in the Center Hall, he casually asked if I would fasten the cuff-links on his shirt-sleeves. And, casually, I obliged!

I never saw Congressional and Senatorial wives upstairs at the White House. But Jackie attended the annual luncheons the Senate Wives gave in her honor on the Hill. On these occasions, Lady Bird Johnson, as the Vice President's wife, was her hostess. Still, I never came in personal contact with Lady Bird Johnson at the White House.

It was in the Monroe Room in May, 1961, during their visit to the White House, that I saw one of the world's most dazzling couples. The President and Mrs. Kennedy, showing them through the living quarters, approached the Monroe Room; and they stood at the doorway, chatting for several minutes.

I looked up from my work to behold Prince Rainier, with his trim, dark mustache, most dashing and charming, while Princess Grace, with her fair, flawless complexion beneath a white cloche hat, gazed admiringly into the President's eyes as he spoke. He seemed to be explaining historical points of the Monroe Room, and she appeared most interested.

Never again, I knew, would I see a more delicate and fragile beauty than hers.

I also remember vividly the day when Commander Alan Shepard (the first space astronaut) arrived at the White House for an official ceremony on the South Lawn. Caroline wanted to go downstairs with her mother, but Jackie preferred that she remain upstairs.

I managed to pacify Caroline by offering to show her some pictures of Tom Kitten and the boys, which I had in my wallet. But at the sound of the approaching helicopter, Caroline's excitement rose, and I knew I could no longer hold her interest.

"Shall we go out on the balcony and look?" I asked. In a split second she was leading the way. We peered down through the iron railing of the balcony to watch the official welcome and decoration of the Commander. Suddenly, hoping to get her mother's attention from below us, Caroline broke her silence and called loudly, "Hi, Mommy!"

Not only did her mother look up, but so did the semicircle of photographers, who instantly clicked away with their cameras.

It appeared—this unexpected picture of us together—in newspapers the next day. One of the captions read: "Meanwhile, up on the balcony, Caroline is held by a nurse." Obviously, my anonymity at this point remained well-preserved.

"T.K."—that stands for Tom Kitten—was Caroline's cat, and she missed him very much when Jacqueline decreed that he had to go—and my home was the logical pet haven.

Tom Kitten was Caroline's very first favorite—she had had him since she was three. It hurt to give him up, even though she knew my sons Chris and Greg, who were close to her own age, were taking good care of him and loved him, too.

When did she first come to visit him? Yes, here it is in my diary.

> Saturday, March 4, 1961: Social visit today—Caroline came over with Miss Shaw, John, Jr., and U.S.S.S. Agents Lynn Meredith and Bob Foster, to visit "Tom Kitten." They arrived @ 4:15 P.M. and left at 7:30 P.M. Caroline was very happy at seeing her cat again. She threw her arms around him and gave him a great big kiss . . .

Pierre Salinger, the President's press secretary, had confessed to the press what had happened to Tom Kitten and another White House pet. Soon a headline said, "White House O.K. for a President, but Not for a Dog or Cat."

The story told that Tom Kitten had begun meowing too loudly when he arrived in February when the children returned from Palm Beach. T.K. searched through the White House and found not another cat for company. He was pretty lonely there. And as for the dog in the headline, that was Caroline's Welsh terrier, Charlie. He had been temporarily shipped out to Glen Ora, the rented weekend retreat in Middleburg, Virginia.

But the story did not say that the President was allergic to dog and cat fur and that his fatherly indulgence was always being put to the test—whether to be surrounded by the many pets the children yearned for, or be kind to his sensitive nose and get them all out of there.

Hamsters outnumbered everything, including people. There was the time when one of them drowned in the President's bathtub. And one morning, as I entered my office and turned on the light by my desk, out ran a mouselike creature. I emitted a wild shriek, breaking the serenity of the most dignified surroundings in the land.

Much to my chagrin, the doorman who came to my rescue could not have appeared more blasé as he prepared to retrieve the squirming culprit. I got the impression that he had been through this before and even expected it to happen again. I was relieved when he had the little rodent cupped securely in his hands at a safe distance from me. Carrying it off to its proper shelter, he said resignedly, "It's only the children's hamster, ma'am. He won't hurt you!"

"He won't help me, either," I retorted. I was still shook as I grabbed up a bunch of folders and headed for Jackie's room.

For the most part, the President succeeded in keeping Caroline's menagerie quartered outside. The dogs stayed in the area of the Flower Room, where the fresh bouquets were made —a sort of greenhouse. The White House menagerie grew with the years, and eventually included Pushinka, a gift from Premier Khrushchev.

Pushinka was the offspring of the first Russian space dog, Strelka, and made big news when she arrived at the White House. Charlie immediately fell in love with her and soon there were four more pups! When they were old enough to be given away, Jackie wanted to be sure they would have good homes and saw to this personally.

One was to be awarded as a prize to the winner of a letter-writing contest. Children from all over the country were invited to enter by writing a letter about the kind of home and care a dog should have. And, of the top contenders, I remember Jackie instructed Pam to check into their home life, warning her to be sure it wasn't given to any child with a drunken father, who might slam it against the wall.

Another she presented to Louella Hennessey, the Kennedy nurse, who she well knew would provide a good home for it. And another she promised to the children of Peter and Pat Lawford, telling them that, as the pups grew a bit older, she would see to it that the children got "the peppiest one." The fourth, as I recall, was presented to a White House employee, Mr. Traphis Bryant, who looked after the pups until such time as they were ready to be given away.

Then, after his trip to Ireland, the President received a cocker spaniel named Shannon from the Prime Minister of Ireland, Eamon De Valera. Shannon soon became the children's favorite, even supplanting Charlie, who was the most written about in the press.

Of all the pets at the White House, Jackie's favorite was her German shepherd, Clipper, given to her by the Ambassador, Thanksgiving, 1961. Few people knew that Clipper was her constant companion and at times was allowed upstairs in the living quarters to nestle contentedly by her feet as she dictated. Because of the President's allergy, Clipper would be sent downstairs before he returned from his office.

Last, but not least, was Wolf, a gray Russian wolfhound, who was very thin and rather nervous.

Macaroni and Tex were Caroline's two ponies. Macaroni, of course, whom she rode around on the South Grounds, was her favorite—and keeping a steady eye on him and her as they paraded the grounds were Miss Shaw and the Secret Service Agents assigned to the children.

Like her mother, Caroline was always very considerate and protective of her pets. One time, I recall, when she thought her little brother was being too rough with Clipper, she admonished him in a grown-up way, "John, you aren't supposed to do that to a dog's tail. Be careful. If you want to pat him, do like this," she said, as she gently stroked away at Clipper's head.

Now and then, it would be Glen Ora, the rented estate at Middleburg, that would claim Jackie's attention. From the outset, the Kennedys used Glen Ora as a weekend retreat, enjoying the respite it offered from the White House.

The clearing of the new groom for Glen Ora through Secret Service was essential. Jackie was happy to hear that he was also handy around the house. Besides being good with horses, he was an engineer.

In the spring of 1961, Jackie would go hunting occasionally, making plans usually with her friend Mrs. Paul Fout at Middleburg. I used to call Mrs. Fout on the phone with messages about when and where the hunts would take place.

From the moment Jacqueline became First Lady, she began changing the White House interior . . . a project that was never completely finished from the day we entered until the day we left. All around in the great house was activity and planning.

I like the way Pierre Salinger puts it in his book, *With Kennedy*—"As the Kennedys moved in, so did the carpenters." It was like the house on N Street. If the President was looking for a familiar spot that would not change, he had again come to the wrong place!

JFK did not raise a fuss until fairly late in 1963. Jackie had about run out of things to redecorate and had finally thought of the President's elevator. She made it very elegant and ornate—very unlike an elevator—she even had it wallpapered. The President put his foot down. He didn't like the wallpaper. He didn't like the green carpeting. And he said the whole effect was too bright.

Soon Jackie asked that the painters go back to work once more on the elevator—this time to change it to the same soft muted white as the State Dining Room.

More than once the President was called upon to decide just how far one could go in re-making a White House into a home for an artistic First Lady with the sensitivity of Jacqueline Kennedy. For example, there was the matter of whether one dared change the color of the Blue Room to white with blue touches—the press had a field day with that one.

And whether it was all right to inaugurate the actual *selling* of guidebooks in the White House to make money for buying more furnishings. It was a tradition-breaking move.

In fact, it all was pretty much tradition-breaking. As Pierre recalls in his book, Jackie later wrote to a friend, "I was warned, begged, and practically threatened not to undertake the renovation."

The President checked with his advisers and trusted friends how best to proceed with renovation, if it should be done at all. His fear was that it would cause the same kind of public furor that President Truman's balcony had caused.

But Jackie had captured the heart of the nation, and could do no wrong. The President was surprised and pleased at the public response, and he was, of course, glad that her renovation chores were keeping his wife busy and happy in spite of her first reaction to the White House, on the visit with Mrs. Eisenhower.

By spring, the renovation of the family quarters on the second floor, though not entirely completed, had reached the point at least where the Kennedys could begin to use the rooms at the West End. The bedrooms at the East End now served as guestrooms for family and close friends who visited.

During the renovation, Mrs. Henry Parrish II, the interior decorator from New York, was of great assistance to Mrs. Kennedy. "Sister Parrish," as Jackie affectionately called her, devoted endless hours of effort and skill to the project.

First came Caroline's room and John-John's room, and then the President's and First Lady's rooms, so they could move out of their temporary quarters in the Lincoln and Queen's rooms.

Caroline's and John, Jr.'s bedrooms were located off the Center Hall opposite the Oval Room. Miss Shaw's bedroom was conveniently situated between the two.

Caroline's room was furnished in a typically feminine theme of pinks and whites, with a white four-poster canopied bed, dressed in the same rosebud chintz material as the drapes and couch. At one end of the room was the huge dollhouse given to her by President Charles de Gaulle. Displayed throughout the rest of the room were many stuffed dolls, animals, and other toys.

John, Jr.'s room, opposite Caroline's, was furnished in a

blue-and-white theme, and typically showed his natural interests in toys and pictures around the room.

President Kennedy's bedroom, directly off the West Hall, was conveniently located nearest the family elevator for quick departures and arrivals to and from his office in the West Wing.

It was handsomely furnished with a large mahogany four-poster bed and matching pieces set against off-white walls. It was finished with accessories to the bed and windows of a masculine, deep blue-and-white design.

At the foot of his bed was a table holding his reading material of daily newspapers and current magazines. *History Today,* I recall, was a favorite. Overseeing the order of the room at all times was meticulous George Thomas, JFK's valet and most devoted attendant. I always had to give *History Today* to him to be sure the President saw it. Jackie had asked me to subscribe to it.

Jackie's bedroom, dressing room, and bath—separated from the President's bedroom by a deep closet that contained a stereo system—were located directly off the West End sitting room.

Decorated in shades of pale green-and-blue, her bedroom contained most of her own furniture that she had used in Georgetown. At the foot of her bed was an upholstered bench that held current issues of magazines—both American and foreign. Among the foreign publications were *Paris-Match, Figaro Litéraire, L'Officiale, Art à la Mode, Femme Chic, Elle, Realités, and Spectator.*

Jackie had rather exacting tastes, of course, when it came to decorating. I remember there was much grumbling by some of the craftsmen at the demands for perfection that were made on them. But the incident that caused the greatest flap was the time the White House painters saw *red* over the *green* walls of Jackie's bedroom!

The painters had taken it as just another job when Mrs. Kennedy gave instructions about how she wanted her bedroom painted. Her choice had been pale-green walls, with the door and window moldings painted white. This was an intricate task, requiring extra care with the use of masking tape, to prevent the two colors running together.

The second important factor was that of time. The job was to be done in her absence from the White House over a weekend and completely finished by her return.

The room was large and, considering the details involved, had required the use of some extra men. They worked feverishly away. By the time Mrs. Kennedy returned, the room was, indeed, ready. How relieved they were to meet their deadline!

However, as she and I stood in the sitting room by the doorway leading into the bedroom, her first glance at the magnificent results was to bring forth only these most unexpected words, "Oh, gosh! I'm not so sure I like the room this way. Mary, do you suppose I could ask to have it all done over in off-white?"

I nearly staggered. I had nursed it along, and it was almost as though I had just completed this laborious task myself. "Oh," I questioned, "don't you like it, Jackie? I think it looks lovely."

She just stood there contemplating it. I could tell that her mind was still working, and I added, "Well, Jackie, if you'd really like it done over, I think the person to ask would be Mr. West." I just knew I had to get out of *that* kind of commitment.

"Oh yes," she readily agreed, "would you ask him to come up here?"

Weakly, I reached for the phone, and within minutes, Mr. West was receiving the same casual question.

He replied without hesitation, "Well, Mrs. Kennedy, if that's what you'd like, all you have to do is say so. I'm sure we can take care of it for you."

My heart went out to the painters. I certainly didn't want to be around when they were given their *new* instructions. Yet, I still wasn't to be left out completely.

Later that afternoon, as I sat at my desk in the Monroe Room, I received a personal visit by one of the painters. As spokesman, he had come to me for verification. "You know, it's not that we mind the work so much—after all, it *is* all in a day's work. But, tell me, Mrs. Gallagher, you've been with Mrs. Kennedy now longer than any of us here—does she *always* go around changing her mind like this?"

I could offer no encouragement. "Well," I answered, "I think you'll find as time goes on that Mrs. Kennedy has definite ideas and tastes when it comes to decorating and furnishing her rooms. So, I guess it's really just a matter of trying to accept things like this as they come along."

This did little to ease him, so I volunteered the story of how, in Georgetown, Mrs. Kennedy had had the wallpaper in the study changed three times within a few months. This, too, neither cheered nor consoled him. He left without cracking a smile. Eventually Jackie's bedroom was handsomely redecorated, and fortunately, it caused no shattering problems.

I always thought that any woman would have enjoyed the chance to step into Jackie's dressing room and glance over the colorful array of clothes that hung in the closets—a real treat to the feminine eye! Provi neatly arranged the garments in their various categories—suits, blouses, slacks, dresses, evening gowns—with matching shoes carefully lined along the floor beneath the racks. One could simply spot the shoes that went with each particular outfit.

In another closet, a walk-in, pretty hats sat on their head forms on the shelves, with even more shelves, holding the assortment of handbags. And it was almost like walking into a little shoe store—even more shoes were lined up along the floor.

Sweaters, lingerie, gloves, scarves, stockings—all carefully laundered and folded—rested neatly on shelves in the dressing room just beyond the clothes racks, always readily accessible. In this same general area were Jackie's jewel cases—about two or three—for her quick selection of an appropriate piece.

The sitting room—spacious, comfortable, and tastefully furnished—displayed, among other things, some of her favorite costly European acquisitions—drawings and paintings. A corner table by the long couch at the end of the room held framed photos of her father, a strikingly handsome figure, and of her father and her. A little picture of her mother, holding Jackie at a very young age, rested on a table in her bedroom, in front of the fireplace.

A large, round table sat in the center of the sitting room, usually holding a floral arrangement surrounded by various large books on art, antiques, furniture, and such.

The two main walls, on either side of the room, were lined with ceiling-high bookshelves and large storage cabinets below. Against the center wall, leading into her bedroom, stood her mahogany secretary with stationery, telephone, incoming mail basket, and the ever-present memo pads that Jackie used for scribbling sundry notes to herself throughout the day. In almost pattern-like form, her quick, fresh reminder headings would be listed each day:

"Phone," "Write," "Do," "Mary."

Under each category, she would appropriately register her thoughts as the day progressed.

The transformation of the "Margaret Truman Bedroom" to the Kennedys' private dining room was, perhaps, the greatest change of all in the family quarters. It was located directly off the West sitting room, opposite Mrs. Kennedy's bedroom. Its scenic, historic wallpaper and its glittering chandelier highlighted the splendor and set the mood for the meals served there.

The large, modern, totally equipped kitchen was installed directly off the dining room so that, unlike previous First Families, the Kennedys enjoyed one of the unique features in dining pleasure at the White House.

There already were two dining rooms in the White House—the formal State Dining Room and the Family Dining Room, both on the first floor. What had annoyed Jackie was that the food had to be cooked in the kitchens on the ground floor and sent up by dumb-waiter to the first floor. Unless it was rushed up, it was never hot enough. So she designed her own kitchen and dining room, right in her own family quarters on the second floor, now referred to as the "Private Dining Room."

In fact, both the kitchen and the dining room were directly off the West Sitting Room—most convenient for sending Provi in with a quick message for the chef. Such as "We'll be having six for dinner tonight," or "Tell him I'll have some hot tea when I wake up from my nap."

Of all the family rooms, my favorite was the Oval Room, located off the Center Hall and next to the President's bedroom. It was, I would say, the most dressed-up of all—simply elegant!

Its tones of gold and orange combined magnificently with the streaming sunshine of the daylight hours, offering a bright and cheerful atmosphere. During the evening hours, its beauty was equally enhanced by the soft, restful lights that shone from the various table lamps. It was the room most often used by the Kennedys for private entertaining, and it reflected the maximum of good taste in its expensive, comfortable furnishings.

The public did not get to see the changes in the family quarters. But as Mrs. Kennedy gradually restored the public, or State, rooms on the first floor, the ladies of the press and the photographers were invited for a preview glimpse. Most of the changes were greeted with great applause from history buffs around the country and from cultural groups, as well as from official Washington.

Newspapers had a little fun reporting the first day President Kennedy used his newly redecorated Family Dining Room on the first floor—where he held his breakfasts every Tuesday with his aides and Congressional leaders. Jackie had kept him out of it for a few weeks so that it could be completely renovated.

First, the elegant antique chair under the President's assistant, Larry O'Brien, collapsed, and he landed on the floor! Then as the President sat down in his chair, it started to crumble under him with an ominous noise. Fortunately, he was saved from a crash landing by Congressional leaders McCormack and Mansfield, who grabbed him on each side.

The antique chairs were quickly moved out.

14 ∾ HOW MANY JOBS IN ONE?

I THOROUGHLY ENJOYED WORKING FOR JACKIE at the White House—whether it was switching from typing to telephoning to bookkeeping, or switching from signing *my* name to *her* name in paying Jackie's bills. Never in my life had I known such swift days as that first year, nor found myself in such a state of perpetual motion.

Details galore. Jackie, as she poured out her steady stream of dictation, would suddenly stop to ask, "Do you have all that, Mary?" or, "Am I going too fast?" Then she would heave a sigh of relief at the end and express her own surprise at having accomplished so much.

How satisfying it was to be able to help Jackie this way— to be able to take her dictation, no matter how fast, without interrupting her as she went along, or asking her to repeat something, which would cause her to lose an important thought along the way.

I realized my responsibility to be thorough, efficient, and accurate, and above all to maintain my cool. It was very important, no matter what happened, to maintain my cool.

Jackie maintained hers, too. The busier it got, the more she called for additional help. She was serene, unruffled, and unhurried as she gave directions to others. In fact, I reflected, her room was the quiet eye in the center of the hurricane of activity that she had inspired.

Sometimes my White House adventures with children and pets seemed to take precedence over my regular chores.

There was the time on Miss Shaw's day off when I was working in the Monroe Room and the President was napping, while Jackie was off somewhere.

The substitute nurse had followed the regular pattern of putting John, Jr., into his pram and out on the Truman Balcony for his afternoon nap. I was catching up on some bookkeeping—avoiding the typewriter, which might awaken the President.

The silence, however, lasted only so long. The clear, sharp, familiar voice of the awakened father bellowed through the empty rooms: "Miss Shaw, Miss Shaw..." And finally, "MISS SHAW!"

Suddenly aroused, I ran out into the Center Hall.

The President, his head poking out from his bedroom door, spotted me and called out, "Mary, do you know where Miss Shaw is?"

I quickly informed him, "Miss Shaw's not here today, Mr. President—it's her day off..."

Now I could hear John, Jr.'s cries coming from the balcony. "Shall I see if I can find the nurse on duty?" I offered further.

"No, no," he said, "I think you'll do just fine. John doesn't sound very happy out there. Will you please see what you can do for him?"

"Oh, yes, sir," I replied, and scurried through the Oval Room to the balcony.

John not being very happy was putting it mildly. As I approached the pram, his cries were reaching their highest pitch, and his little feet were kicking madly away at the covers. "Now, now, now, John-John," I cooed, leaning over the shaking pram, "what seems to be the big trouble?" As I prepared him for the quick, dry change, the substitute nurse suddenly appeared from nowhere, dutifully taking over and thanking me for my assistance.

It was in my office in the Monroe Room that I launched into a tremendous project—the typing of a "Menu Book" for the newly hired French chef, René Verdon. It contained all of Jackie's favorite menus—for all occasions. There were close to a thousand in all.

In spite of all of the French words, unfamiliar to me, I had somehow managed the feat in ten days. With relief, I presented the completed notebook to René, trusting that he, at least, would understand its culinary jargon.

The hiring of Chef René was one of the things that had commanded Jackie's attention when we were at Palm Beach before the Inauguration. Tish had been directed to have someone at the White House show René through the kitchens. The ushers were instructed to have most of the kitchen staff on hand that day, so that René could see how the kitchens were run.

I remember what a furor it caused in the newspapers when an Indochinese chef, named Bui, said that he was supposed to go to work for the White House. Then, suddenly, it was René Verdon who was appointed.

It was indeed true that Bui was being considered. In Palm Beach, Jackie had instructed me to tell Tish that she could continue to check into the Indochinese in case they didn't hire René after all.

It was Mrs. Auchincloss who innocently got Jackie more publicity than she wanted by recommending Bui. Trying to be helpful, her mother told Jackie that her Vietnamese manicurist had a chef friend who wanted to come to America. He was the chef of the French Ambassador Chauvel in London, and, later, Bui had informed newsmen of his possible appointment.

But Jackie said that René was from the exclusive Pavillon restaurant in New York and had been recommended by her father-in-law, Ambassador Kennedy.

Most recently, René had been at Essex House on Central Park South. Thorough expert that he was, René had "studied up" on the Kennedy tastes at the posh Caravelle restaurant, which was the Ambassador's favorite. From its kitchens came dishes that JFK loved, such as chicken in champagne sauce.

They had been served aboard the *Caroline,* when the Senator was campaigning in New York.

Before we left Palm Beach to return to Washington, it was all over. René had definitely been hired. Jackie told Tish not to bother any more about Bui, because René was a "naturalized American," and that would simplify everything.

"So just forget about Bui," Jackie told Tish. She told her to handle it in the way she felt is the most tactful and to make sure he didn't speak to any newspapermen.

But, of course, he did.

Jackie and I had quietly planned for her first visit to my house on Friday afternoon, April 14th. She wanted to come with the children to see Tom Kitten. But at the last minute, Tish had advised Jackie of some social commitment, necessitating the cancellation of her visit.

Jackie was quite irritated and expressed apologies. She said it was one of the things that irked her about the White House, having to give up her personal life when it meant having to do something official. She asked that I remind her about it again sometime after May 11th, "as my schedule is pretty tight till then." So, Caroline came without her mother.

It was to be much longer than that before Jackie came to my house.

Meanwhile, another pleasant routine was changed. Until now, I had been enjoying lunches served to me on a tray at my office in the Monroe Room.

But suddenly Jackie felt compelled to change this arrangement with the explanation, "If the *others* know you are eating up here, they'll think I am showing favoritism."

I told her I understood, and that I wouldn't mind at all eating in the White House Staff Mess. It would actually give a little break in the day for me, at that.

Jackie did not seem to want unauthorized stories or pictures of Caroline and John-John published. I recall how, this first spring in the White House, she answered a newspaperwoman, who had sent pictures of Caroline with the request for permission to use them.

Thanking her for the pictures and praising them as so poetic, Jackie finally said no. She was afraid that others would expect to do the same when they photographed Caroline through the railings of the White House lawn.

My day at the White House normally began about 9 o'clock, when I would swing my little red Jet into a "no parking" area on East Executive Avenue near the guards' gate where the tourists enter the White House. Officer Adams, of the National Park Service, would save me a little space in the area reserved for White House personnel only. Upon spotting my car, he would immediately step out into the middle of East Executive Avenue and halt traffic both ways while I made my U-turn and backed into my place.

He was always very pleasant and often complimentary about my parking. One particular morning, in fun I responded rather loftily, "Oh, don't worry about me. I can park this little Jet on a dime."

He took me up on it—literally! Soon after, I kept noticing that the spaces were getting smaller and smaller—as Officer Adams's smiles became broader and broader. Finally, one morning, I found I had but the barest minimum of space left —and there he stood, watching like a Cheshire Cat.

I wasn't about to let him have the last laugh. With two sharp turns I made the grade. He must have been impressed. As I got out, he said rather sheepishly, "All right—you win— you've proved it to me now."

I would slip inconspicuously into the White House and wend my way through to the Mansion.

Except for the ushers, guards, and the Secret Service Agents posted in various spots, Tish and the press aides— JFK's and JBK's—and the domestic help within the Mansion proper, there was hardly a White House person who knew that I was upstairs.

In time, as I became acquainted with various members within the White House itself, I was met with expressions of surprise and even disbelief that Mrs. Kennedy actually had a secretary working for her upstairs.

I would be asked, "Whose office do you work in?" or "How long have you been with Mrs. Kennedy?" or, "Really? You mean it?" or, perhaps most common of all, "How come we never read about *you?*"

And then, there was the incident when the matter of my identity not only carried more serious overtones but required positive proof, as well.

One morning in June as I entered the East Gate, I offered my usual, cheerful greeting to the guard in the security booth and continued past him. I didn't recognize him as one of the regulars, and it became obvious that I was a stranger to him.

With a fingering motion to me, he called out, "Ma'am, do you have a White House Pass?"

I said yes, but he challenged me: "May I see it, please?"

Confidently, I reached into my handbag, pulled out my wallet, and displayed it to him from within its plastic flap. But this wasn't sufficient for him.

"Would you mind removing it for me, please, ma'am?"

I was getting a bit leery at this point. "Is something wrong?"

He studied both sides of the pass for a minute or two, then said dubiously, "Well, ma'am, the description seems to fit you all right. But this picture—I don't know—it doesn't look quite like you."

I took a closer look at the picture now that he held it before me. To my own surprise, I hardly recognized myself— I looked like a skeleton! "Oh," I said, remembering, "this picture was taken during my first week here in January when I weighed only 115 pounds."

I was now back to my normal 130 pounds, having lost 15 pounds during the campaign and pre-Inaugural weeks.

"Ma'am," he suggested, "if I were you, I'd arrange to have a 're-take' real soon. You know, you might just run into this situation again."

It was good advice, and I immediately followed through. But not without facing the disbelief again in the photographer's office. Did I really work for Mrs. Kennedy? By this time, however, I was well geared to the situation and simply resigned myself to it.

When I first started working at the White House I asked Tish about the possibility of a White House car to drive me back and forth from my home. I knew this was being done for Tish as social secretary and Pam as press secretary, but she had said she knew of no such arrangement for me. Toward the end of that first year, John McNally, who was in charge of the smooth operation of the White House, including the motor pool, was shocked one day to find that I was driving myself to work.

McNally immediately ordered that a White House car pick me up every morning and evening, too. "After all, the personal secretary to the First Lady *should be* driven." Thereafter, my driver would arrive outside my house every morning at 8:45.

I still was careful not to be seen by the press. The driver would go through the northwest gate on Pennsylvania Avenue, pass by the West Wing where the press waited with cameramen to catch a glimpse of the President, and swing down underneath the portico. I would enter through the Tradesman's Entrance.

This brought me into the ground-floor hallway on the route that led from the Mansion to the President's office in the West Wing. Often, he and I would run into each other along the way, going in opposite directions, and he'd say, "Hi there, Mary," or "How are you doing? How are the bills coming along?" He was never too busy to say something.

In June, 1961, I took Chris and Greg to the White House for their return visit after Caroline's visit to our home. It was a little bit touch and go. After all, the boys had to go to the bother of putting on Sunday clothes, and only for lunch with a girl, who was still a *girl*, even if she had given them a kitten. Fortunately, they had a certain amount of

126 ৪৯

curiosity to see where Mother worked. And the best incentive was the chance to ride into Washington—a good twelve miles.

As it turned out, Chris and Greg were fascinated by the unusual array of stuffed animals and creatures in Caroline's bedroom, especially one of her Raggedy Ann dolls that was taller than she, and a giraffe that stood even taller. Then there was the rocking horse that survived all their clambering around on it. But they snooted her tremendous doll collection completely and hopefully searched for little cars and trucks!

Whenever Jackie was away from the Mansion, she liked to arrange for Caroline and John-John to have plenty of company so they would not be lonely, and Chris and Greg returned again and again to share the part of Caroline's play world that really fascinated them—her outdoor playground.

They rode Macaroni, the pony, jumped on her trampoline, rocked in her outdoor boat rocker and, best of all, climbed into her treehouse from which the exit, I recall, was a playground slide on which they slid directly to the ground.

Naturally, the boys had to try a variation of climbing back up to the treehouse the hard way—up the slide. Caroline went up the ladylike way, by little steps.

Caroline could not interest the boys in having tea in her little dollhouse, which was built on the South Grounds near the treehouse. She liked to have teatime like her mother, but she would have to wait for girl visitors to pour her imaginary tea.

In July, 1961, when we were getting adjusted in the White House, United Features wanted to feature "America's luckiest working girls—top level assistants to Jacqueline Kennedy."

They wanted the First Lady's press secretary, her social secretary, and her personal secretary. So I came out of hiding and the third part, for which I had been interviewed by Ernie Barcella, was about me.

In the advance publicity, they described Pam as "attractive" and "trim" and Tish as "possessing much of the poise and charm of the First Lady, herself." Concerning me, they said that I had been a close friend of the Kennedy family for years and that I was the only aide of the First Lady to have an office in the Kennedys' White House living quarters. The advance went on to say that "as a housewife and mother herself, she has personally experienced many of the problems that are passed on to her as Mrs. Kennedy's personal secretary."

I still have the clipping from the Philadelphia *Daily News*, Tuesday, July 27, 1961. The series was called "The First Lady's First Ladies," and my story was entitled, "Immigrant's Daughter in White House."

After that, I returned to my old policy of avoiding the press.

In fact, once when I was going on a trip with her, Jackie asked me to use my maiden name, Barelli, so nobody would know who I was.

As I was working in Jackie's sitting room one day in the fall, Dave Powers came by and called cheerfully, "There's a *paisan* of yours in your office. I think you should meet him."

When I entered the Monroe Room, there were Eunice Shriver and a man whose back was turned as he peered out the window at the South Lawn. When Eunice and I greeted each other, he turned, and I found myself shaking hands with the very personable Frank Sinatra, as Eunice made the introductions.

By now, I was getting more blasé; I didn't even *think* to ask for his autograph!

Suddenly, I was to be evicted from the Monroe Room—because Jackie had decided to redo it and give it a new purpose and a new name. As she explained, it would be used by the President as his Cabinet Room, and it would be re-named the "Treaty Room."

So, in October, 1961, Jackie again faced the problem of what to do with me. She pondered my using the Lincoln Sitting Room, but changed her mind.

"It would mean rolling out your typewriter and swooping up arms full of stationery whenever we have guests," she said.

She still preferred, however, that I remain within close

128 &

reach and, with no other spot available on the second floor, suggested the east solarium, located on the third floor directly above us. Once settled there, I thoroughly enjoyed it—so spacious, airy, and light.

When completed, the Treaty Room showed the same fine attention to detail that marked other rooms. Its walls were covered with a paper resembling deep-green velvet, bordered in a red-and-white pattern. This was copied from the wallpaper in the room across from Ford's Theatre where President Lincoln died.

The Victorian furnishings included some of the original Lincoln period pieces, such as the table, the swivel chair, the sofa, and the marble clock on the mantel. A deep-green rug matched the walls and the dark-red velvet draperies were also Victorian in style. The treaties were grouped on the wall.

With the huge, magnificent chandelier, hung above a tremendous table (brought from the Capitol, as I recall, with the help of Vice President Lyndon Johnson), the room was completely transformed from what I had known when I first worked there.

I remember when Jackie was finally going to unveil the Treaty Room to the press. Only minutes before her scheduled appearance in the room, she had a sudden inspiration and sent me in to "copy the names of all the signers of the treaties in there."

I jotted down the names and rushed back to her. As she stood before her mirror, making last-minute adjustments to her hair, she quickly memorized the names as I read and reread them all to her. Then she went in and made a brilliant presentation that sounded as if she had been studying it all for months.

I felt very proud of her that day.

It wasn't long before Jackie decided to use the Treaty Room again as an alternate spot for her daily dictation. She preferred it, she explained, because it was "away from the rooms where we actually live." And anyway, the Man of the

House didn't seem to be using it much for signing documents, after all.

So now I was back in the Monroe Room, converted into the Treaty Room, except that I brought my baskets and folders down there from the solarium, when Jackie didn't want to dictate in her bedroom.

In the Treaty Room, Jackie would sit on a green-velvet-covered armchair at the end of the long center table. I sat in the first chair to her right, and we would gradually go through the accumulation of things—well lighted by the sparkling chandelier.

There were many times after our working sessions in the Treaty Room when the overload—the voluminous folders, pieces of china, table lamps, State gifts, and the like—was so great, I would require the assistance of a doorman to help carry them all back to my office.

Eventually, Jackie obtained a little antique gold French telephone, installed with a very long cord so that it could be carried from the corner desk to the table and wherever convenient to her.

Then, suddenly, I was to be evicted from the east solarium! Mrs. Kennedy had plans for it to become a little classroom for the children.

My desk went out, and in came the little bowls of clay and the fingerpaints. So, off I went to share Provi's quarters with the racks of clothes and the couch full of gloves.

There were gloves of every length—wrist, above-wrist, elbow, above-elbow, arm-length. Black gloves, white gloves. I don't believe that I have ever seen the couch in the room when it was not covered with dress boxes, lingerie, and gloves, gloves, gloves.

My new office suddenly looked like a dress shop with the overflow clothes from the closets hung on racks. And the new clothes coming in from New York, Washington, and Paris. And the endless accessories that went with each outfit—the hats, the shoes. The gloves.

Once Jackie, concerned that I seemed to be getting thinner and thinner again, said, "Oh, Mary, why don't you just take yourself a little rest on that couch sometime!"

I hated to tell her that it was hard to find the couch. Anyway, there just was no time.

And, of course, there were the financial accounts, which I would work on at home and which I never left out of my sight. They were done on the President's directive and were one of my greatest responsibilities.

As for Provi, every year it seemed she had more work to do, more clothes to care for. And Jackie became more certain in her demands, more used to issuing orders to both Provi and me at every moment. We would run our legs off, upstairs and downstairs and back to Jackie's room. Provi would say to me frequently, "Oh, Mees Gallaga, how we gonna keep thees up another year? I don' think I can keep it up like thees." And just then, Jackie would call again, wanting something, and Provi would go running.

Jackie somehow became aware that clothes were suffocating me. She toyed with the idea of putting me in the Map Room on the ground floor, the room that had been FDR's strategy room, filled with maps during World War II. I didn't like the idea at all, and at a crucial moment, Mr. West, the Chief Usher, saved me.

He came in one afternoon and was unable to believe his eyes. "I don't know how you can operate well in here," he said. "Wouldn't you like to have a better office with less congestion?"

I didn't want to hurt Provi's feelings, but I told him I certainly could use a little more space. Soon he was back. He had found the perfect office for me—a lovely room, still on the third floor, next to the seamstress, Lucinda Morman. It was directly above Mrs. Kennedy's bedroom on the second floor, and with the elevator so near, I could be at her side in a minute.

Meanwhile, little Caroline's classroom was moved again—

from one solarium to another. This one, directly above the Truman Balcony, faced the South Lawn.

The balcony off the south solarium had one of the most magnificent views of Washington, since it was on the third floor and looked out on the Washington and Jefferson monuments. No one glancing up would suspect the activity that went on up there at times.

Here, on occasion, Jackie would come up to enjoy the sunshine and fresh air while she dictated.

Here, Caroline and her playschool friends enjoyed riding on tricycles and hobby horses that were mounted on huge springs.

Here lived a hutch of huge gray-and-white rabbits in full view of the little children in their classroom.

Here Ray and I brought Chris and Greg on Easter Mondays to watch the traditional Easter Egg Roll on the South Lawn. It was, as I have said, a busy house.

Caroline's home was certainly not like other children's. She did not sit at the table with her parents for meals, nor did John-John. They had their own schedule with Miss Shaw and sometimes saw her and their Secret Service men more than they saw their parents.

The stories I told Caroline about Tom Kitten seemed to satisfy her pretty well. She was always most attentive—popping up with a little question here and there—and apparently always sufficiently amused, as well. With a little crinkle in her nose, she would smile and ask in anticipation, "Can you think of any more?"

Usually, my reply was based on the amount of work facing me on my desk. And eventually she'd go scampering off with the reminder that I bring Tom Kitten to the White House to visit her.

Then, a little later, she'd be back, wanting to draw pictures. Her interest in "drawing pictures"—birds, cats, horses, flowers—whatever her mood—though really never wavering since her Georgetown days, now became second to the "little stories about Tom Kitten."

It was a very sunny and cheerful classroom where Caroline and her friends were encouraged by her teacher, Miss Grimes, to exercise their imaginations. The day I happened to visit, they had constructed a story, with each child contributing one line as Miss Grimes chalked their immortal stanza on the blackboard:

> We have a surprise, said Caroline,
> A surprise for dinner, said Avery,
> It is something for me, said Nelia,
> Come for dinner, said Chris and Agatha.

I don't recall the names of all the children, but Avery was the son of the assistant press secretary, Andrew Hatcher, and Agatha was Agatha Pozen, Caroline's best friend. They visited each other's houses frequently, and a few times, Caroline even brought Agatha along to our house, where they played happily on the "Jungle Gym" set in the back yard.

Caroline had a bright little mind and, in her utter innocence, she managed to cut everyone in turn right down to size.

When she met John Glenn, the famous astronaut, she asked, "Where is your monkey?"

When the press asked what her daddy was doing one day, she treated it equally lightly and said he was upstairs not doing *anything*—just sitting there with his shoes off.

When she came to my house for the first time in March, she walked into the kitchen and said, "Where is your cook?"

She looked at me in amazement when I said, "You're looking at her."

It was a new concept for Caroline.

15 ∿ JACKIE'S WHITE HOUSE

FROM THE MOMENT WE WERE IN THE WHITE House, we were involved in ordering and moving paintings and furniture. Crates of paintings were always arriving or leaving, to be returned, to be framed, or to be retouched. And if it wasn't paintings, it was antiques.

I was forever giving careful instructions on how things were to be packed, where they were to go.

Meanwhile, back at the West Wing, Pierre Salinger was assuring the press that Jackie was not going to disturb the appearance of the White House. She was just going to make her own quarters a little more livable.

But even at the beginning, Jackie was hard at work planning what to do, how to change the White House room by room, family quarters, public rooms. She was not content even with the swimming pool area, which looked rather drab —or "like an institution," as she put it. A tremendous mural of sea and shore was eventually painted all around its walls— a gift of her father-in-law, the Ambassador.

Whether Jackie was collecting art and antiques for her own private art collection or for the White House collection, my days became unlike anything I had ever known or would know again.

And she expressed herself so amusingly and uninhibitedly. "I think you should ask for a bicycle!" she told Henry du Pont, the great expert on early American homes and director of Winterthur Museum of Delaware. Early in 1961 he had spent a day "tramping around the White House," as she put it, and was due to return for another day of it.

The details of art collecting were almost a full-time job in themselves! There were fifty Catlin Indian paintings loaned to the White House, and the problem was how to frame them. Two drawings needed to be framed and hung in the Oval Room. Jackie was keeping six watercolors while returning the photographs of those she did not want.

One of her personal art scouts was Roy Davis of the Davis Galleries in New York, and another was Herbert N. Bier of Hyde Park Square, London. She kept them both pretty busy!

In the shuffling of paintings that were coming and going, Jackie's frequent message would be: "Send up a man to hang some pictures," or "Tell Mr. West I need some men to move things around."

Every gallery and museum in the country, it seemed, was laying its treasures at Jackie's feet for her to pick and choose from. The Boston Museum of Fine Arts had captured her heart. Included among its offer of pictures to be loaned were two watercolors of Villa di Marlin, a place where she had stayed when she was a young girl with her friend Carmilla Becci-Becci-Blunt, whose family owned the villa.

Jackie thanked the director, Perry T. Rathbone. She wanted to keep some of the pictures until she had made up her mind and returned others she was sure she did not want. In all, Jackie borrowed eleven paintings from the Boston Museum of Fine Arts, including "Indian Camp" by Winslow Homer and "Bathing, Marblehead" by Maurice Prendergast.

Then Jackie was looking for more Sargent watercolors, and got in touch with Roy Davis, saying that she had one on loan from the Boston Museum and both she and the President loved the painter's work. She wanted him to let her know what he could find and how much it would cost.

Seven watercolors arrived early in 1961 from the Maynard Walker Galleries, which Jackie put in the Map Room so she could study them at her leisure. It didn't take her long to make up her mind. One was kept, and six were returned. And, soon after, the familiar request: "Send up a man to hang pictures."

Jackie had a remarkable memory for paintings she had once seen and liked, but had not bought at the time. When she was ready to consider the purchase, she would simply send a quick follow-up. For example, remembering a Guido Reni drawing that had greatly impressed her on an earlier occasion, she communicated with Mr. Bier in London, to find out whether he still had it.

On another occasion, as she leafed through a magazine, she asked that I call Roy Davis to let him know that she "got *Esquire* and would like to know if she could buy the David Levine picture of Hatfield House. If already sold, what else could she buy? Save something pretty 'til she decides..."

For her family quarters, Jackie bought a child's patchwork quilt that had been on display at the Pittsfield, Massachusetts, Museum. Dating back to the 19th century, its design bore the names of former Presidents.

Most touching of all in that first year of art collecting was Jackie's desperate attempt to get an oil painting by Schreyer that, obviously, meant something special to her. And understandably so. It had formerly belonged to her father's estate, and she was pressing the Palm Beach Galleries to see if it could be bought back from the private collector to whom it had been sold in February, 1958, for $600. "Our Warriors" was the name of the painting, and a year had gone by now since she had last appealed to the Galleries in the matter.

She wanted it, she explained, because it had belonged to her father. As one last measure, she asked the gallery whether she might get in touch with the present owner. Jackie, I knew, could be very patient when it came to getting a painting she wanted, but many times I have wondered if she ever was successful in her efforts to get "Our Warriors."

Jackie loved animal paintings, too. One of her favorites was her "Oudry Dog," as she called it, which she went to special lengths to have reframed more to her liking, for the family quarters. She could hardly wait to have it back, telling Roy Davis that she wanted it back as soon as possible, because she had a place specially reserved on the wall for it.

136 ໄ

One of Jackie's greatest helpers in locating art for the White House was the modern abstract painter, Bill Walton, the Kennedys' Georgetown friend. He especially looked for naval scenes for the President's office and came up with two pictures depicting the battle between the *Constitution* and the British frigate, *Guerrière*, in the War of 1812.

The youthful-looking, pug-nosed Walton was the son of a newspaper publisher. He had given up his own writing career to devote full time to art. Before then, he had written for the Associated Press in New York and Chicago, as well as for *Time* magazine. As a *Time* correspondent in World War II, he had parachuted into Normandy. After the war, he wrote for *Life* and *The New Republic*.

But he had dropped even his beloved art when JFK needed him in 1960, and he went from state to state, helping in primaries and campaigns. He had also manned the New York City headquarters.

To be Curator of the White House, Jackie chose Mrs. John Newton Pearce, wife of the assistant curator of the Division of Cultural History at the Smithsonian. She had worked at Smithsonian as a historian, and she was on loan to the White House.

Mrs. Pearce's office was in the Map Room. It was filled with paintings of former First Ladies—Mrs. William Howard Taft, Mrs. Rutherford Hayes, and President Jackson's hostess—daughter-in-law, Mrs. Andrew Jackson, Jr.

One of the biggest jobs Mrs. Pearce undertook was writing the official guidebook on the furnishings of the White House. She was assisted in the Curator's Office by Janet Felton, a friend of Jackie's from New York whom she had summoned to Washington for the job. A third girl, Blair Whitehead, and two men, Jim Ketchum and Bill Elder, eventually became part of the Curator's Office, too, as the White House exploded in a flurry of decorating activities. Jackie needed all the help she could get on the many plans she had.

The Blue Room had been her pet peeve—she called it "depressive." She studied thoroughly the old records of early plans and decorations of the White House, and she became convinced that the Blue Room was not intended as a "blue" Blue Room at all, and that it should have "whitish silk walls" with only blue touches to fulfill the original intent.

In justifying her desire for changing the color in the Blue Room, she turned to David Findley, the chairman of the Fine Arts Commission, which had to approve all changes in public buildings. She said that after walking through the succession of the Red Room, the Blue Room, and then the Green Room, all in strong colors, "one feels a bit shell-shocked when one finally staggers into the peaceful white of the East Room."

The Commission approved her change.

Endlessly, she tried switching the furniture around, and I would instruct the men to try the sofa and chairs in the hall instead of in the Diplomatic Room where Mr. du Pont had put them.

I would follow Jackie with my notebook and pencil, jotting down all the instructions and making sure they were carried out while they still made sense to me. There were dozens of things to do, such as telling Janet Felton to reassure Mr. Findley that the Blue Room chandelier will be placed in the Green Room.

Jackie was thrilled when she learned from James Biddle, of the Metropolitan Museum of Art, that the White House was really an English house. She told him that she had felt it instinctively because all the pieces of furniture she visualized for the rooms were English in her mind.

It was a Frenchman, strangely enough, who was her confidential adviser on how to restore the White House to the elegance of long ago, in the days of President Monroe. His name was Monsieur Stephanie Boudin, and he was a decorator from Jansen of Paris. Whenever he could, M. Boudin came flying to Washington to help her, and Jackie assured David Findley that Boudin would give them a plan for the Blue Room without expecting credit.

Jackie laid her plans carefully, step by step, even to organizing a special committee to help her achieve her ends. She told James Biddle that in organizing her special committee to acquire period furniture, she had to have everything well done from the start. And that if she didn't, it would all end in confusion and "silly stories" in the newspapers. She also didn't want the bad press and hard feelings Dolley Madison had been subjected to.

Dolley Madison had bought a mirror in Paris for $50 without authorization, and Congress had become so incensed that they had investigated it and the investigation had cost $2,800.

Every move Jackie made was approved by two committees.

It was rather confusing—two committees with titles almost alike. Before Jackie came on the scene, there had been a Fine Arts Commission for years, headed by David Findley.

Then on February 23rd, Jackie announced her own Committee, named "The Committee on the Fine Arts Commission for the White House," for the purpose of locating furniture from the period of Jefferson's occupancy of the White House—1802—and raising funds to purchase it.

Jackie's committee consisted of Henry du Pont, the chairman, and three other men and seven women, including Jackie's friend Jayne Wrightsman. David Findley was also on Jackie's committee, as was "Sister" Parrish, her decorator.

The first great painting to be acquired by the new committee was hung in the Green Room—a portrait of Benjamin Franklin painted from life in London, 1767, by a Scottish artist, David Martin. The National Gallery of Art came up with two more modern paintings—Cézanne's "The Forest" and "House on the Marne." These Jackie was most fond of, and she had them hung in the Green Room also.

Pictures marched around the White House: Andrew Jackson moved to the Cabinet Room after being in storage all during the Eisenhower Administration. The famous Christy painting of Mrs. Calvin Coolidge was shifted from the China Room to the Red Room. The McKinley portrait that had been in the Red Room went to the ground-floor corridor. Harry Truman's portrait was off to the head of the stairs.

And so it went. Jackie would always explain to those who got excited about the changes and asked questions that "it isn't necessarily permanent. We are just getting the scale, testing to see where they look best in each room."

I was especially interested in seeing which paintings Jackie used for decorating the dining rooms on the first floor. In the State Dining Room, after she changed the Williamsburg Green, which she detested, to a soft off-white, she removed a green landscape painting by Innes and placed a huge George P. A. Healy painting, a brooding figure of Abraham Lincoln, seated in a chair with hand to chin. It rather dominated the room in a very thoughtful way, adding a somber note to the gold-upholstered chairs.

In the Family Dining Room, she hung another outstanding Healy, one of President John Tyler.

JFK applauded Jackie's choice of Lincoln for the State Dining Room, saying, "Lincoln not only had nobility of character, but he loved politics with the passion of a born practitioner." That Lincoln portrait, incidentally, had been taken from the White House foyer.

Another Lincoln portrait, by George Henry Story, was hung in the Cabinet Room.

Eventually, one more committee was formed and compounded the confusion—The Committee of Americana Antiques Advisors. It included Malcolm Watkins, Head of the Division of Cultural History of the Smithsonian, Nicholas Biddle of the Metropolitan Museum, and Marvin Schwarz of the Brooklyn Museum.

As people were added to the ranks of Jackie's committees, she would explain to them how they could best help, and she would tell them how duplication was being avoided. All the members, she explained, were sending to Jayne Wrightsman at Palm Beach lists of prospective donors, who might have appropriate period furniture for the White House or might be willing to donate money. It was Mrs. Wrightsman's job to screen the lists so that the same person would not be solicited over and over again.

Jackie explained, too, that the committee had been busy getting rulings from the Internal Revenue Service so that people who gave things to the White House could get a tax deduction. Eventually, Congress passed a law to make the donations to the White House tax deductible.

Great secrecy was required, because every time it was learned in the trade—or even rumored—that Jackie's committee was interested in a certain piece of furniture, the price went up and up.

As I recall, about the biggest leap in value involved some 19th-century wallpaper printed in 1834 by Zuber and entitled "Scenic America," showing views of early New York City, West Point, Boston Harbor, Niagara Falls, Natural Bridge, and other sights.

A young man, a Harvard Business School student, had bought the panels for $50 and sold them to the White House for $12,500. He first showed the wallpaper to the Curator of the White House, spreading it out on the floor of her office. Jackie walked in, took one look, and made her decision on the spot.

To get the money, Jackie informed the president of the National Society of Interior Designers, Edward F. White, that the White House had no historical wallpaper and that Zuber's "Scenic America" would be another significant contribution. Would the Society like to buy the wallpaper for the White House? They would and did.

Before 1961 was over, the wallpaper was on the walls of the Diplomatic Reception Room, above the oval rug with its stars and insignia of all fifty states. The rug had been specially woven for the room and presented by the same Society— during the Eisenhower Administration.

I remember the times I passed through the Diplomatic Reception Room as the old wallpaper was being applied. I would stand in awe, watching artists with their pinpoint paint brushes, painstakingly filling in the little cracks and missing chunks in the old paper, which was actually shredded. They had to re-create the original design. I was simply spellbound by their expertise!

When they were through, I was sure that not even the most critical eye could detect the "patchwork."

In that happy first year of redecorating, Jackie had come into several windfalls. One was an historic 1817 pier table, which she found in the basement of the White House, hidden away and looking worthless because, in 1924, someone had covered it with gold radiator paint.

The table had originally been ordered by President James Monroe from Parisian cabinetmaker Pierre-Antoine Bellange for the Blue Room. The 144-year-old table was restored by the firm of Jansen, of New York and Paris, as a gift to the White House from Stephanie Boudin.

Then came the great discovery of the desk President Kennedy was to use thereafter—a mammoth desk elaborately carved from the timbers of H.M.S. *Resolute*. It was originally a gift from Queen Victoria to President Rutherford B. Hayes, and President Kennedy was thrilled to have it, especially because FDR and Wilson had used it in the past.

A project that was not as easy as it seemed was the dream that dated back to Jefferson, concerning the proper kind of library a President should have at the White House. It was Henry du Pont who had actually arranged for Jackie to get Jefferson's papers on the guiding principles to be followed in selecting suitable furnishings for the library, and on the appearance and selection of books.

Jackie formed still another committee to help round up the books and plan the proper décor for the room.

Enthusiastic as she was, however, her projects seemed to be dragging, and she once complained that there was a great deal of confusion, with many things going on at once—finding furniture and pictures, and always having tea with reluctant donors.

Jackie was fascinated by all that Jefferson wrote about his selection of furniture for the White House. He had come back to America, after serving as Ambassador to France, with 86 packing cases of house furnishings, some of which he eventually placed in the White House.

Jefferson had used the Blue Room as his drawing room, and the Red Room as his sitting room. Jackie had his description of how things looked in his day. "The Great Hall of Entrance," for example, had held "eight fire buckets," as well as 28 mahogany chairs with hair-cloth bottoms, an eight-day clock, 2 large mahogany tables with leaves, 4 settees, and 2 side tables.

Jackie was interested to learn that he had designed his own cornices in the State Dining Room and had used *toile de Jouy* fabric at the windows of some rooms, chintz and dimity at others.

One Jefferson touch I was sure she would not follow, however, was canvas covering on some of the floors. It was then called "floorcloth" and painted green.

Gifts and offers of help of one sort or another came from all corners of the country. An ornate Baltimore desk, early 19th century, came from Des Moines, Iowa, from Mrs. Maurice Noun. That desk, which was said to be worth $20,000, had three glass panels decorated with the figures of "Fame, Temperance, and Justice" scratched in gold leaf and backed in blue.

Bill Green, of Fairfax, Virginia, presented Jackie a 200-year-old, mahogany high chair for little John-John. It had a compartment in front to place a hot brick as a footwarmer.

For the President's office, Jackie took his old North Carolina porch rocker that he had used for five years in the Senate and had it upholstered to fit in with the more elegant surroundings of the White House. She ordered the frame stained and the cane back padded with foam rubber and covered with oatmeal-color monk's cloth. The papers liked that, headlining the story, "JFK IS ROCKED BY WIFE'S THOUGHT-FULNESS."

For a while, the White House was overloaded with rocking chairs. Everyone wanted to contribute one. A 16-year-old boy, Thomas Brown, from Olathe, Kansas, got to come to the

White House to deliver his prize-winning rocker, which he had carved himself, competing in the National Industrial Arts Award Competition.

Jackie's success in finding the President Monroe pier table in the White House basement had spurred her on to expand her personal search.

On June 23rd, she ventured across the street to Blair House. It was her first tour of Blair House, and Blair Lee House rooms, where State visitors stay. She stayed forty minutes and came up with some thrilling discoveries: a highboy and a lowboy that she ordered moved to another room; some Lowestoft ashtrays in a cupboard which she placed on tables where she felt they should be displayed.

Then she made a safari in August to Fort Washington, Maryland, where all the "white elephants" of the White House are stored. Here were row on row of chairs discarded by the White House, including Woodrow Wilson's wheelchair, and an armchair possibly used by Ulysses S. Grant; stacks of paintings; a cedar chest still labeled to show it had contained the Franklin D. Roosevelts' children's bathing suits and other woolens.

The Green Room and the Red Room were the first of the public rooms completely redone by Jackie's committee. Gradually, all the bits and pieces fell into place. Committee member Mrs. C. Douglas Dillon and her husband, the Treasury Secretary, gave many things, including a sofa that had belonged to Dolley Madison, which ended up in the Red Room.

Sometimes, the gift was a small thing, like a piece of velvet of exactly the right period to cover two chairs Lincoln had used. Sometimes it was a big thing like the $165,000 painting donated by publisher Walter Annenberg of Philadelphia.

Of course, not everyone agreed with every change. Some people wrote that what had been good enough for the Republicans should be good enough for the Democrats. Some objected to moving various paintings from old familiar spots.

144 ह॰

Some complained that Jackie had ruined the natural wood finish by painting the doors in the foyer, which had been made of the original White House beams. Even the old nail-holes had been filled in and covered with paint, taking away the old historic quality.

But Jackie's search for the finest impressed the public. Crowds became fantastic. A line of 8,074 tourists waited to see the White House on April 2, 1961, and it stretched down the sidewalk as far as the eye could see.

That was just the beginning. Later in the month, there was a record 13,575 in one day!

After that, I took crowds for granted and didn't bother to check the tourist figures—men, women, and children were lined up not only on the sidewalks at the East Gate, but winding around whole city blocks, as well.

Eventually, the public rooms looked completely different—the Blue Room was white with blue touches, the Red Room was cerise, and the Green Room was soft and gentle as a spring garden, with the two landscapes by Cézanne to enhance the effect.

Jackie's final triumph came not from the general public, but from the President himself. I remember it happened one day that Alice Longworth came to visit Jackie in the afternoon to see the changes, and the President had happened by.

Right afterward, while Jackie sat listening with a happy and proud smile on her face, the President dictated a statement to me which would serve as a press release or for other general use to explain to the public what Jackie had been doing:

"Through a wise provision of the Congress at its last session, the White House, which had become disfigured by incongruous additions and changes, has now been restored to what it was planned by Washington. In making the restorations, the utmost care has been exercised to come as near as possible to the early plans and to supplement these plans by careful study of such buildings as that of the University of Virginia, which was built by Jefferson.

"The White House is the property of the Nation and, so far as is compatible with living therein, it should be kept as it originally was for the same reasons that we keep Mount Vernon as it originally was.

"The stately simplicity of its architecture is an expression of the character of the period in which it was built and is in accord with the purposes it was designed to serve. It is a good thing to preserve such buildings as historic monuments, which keep alive our sense of continuity with the Nation's past."

Hearing that, I had new appreciation for what Jackie had done.

The effort had really been worthwhile, not just for today, but for all time.

16 ∽ THE FACE OF FASHION

WHEN JACKIE FOUND THAT HER CLOTHES were being copied and sold at bargain prices to every stenographer and shop girl, she was annoyed. But when she found that Caroline dolls were being displayed in every dime-store window and that her very own look was being captured in wax so that she was standing in every store window as a mannequin, she was furious.

"I feel as if I've been turned into a piece of public property," she commented bitterly.

Ironically, Jackie was not thrilled to be the pacesetter for a whole nation.

Despite her annoyance, her clothes continued to dominate the fashion scene. America's young females were caught in the rage of her "latest" styles, and hairdos. But, then, being the youngest (31 years old), most glamorous, First Lady to occupy the White House in generations, this was understandable.

Quite noticeable, too, was the influence that such modes seemed to have on all the girls who worked in the White House, especially Jackie's own press secretary, Pam Turnure.

As she walked through the halls of the White House, Pam could almost be taken for Jackie's double—except for being a bit smaller in size. But the sleeveless dresses, the low-heeled pumps, the "Jackie coiffure," the whole works, were quite obvious. To those with whom Pam dealt daily, perhaps even a trace of Jackie's mannerisms in speaking could be detected.

It was impossible to keep *Women's Wear Daily* from ferreting out many of her fashion secrets and springing sketches of what she planned to wear. Sometimes she would tell any designer or fashion house that she would cut him off if he did such a thing.

Some she gave another chance. For example, even before the White House, when we were in Palm Beach, she warned Oleg Cassini not to let *Women's Wear Daily* know about the clothes she would wear in the White House, and that included sketches.

As First Lady, Jackie no longer gave away or sold clothes through Encore. Dresses and gowns used at State functions and in travel were stored in the cedar-lined storage closets on the third floor, and Jackie had a remarkable memory for knowing exactly what was there at all times. "Get me this or that dress," she would say, giving a complete description of how it looked and where to find it.

I remember that she sent a collection of her informal clothes to Prince Radziwill's relatives in Poland in my name, as if they had come from me rather than from the First Lady. But, in this case, the recipients were aware of the "real" sender—advance notice was arranged through Lee.

Sometimes I thought that all of Jackie's historic clothes used on State occasions and in her travels with the President should be placed in a special museum to show her effect on fashion. And I still believe they should.

I can tell you that the Inaugural Ball gown was not Jackie's favorite. She much preferred the Gala gown, the utterly simple white one—unrelieved except for a geometric design, of the same material, at the waist—which had been made by Oleg Cassini.

In fact, Jackie wanted to have the Smithsonian Institution display her Gala gown instead of the Inaugural one, and I was still fighting that battle for a long time after the Kennedys had moved into the White House.

Jackie asked me to have Tish contact the Smithsonian about this and said she was offering it because she thought it was by far the prettiest. If they liked, she said, she could show it to them. She would be glad to send it over. And she wanted to be sure they knew Oleg Cassini had made it.

The Smithsonian, in making up its exhibit, still preferred sticking with tradition. So Jackie gave up, and her Inaugural outfit was put on the Jacqueline Kennedy mannequin.

I always thought of that when I saw the many clippings and items about Jacqueline Kennedy's Inaugural gown at the Smithsonian, that it was the single most popular exhibit there. In fact, there was even an item about how the Smithsonian had bought and installed heavy-duty carpeting "that could not be worn out" in front of the display of "Gowns of the First Ladies." Even so, right in front of the Jacqueline Kennedy mannequin, a hole had developed in the *indestructible* rug, so great was the traffic there.

When we were at Palm Beach prior to the Inauguration, it was formally announced that Oleg Cassini would be Jackie's clothes designer. For the most part, he was. To accentuate an image of "American patriotism," I recall Ambassador Kennedy's suggestion at the time that she alternate with other American designers, as well, changing with the various seasons. A clever idea, I had thought, but then, Jackie apparently thought differently. She kept on with Mr. Cassini—but simply could not resist getting things from her favorite couturiers abroad, too, using her dress scouts to order, so it would not be known the gown was for her. Sometimes the gown was supposed to be for her sister, Lee.

It was no wonder that, as the months went by, Jackie was faced with the financial clamp-downs by her husband that gradually came into play, hand-in-hand with her fabulous wardrobe.

Cassini had color photos made of his collection and Jackie sometimes ordered from Cassini's by looking through a viewer at the color slides he had sent her.

Dress models were ordered by number. Typical of the shipments that would arrive in the long, heavy cartons was this for which I had sent the instructions to Kay McGowan:

#194—Green zibeline suit
#153—Dress and coat for travel
#751—Beige dress
#162—Long gown with embroidery on hem and cuff of jacket
#140—Pink lightweight dress
13—Lesur wool outfit in pistachio or Chartreuse for traveling

There were two dresses in the shipment, not numbered, but made just for her, one in "shocking pink with matching jacket," and one in "white crepe."

Of all the beautiful dresses and gowns that hung in Jackie's closets, one of my own favorites happened to be a stark-white theater or cocktail suit. It was short length with simple straight lines. The dress was collarless, with short sleeves, and was adorned with rhinestones around the hem. The jacket to match was completely edged in rhinestones, too—around the mandarin neckline, down the front opening, and around the bottom edge. Even the cuffs of the long sleeves glittered and sparkled with rhinestones.

I don't recall that I ever saw a single bill from Cassini, in spite of the many gowns he made for Jackie. However, I do remember that we sent checks for the countless pairs of gloves we were always ordering through his establishment.

Oleg Cassini would send his Girl Friday, Kay McGowan, to the White House to check the fittings of Jackie's new gowns.

I recall that once he sent eleven pieces at one time; and this was not unusual.

Before Cassini cut the precious material for outfits being made specially for her, he would have Jackie's complete instructions. First he would send Jackie swatches and sketches beautifully rendered, and Jackie would study them carefully as she dictated her comments on them to me. She liked sketches A and B, but wanted the shoulder changed, or the neckline a bit higher. He also sent her swatches of gorgeous materials in the color in which he thought each dress would look best on her.

Jackie was trying very hard to keep an American label on her clothes, but she was not above checking on what Balenciaga and Givenchy and others were doing and drawing, and bringing particular sketches to Cassini's attention with suggestions about how he could incorporate certain points in what he was planning for her.

Once I called Cassini to tell him that as a special favor to Jackie, one of her favorite photographers had taken photographs of the Dior collection for her when he was in Paris. Cassini was to keep the photographer out of trouble, I cautioned, and only call him at home.

Clothes and more clothes—stockings from Garfinckel's, underwear from Bonwit Teller, "pretty night gowns—long, not too décolleté"—from Elizabeth Arden.

Jackie loved Chanel suits. She liked their comfort and style and often made her own choice of piping or braid edging to be used. I recall she wore an off-white Chanel suit with black braid edging when Empress Farah Diba and she walked around the White House grounds during the State visit of the Shah of Iran in the spring of 1962.

Shoes came from Eugenia of Florence and were made to order three and four pairs at a time. In a note above my own signature, I wrote, "Mr. Mario [Eugenia of Florence]: Under separate cover, I am sending you today three pairs of shoes which Mrs. Kennedy has asked me to return. She does not wish to keep the two white pairs and, with regard to the black shoes, she claims they are still a bit too narrow. Mary B. Gallagher."

For riding at Glen Ora, Jackie was ordering from Gordon's. She wanted a navy blue gabardine coat with double vents, as well as a tan pure silk coat. She also wanted Bombay jodhpurs, canary yellow breeches, and a pair of dark-brown breeches.

And Jackie also wanted Bombay jodhpurs for Caroline—something lightweight and washable. The first fitting was to be set up for the following Saturday.

Every dress Jackie wore that first year caused a great commotion and was generally greeted with wild applause by the fashion industry.

For the Judiciary Reception of 1961 in the White House, Jackie wore a beautiful black ottoman skirt and sleeveless camisole top with jet beading. I liked the severe square neckline on her. To entertain the Trumans during the Kennedys' first year in office, she wore a dramatic white satin dress with straight boat or bateau neckline and straight-line skirt, with nothing to relieve the effect but a pair of diamond pendant earrings and her own beauty.

Jackie always put her best foot forward at the White House. She also put a pink shoe forward for the Congressional Reception on April 16, 1961. She wore a sensational pink-and-white straw lace with shoes to match. The dress was sleeveless with a bateau neckline. This time her ornament was a feather-shaped diamond clip in her bouffant hairdo.

In May, Jackie started a fad for dresses with only one shoulder covered. She wore one—a flowing chiffon—to the State dinner when they entertained the Tunisian President Bourguiba on the 4th. And she was again a "one shoulder bare" sensation two months later wearing a one-strap gown at the dinner given for the Kennedys by Pakistan President Ayub Khan and his daughter, Begum Nasir Akhtar Aurangzeb, at the Mayflower Hotel.

At that party, Mamie Eisenhower was present, too, and it was fascinating to see the difference in the First Ladies,

Mamie's dress so bouffant and tucked and Jackie's so slim and severe.

But there was one time Jackie was fluffy, too. That was on the lawn of Mount Vernon. Then her gown was most romantic, making me think of a modern-day Southern belle on the order of Scarlett O'Hara, posed in front of the tall pillars. The scene could have been right out of *Gone with the Wind*.

For that super lawn party, Jackie wore a full-length sheath of row on row of narrow ruffles—lace on white organza. The neckline was her favorite—bateau—straight across the front. Adding a dramatic touch for dealing with evening breezes off the Potomac was a Chartreuse silk stole that was worn tied in back, so as not to disturb the severe straight lines of the front. The stole matched the wide severe belt that nipped in the waist, one of the few times to my knowledge that Jackie wore a tight waist.

The occasion made fashion history in still another way, much to Jackie's annoyance. Jackie did not know that her Social Office had told all the female guests to wear short skirts. Alice Roosevelt Longworth had even turned up the bottom of a floor-length gold lamé gown in order to conform.

Only Jackie and her ranking feminine guest of honor, who was wearing a sari, were in long gowns. Everyone else, with the exception of Mrs. Franklin D. Roosevelt, Jr., was in a short skirt.

17 ~ THE KENNEDY CIRCLE

*J*ACKIE WAS "LACE."
The President was "Lancer."
Caroline was "Lyric."
John-John was "Lark."
The Secret Service men could be talking about the Presidential family as strangers walked by, and it would make no sense at all to them. All the Kennedy code names started with the same letter of the alphabet—the one after "K."

Jackie loved nicknames, too. The whole White House was name-happy.

To her, I was "Little Mary."

"Pekes" was Jackie's nickname for Lee, her sister, and Lee called Jackie "Jacks."

Provi got her nickname, "The Mexican Princess," from "Muggsy," and Provi referred to Jackie as "The Lady."

"Muggsy," of course, had been with the family from way back, and most people didn't even know he had a last name —O'Leary.

Ted Reardon was "T.J." to everyone.

A pair of secretaries were nicknamed "Fiddle" and "Faddle," because they were together all the time and even shared an apartment.

Two Filipino Navy stewards, "Quemoy" and "Matsu," had been nicknamed by Dave Powers. That was all I ever heard them called.

And Dave Powers, in turn, was stuck with the nickname of "Court Jester," because of his skillful storytelling, especially jokes about the Irish of Boston. That was his specialty—that and being able to win any argument on sports events and baseball scores.

And "JFK and JBK" took care of the President and his wife in one breath.

"Buttons," of course, was the President's nickname for Caroline, and sometimes he was "Silly Daddy" to her. I believe it was also the President who gave the nickname of "John-John" to John, Jr., and that's how he was known to everyone in the White House and to the nation.

It was all like talking in code.

The Irish Buddies or "In-Group" were known as "The Irish Mafia"—Ted Reardon, Dave Powers, Larry O'Brien, Kenny O'Donnell, and yes, Muggsy.

JFK enjoyed his "Irish Mafia"—especially Dave Powers, who was always up to some mischief or other. One day, the President commented that he was going to bestow an award on Dave "for his ability to find his way to the refrigerator at any time of day or night."

He was also able to find his way around my bailiwick, and one day left me in rather a frenzy. When I went to Jackie's sitting room to get something from her "Antiques" file box on the shelf of her cabinet, it was missing. There were the "House," "Clothes," and "Food" flowered boxes with their ribbon ties—but no box in which we filed our clippings and photos of "Antiques."

I searched high and low, and I was frantic! For several days, I searched. Then, one afternoon, when I stopped in to see Evelyn Lincoln on the way back from the Staff Mess, I happened to mention my dilemma. "Eve, I just don't know what's happening to me. For some reason, I just can't find Jackie's 'Antiques' box . . ."

A strange look came over Evelyn's face. "Oh, wait a minute. Do you mean this?" She walked to the bathroom of her office and reached up on the shelf. I couldn't imagine how that box could've ended up here in *her* office! And the expression on my face spoke its own question.

"We had a little party here in the office last week, and Dave borrowed the box to carry over two bottles of liquor from the Mansion. They just fit perfectly!"

At the Staff Mess, Dave Powers usually had some funny "story of the day" and at times, he would turn it on himself. I remember one Friday afternoon, when fish was the order of the day for all Catholics, and Dave's platter was put before him, holding a full-length fish.

He studied it awhile, then called the steward back and said grimly, "Would you mind taking this back to the kitchen and ask them to remove the head, please. I just can't bear to eat this thing with his eyes looking up at me like that!"

There was often trouble with formal titles—there were so many to remember and so many problems of how to address each dignitary. "His Royal Highness," "The Honorable," "The Right Honorable." Dave Powers may have had the right idea. When the Shah of Iran arrived, in 1962, he stuck out his hand and said, "You're my kind of Shah!"

Much has been made of the fact that the President smoked a cigar, but I very seldom saw him smoking. Though, when he did—he did smoke a cigar. Only once did I ever see him with a pipe—in a picture taken at Camp David.

I never knew the President to be a spendthrift. Nor was he a vain man. But the one area in which he did spend money rather generously was in the grooming of his hair.

I once saw him pay $20 to the barber who had come to the Ambassador's house at Palm Beach.

All through the White House years, as on Capitol Hill, Kennedy valued humor and enjoyed around him people who could make him laugh. Humor was infectious throughout the White House!

I came to the office each day not knowing what new episode lay ahead. There was always something to keep you going.

Tuesdays turned out to be "Stuff Mary Days!" The whole kitchen staff entered into a conspiracy to fatten me up. After the President's Congressional Breakfast on Tuesdays, the butlers would bring a silver service with everything the President and the legislators had ordered: juice, scrambled eggs, bacon, ham, sausages, buttered toast and rolls and jelly and pot of coffee. Enough to carry me through the day, if not the year.

Muggsy O'Leary joked with the President, and was known as a great kidder. His special target was Provi, and he would tease her mercilessly until she would say, "Muggsy, you get out of here. I got too much work to do."

That was exactly the point of Muggsy's teasing. "Come on there, Provi, let's get busy! When are you going to do some work around here?"

To see Provi laboring over an ironing board, surrounded by racks and boxes and darting in and out of the room to answer "The Lady's" call, made his taunting absolutely hilarious.

The Secret Service men, too, had a good sense of humor, but that was not what they were chosen for. When they were around the Presidential family, they were very close-mouthed and sharp-eyed, with full attention to duty.

Muggsy was part of the Secret Service, too. When he was first assigned to the Secret Service detail at the White House, he was assigned to the Kennedy children, working with Agents Meredith and Foster. But, after Mrs. Kennedy's edict that the Secret Service men were not to stay too close to the children as they played outdoors, Muggsy asked to be transferred to the President's Secret Service detail.

Muggsy was too much the affectionate type to be stand-offish with the children. He must have felt the job could only be carried out with warm friendliness, and he couldn't be happy keeping a restricted distance.

Later, the order for Secret Service men to keep some distance from the children was rescinded because of the swimming-pool incident, which made the newspapers across the nation.

On Miss Shaw's day off one summer afternoon, Caroline had been taken to Virginia to swim in Nina Auchincloss's private pool. At one moment, she lost hold of a float and went under. A guest jumped in with her clothes on to fish Caroline out.

After that, Jackie decided to have the Secret Service Agents as close as necessary to protect the children at all times.

Jackie once used her Secret Service Agent, Clint Hill, as the advance public relations man for one of her foreign trips. She later told Treasury Secretary Dillon that he was so good at it that instead of using the Embassy men she turned all official details over to the Secret Service man.

In contrast to this, Jackie sometimes seemed to be almost merciless in resisting security. Once a security man was carrying out his duty in checking out an item that had looked rather strange to him, as routinely as he had always checked out everything else. Unfortunately, this happened to be one time when Jackie apparently felt that the item was none of his business. In short order, Jackie decreed that he be replaced, and he was quickly transferred to another division. He never had a chance to explain.

At the same time, Jackie's frustrations drove her to be acidly humorous about the security restraints in being a First Lady. She had her heart set on serving soft-shell crabs one day and thought the best ones were obtainable only at a particular market that had not been cleared for purchases by the White House. So she ordered the Staff to "send someone in disguise"!

Jackie was totally unpredictable, sometimes doing the opposite of what her husband wanted, sometimes trying to please him in the minutest detail. When JFK liked a particular picture of her—one in a yellow check dress, taken by Jacques Lowe—Jackie went out of her way to get the message to Molly Thayer, considered the family social historian, who was working on her three-part series for the *Ladies' Home Journal*. She told Molly that the picture of her in the yellow check dress had to be used.

The lunch hour was one of the few times that the President could have a little privacy with Jackie. After his swim, he would come to the Mansion for lunch and she would join him for a little while before his nap. One time Jackie was so absorbed in what she was dictating, as we sat in the sitting room, that she forgot the President was waiting for her. He had come and gone. Finally, George Thomas came to the doorway and announced, "Miz Kennedy, the President says if you don't hurry, he'll fall asleep." She hurried off.

Jackie loved to come up with surprises for her husband—little gifts that would amaze him. And she loved intrigue and outwitting the press or anyone she considered nosey—including the general public. Sometimes she would act like Secret Agent 007, such as the time she wanted me to send a cable to a friend traveling through Switzerland, asking him to bring home 10 monogrammed shirts for your friend JULIUS FISCHER KOVAK. Having trained in Jackie's special school of intrigue, I immediately caught her code and smiled. "*Julius Fischer Kovak*"—*JFK*.

Jackie was very proud of her family heritage and once commented that she must "someday" move to Caroline County in Maryland, because it was connected with her family history on the Bouvier side.

Michel Bouvier, a favorite cousin of Jackie's lived on the rue Adolph-yvon in Paris. He enjoyed being the family historian, and Jackie was interested in what he could tell her about family history. She learned that Caroline County in Maryland was the source of family names: both her sister and daughter were named Caroline.

Jackie was thrilled when Michel came to visit her in March of her first year at the White House and brought a "Cincinnati Lineage." She assured him that it would be saved for little John to see when he was old enough. I recall that she also mentioned to him that she would "adore having" copies of the family coat of arms.

Jackie was annoyed once that a particular girl claimed to be a relative. She told someone to get the girl out of her hair, saying that she was some dreary girl who kept claiming she was a cousin. Jackie gave instructions to send her a nice letter—"PBO." The initials stood for Polite Brush-Off.

The press made much of the fact that the Kennedys as a whole family did not go in for expressions of affection in public. They seldom kissed when meeting each other, even after trips. I felt they simply had followed the New England tradition of reticence.

Nor were the Kennedy wives and in-laws at the White House as often as the public thought they were. Jackie Kennedy was not one to call her sisters-in-law in the middle of the day and say, "Come on over and talk."

She had no close relationships with in-laws or women friends. Jackie lived a strangely remote life in the White House, busying herself with official entertainment, her own little family, and the projects of her own choice. If she didn't want to participate in some activity, nothing could drive her to it. She had no compunction about saying no, though she preferred to let someone like Pam, her press secretary, say it for her.

She did not want to go to the Distinguished Ladies Reception, which was in her honor, at the Inauguration of her husband. And she did not go.

The press pleaded with her to have press conferences. Tish, her social secretary, in a meeting with women reporters just prior to the move to the White House, practically committed Jackie to holding press conferences.

Jackie did *not* hold press conferences.

When Jackie's love of interior decorating turned to the White House, she worked harder and longer and more painstakingly than anyone could imagine. And that was because she wanted to. If anyone had tried to stop her from redecorating the White House, he would have had a hard time.

As she herself once said, when briefing Nancy Tuckerman about her obligations as First Lady, "People told me ninety-nine things that I had to do as First Lady, and I haven't done one of them."

When Jackie's mother would phone her, she could seldom reach her and would have to give me the message. Sometimes she avoided her mother; other times she sought her out.

Often I would be the one to relay Jackie's message to her mother, as Jackie herself sat in the same room. Once Jackie wanted me to call her mother and tell her not to show Molly Thayer any more letters, "no matter what she does"—while Molly was writing her biography of the First Lady. On another occasion, she asked me to say to her, "Jackie wants to know if you would bring Mrs. Harriman with you when you next come over to see the babies." I was to say that, in this way, Jackie wouldn't have to issue a special invitation to Mrs. Harriman at another time.

Mrs. Auchincloss was always helping Jackie in any way possible and always tried to be completely loyal to her, it seemed to me. At times, I would find myself wishing that her daughter could be a bit more considerate of her mother.

From what I had observed, Jackie's relationship with her mother-in-law was not too close, either.

Ever since the Palm Beach luncheon incident between them—when Jackie did not join her mother-in-law and her guests at luncheon—it seemed that the senior Mrs. Kennedy must have stopped trying to draw Jackie into her activities.

After the Inaugural, I noticed that the President and Jackie, seemed to prefer spending future winter vacations at the homes of friends nearby, rather than at the senior Kennedys' as had been the tradition.

When I went down to be with Jackie one Easter, she stayed at the residence of Colonel Michael C. Paul. In my albums, I have several lovely pictures taken during my visit there.

At times the President became the intermediary between the two Mrs. Kennedys.

The President would sometimes invite Mrs. Rose Kennedy to be his hostess at the White House when Jackie was away, as in 1962 when Ecuador's President Carlos Arosemena visited.

And when Mrs. Kennedy was coming to visit a White House chauffeur or aide would be assigned to escort her to the White House. Sometimes, General Clifton would meet her plane.

Mrs. Rose Kennedy liked to sleep in the Lincoln Bedroom, and I recall the amusing episode when the President wanted to show some visitors the Lincoln bed, which they had asked to see, and popped open the door. He popped right back out again, because his mother was taking a nap on the Lincoln bed!

I was so amused, too, when I read the delightful story in *Look* magazine—"A Visit with the Indomitable Rose Kennedy"—telling how "penny-wise" she was and how when the local candy-store man sent her a $38 bill run up by her grandchildren the previous summer, she asked for an *itemized* account.

It reminded me of one afternoon in 1963, right after Jackie left for Greece, when the President's mother was acting as his hostess. I received a telephone call from the White House telephone operator, asking if I knew of a masseuse whom I could recommend for Mrs. Rose Kennedy, and would I please go down to the Lincoln Bedroom to let her know.

I found Mrs. Kennedy standing at the doorway of the Lincoln Bedroom in a lovely short robe, looking elegant, as always, except for the incongruous touch of stocking feet. She explained that she was about to take a nap, having been up since early morning to go to Mass, and how nice it would be to have a massage to relax her.

When I suggested someone from Elizabeth Arden, she seemed rather concerned about the expense that might be incurred, stating "Oh, but they charge $17. I realize they have to charge for their time in coming and going, but I'd rather have someone who could just come over and do it for about $7.50."

I quickly ran upstairs to my office, checked the Yellow Pages of the phone directory and, in short order, I managed to locate such a person.

Later, I received Mrs. Kennedy's thanks—she was well pleased: "Oh yes, thank you so much—she was just great!"

The situation was quite different between Jackie and her father-in-law, Ambassador Kennedy. Perhaps the one thing I remember most when I think of Mr. Kennedy is the great fondness Jackie held for him. They could sit and happily scheme together and be as playful as two little children.

After Christmas, 1960, Jackie reported to Ethel on a new game which Grandpa enjoyed most of all. The Ambassador and Jackie would see who could first hit Evelyn Jones with their lamb chop bones before she could get to the pantry door. Evelyn Jones was the head housekeeper at the Ambassador's residence in Palm Beach.

I had heard of the Trumans' game of throwing bits of bread at the table, but I'd never heard of throwing bones!

My own contacts and direct associations with the Ambassador were rather limited in that he never appeared too often at his son's home in Georgetown or even at the White House. But I would see him at his home in Palm Beach when I spent time there with Jackie. I found him to be gracious and sociable at all times. My first day there when I was working away in his study on the first floor, he came in to fix himself a cool drink from the bar. Upon meeting me, he offered me a Coke, then sat for a little while talking to his niece, Ann Gargan, who had come in with him. They seemed to enjoy each other's company very much and had a great rapport. Incidentally, it took a few days before Ann, herself, began any conversation with me. And when she did, her first question was, "How long have you been with Jackie?" From then on, she was most sociable toward me.

Of the Kennedy sisters, it seemed that Jackie was closest to Jean Smith. We would often call her to arrange having her children come to the White House for dinner and movies with Caroline and John.

Stephen Smith, Caroline's cousin, was Caroline's favorite playmate, and her "boyfriend." They were the same age. Frequently, Jackie asked me to call Jean to make arrangements for Stevie to come and play with Caroline.

Jackie truly loved horses, and Caroline was like her. I was entertained by memos I sent concerning how many horses could go in the vans that the Kennedy women were sending back and forth to the Cape. Preparations for the animals were as important as preparations for the people!

Pat Lawford lived in California—away from the scene—so it was seldom that she saw Jackie. But when the Lawfords came to Washington, it was fun having Peter Lawford around the White House. He was very friendly and sociable and seemed to keep Jackie in good spirits, kidding with her. He was also good company for the President, when they relaxed in the family quarters. Peter wanted a print of the President's favorite picture of Jackie, and I arranged to get one for him.

Eunice Shriver was busy with her pet project of working with handicapped and retarded children. In the summer, she opened her home and swimming pool to mentally retarded children for swimming, picnics, and fun.

During my last year at the White House, she got her brother's ear, persuading him to set a good example for the nation by starting a program of hiring the handicapped to work at the White House.

I remember that we were just at the stage where Larry Arata, the White House upholsterer, had approved of one particular lad for his shop in the White House. But then came the terrible tragedy . . .

I saw with admiration the story in the newspapers about Eunice continuing her work with the retarded as the wife of the American Ambassador to France, Sargent Shriver. "One morning a week," the story said, "she gets into her slacks, sweatshirt, and sneakers and drives a distance of about 45 miles to help train young retarded children."

At the White House, because her husband and Robert Kennedy were so close, Jackie saw Ethel perhaps more than her other in-laws. With her, Jackie was especially uninhibited. When she thanked her for a blue robe that Ethel had given her, Jackie vowed that since she had received it, she had never been out of it, like the slovenly heroine in the movie *Come Back, Little Sheba*, who never got out of her wrapper.

But, as with her own sister, Lee, a little competitiveness occasionally crept into Jackie's relationship with Ethel. I remember once, when her sister-in-law's outfit had been a great hit at a Senate luncheon, Jackie made a point of asking me to call Ethel's secretary and ask her where Ethel got the pink suit she wore to the affair.

A few minutes later, I had the answer for Jackie, "Madame Paul's, St. Aubin de Paris on Wisconsin Avenue in Georgetown."

Within her own family and wherever she went, Jackie had an electrifying effect on men. It wasn't just that she was the First Lady, to whom deference was due. Her breathless little-girl quality combined with her witty sophistication made for an undeniable charm. They wanted to protect her. Men hovered around her and listened to her sensuous voice. They wanted to amuse her and to hold her attention.

I think Secretary of Commerce Luther Hodges at a diplomatic reception explained it best, "She looks right at you while you're talking and makes you feel as if you are the most important person she ever met."

There was something about the way she said things that held people spellbound. It was a sort of breathless way, but she spoke almost in a whisper so that you had to lean forward sometimes to hear her.

What most people didn't know, however, was that behind that pretty face was a steel-trap mind. Jackie was an inveterate reader, spending many, many hours, when people thought she was having gay times, reading books on many subjects.

What amused me was that Jackie was worried about being a slow reader. She once said, "Knowing Jack devours 1200 words a minute throws me into a state of depression. When we leave here, he will know everything, and I will be illiterate."

Jackie appreciated clever minds in every field. For example, she asked McGeorge Bundy to keep her supplied with Ken

Galbraith's intelligence reports from India because they were so fascinating.

What she enjoyed most, as she put it, were his "impertinent cables." But when she learned Galbraith was leaving that post, she told Mr. Bundy that he could forget about the State Department reports—they would no longer hold the same interest.

Secretary of Defense Robert McNamara was another great favorite with Jackie because of his sharp wit and fantastic memory—he could instantly recall a person's name even if he hadn't seen him for several years. When Jackie wanted to be especially nice to one of her feminine dinner guests, she would arrange to seat her next to McNamara—it was the mark of Jackie's favor.

During the Shah of Iran's visit in 1962 with his beautiful young wife, Farah Diba, I was to call Anne Lincoln for Jackie and ask, "Is it possible for either Jackie or Farah Diba to sit next to Secretary McNamara tonight?" But, on second thought, realizing that protocol might become involved, Jackie wanted Anne to know that if there was any problem, she should just "forget it."

As it turned out, protocol prevailed, because Anne soon called back to say, "No, the Empress is on the President's right. And on the Empress's right will be the Vice President."

The Under Secretary of the Navy, Paul "Red" Fay, was a very good personal friend of both the President and Mrs. Kennedy and would often be invited to join them on weekends either at their country home in Virginia or up at Cape Cod.

Fay's book, *The Pleasure of His Company*, written after the President's assassination, clearly reveals this close personal relationship between them. I first had the "pleasure" of Red Fay's company during my summer with Jackie in 1963 at the Cape. He was in the foyer of the house when I arrived there one day, and we were introduced.

Considering the fact that he was such a good friend and

165

made a generous donation to the Kennedy Library from the proceeds of his book, I was shocked at Jackie's displeasure that he had written his book at all. I later heard—and it was reported, too, in the newspapers—that she had sent his check back to him.

Jackie, for the most part, instead of bringing in new friends of her own, spent her time entertaining the President's friends and associates. The small group of intimates who were their closest friends, invited to their small dinner groups in the evening, included:

The Charles Bartletts, who originally played Cupid in bringing JFK and JBK together—he is a newpaper correspondent; the Benjamin Bradlees, Georgetown friends—another writer; Bill Walton, the artist; Charles "Chuck" Spalding of the Harvard class of 1940; and Lem Billings, who had been JFK's roommate at Choate.

Lem Billings, incidentally, was a frequent guest at the White House and would occupy one of the guestrooms on the third floor—barely bothering to call to make sure his room was ready. I remember on one occasion that, as Jackie and I waited for the President's elevator on the second floor, several minutes passed and still the elevator did not descend from the third floor.

Jackie became more and more impatient, so I left her and took to the stairs to investigate.

I questioned the doorman holding the elevator, apparently waiting for someone. "Yes, ma'am," he confirmed, "Mr. Billings asked that I hold the elevator for him—he'll be right back."

He was one guest who really knew how to make himself at home at the White House.

Among the things that never failed to surprise me were the movies that Jackie called for to be shown in the private theater at the White House for friends, such as Arthur Schlesinger, the Max Freedmans, the Gilpatricks. One day she wanted me to inquire about three movies: *Black Tights*, *Last Year at Marienbad*, and *Walk on the Wild Side*. Another

166 ॐ

day it was the French movie, *Jules et Jim*. Her tastes in movies was definitely sophisticated, rather than goody-goody. She wanted *The Conjugal Bed* shown over the weekend in the country.

The President and she, however, did not share the same movie taste, and sometimes he would leave before the show was over.

The President was so busy that Jackie occasionally had to make a date to get to see him in the evening. I would call Evelyn and ask, "Has the President anything to do Thursday night?" And another time, "Has the President anything on his schedule for Saturday night? Would he like to go to a dinner dance?"

Jackie was clever with words and occasionally took special interest in a toast that her husband would be making at a State dinner. In May, 1962, she asked Arthur Schlesinger for help on a toast for André Malraux, the French Minister of Culture.

Sometimes her generous gestures backfired. When her dear friend, Franklin D. Roosevelt, Jr., was sworn in at the White House as Under Secretary of Commerce, she thought it would be suitable to present him with the Bible that had been used. Then she learned—too late—she had given to Mr. Roosevelt the Bible that had been used in the White House since 1948.

Jackie later asked me to get in touch with Evelyn Lincoln to get a new Bible that would be used for future swearing-in ceremonies, which each appointee would sign after he had been sworn in. This Bible would belong strictly to JFK, and they would take it when they left the White House.

I was amused when Jackie mentioned that the President wasn't too crazy about the Bible idea. "He told me I'm getting to be just like his mother," she said, "worrying about little things, and pretty soon I'll be going around with notes pinned all over me."

To prepare for Jackie's travels, I always packed in her brief-case a good supply of PT-boat tie clips for men and PT-boat pins for ladies, the same items that Evelyn Lincoln packed for the President when he traveled.

The man behind this popular Kennedy memento was Frank Allen, who designed the pins and the clips, as well as other items that had been used in the 1960 campaign—the Kennedy-girl hats with streamers down the back, "Jacqueline" perfume, ballpoint pens engraved with the President's name, and various buttons and badges.

But his greatest triumph was the PT-boat tie clips and pins, which he donated from time to time in generous supply. I can recall at Georgetown, during the campaign, when these items were received directly at the house. Jackie would say, "Mary, will you please write a nice note to Frank Allen in New York today, thanking him?"

After we were in the White House, he continued to send them, but Evelyn Lincoln took care of thanking him for the President. Actually, this was a sideline with Frank Allen, who received no compensation for them. He had a thriving dental laboratory and just seemed to enjoy having this little hobby. He was also a long-time friend of Ambassador Kennedy.

A pattern was established with the President that was to continue throughout his "thousand days." No matter how busy he was, he *always*—somehow—took a moment to meet the members of my family when they came to Washington to visit.

Strange as it may seem, I never had the courage to take them in to meet my lady boss, no matter how much they pleaded for just one moment, or one glimpse of Jacqueline Kennedy. I would shift them instead to the President, because there was never any doubt in my mind about his saying yes.

I recall especially the visit of my sister Eva and her husband, John Coughlin, with their two children, John and James, from Worcester, Massachusetts. As loyal supporters (and fans) of JFK, they said their trip to D.C. "would not be complete" if they couldn't at least shake a Kennedy hand before going back.

I checked the possibility with Evelyn. "Oh, sure," she readily agreed, "I know he won't mind at all."

She went over his schedule for the day, then suggested we arrange it for right after his nap. "George, his valet, will set it up—I'll call him now."

Sure enough, the Coughlins' big dream came true. JFK saw them in the West Sitting Room, looking his usual refreshed self—and upon catching their names, quickly came back with a typical quip: "So," he said, in a broad smile, "another member of the family went off and married an Irishman."

To put it mildly, Eva almost went into a slight faint, murmuring, "Oh, Mary, he's even handsomer than his pictures."

I squirmed, embarrassed that he might have heard—needlessly, at that. He not only heard, but obviously loved it. His eyes seemed to take on an extra twinkle, and his parting handshakes revealed his truest warmth. All of Worcester, no doubt, would get to hear about this!

This remarkable trait, which truly seemed a natural gift of the President, was noticed and appreciated by others. When my former roommate, Lois, returned to D.C. with her husband, Colonel Alfred Strode, on leave from overseas duty, she came to see me.

It was her first visit to the White House since her former boss had become President. Of course, more than anything, she hoped to see the President for at least a moment.

Reluctant to interrupt his busy schedule by requesting an appointment, Lois settled for just taking her chances with me. After lunching at the Staff Mess, we stopped by to say hello to Evelyn Lincoln, whom Lois also wanted to see. She had no sooner embraced Evelyn with a friendly hug than emerging from the Cabinet Room was the President, himself.

He was pleasantly surprised to find Lois standing there, and her shock and delight were visible as she feasted her eyes on the tanned and handsome man before her.

For several minutes, he displayed his usual charm in greeting her, asking questions about her travels. Then, showing his real concern, came the pièce de résistance, "You're not looking for a job by any chance, are you, Lois?"

Lois smiled and replied, "Not at the moment, Mr. President."

"Well, if you ever are," he went on, "you know you can come back and work for me. I'm sure we can find a good spot for you right here."

Lois was shining like a silver dollar!

He reached for a newspaper on Evelyn's desk, entered his office and, as usual, had left his indelible mark.

"Oh," Lois sighed, "what I wouldn't give to be able to come back and work for that man!"

Only on one occasion did I build up sufficient courage to request a favor of Jackie—that she autograph a White House Guide Book for one of my nieces, Sister Constance Marie, a Sister of Charity of Nazareth.

It happened in August, 1962, when I was leaving to spend a few days in Kentucky, visiting with her. I had forwarded a copy to Jackie at the Cape with a note, explaining that it was so difficult to know just what to present to a nun in a convent and that this was the one thing I knew she would really love and cherish.

It was a little victory when I received the book a few days later, bearing Mrs. Kennedy's neatly inscribed message of good wishes. So Connie remains the one and only member of the family to score on this point!

18 ∽ THE JACQUELINE IMAGE
AT HOME AND ABROAD

*J*ACKIE WAS VERY CONSCIOUS OF HER PUBLIC image in the White House right from the very beginning. When the author Mary Van Rensselaer Thayer, her mother's friend, was doing a three-part series on her for the *Ladies' Home Journal*, Jackie informed her, even from Palm Beach, that she would never forgive her or the magazine if they used an unflattering picture of her as the Inquiring Camera Girl using a Speed Graphic.

Instead, she wanted Molly to use a snapshot she liked that showed her interviewing some British bus drivers who were touring the Capitol. I recall Jackie had me mail it to Molly from her own scrapbook.

There was another picture she asked Molly not to use because it had been taken when she was an awkward adolescent —and another that made her look, she thought, like a "stupid glamour girl." Jackie had sharp wit and did not hesitate to use it, even against herself.

I tried very hard to understand Jackie. She was a very complex person—not at all the helpless little girl she sometimes portrayed, and which was so appealing to the public mind and to all the men in any gathering.

She was completely organized, always planning her life, always looking ahead. I believe that her aura of helplessness could get her anything she really wanted, and she seemed to enjoy the role when it suited her. I used to reflect that Jackie was spoiled by having her way too much, but she was never naive.

Her husband would agree with almost anything to please her. But sometimes he had to press her to do what she didn't want to. Once, the help came back from Florida talking about how Jackie had not wanted to go to church. When the President insisted, she had ignored the Sunday clothes that had been laid out for her, choosing instead to go in the most casual get-up—a sun dress, flat sandals, and a kerchief tied around her head. The press was on hand, as usual, and didn't fail to mention that the outfit hardly seemed appropriate.

Jackie saw herself as someone remote from the common herd, and did not want the public to think there had ever been any hardship in her life.

Also, Jackie did not want her image to be de-glamorized with too many obstetrical details, or want it stressed that she had had difficulties in having children. She had lost two before having Caroline in 1957—one in 1955 and one in 1956.

In another vein, I recall that Jackie gave Mrs. Alice Longworth a copy of the funny book about the Kennedys, called *Who's in Charge?* which had been autographed by the author, Gerald Gardner. Jackie liked that kind of fun-making so much that she asked for another autographed copy to replace it. But strangely enough, it infuriated her to hear or even see the Vaughn Meader record that poked fun at the First Family, in which the impersonators were shown standing in front of the White House.

She got in touch with Pierre Salinger, asking him if he couldn't do something about it. She felt there should be some rule about the White House as there is for the flag, so no one could use its picture for what she called cheap jokes.

Jackie's pride of family was stung when Vaughn Meader brushed his hair over his eyes and made light of her husband and the Presidency, in a devastating imitation of JFK's appearance and voice. But she became even more incensed when he decided to include a child named "Caroline" in his act.

She told Pam that she didn't care what he did with the

record he had already cut, but she definitely did care about his making money by mentioning the children's names. There were very few things that got Jackie as excited as the subject of Vaughn Meader.

Jackie took a good hard look at everything written about her or the Kennedys. She was frequently concerned about her husband's image, and would look over books that purported to tell what he was really like. When Jim Bishop's book *A Day in the Life of President Kennedy* came out, she said, "There would have to be forty-eight hours in a day for the President and me to do all the things he wrote about."

She read the local papers and even took a searching look at the women's section of *The New York Times* with her morning breakfast tray. Frequently, I would send word to Pam to get additional copies of something Jackie liked or didn't like.

We were always getting copies of photos that appeared in papers and magazines, for the children's albums or for her own collection. She kept her photos in attractive-looking boxes on a shelf arranged by event and by date.

Bachrach called, wanting to do a formal photographic portrait of the First Lady in her Inaugural gown before it was given to the Smithsonian. They had tried to pin her down even before the Inauguration, but she had not been in the mood then. They had already taken the portrait of the President that was used all through the campaign and the Inaugural. Now they wanted hers.

Jackie seldom mentioned her own ability as a photographer. I can say I never in all those years saw her snap a picture, although her personal photographic equipment, including several cameras, was kept in a lower cabinet in her West Sitting Room, along with films and bulbs. But she once mentioned that she had taken a picture of the same fountain that Sargent had painted in the watercolor that was loaned to the White House by the Boston Museum of Fine Arts.

It was my feeling that Jackie was a frustrated artist, who might one day gain unexpected fame in this field. She sometimes kept an easel set up, especially at the Cape, and had an album of her drawings of animals.

My diary shows that in July, 1962 Jackie expressed interest in taking some lessons in watercoloring from the French artist, Jacqueline Duheme. As a result, her talent found expression in two paintings that were used as Hallmark Christmas cards for the benefit of the National Cultural Center—"The Journey of the Magi" and "Glad Tidings," which showed an angel blowing a horn against a turquoise sky. I thought they were delightful. They showed an ethereal quality and great delicacy.

This was just another facet of a fascinating personality.

Jackie's sense of dignity was not superficial. There was an inborn refinement, even though she could express herself in sharp and colorful words. She wanted her surroundings to be serene and genteel. She told Anne Lincoln, the housekeeper, she found it abhorrent "to hear loud jazz crashing through the East Room."

From the beginning, Jackie's entertainment at the White House was opulent and elegant. Her first White House party—ten days after they moved in—was precedent-shattering. Instead of the traditional little cakes and party sandwiches, there was a heaping buffet table of cold foods and various hot and cold dips. It was the first time a bar had been set up at the White House in anyone's memory. The papers didn't fail to point out, too, that liquor had been served on Sunday. There were even editorials about that.

Jackie and the President broke tradition with their naturalness and informality. Up to this point, guests would be lined up four abreast, waiting to be received. Now, the guests could mill around and have a drink at the White House, just as if they were at a little neighborhood cocktail party.

When the President, wearing a gray business suit, and Jackie, wearing a black velvet sleeveless sheath, entered the room, they simply mingled with the guests, shaking a hand here and there, as they moved around from group to group,

174 ੬❧

eventually ending up in the Blue Room, where they formed a receiving line.

Soon, at later parties, the Kennedys completely dispensed even with the receiving line at their formal receptions and just walked around the rooms, talking to this guest and that— taking a hand or not, as seemed natural at the moment. Though the actual bar disappeared from the scene, cocktails remained very much a part of the party, served on trays by butlers who passed among the guests.

I remember the private party at the White House on March 15th in honor of Prince and Princess Radziwill. This was one of Jackie's very special affairs, and she wanted it to be strictly *haute cuisine*. Perhaps she could not help "showing off" for her sister, and the food was in the best French tradition.

Salmon Mousse with Cucumbers
Poulet à l'Estragon
Grilled Tomatoes
Mushrooms in Herbs
Casserole Marie-Blanche
Baba aux Fraises
Demi-tasse

The household had a festive air whenever Lee was there. I remember how Provi walked by one day with a bottle of beer on a tray, heading for the Queen's Room. I thought the Princess wanted to drink it. But, as I learned from Provi, it was to shampoo her hair. I never knew to what use beer was being put around the White House.

One morning a butler walked by with a bottle of beer on a little silver tray. It was for Peter Lawford. And a little later, there Peter was, padding down the hall in his black velvet slippers, which he wore even with his regular suit. Those slippers reminded me that down in Palm Beach I had learned of Peter Lawford's dislike of wearing shoes. Someone told me how the President made him keep his shoes on when he started at the first tee on the golf course and wouldn't let him take off his shoes until they were away from the clubhouse.

In April, the President gave a stag luncheon in honor of Prime Minister Macmillan on the 5th. It was quite British, though the menu was certainly not as impressive as what the Radziwills had.

At the same time, Jackie gave a separate tea for Lady Dorothy Macmillan in the Mansion.

Then came a stag luncheon for Konrad Adenauer. The first formal State Luncheon on a grand scale was for the Prime Minister of Greece and Mrs. Karamanlis, on April 17th. The menu was sumptuous.

How ironic it was that one of the most important functions of the year, the Congressional Reception of April 18th, coincided with the Bay of Pigs disaster. The poor President had no time for dancing in the East Room with his guests; he was busy at his office most of the night.

The year was filled with many notable guests—King Ibn Saud of Saudi Arabia, President Sukarno of Indonesia, President Fulbert Youlou of the Congo. Governor Nelson Rockefeller and Prince Bernhard of the Netherlands appeared at the White House on the same spring day. On May 3rd, it was the President of Tunisia and Mrs. Bourguiba, honored at a State Dinner.

During the first few months of 1961, the President and Jackie stayed close to the White House. It was not until May that their foreign trips began—then Jackie really hit her stride and was abroad more than the President himself. I kept up with her as best I could, from my office.

It started with Canada in May, the first State visit to a foreign country. As she went with the President, I took the opportunity to sneak out of Washington myself for a quick vacation in Bermuda, with the excuse that Ray wanted me to join him at his company's convention.

How strange it was to see in the local paper there, *The Bermuda Mid-Ocean News*, Friday, May 19, 1961, that Jackie was visiting the Royal Canadian Mounted Police Barracks at Rockcliffe to inspect their magnificent horses. There was my boss, smiling as she posed, nose-to-nose, almost kissing one of the Royal Mounted horses. Knowing how she loved horses, I knew the smile was sincere.

She returned just in time to entertain Prince Rainier and Princess Grace of Monaco on May 24th, with intimate Kennedy friends—the FDR, Jrs. and artist Bill Walton—among the guests.

Almost immediately after she returned from Canada, Jackie began preparing for her next trip abroad, a fabulous one, to Paris, Vienna, and London.

When Jackie learned about JFK's projected trip to Europe, she excitedly sent Lee a cable saying that they would both be coming to London for the christening of her new baby.

Again, I followed Jackie's triumph in the newspapers, "emoting" over it as only another Latin could. She was a Bouvier in Paris, and the crowds greeted her as their own. It was Jackie's milieu. It was a place where she was far more in her element than the President could possibly be. In the first place, she knew Paris as he never knew it. She had gone to the Sorbonne there, and as a student she had lived there with a French family.

I was hoping the President could manage to get his political homework in, because the headlines were all for "Jacqueleen." I laughed as he gave a typical Kennedy punch-line. "I do not think it altogether inappropriate," he announced as the crowd roared, "to introduce myself. I am the man who accompanied Jacqueline Kennedy to France." Only my old boss could come up with that one.

If ever there was a moment to match Marie Antoinette's in the Hall of Mirrors at Versailles, it was Jackie's when she had the full attention of General de Gaulle and one hundred and fifty guests at the formal State Dinner in that same magnificent chamber.

She was the bright star, and even though I wasn't there, I felt as I looked at her pictures that she had never looked more beautiful. I knew the dress well. The papers were making a fuss about its being a foreign creation—a Givenchy gown—after everyone expected that she would wear only American gowns. It was a white satin, with bateau neckline, embroidered over the bodice with colorful paillettes. On her head, crowning her new Louis XIV hairstyle, was a little tiara. I wondered where she got it.

And what a follow-up—she and the President flew on to Vienna to meet the Khrushchevs, where the crowds in the court of the Hofburg Palace screamed so loud and so long for Jackie that she appeared at the window to quiet them.

She graciously took Mrs. Khrushchev to the window to wave to the crowds also. I smiled as I read that.

On that same trip came London and more glamour. At dinner in Buckingham Palace, Queen Elizabeth's tight bodice and full-skirted effect were in direct contrast to Jackie's severe white gown that seemed somehow even more regal.

I remembered having seen that gown on the rack in Provi's headquarters on the third floor when she unboxed it. It was pale-blue satin with little bows on the shoulders, but no other decoration. The neckline ran in a straight line from shoulder to shoulder.

The papers also reported the christening of her sister Lee's baby, Anna Christina, the day after the visit to Buckingham Palace. The President was godfather. I knew how pleased Jackie must have been. Anything that involved Lee was so important to her. The President and she had stayed with Lee and the Prince instead of being guests of the Queen and Prince Philip. Ironically, the address for Lee and "Stash" was Buckingham Place.

The President returned to Washington, and Jackie continued a semi-official visit on her own.

She went to Athens with the Radziwills, at the invitation of the Greek Prime Minister and Mrs. Karamanlis, and then went yachting in the Mediterranean with the shipping magnate, Niarchos.

By mid-June she returned, but not in time to help the

178 ૱

President entertain the President of Italy, Amitore Fanfani. Naturally, since he was Italian, I longed to shake his hand, but didn't get that near to him.

After spending the Fourth of July holidays at the Cape, Jackie was back in Washington for her history-making event of the year—the dinner reception and concert on the lawn of Mount Vernon in honor of the President of Pakistan, Mohammed Ayub Khan, July 11th.

Never did the White House staff work harder against greater odds and hazards from heaven, man, beasts—or, at least, insects—than they worked there. The guests were transported down the Potomac to Mount Vernon by boat, and Jackie had a new nickname around the White House for a while, "Cleopatra on her Barge." But Jackie's barge was the Navy's *Sequoia*.

It was one of the four yachts carrying guests down the Potomac to Mount Vernon. The President arrived aboard the Presidential yacht *Honey Fitz*. The Robert Kennedys and Stephen Smiths were among his guests.

What a party that was! No effort was considered too great. The logistics of the food alone were unbelievable: since there was no electricity at Washington's old home, huge generators had to be carted in to supply the heat for the portable kitchen, as well as light. The food was hauled down in special trucks.

Then the insects took over, especially gnats from the riverbank, so workmen sprayed the grounds twice. Chef René was most annoyed about that, claiming his food was being poisoned.

Even worse was the problem of indoor plumbing. Portable bathrooms had to be set up. Unfortunately, the workmen had placed them in the most obvious places, making them an eyesore. At the last minute they had to be moved and placed more appropriately behind bushes.

The guest of honor, Ayub Khan, was enchanted, and Jackie was delighted, and so it was all worth while. Even the President in his toast had been moved to agree with the Father of his Country. "George Washington once said, 'I would rather be at Mount Vernon with a friend or two about me than be attended at the seat of government by the officers of state and the representatives of every power in Europe.' "

Fortunately for me, I didn't have to account for expenses involved with such State entertainment. That went through the Housekeeper's Office. I had enough to do just keeping track of Jackie's personal entertainment, as when she gave the private party for her sister, Lee.

The newspapers were forever getting excited about the cost of Jackie's entertainment, especially that Mount Vernon dinner.

Pierre Salinger, the President's press secretary, explained that most of the extras had been donated by public-spirited citizens. He said, "The only costs were for the food, and these were within the normal State Department allocation for the entertainment of State guests."

Pierre said the special green tent pavilion had been contributed by the Philadelphia firm of William H. Vanderherschen, Inc. The entertainment had been provided free of charge by the National Symphony Orchestra, and the band leader, Lester Lanin, had contributed a trio for incidental music. Furthermore, the fabulous decorations for the flower-bedecked, candlelit tent had been done free of charge by Tiffany.

"It would be impossible to give such a dinner," said Salinger, "unless we had the help of public-spirited citizens. It will continue to be Mrs. Kennedy's policy in the future to call on such citizens to help our country put its best foot forward."

With this big event behind her, Jackie went back to Cape Cod for the rest of the summer, keeping in touch with me by courier mail. It was like our own personal post office service. Planes shuttled back and forth during the week with mail from Washington to Hyannisport.

A special desk folder was designed by Jackie for her personal use, and she sent instructions for it by courier. Originally, it was to have an inset of the Inaugural medal, but

Jackie thought it had "such a ghastly color" that she decided to use a Treasury medal instead.

Lee Radziwill was having it made in London for her, and Jackie asked me to send the Treasury medal with a note of instructions. Jackie, being a perfectionist, wanted the cover made in a very special way—the President's face on the medal should show on the front side, and the reverse of the medal should also show through on the inside of the cover.

By mid-September, Jackie was back in Washington to settle down to domestic affairs once more, arranging to greet the President and Mrs. Prado of Peru on September 19th.

Then, she went to New York with the President, staying at their suite at the Carlyle, in preparation for his address to the United Nations. I had not seen the suite, but I knew it must be something special from all I had heard when the Secret Service men arranged security matters there. It was a two-level apartment, located in the penthouse of the hotel, and had as many rooms as a small house—living room, dining room, library, kitchen, two bedrooms, and two baths—Jackie's room in her favorite off-white. An expanse of glass revealed a magnificent view of the New York skyline overlooking Central Park.

Then, it was on to "Hammersmith Farm," Jackie's childhood home in Newport. I knew it, having attended her lavish wedding reception there.

October was fall cleaning month for me at the White House, because Jackie wanted all the shelves and cabinets in the sitting room rearranged. The worst part of the job was sorting the innumerable books, to separate Jackie's personal library from that of the President. Before I was through, I realized what a back-breaking, time-consuming job a library can be and was lucky to enlist a houseboy to help me along.

Jackie had ordered special personal bookplates from Tiffany. After sorting the books into "his" and "hers," I pasted the beautiful seals on the inside front cover of each volume.

Besides the art books, Jackie's library reflected her major interests, covering poetry, history, biography, and a number of volumes on horses, as well as books on antique furnishings—especially French. There were some current novels, but predominantly older books. Some were in French. Few had dust jackets. I had the feeling that these were the books she had collected over her lifetime.

Jackie's books were kept in two large bookcases above cabinets in the West End Sitting Room. Most of her art books were in the open bookshelves and about a half-dozen, far too large to fit the shelves, were arranged on the round center table. The President's books were moved from the Center Hall to the Oval Room. Those left in the Center Hall belonged to the White House Library.

And pictures—what a mountain of pictures I sorted in the course of the year. For Caroline's albums, for John-John's albums, and boxes of loose photos.

The famous Richard Avedon had taken some photographs of Caroline running, and these especially thrilled Jackie. She congratulated him and asked for copies.

Jackie mentioned two of them as the most enchanting children's pictures she had ever seen.

What a thrill it was on the first day of November to know that President Truman and his family were "in residence" again at the White House, especially since *my* Blue Toile bedroom on the third floor was one of the suite of rooms being used by the Presidential family.

When the Trumans descended the stairs to dinner, the Marine band switched from "Hail to the Chief" to the "Missouri Waltz."

Though JFK was not up to his old trick of making his guest sing for his supper, as he had up on the Hill, he did make this one play the piano. Harry Truman entertained the President, Jackie, and their guests with Paderewski's "Minuet in G."

Afterwards, the White House staff had a good laugh about the punchline of the evening. Just as Harry Truman was about to strike the first chord on the piano, a protesting voice rang out from the audience, "But you're not a member of

Jacqueline Kennedy

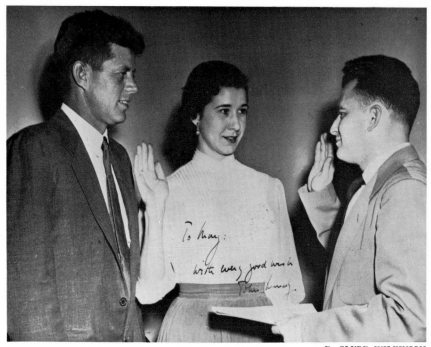

I am sworn in as secretary to Senator John F. Kennedy, January 1953.

George Thomas, valet to JFK, and Provi (Providencia) Paredes, Jackie's personal maid, at the party for JFK's 46th birthday, May 29, 1963.

left: The Senator and his administrative assistant, Timothy 'ed) J. Reardon, Jr., greeting his office staff. (*Right to left*) I am the wheel; Evelyn Lincoln, JFK's personal secretary; Betty arley; Lucy Torres; back seat, Jean McGonigle; Lois Strode; ne Williams; Dorothy McCann.

Tom Kitten, Caroline's favorite pet, at home with the Gallaghers, to whom he was given after only one month at the White House.

STOUGHTON

The Kennedy's most famous pet, Pushinka (daughter of the space dog Strelka), given to Caroline by Nikita Khrushchev. The pups were fathered by Charlie, the Kennedy's Welsh Terrier.

A playtime afternoon at the Gallagher house—Secret Service Agent Lynn Meredith plays for Caroline Kennedy, Greg and Chris Gallagher.

My mother-in-law Ann Gallagher (Grammy) looked after my boys while I was at the White House. Grammy and Gregory at my house with Caroline and John-John.

Pierre Salinger, one of the emcees at the Staff Mess for JFK's 46th birthday party, enjoys the humorous present.

I lunched at the White House Mess with members of the Presidential staff. (*Left to right*) Myself, Carson Howell, Homer Gruenther, John McNally, Roy Killerman, Floyd Boring, John Campion, Gerald Behn.

At Squaw Island, near Hyannisport, Cape Cod, a trailer served as office for the Secret Service detail and myself. (*Left to right*) Top, unidentified, Paul Landis; 2nd row, Floyd Boring, Tom Wells, Ensign George Dalton; 3rd, myself 4th, unidentified, Clint Hill, Louella Hennessey; bottom, John J. (Muggsy) O'Leary, Lynn Meredith, unidentified.

During Jackie's official trip to India and Pakistan, with her sister Lee Radziwill, this snapshot caused widespread controversy among columnists criticizing and defending the length of her dress.

This informal photograph of the world's most popular couple, their favorite, was sent to thousands of people all over the world, who requested one.

White House entertainments became cultural events. A stage was set up in the East Room where such celebrities as Pablo Casals (*above*) performed.

Our most prized photo, taken by Provi when the Gallagher family visited the President-elect in Georgetown, November, 1960. Jackie was away. Caroline would not turn around.

Among the many offices I occupied in the White House, this was one of my favorites—the East Solarium.

My husband and I attend the Inaugural Ball, January 20, 1961, with our closest friends, Mary and Peter Kosak.

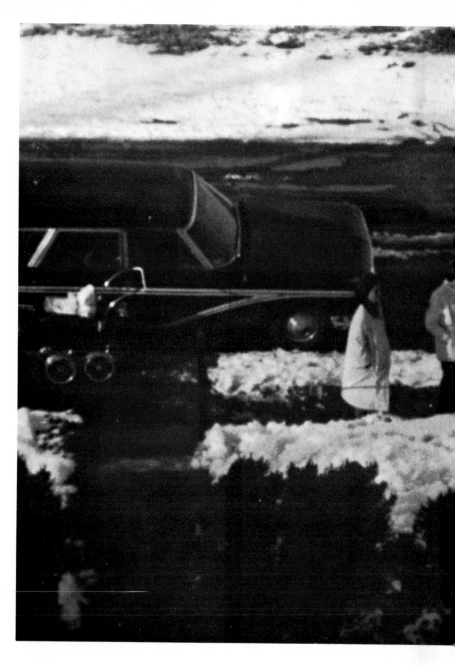

The unexpected visit. Jackie brought her children to my house for a str[and relaxed afternoon on March 7, 1962, the day before she left for Ind[

The first home that the Kennedy's built at Atoka in the Virginia country-side. There the family escaped the White House pressures.

The Georgetown house where JFK and Jackie lived during the Presidential campaign of 1960.

The Georgetown home that Jackie bought after leaving the White House. From there she moved to New York City to live.

A study in regal style. The simplicity of Jackie's gown contrasted magni
cently with Queen Elizabeth's bouffant creation. This picture was taken
Buckingham Palace during the State visit in 1961.

We gathered in the center compartment of Air Force One to watch the swearing-in of Lyndon B. Johnson as President. Jackie is standing beside Mrs. Johnson. I am looking over the head of Mrs. Johnson.

When Air Force One arrived in Washington, Bobby Kennedy escorted Jackie off the plane. I am standing just behind them.

U.P.I.

Jackie and the children as they enter their new life in the Georgetown house shortly after the assassination. This picture was taken as they are leaving the Harrimans' where they temporarily stayed.

Equity!" It was daughter Margaret, and she brought down the house.

It was a great year for entertainment—not without snafus, of course, but these had added something to the flavor of the time.

My favorite had occurred just before the Trumans came, at the reception in honor of the Chief Justice in October, when the Marine Band three-man combo had played hot jazz during the time that the President and Jackie and their guests of honor descended the Grand Staircase. A substitute Marine Band director had not understood and was still waiting to stop the combo and strike up "Hail to the Chief" long after the President and Jackie were greeting guests.

In the fall, Jackie was hostess again to several foreign dignitaries: Gromyko of Russia, the presidents of Finland and Liberia, and President Leopold Sedar Senghor of Senegal.

Jackie wasn't afraid of tackling big problems, such as providing a suitable stage worthy of great performers. She was distressed that her guests in the back rows could never see the performers who were on the floor level.

By October, a special stage had been built in the East Room. It was elaborate, heavy, made up of many segments, and took a half-day to put up or take down—a job that required many men.

The portable stage was first used for the performance of Shakespeare after a dinner honoring the President of the Republic of Sudan, Ibrahim Abboud, on October 4, 1961.

It was a cultural triumph for Jackie—the appearance of the American Shakespeare Festival Theatre from Stratford, Connecticut. As I recall, there were scenes from *Macbeth*, *As You Like It*, and *The Tempest*.

In November, Pablo Casals made history by breaking his self-imposed "exile"—he had vowed not to play in any country that recognized Franco—to play for the Kennedys and the Puerto Rican Governor, Luis Muñoz Marín, and his wife. To top it off, Alice Longworth was in the audience hearing Casals perform in the East Room just as he had once before, when she sat beside her father, Teddy Roosevelt, in 1904!

The children's entertainment presented another kind of history-making. It was at Caroline's and John-John's first White House birthday party in November that a monkey named Suzy, dressed in a little child's dress, arrived from the Baltimore Zoo to perform for the children, accepting their favors, eating and shrieking with them. It all turned out to be Suzy's party, and Jackie wasn't too pleased with the "publicity" that the monkey received in the newspapers after the party. She later put the clamps on Suzy's reappearance.

Jackie made up her mind that the next year she would have a hurdy-gurdy or organ grinder and handle it more discreetly. As she told Tish, "Maybe we can get one of the policemen to play it!"

Thanksgiving had seen the annual "Meeting of the Clan" at Hyannisport. That was the only occasion when all branches of the family came together at one time. They stayed at the compound, which consisted of three houses—the President's house, the Ambassador's house, and Robert's house. With all the children of the various families—the Shrivers, the Smiths, the Lawfords, and the brothers Kennedy—John, Robert, and Edward—it was quite a hubbub.

I had heard a lot about the compound, but I had not yet seen it. Just before Thanksgiving, Jackie had gone with the President to Hyannisport, then to Newport to greet Prime Minister Nehru and his daughter, Indira Gandhi, who was destined to become Prime Minister herself. They brought them back to Washington for festivities in their honor.

In mid-December, Jackie again logged thousands of miles, traveling with the President—first to Puerto Rico, then to Venezuela and Colombia.

I noted when I saw the pictures of Jackie at the formal dinner given by Venezuelan President Betancourt that Jackie was wearing a gown that left her shoulders completely bare. I remembered how she had gone to considerable pains to warn Cassini that as First Lady she could wear only gowns with "that covered-up look." But then, even a First Lady could change her mind.

One afternoon in December, 1961, as we wound up our working session, Jackie asked, "Mary, are you going to the Christmas party this evening?"

With a blank expression, I replied, "Christmas party? Where?"

She seemed rather surprised when she realized I hadn't been informed of the staff Christmas party, and proceeded to fill me in with the details of time and place—expecting, perhaps, that I might yet be able to make arrangements to attend. But by now the hour was too late. Thanking Jackie for mentioning it to me, I gathered up the material she had just finished dictating and returned to my office.

I'm sure that it was because of Jackie's memory that the Social Office made no slip-up of notifying me about the following year's Christmas party. A mimeographed announcement was forwarded to me days ahead, and on the outside flap of its fold were the clear, handwritten words: "Mary Gallagher, this is for you."

The party was scheduled from 6 to 8 P.M. And, sensing the busy workday ahead, I took a fresh change of clothing with me that morning. When the time drew near, I had a few moments to slip into them—and made it to the party on the dot.

I had a wonderful time and enjoyed my very first dance in the East Room of the White House with none other than Caroline's Secret Service Agent, Lynn Meredith.

While Jackie was in Palm Beach, for Christmas, I arranged for Chris's kindergarten class at St. Mary's School to come to the White House to see the most unusual Christmas tree. Jackie had dreamed it up, basing it on the *Nutcracker Suite* ballet.

How the little children had stood open-mouthed at that wonderful White House Christmas tree. I had never seen a tree like that before, either. Every imaginable toy soldier, sugar-plum fairy, and elf perched on the branches, interspersed with candy canes, drums, sugar cookies, exotic birds, hearts, bells, little wrapped packages, candles, and mammoth snowflakes. Instead of the usual icicles, there were soft satin streamers.

Even the nuns were absolutely awed by it and grateful to be seeing it, too. As the children stood admiring the tree, the nuns stood chatting with the White House guard. I couldn't help overhearing them talking about me and smiled when I heard the guard say, "Outside of the First Lady, Mrs. Gallagher is the only one we say 'yes, ma'am' to."

It was on the 21st that I took Chris's class to see the White House, and it was on the 21st that the President's father suffered his stroke. He had seen the President off on Air Force One on his way to Washington and had gone to play golf, when it happened right on the links. The poor President was very upset and turned back to reach St. Mary's Hospital in Palm Beach. Jackie was still there, waiting to take off with the President for his trip to Bermuda some days later to meet with Prime Minister Macmillan.

After seeing his father, he carried on with the conference, but I'm sure his heart wasn't in it.

Dressing for our traditional New Year's Eve Gala at my husband's club, I felt the effects and wondered what kind of New Year's Eve the Kennedy family was having. At this very moment, probably Jackie must be dressing for her New Year's party, too. She and the President traditionally spent every New Year's Eve with the Wrightmans, just as Ray and I were always with our friends, the Kosaks.

I suddenly got that lost feeling. What had happened to 1961? What had happened to everyone? It seemed that all year the Kennedys had been rushing away somewhere, alone or together—England, France, Greece, Hyannisport, Palm Beach. And all through the year, the great and famous had been coming and going from all parts of the world, entering and exiting, entering and exiting.

186 ଛଚ

I felt like a bit actress who only knows her own small part. Too much had been taking place on all parts of the stage. Jackie was the main character, as far as I was concerned, and just keeping up with her kept me busy enough. It had been quite a year. A vintage year.

19 ᕲ UNEXPECTED VISIT

I SEE BY MY DIARY THAT 1962 STARTED OFF quietly. Jackie returned from Florida on the 10th of January, and on the 20th she accompanied the President to the First Inaugural Anniversary Banquet held at the Armory. Ray and I attended with our next-door neighbors, retired Brigadier General Cornelius J. Mara and Mrs. Mara. The General had been President Truman's Air Force aide at the White House and remained his close friend long after the former President moved back to Independence.

In February, the man of the moment came to the White House—astronaut John Glenn. When I saw him, I thought he resembled Ray in appearance.

On Valentine's Day came Jackie's big moment on TV— her tour of the White House—in which she shared the restoration changes with the public.

It had been filmed in January. It was her show. Acres of cables and a stand-in model of the same size, with a "Jackie hairdo," holding the pose and walking through the things Jackie would do before the cameras.

The Monroe pier table. The Red Room. The Green Room. How strange I felt, watching it at home, like millions of other Americans. But I knew as few knew how much time and effort had gone into making those rooms echo the past, when

Dolley Madison had lighted candles in the gold vermeil candlesticks of the State Dining Room. Jackie moved from room to room like a queen, dressed in a plum-colored wool dress, her voice dramatically low, but vibrant.

Naturally, Jackie talked only about the history of each piece, not having time for fascinating little tidbits, such as why the dining-room centerpieces were vermeil—gold on sterling silver—not solid gold. It had come into vogue to discourage looters in the old historic days when thieves were snatching only solid gold objects.

She couldn't tell how hard her Fine Arts Committee had worked to get each object, twisting arms for donations, scouring the country to get the best of kind.

Though her whole restoration had attempted to bring the White House back to Jefferson's days, it was ironic that Jackie had only one little object of Jefferson's to show—his bronze inkstand inscribed "T. Jefferson, 1804."

I liked the point Jackie made about Thomas Jefferson—that he had considered the White House "big enough for two emperors and the Grand Lama."

It was a delight and a revelation to see the big and little happenings—the big and little emergencies—that filled our days at the White House. Many times Jackie would ask my opinion when there was something such as a State gift that had to be approved. She would ask whether I thought the samples that had come down from Tiffany's—the usual supplier for State gifts—were "suitable." Jackie knew I would give an honest opinion. Once, when the gifts were pieces of mineral ore wrapped in gold twine to be used as paperweights, Jackie said, "I'm not too crazy about these."

March 2nd was one of those times when the Treaty Room table couldn't have been more crowded. I had been so busy preparing for Jackie's departure for Rome and India on Thursday, March 8th, that I had been sleeping over at the White House out of sheer necessity.

That morning when Jackie came into the Treaty Room and saw the table so loaded, she held her head. "Oh my," she said, "I just don't know where to begin, but we'd better get started."

As she settled in her usual chair at the far end of the table, she began the morning's work in her methodical way. I was to ask Ethel Kennedy's secretary whether Ethel and Bobby would like to "come for dinner tonight—7:45." And would Ethel lend Jackie a big comb to wear under her veil for her audience with the Pope? Ethel was to bring that along so Jackie could pack it for Rome.

Also I was to request Jackie's clothing scout, Letizia Mowinckel in Paris, to get the white crepe blouse that went with the white Chanel coat she had ordered.

Then she asked that I call Eve Fout in Middleburg to see what time the Hunt was scheduled for on the following day.

I phoned while she looked through her papers and came back with the answer that the Middleburg Hunt was leaving from Pott's place at twelve and the Orange County Hunt was leaving at eleven. This required another call back to tell which Hunt Jackie was planning to join.

On and on it went all day. Details, details, details.

As Jackie made preparations for her trip to India, she also planned ahead for Caroline and John to spend some time in Palm Beach with JFK during her absence.

Remembering that Wednesday was nurse Shaw's day off, Jackie also asked that I have Miss Shaw arrange to get Mrs. Deedle to take care of the children on Wednesdays while she was away in India those few weeks in March.

Just as Jackie could at times treat the most trivial matters as of utmost importance, she could at times handle the largest matters with most exacting detail. She was trying to save the character of Lafayette Square across from the White House and so informed an official of the General Services Administration. New buildings were to blend in with the old. She wanted the architects to resubmit plans that would not be modern and yet not be so old-fashioned that they would resemble a 19th-century institution—such as, she said, "some State School for the Deaf."

Jackie said her thoughts concurred with the President's, and she wanted the architects to come up with a design for the Court Building that would be in keeping with the 19th-century architecture of the Square. When the designs were ready, she wanted to see them.

And she wanted Dolley Madison's house saved. I remember and love her bitter comment about the Dolley Madison House and the rumor that it would be torn down: that it was a shame to demolish it unless it was now *against the law* not to do so.

With that taken care of, Jackie tackled her hat problem, telling me to send back a couple of hats to Marita, her hat designer, at Bergdorf Goodman.

I was to explain that Jackie had made a mistake in the aqua roller brim hat and that she wanted Panama straw to match the sample I was sending. The other was to be in shocking-pink straw, and they were both needed for the following Thursday.

Then there was a message to Kay McGowan to bring a fitter with her when she delivered the black dress for Jackie's audience with the Pope on Thursday.

And that was only the start of the morning's work.

After this session, I returned to my desk, my arms loaded with folders and notes and reminders. I knew there was no use putting anything off. Jackie had a fantastic memory and always knew what matters were outstanding. She also wrote reminders to herself.

But at least this day I didn't have far to go to my desk. Jackie didn't want me to waste time going from one floor to the next and had ordered my typewriter temporarily transferred to the second-floor Center Hall in the family quarters —giving it a very lived-in look, indeed! Here, within steps of her bedroom and sitting room, I was more readily available for her every need.

That night when I saw Bobby and Ethel come upstairs to the family living quarters, I was still banging away on the typewriter.

As they emerged from the elevator and entered the Center Hall, they both greeted me warmly and Ethel in her typical vivacious, effervescent way exclaimed, "Gosh, Mary, what are you doing working so late?"

They looked so young and happy, it was hard to believe they had so many children and so much responsibility. The Attorney General walked ahead, and Ethel hurried to catch up with him.

The President was already in the Oval Room, waiting for them, but Jackie was making a late entrance. As she walked past me slowly with measured steps, it suddenly struck me how different the sisters-in-law were—Ethel so peppy and Jackie so subdued.

As George, with a tray of drinks, was the next person to pass, it suddenly dawned on me that the typewriter clatter was scarcely the right background music for cocktails. I quickly retired to the blue bedroom upstairs.

Preparing for bed, I realized that the next day, Saturday, would be another busy one. And looking at my diary, I can see that it was—and full of surprises.

I didn't get to go on Jackie's trips to foreign countries, but I got involved in all the problems that faced her before she took off, all the side issues that brought each trip to life for me—and which highlighted Jackie's meticulous attention to detail.

My diary entry for March 6, 1962, shows that Jackie wanted to make sure that someone would go along with her to Mass at St. Peter's—"either S.S. or Monsignor who would know when to stand up and when to kneel down."

She asked me to wire Tish, who had gone to Italy in advance, to make arrangements for her to go to a regular Mass at St. Peter's, not a high Mass.

She questioned whether she could either go in street clothes and change in a small room before seeing the Pope, or see the Pope first and change for Mass.

Suddenly that afternoon Jackie and Caroline appeared in my office, hand in hand.

"Oh, Mary," Jackie asked with a girlish smile, "do you suppose I could take you up on your invitation and come out to your house tomorrow with the children? Caroline says she wants to see Tom Kitten, and I'd like so much to just spend a nice quiet day with the children before leaving for India."

I looked up from my typewriter. I couldn't believe my ears. It was Tuesday afternoon, the 6th, with only one day left before the zero hour; Jackie, I knew, must be aware of it.

It was a year since our original plans for such a day together had been canceled because of a social commitment. But I never dreamed that, when Jackie promised "We'll do it another day," she would choose a time like this. I was both happy and proud that she was even considering the visit, but I was simply dumbfounded! My house had been getting along without me—while I slept at the White House—and who knew how it looked?

Yet, my response was as enthusiastic as if this was the one question I was expecting and hoping for. "Why, yes, Jackie," I said, "you certainly may...we'd just love it!" Caroline beamed.

Jackie set the approximate time of their arrival at "somewhere around 3:30—after the children have had their naps."

My thoughts raced furiously over the next 24-hour span, and I found myself compelled to ask a much-dreaded question, considering the amount of unfinished business before me. But I had no choice.

"Would you allow me the day off tomorrow, Jackie?" I asked. "I'll need a little time for preparations, you know."

She readily agreed, of course, and I was grateful. To have asked for a day off for any other reason, when she was due to start a trip such as this, would have been sheer folly. I shuffled through the mountains of work on my desk, pulled out only the "musts" to be handled before leaving that day—and silently prayed that my judgment would not betray me. By 5 P.M., I covered up my typewriter.

It's one thing to work for a First Lady, but quite another to have her come to your house!

At home, I quickly changed into comfortable work clothes, and found myself working almost around the clock. It was to be a casual affair, of course, so I had suggested to Jackie that she "just come in slacks." And, she, in turn urged me "not to fuss . . . we can have hamburgers for dinner."

After a scant few hours of sleep, the big day was now upon us—Wednesday, March 7th. Despite Jackie's suggestion that I not "fuss," I was right back in a whirlwind swing. Even the windows got washed.

Despite her other suggestion that I just serve "hamburgers," the meal I had planned was to suit my Italian taste: rigatoni macaroni and meatballs, Southern fried chicken, salad platter, stuffed celery, relishes, Italian bread and butter, Chianti wine, milk for the children, dessert, and coffee.

Chris and Greg eagerly awaited the arrival of their little friends, although I warned them not to mention the Kennedys' visit to anyone in the neighborhood. The success of the visit, I realized, depended on protecting Jackie from a crowd of curious people, and to this the boys gave their youthful solemn promise.

Tom Kitten, completely oblivious of the honor being bestowed on him on this exciting day, was spending the afternoon on his favorite bed upstairs, snoozing away!

To complete the family picture waiting for the arrival of our "special guests," there was Ray, who had declared a holiday for himself, as well as my mother-in-law, Ann Gallagher, who we felt more than deserved the honor of meeting Mrs. Kennedy and the children. She had faithfully dedicated herself from the beginning to the role of baby-sitter for Chris and Greg—and naturally, Tom Kitten.

As luck would have it, after a fast shower and donning my magenta wool slacks with colorful matching top, I made it back downstairs just in time. At 3:30 P.M. Jackie's station wagon was pulling up in front of the house—she was prompt to the minute.

She, wearing slacks too, and with John-John in her arms and Caroline following, got out of the car and made her way up the twenty steps to our front door. Behind them came the two Secret Service Agents, lugging the empty pram up to the front porch, then returning to the sidewalk to keep watch outdoors.

Entering the living room, Jackie immediately made my pace-setting record seem a triumph. With one quick glance around, her first words were: "Oh, Mary, how pretty!" Suddenly I looked around as if seeing the room for the first time. I quickly thanked her and offered to take her coat.

If I could only rest a few minutes, I'd revive, I thought, happily anticipating the next hour, when we would simply sit and relax with a nice drink before dinner.

But what was she saying? Before relinquishing her coat, Jackie asked casually, "Mary, it's such a nice day . . . do you suppose we could go for a little walk before we get our boots off?"

There was *snow* underfoot! And, just the thought of going into it for more exercise practically numbed me. I looked at the chair.

"Just give me a minute to get my boots on," I ventured, "and I'll be right with you."

Now the pram, which had just been hauled up to the porch by the two S.S. Agents, would have to go back down to the sidewalk again. Only, this time, it was my husband who was called on to do the honors—single-handed. Ray wobbled and clanked it down all twenty steps. Jackie placed John-John in the pram, covered him snugly, then took hold of the handle and pushed him along as I walked beside her. The walk was brisk and quite invigorating, and I marveled at my own renewed energy.

What a picture we made. Caroline, Chris, and Greg trotted merrily ahead, while the two Secret Service Agents followed at a discreet distance behind.

Pushing the pram along required extra effort on Jackie's part, since snow kept clogging the wheels.

I offered to help her as we left Belfield Road for our climb up Woodmont, but she said, "Oh, no, thanks, Mary, I think

I can manage just fine!" She seemed to relish the privilege of hard work, and I was impressed.

Within a few minutes, I found myself facing another concern. Several cars passed us in their descent of the snowy hill, with sudden reactions from the drivers. As they caught sight of the distinguished pedestrian, their "double takes" were so spontaneous that I was afraid of a collision with the nearest tree!

From Woodmont Road, we turned on to Grove Drive, a long dead-end street with less moving traffic. I didn't notice anyone looking from windows, and I was truly proud of Chris and Greg for not spreading the word. No neighbor had seen us. Or so I thought, for the moment.

But, at least, Jackie and her children were spared the usual gaping crowds, clicking cameras, autograph requests, and the rest.

After I gave Jackie a quick tour of the house, we joined the children in the playroom upstairs, where Tom Kitten was fast asleep. Jackie sat on the floor beside the bed, stroking Tom Kitten while watching the children at play.

Ordinarily, Chris and Greg proffered their wild array of cars and trucks to interest their friends, but attempts to interest Caroline in cars had proved as unsuccessful for them as hers to hold their interest in her collection of dolls at the White House.

Instead, the three became completely absorbed in Tinker Toys. Typical of little four- and five-year-olds, they were applying full concentration to the hundreds of little pieces before them and were soon proudly showing their models of airplanes, swings, windmills, and so on.

Jackie remarked in amazement that she had never seen Caroline so completely interested in working at any one thing before, admitting that she'd never seen or heard of Tinker Toys before now.

"I really think we should get some for Caroline's play school," she suggested, asking that I purchase "about a half-dozen boxes," which I assured her I would be happy to do.

I remembered how hard Jackie tried now and then to do what the "average person" did. There was the time that she discovered a contest advertised in a magazine. You filled in a coupon and sent the label from a can of tobacco in a name-the-horse contest. As "Mary Gallagher," Jackie entered the contest. She had several ideas for names of horses, and for each name I had to get another can of tobacco—a rather large size.

If you won, you got the horse.

Jackie wanted the horse, and accumulated a half-dozen or so cans of tobacco. They lay around for quite a while, but she never became interested in making any use of them. Eventually, to get rid of them and not waste them, I packed them off to my brother-in-law, John Coughlin, in Worcester, Massachusetts, with a note:

Dear John:
    I hope you enjoy this. It may taste better than your other brands.
    It came directly from the White House.
                                        Love,
                                        Mary

I never did tell John the story behind his windfall.

For now, however, there was more immediate business at hand—it was time to think about getting dinner on the table. As I headed for the kitchen, I suggested to Jackie that she make herself comfortable in the living room with a magazine. Instead, she grabbed a magazine, and followed me into the kitchen, exclaiming rather breathlessly, "Oh, Mary, your wallpaper is so beguiling!" And then she chose a chair at the kitchen table.

As I prepared the food, we were joined by the children, as well. John-John came crawling in on all fours, and my first thought was to manipulate him to a spot out of harm's way.

Remembering an old Italian custom, I reached for the bread drawer, ripped off the "heel" from a loaf of Italian bread, placed it in his hands, then propped him up on the floor beside his mother's chair. This would, I knew, keep him happily occupied for a little while.

"Mmm-mmm, that looks good, Mary," Jackie said, "could I have some, too?"

"Why, sure," I answered, and with another strong twist at the bread handed *her* a chunk to munch on. "Would you like a nice glass of Chianti to go with it?" I offered.

"No, thanks, but if you have some milk to spare, I'll take a glass."

There was plenty of milk and, after placing a tumblerful before her, I couldn't help feeling that she was thoroughly enjoying this rare chance to be sitting at an ordinary kitchen table.

The tranquil kitchen scene was shattered when suddenly three noisy, energetic children entered, "following the leader" from the floor onto a stool, to the top of the kitchen counter, down to the stool again, with a jump to the floor.

Then, a quick run around through the rooms, shrieking with joy, and back to the kitchen again for another stool-to-counter session, which stopped only when they ran out of wind. Since Jackie didn't stop Caroline, I didn't stop my two, either.

For the children, the rigatoni was easy to manage. When it came to the fried chicken, I suggested they "just pick it up and eat it with your fingers."

Jackie seemed pleased and exclaimed, "Oh, great, Caroline—we can eat it like we do when we're on a picnic!"

Toward the end of the meal, Tom Kitten was allowed to join Caroline at the table. Sitting on the chair beside her, he nibbled at the little bits of chicken she handed him, and she laughed each time he licked her fingers.

By 6:30 or so, their little visit had come to an end; and, thanking us "for such a good time," they slipped away as quietly and unnoticed as they had arrived.

The next morning—Thursday—the "big day" of Jackie's departure to India, I forced my last ounce of energy into action. Arriving early at the White House, I quickly tied up all loose ends left dangling the day before and packed Jackie's brief-case with her various types of stationery, calling cards, photo-graphs, PT-boat tie clips, and so on.

I also slipped in a little personal note that I knew she would find and read en route. I thanked her for having honored us with her visit the day before.

The greatest joy was seeing Jackie completely ready—no delays. It was 12:30 noon.

At the elevator door, we bade each other a fond farewell, and with a last wave as the doors closed after her, I returned to my desk. But, within minutes, I was completely overcome with a sudden wave of weakness. By 2 P.M., I found myself placing an emergency call to Dr. Donnally. He ordered me home to bed, where I remained for the next full week—resting and consuming all of four prescriptions to put me back on my feet again!

It was some weeks later when I learned of at least one person who did notice and recognize Jackie on that Wednes-day afternoon.

It was Mrs. Wayne Hawks, whose husband had been em-ployed at the White House for many years under five Presi-dents, and with whom I had shared many a lunch hour at the "Members' Table" in the White House Staff Mess. Their home was located on Grove Drive, the long dead-end street where Jackie and I and the children had walked on that par-ticular afternoon.

Later, as we lunched together, Wayne mused, "You know, Mary, a funny thing happened not too long ago. When I came home from the office, Betty told me that when she looked out of the window that afternoon, she could have *sworn* she saw Mrs. Kennedy walking along our street pushing a baby carriage.

"She said there was another woman with her, too, and several children. But, I told her she must have been seeing things."

I laughed. Now that it was over, I felt there would be no harm in divulging our little secret.

"Betty wasn't 'seeing things' at all!" I confessed. "Mrs. Kennedy *was* on Grove Drive that afternoon—I happened to be the 'other woman'—and the children were Caroline, Chris, and Greg, and, of course, John-John, in the carriage."

Wayne practically choked and quickly came back with: "She *was?*"

The next expression of curiosity came from, perhaps, the most logical person of all—Andy Hatcher, assistant press secretary. He was sitting next to Wayne, taking in the whole conversation.

"I don't understand it," he said. With a quizzical look, he mused, "How come the press didn't get hold of *that?*"

"Well, Andy," I explained, "it's really very simple. The purpose of Mrs. Kennedy's visit was to spend a nice, quiet day with the children and Tom Kitten before taking off for India. So, I didn't mention it to anyone."

Wayne listened no more. Leaving his lunch, he sped off. "Excuse me while I call Betty. She'll be happy to hear she was right after all!" Soon he was back again, satisfied at having set his wife's mind at ease again.

20 ∾ ROME, INDIA, PAKISTAN

I USED TO WONDER HOW A PERSON COULD possibly remain unspoiled when one read such headlines about one's self as Jackie had in the triumphant trip of 1961. "She Came, She Saw, She Charmed [Paris]," "Jacqueline Charms All Vienna," "Jackie Dazzles in London," "After the Peerless Helen—Athens Prepares for a Jacqueline Conquest," and "First Lady Lunches with Queen Today."

Jackie had become an American phenomenon, an international event.

And now she was undertaking such a journey alone, a "return engagement," so to speak, to visit Nehru, who had been in Washington the previous November, and Ayub Khan, who had been taken down the Potomac to Mount Vernon in June.

In Rome, Jackie met the first "official" hazard. Before she left, Tish had made some arrangements concerning President Giovanni Gronchi, but Jackie had me tell the Social Office to straighten out the mistaken impression that the First Lady was having "Tea with Gronchi at 4:40," as they had cabled us.

Jackie's reply was that she was to see him on her way from the airport, not for tea. So she stopped off to see him on her way to the Vatican. Somewhere she changed her costume to a black gown with Ethel's comb and veil before entering for her audience with Pope John XXIII.

Jackie did not forget her mentor and counselor, the man who almost filled the place of her father and who was most dear to her, the Reverend James Leonard of Dublin, Ireland. She asked the Holy Father for a special blessing for him and mentioned that the Pope had been pleased to give it.

That was Jacqueline—sophisticated and blasé one minute, and warm and spiritual the next.

About a week before Jackie left, I had her India-Pakistan itinerary, and it made me tired just looking at it. As it turned out, she had a little cold, and the trip was delayed a few days, but after being joined by her sister, Lee, she kept her 21-day schedule: New Delhi, Mysore, Calcutta, Benares, Agra and the Taj Mahal, Udaipur, Jaipur. Then on to Pakistan for Rawalpindi, Peshawar, Khyber Pass, Karachi.

Even the great economist and ambassador to India, Ken Galbraith, dropped everything to accompany Jackie not only to India, but to Pakistan.

Galbraith did everything he could to make Jackie's Indian trip a success, even the press briefings twice a day.

Provi was along to take care of Jackie's clothes, which she

had chosen in brilliant colors, befitting the bright saris of the country. Jackie brought saris back to make into dresses.

The hall in the palace of the President—with its many chandeliers and brilliant Oriental rugs—was as impressive in a different way as the Hall of Mirrors in Versailles had been.

Jackie had learned the palms-together Hindu greeting, and I saw by the papers she was using it. She also wore a red dot— the *tilak*—on her forehead. She had an adventure I'm sure she hadn't been prepared for—witnessing a fight to the death between a cobra and a mongoose. The battle was put on for her in Prime Minister Nehru's garden after she had returned from a horseback ride. Jackie was horrified. She cringed and turned to Nehru, and he put his arms around her reassuringly. But, of course, it was perfectly safe with the snake-keeper watching every minute.

Somewhere she had found time to buy an astrakhan hat for the President. She had gone with Lee to ride an elephant in Jaipur. And she visited the Taj Mahal, both by day and by night. I always visualized how beautiful that must have been and how lovely she must have looked in her bright colors in the moonlight.

In Pakistan, Jackie and her entourage were objects of great curiosity to the crowds in the streets. Jackie and Lee rode a camel, and even before Jackie got back, the newspapers were commenting about the shortness of her skirts and whether too much knee had shown. Oleg Cassini rose to her defense to say her skirt length was "just right."

When she went riding with the President of Pakistan, Ayub Khan, he was so impressed with her horsemanship that he gallantly gave her the steed—a bay gelding named Sardar. Afterwards, she rode Sardar around Glen Ora with Caroline following behind on little Macaroni.

Jackie began to grow weary of the trip, and wanted to steal away to visit with her sister and brother-in-law in London. The helpful Galbraith wanted to accompany her to London and return to Washington in the same plane.

Jackie S.O.S.ed the President to call Galbraith home earlier. She simply needed a little rest, and everyone was always trying to get closer to her, to help her or just gaze at her beauty and see what she was all about.

When Jackie returned from London at the end of March, she sent a very sweet letter to the Vice President and Mrs. Johnson, thanking them for the red roses that had been waiting for her on her return. She revealed her typical humor, saying the President had shown their roses to her first, even before she saw the children.

Nineteen hundred sixty-two was another cultural feast in White House entertainment.

After Jackie returned from India, forty-nine Nobel Prizewinners came to dinner on April 29th. The President, in his welcoming toast, called it "probably the greatest concentration of genius and talent in this house with the possible exception of those times when Jefferson dined alone."

Then there was the arrival of the Mona Lisa at the National Gallery of Art on a visit timed to coincide with the arrival of Cultural Minister André Malraux of France, May 11th. Jackie had arranged this loan of the world's most famous painting while she was in Paris in 1961.

But there had been one sour note earlier when April 10th had brought the annual Reception for Congress and the steel crisis simultaneously.

During the crisis involving a steel price increase, the Shah of Iran and his beautiful wife, the Empress Farah Diba, arrived for a State visit. For them, the new stage had a good workout, with the Jerome Robbins dancers performing *Ballet USA*.

I wondered how the President could concentrate on the social and diplomatic events at such times, knowing the problems that he had left behind in his office. But he did and always appeared smiling.

Jackie and Farah Diba both had small children, so the

day after the State dinner, Jackie took her to see the White House nursery school.

It was in the spring of 1962 that jewelry seemed especially important to Jackie. At Wartski's, in London, she had seen and fallen in love with an antique 18th-century sunburst clip, and she wanted it to wear in her hair. It was priced at £2200. She had me find out exactly how much that amounted to in dollars. The answer was $6,160.

Jackie wanted to make an exchange, or at least, to trade a few pieces of her jewelry and make up the difference in cash. She asked me to have her jewelry appraised. Soon my private office looked like a jewelry store; Charles Ernest Jewelers arrived one afternoon to look it all over with their jeweler's glass and other paraphernalia. As they examined the jewelry, I watched. It took several hours, and I could tell they were fascinated, complimenting various pieces.

There was a big aquamarine given her by the Brazilian Government and the diamond wedding-present clip which the Ambassador—Joseph Kennedy—had given her.

There was a sapphire and diamond bracelet from Van Cleef & Arpels, and a gold pin, given her during her visit to Greece in 1961—gold laurel leaves with an emerald.

There was a ruby and diamond pin of two strawberries that the President had bought Jackie for Christmas in 1960, and Jackie wanted to check Tiffany to see what it was worth.

And finally, there were what Jackie called "bits and pieces of gold jewelry."

After their appraisals were submitted, copies of them were sent to the Kennedy office in New York, to be filed with Jackie's jewelry inventory.

Jackie was especially interested in the appraisal of the Brazilian aquamarine. After much discussion and negotiating, Jackie got something close to $4,400 in cash for the aquamarine, the diamond wedding clip, and the gold jewelry, and had to pay less than $2,000 difference. She checked the transaction with the New York office, and she got her antique 18th-century sunburst clip.

Besides the sunburst business, she was involved at the same time in other jewelry matters. There was a gold minaudière from Paris that Van Cleef & Arpels had, and Jackie wanted to know the price of it.

About the same time, Jackie was also concerned about the price of still another piece of jewelry she had chosen, and she was most precise in regard to its value.

I didn't fully realize how much precious gems meant to her until she called me into the Oval Room one day that spring —1962—and showed me a diamond-encrusted sword that had been given to the President by Ibn Saud, King of Saudi Arabia.

Jackie asked me to call New York and have Tom Walsh come to the White House in strictest confidence. I was to show him the sword and find out whether the diamonds could be taken out and glass "gems" be substituted in their place.

Jackie told me to explain to Tom Walsh that the President says okay, and that when Walsh came to Washington, he was to take the sword to a discreet jeweler and watch the man take out the stones. Then Walsh was to keep the jewels for Jackie. He came to the White House alone, and I showed him the sword. He did not take it with him.

I sighed with relief when he eventually reported that it would not be worth while to take out the gems. They would be too difficult to get out, and the cost would be prohibitive.

The most amusing part of the story to me, knowing Jackie's cleverness, was the explanation to be given to the artisan —that the sword was an old thing Ambassador Kennedy had, which Mrs. Kennedy wanted made into something else.

The President now entered her jewelry saga. Jackie had decided she didn't like the emerald engagement ring he had given her, and he let her go ahead to see what the jewelers could do to make it more suitable to her taste.

Early in 1962, this was one of Jackie's big projects—the problem of re-designing her ring. She asked Van Cleef & Arpels in New York to do a wax model—in fact, three wax models.

One day's diary entry, in particular, tells the story:

June 15, 1962: Upon receipt of JBK Emerald/Diamond Engagement Ring, "re-mounted" into a Wax Model of her choice, Jackie asked for my opinion before making a definite decision. As I studied the extra rows of little diamonds, which now surrounded the two beautiful, initial stones, they seemed to detract from the true beauty of her ring in it's original state. "Oh, no, Jackie—I think you'd be making a big mistake to change your ring this way," I told her. "To me, it looks much too bulky and takes away from the whole beauty of the ring." Her disappointment could not have been more obvious. "Oh," she stammered in disgust, "You're just like Jack."

She returned the ring, and wax models continued to go back and forth. In the end, Jackie finally gave up. She seemed to realize, as had the President and I, that her lovely ring required no further adornments, after all!

21 ∾ IDYLLIC SUMMER

I COULD NEVER TELL WHICH OF JACKIE'S moods to expect next.

One day, she would be exasperated because an unopened box of gifts from an Ivory Coast dignitary "hung around for three days until someone finally gave it to George [the President's Valet]." She disgustedly ordered the Social Office to make sure that in the future someone would collect presents, make a list of them, and write thank-you letters.

The next, she was ordering "dust for eyelashes," which she had read about in an article by Eugenia Sheppard in the *Herald Tribune*.

And the next, she was going full speed ahead with language records as part of a cram session in Spanish preparatory to her trip to Mexico in June, and practicing on Provi. She also studied Portuguese for a trip to Brazil in the summer, but it was called off.

Then it would be back to clothes, clothes, clothes. They would be so photographed and inspected around the world that Jackie felt she could not wear them again. So she made an arrangement with Oleg Cassini, to select her clothes for her Mexican trip, but he could keep them in his collection, and she would return some of them to him.

All spring and summer, Cassini would be making sure that the right clothes got on the right plane at the right time— bound for Washington—to be met by a White House car.

For Brazil, Jackie wanted pink brocade; for Mexico, the green Gazar dress and coat with a hat in matching flat, shiny straw.

To me, Jackie seemed to wear every color beautifully. But I noticed, as time went on, that her "fashion rainbow" never seemed to include turquoise.

One day, my curiosity got the best of me and I asked, "Why don't you ever wear turquoise, Jackie?"

"Oh," she answered, "that's one color I just can't wear— it makes me look yellow."

There were countless odds and ends of things that season, concerning clothes and the logistics of deliveries—a check went to Lee for $175 for something she had picked up for Jackie; Cassini clothes had been put on an American Airlines plane at 1:30 by the flight manager at LaGuardia; Bergdorf was sending a collection to Glen Ora so they could be tried on there one Saturday. The heavens seemed to have opened up —it simply *rained* clothes!

June 2, 1962: (Saturday)—Huge collection of clothing arrived from Oleg Cassini—JBK called me to W.H. As she tried on each and every model, she would ask both JFK and me for opinions and/or suggestions. Stepping from each as it dropped to the floor to be swooped up by Provi

206 ह॰

and put on its hanger again, JBK dictated her likes, dislikes, particular preferences.

I took pages and pages of corresponding notes on each particular design by number and description, with added innovations showing her individual taste in textures, colors, and styles.

Poor Kay McGowan, I thought, she's going to have enough here to keep her busy right through this season and into the next.

When her daddy was receiving State visitors, Caroline and her whole class would come to the Monroe Treaty Room to watch the activities on the South Lawn from the windows. I would join them, listening as she and her group excitedly counted out the 21-gun salute!

When her parents were away, Caroline would sometimes be permitted to come out to our house for the day.

My diary tells of another of these memorable occasions:

> June 6, 1962: JBK left for NYC 3:00 P.M. Caroline and her girl friend, Agatha Pozen, came to our house to spend the afternoon. After the usual visit with Tom Kitten, we set out for a picnic along Mt. Vernon Boulevard. Chose a most secluded spot, and enjoyed hot dogs and hamburgers and milk shakes along the river bank...

While Ray and Agent Meredith went in to order the picnic lunch, a parishioner friend, Mrs. William Speck, saw me in the car and came over to say hello to me.

Peering into the back seat, she spotted the famous face of Caroline, and her eyes widened with immediate recognition. But, to protect Caroline from exposure, I did not make an introduction.

It was a happy, fun-filled time. Returning to our house, Lynn Meredith, the S.S. Agent, entertained the children at the piano, providing all the snappiest tunes the children loved most, and marches to which they marched themselves through the rooms.

Before they left, I helped the children wash their hands and faces in the upstairs bathroom. As we finished, Caroline seemed rather perplexed.

"Is this the *only* bathroom you have upstairs?" she asked, after checking each of the three bedrooms to see if there might have been more that she'd possibly overlooked.

"Yes, Caroline," I answered, "this is the only one up here. This isn't quite like the White House, where you have a separate one off each bedroom—the house just isn't large enough. But," I added, in hope of measuring up to her standards, "we do have another downstairs, too—so if you're on the first floor, you don't have to come running up the steps to use this one."

She seemed to grasp this in her usual understanding way. But I still had the feeling she considered it all rather strange that such facilities were not quite up to the standards she was used to at the White House.

Another time, Caroline brought her friend, Sandra Eischhim. Lynn Meredith did the honors again at the piano, and the children paraded through the house to his "marches." They enjoyed dinner, too; we ate informally around the kitchen table.

Caroline was a playful child. She liked playing games with people, and she liked to hide. At the office, she would hide under her father's desk. When she came to our house, she hid under a card table until I "found" her.

As he learned to toddle around, John-John was emerging as an interesting personality, too, a mischievous little boy.

One day, I came into the sitting room to find him sitting near his mother, happily occupying himself by breaking up a whole container of cigarettes, one by one, and dropping them on the floor. Since his mother did not stop him, I didn't feel free to, either. But a week or so later, I came in to find him doing the same thing—and his mother was not there. I thought it wouldn't hurt to exercise a little authority. I tapped him on the shoulder and said, "John-John, you mustn't do that—that's a 'no-no.'"

He looked at me in amazement, and I could understand why. Almost no one ever dared to tell him that things shouldn't be wasted.

In fact, in the whole White House, there was only one person I ever saw who was firm with the children—their Nanny, Miss Shaw. Her word was their law.

I never saw Jackie reprimand or spank the children. If they became noisy or irritated her in any way, she would call out, "Miss Shaw, please come in and take them away."

Miss Shaw had such an effective way of rearing children that she could justly boast about not having to spank Caroline for misbehaving. With words alone, she could master the situation.

Miss Shaw and her mistress did not always agree on how the children should be raised. One of the greatest bones of contention between them was the matter of fresh air. Jackie was forever sending the children out with their Nanny to get "fresh air."

They would hardly be up and organized before they would be rushed out, no matter if it was too cold or too hot outside, or whether the children wanted to stay in and play or build something exciting together.

So many times, Miss Shaw would come to me after one of her "sessions" with Jackie and say, "If only Mrs. Kennedy could realize that children do need some time to just settle by themselves, doing little things with their hands, using their minds on something they enjoy working at. They need that just as much as they need being out in the fresh air."

As John-John got a little older, his hair became somewhat of a problem between the President, who wanted it cut short, and his wife, who preferred it long, right down to his brow. I became involved when Jackie asked me one afternoon what I thought of his haircut—did I think it was too long?

I had to be frank; I told her, "Yes." I went on to suggest that, perhaps, she should have it cut—if only to avoid criticism from the press about his wearing a "British" haircut.

Making a little face, she quickly came back with, "You don't mean a crew cut?"

"Oh, no, Jackie," I said. "What I meant was a *regular* boy's haircut...you know, parted on the side and brushed away from his face."

My suggestion must have passed through deaf ears.

As guests of President and Mrs. López Mateos, Jackie and the President flew to Mexico City for the June 28th weekend. She had practiced her Spanish for the short speech she gave there—and she made a tremendous hit.

Soon after their return, the White House began printing hundreds of copies of a lovely photograph of the President and First Lady snapped during their visit there. It turned out to be extremely popular, showing Jackie in a wide-brimmed hat, and both of them wearing happy smiles. It became the authorized mail-out in answer to the many requests for an autographed photo.

Jackie took the children to spend the Fourth of July with their father at Camp David. Then they were off to the Cape for the rest of the month.

Instead of staying at the Kennedy compound, Jackie and the children settled more peacefully at the home of their friend Morton Downey, on Squaw Island—a little neck of land just around the bend from the compound, where they could be safe from tourists and crowds.

By August, it was off to Italy for Jackie and Caroline for a little vacation at a secluded spot with Lee and her children. Caroline was thrilled, not as much by the fact that she would see the world as that Mommy was taking her and not leaving her behind.

Caroline had finally caught the glove fever, too. I saw her one day not too long before, parading into her mother's dressing room with her little hands held up daintily. "Look, Mommy, do you like my new gloves? They're just like yours." They were, too. White kid.

Jackie had come up with an idea for saving enough money

for the special trip, so it wouldn't interfere with the budget.

She had decided that if a couple of her sisters-in-law paid rent on the JFK house in Hyannisport for a vacation, sharing the rent of $1800 between them, then she and Caroline would have the money for their round-trip tickets. The deal went through somehow with Eunice Shriver and Pat Lawford sharing the expense, and soon Jackie was instructing me to tell Bob Luddington what to do to get the house ready for its summer tenants.

She wanted the newer, pink-flowered, cushions for the porch furniture stored away downstairs in the basement and the older, white sailcloth, set put on the chairs.

She wanted the old green chintz slip covers on the furniture.

She wanted all the glass and china ornaments, including some urns on the dining-room mantel, stored and only unbreakable pewter ashtrays left out.

She wanted all the towels, including beach towels, and bed linen packed and put away. She even wanted Luddington to store her huge beach toys, but she *was* leaving the croquet set. You couldn't beat Jackie for thoroughness—as an afterthought, she wanted me to make sure that he made an inventory of flower vases and equipment in the laundry room.

The last thing Jackie did before leaving for the Cape, preparatory to her trip to Italy, was to extend an invitation to me to "come over to the White House any time and swim in the pool. Bring Ray and the boys."

Jackie's instructions to me kept flowing by phone and by courier plane. I was to file clippings, order chiffon scarves for her sent to the Cape, send her wig up with JKF, and a long hair-piece from Alexandre's.

In Italy, the crowds that greeted Jackie and Caroline were fantastic, and I noted in one exuberant UPI story from Ravello, August 31st, "Roses, skyrockets and music from a brass band closed out Mrs. Jacqueline Kennedy's three-week Italian idyll today."

While Jackie was away, Ray and I decided to take the

opportunity for a nice, long vacation. We didn't quite succeed—because Tom Kitten died on August 16th. We were
visiting in Poughkeepsie when Ray's mother called. I remember how we rushed right home, cutting short our stay.
I never dreamed we would give up a vacation for a cat—but
this, of course, was a White House cat!

I hated to spoil the good time Caroline and Jackie were
having, but I felt that Jackie would want to know. So I wired
her the news directly from the home of our friends, the John
Rinaldis.

She replied, thanking me for wiring her, and saying that
she was very sorry about Tom Kitten. From my window today, I can look at Tom Kitten's little grave on a gentle rise
in our backyard—alongside the grave of Tippy, the Golden
Retriever dog the Kennedys gave us.

It was fantastic how many gifts, especially paintings, poured
in for Jackie after this particular trip. Several months later,
when I was working late in the evening with Jackie at the
White House, she offered me a large, colorful oil painting
of Ravello, Italy, where she and Caroline had vacationed in
August.

I often look at it now. That was as close as I got to the
blue Mediterranean that year!

22 ∼ THE BATTLE OF THE BUDGET

I NEVER DREAMED I WOULD BECOME SO DEEPLY
embroiled in the economy measures of the White House.
But it seemed to be my fate.

What really hurt was the feeling that now I represented

to the President just a big dollar sign. I valued my wonderful relationship with him, and I wanted him to associate me with the good things in his life, not his headaches.

My battle with the President's budget—or, I should say, his wife's—became so serious that I would take the long way around in the White House halls to avoid meeting him. I just couldn't stand the reproachful look on his face. And besides, if he spied me, it usually meant more bookkeeping homework for me that evening.

In July, 1961, I had been obliged to report to the President that Jackie's personal expenses for the second quarter of the year had totaled about $35,000. Almost half went for clothes.

The amount we had sent to one couturier alone—Givenchy of Paris—stands out in my mind: over $4,000. I haven't forgotten that because at the time it occurred to me that I could dress for years on what Jackie had spent in this 3-month period with Givenchy.

On March 21, 1961, Tom Walsh had helped to set up a new bookkeeping system for me to follow, and Jackie had followed through with a few economy measures. Every member of the household, including the kitchen help, was ordered to cut down in every possible way. After July, Jackie wanted itemized accounts of food and liquor, with the names of the stores where these items had been bought. And more and more bills would be sent over to JFK's secretary, Evelyn Lincoln, to go into the President's expenses, so they would not show up in Jackie's.

At this time she made some vague promise to improve her spending habits. But over the ensuing weeks and months, it was President Kennedy himself who turned out to be the monitor of her expenses, though it was hard for him to keep her down. Jackie seemed to be a compulsive buyer.

She had the habit of checking the newspapers, for items— big and small—from the department stores. She would tear out ads as she read the paper and ask me to order for her from the "Mary B. Gallagher—Special" account. In a typical month, I would order from Bloomingdale's, Bergdorf Goodman,

Gimbel's, Bonwit Teller, Best & Co., Lord & Taylor, and others.

There was one period, I recall, when she seemed to be going through a boots craze—I ordered pair after pair of them!

Often, when Jackie would go over the books, she would say to me, "Mary, where do you think my heaviest expenses lie?" Invariably, I would answer, "Clothing." She would seem not to hear me, and would go on questioning how she could economize, picking such other areas as Food and Liquor and usually ending up with the little items in Miscellaneous.

Clothing was her blind spot. So were paintings and house furnishings, especially antiques. If Jackie liked something, she ordered it and coped with the bills later. Then, when she saw the totals, she'd get economy-minded again.

She was delighted when her love of animals and efforts at economizing added up to a possible tax deduction. As explained to Tom Walsh in May, 1962, the four cows that Lyndon Johnson had given her and the President had expanded to four cows, three calves, and a bull, which she was thinking of turning into a steer to sell for beef. And there was every possibility that, by the next year, she would have eleven cows. The cow family, of course, roamed around Glen Ora. And Jackie wanted to know from Tom how to go about getting a tax deduction on Glen Ora as a farm. He was to tell us what she needed as proof.

Sometimes, the expenditures for the animals rivaled the expenditures for the children. Or exceeded them! One month in 1963, I recall, the children's bills came to $300 or so—but the animals totaled almost $1,500!

For the children, this covered such items as toys, clothing, books, etc. On the other hand, items for the animals included hospital bills; bills for straw, feed, lime, etc.; and riding accessories and supplies, including a horse vacuum cleaner.

But the main categories, which so tellingly reflected all aspects of Jackie's life, were "Clothing," "Art," "Food & Liquor," "Medical," "Jewelry," "Beauty Salon," and "Gifts."

It was during this time, too, that Jackie was ordering and

buying heavily for the country home that she and the President were building at Atoka, with every indication that this would surely be the record year of bills, bookkeeping, and even more headaches!

It came as no surprise when Evelyn Lincoln called me one day with a message from the President. I can't remember her words exactly, but the call came right after I had delivered the most recent statement of expenses to him. He blew up. He was questioning one item in particular through Evelyn, and I could hear his voice as though he himself had been on the line, "What the hell are we paying Janet Felton over $1,000 for?"

I immediately checked, gave Evelyn the answer, and was sure that it wasn't going to help matters any when she gave "the boss" my message. The money was for a Diette clock with a horse design. Jackie had ordered it through Janet, who had formerly worked for her in the Curator's Office and was now married and living in France.

For a while after that Jackie seemed to become unduly meticulous: I found myself itemizing such trivial things as powder puffs from Julius Garfinckel's—$1.13.

From the beginning, Jackie gave due attention to separating the expenses for official entertainment—which came under the President's allowance—from the expenses of their private entertainment, which of course came out of her own allowance, like the private party she had given for her sister, Princess Radziwill.

By October of the first year, she asked that I check with the housekeeper to get a look at some itemized bills of official White House entertainments, not paid out of the private account, and she asked that I have the housekeeper send her a memo explaining how to separate the accounting. For instance, did lunch for ten publishers go into Private Account? White House Entertaining?

And I see by my diary, the next summer she was asking me to inform Tom Walsh that the parties for Ambassador Galbraith and Ambassador Gavin should be deductible—most of the guests were official, and that was why the parties had been given.

Jackie juggled somewhat with certain art items, too. In the spring of 1962, when she discovered she owed a bill of over $600 to her scout, Herbert Bier of London, she wanted to send some paintings to him to be sold and have their price applied against the bill. She was willing to sell a Rodin watercolor of a dancing girl and a watercolor of St. Paul's done by an American artist, Levine.

But even with the President's watchful eye upon her, Jackie couldn't be completely constricted. In October, 1961, she told me to ask Ted Kahn, of Ben Kahn Furs in New York, to come to the White House with a selection of fur coats. The coat incident had started as an economy move, too. Jackie planned to trade in one of her old mink coats, and Kahn, a former Harvard classmate of the President's, was going to allow her a good price for it. He arrived, heavily laden, on December 5th.

Then came the big decision. Mink or leopard? Jackie couldn't make up her mind. She called the President over from his office to help her decide. She liked the rare Somali leopard, but of course it was much more expensive, too. It was also a fresh idea for her wardrobe.

Jackie modeled the various coats, and the President immediately chose the mink.

But, Jackie ended up with the Somali leopard. Later, I was to learn from Ted that she had caused such a craze for leopard coats across the country that his life became almost unbearable. Skins were in very short supply, and he had trouble filling all his orders. It wasn't too easy to make his customers switch to mink when Jackie had leopard!

This wasn't the only time that Jackie didn't follow her husband's suggestion. I remember a similar incident when the President was trying to do a favor for the hat industry. A hat firm representative had come to see him at his office, hoping to get Jackie to wear more hats, which he was willing to supply. The President called to let her know about the offer, suggesting that it might be nice for her to accept. But she had her own hat designer, Marita, and was not about to change.

As I look back now, I can't help feeling what a tremendous favor Jackie could have done for herself, as well as the hat industry, had she gone along with that idea.

But, then, when it came to coping with expenses, it wasn't the "Clothing" category that seemed to concern Jackie at all.

During those first two years at the White House, I became used to the continuous round of the "Battle of the Budget" between Jackie and her husband, and I took the whole situation pretty much for granted. But, by November, 1962, it reached soaring heights—and I was caught smack in the middle.

On the evening of November 15th, as Jackie and I came to the end of our working session in the Treaty Room, she inquired about her personal bills. As usual, I simply reached for the black-leather three-ring binder, which told all, right down to the final penny.

She spot-checked a few items, asked a few questions—and told me to leave the book with her to look over more carefully that evening.

The following morning, it suddenly became quite apparent that the President had taken a look at the "Black Book," too! As I waited for the elevator on the ground floor, three quick buzzes sounded, indicating that the President was on his way downstairs.

As the elevator doors slid open, however, I faced Jackie instead, with JFK close behind; he looked as serious as I had ever seen him. Jackie practically leaped at me. "Oh, Mary, thank God you're here!" she said. "Jack's going to get Carmine Bellino after me."

Instantly, the name Carmine Bellino told me something was up! He was a long-time friend of the Kennedys and, among the clan, was commonly known as the "figure expert." It appeared that he was being called to rescue Jackie from going off the deep end!

A sweeping glance quickly confirmed my suspicion—the President was on the financial warpath again, but good! First, there was the look of relief on Jackie's face as she bounded toward me. Then, the obvious give-away—the "Black Book" —was tightly clutched in Jackie's arms.

During this moment, my sympathy was torn between Jackie, who suggested, "Let's go back upstairs and go over the books," and the President, who I had never seen look more distraught.

His Secret Service Agent had joined him for the walk to his office in the West Wing, but he wasn't about to leave without at least a few words.

"Oh, Mary," he said, "would you please send over to me a current statement of Jackie's expenses?"

Just two weeks of the month remained when he would automatically receive his copy of the Monthly Statement of Expenses, and I wished that he would wait until then to pursue the matter further. But he couldn't have made it any clearer that he wasn't going to wait more than a day. I followed Jackie into the elevator, ready to face our next question-and-answer session, and geared myself to another strong economy move!

Jackie's first question: "Mary, where do you think we should begin?"

"Clothing." I tried again.

My spontaneous reaction was based not so much on the endless ordering we had been doing, but on the daily sight of her dressing room closets, the day-after-day assortment, hanging rainbow-style on the racks in Provi's room upstairs, and the array of reserves that filled to capacity the huge closets in the storage room on the third floor.

Surely, if Jackie called a halt to ordering even a belt for the next year, it seemed the supply would carry her over without fear of being seen in the same costume twice.

"Oh, yes, Mary," she readily agreed, "and from now on, if I ever order anything you think I really don't need, just slap my hand."

Just as quickly, she dropped any further consideration of it. Instead, she chose her own area of attack, immediately delving into their personal "Food & Liquor" expenses.

As with "Clothing," the figures for "Food & Liquor" were also running into five digits for the past ten-and-a-half months. These were quickly receiving the most careful scrutiny.

Fortunately, all statements were precise and up to date. For every question Jackie raised, a quick flip of the pages revealed the answers. Everything she asked for, she found. Finally, she gasped, "Gosh, Mary, your records are just fantastic!"

But the gruesome fact remained. The "Food & Liquor" expenses were exceptionally high.

Now we turned to the third category—that "catch-all" of household and personal items—called "Miscellaneous." It was running slightly ahead of "Clothing," yet somewhat behind "Food & Liquor."

As we all know, of course, it's the most nondescript items that have a way of adding up. But, to Jackie, it seemed all too incredible! She nearly floored me with her new request.

For each and every one of the bills listed under "Miscellaneous," she asked that I prepare an additional statement each month, breaking down even these little bills into their various categories. And then, under each category, I was to itemize each and every specific purchase with its exact description, "right down to the last thumbtack!"

She ended the session by suggesting that I follow through in getting in touch with Carmine Bellino for his thoughts. As for me, I could quickly form my *own!*

It looked at this point as if I would never again be able to call one evening at home my very own! And, as it all turned out, I wasn't far from wrong.

Within the next week, Jackie and her family were on their way to Hyannisport to join the Kennedy clan for the Thanksgiving holidays, and I was grateful for the few days of peace and quiet. However, she was no sooner back, the children's lovely birthday party no sooner over, than the real budget storm hit!

November 28, 1962, was, as it turned out, a "day of days" with Jackie! I'll never forget those fast, colorfully worded, endless memos!

She informed Tish Baldrige that food and liquor had been flowing as though it were the last days of the Roman Empire, and that the drinks were far too strong and served too frequently. No one, she felt, should have too much to drink at official functions; she found this appalling in the White House.

She went on to give Tish her new plan to set a limit on the number of cocktails or drinks served to any guest: one— and two if he or she really insisted on it.

Also, Jackie felt that from then on, only two wines should be served at official stag luncheons, so that men who had to work all afternoon wouldn't go back to their offices groggy from cocktails and three wines.

Among other things, she also directed the housekeeper, Anne Lincoln, to make a weekly check on the liquor cabinet.

But the suggestion that really staggered me—whether she meant it in dead earnest or tongue-in-cheek, I don't know— concerned her private parties or other occasions where guests might leave glasses, wander off, and order another drink. She instructed Anne to tell the butlers to refill those glasses that looked relatively unfinished and didn't have lipstick marks on the edge. Jackie said to pass them around again—even if a few people got hepatitis. Jackie really had a way of getting her point across, and sometimes I would chuckle inside at the straight face she kept when she said something like this.

Jackie later decided to have Anne Lincoln not only check the liquor cabinet weekly, but also keep the key.

Jackie elaborated even further then on how liquor should flow at stag affairs and official receptions at the White House, telling Anne that people could have one drink immediately, then should have to wait or go after another one, and as for a third, they shouldn't be able to get it at all. She thought this would be fair and that anyone could have a friendly time without getting drunk.

Still, she was willing to make two exceptions to these rules. She said she wanted people to have as much as they wished at the Staff Christmas party. Also, whenever there was a fund-raising event, they could have as much to drink as they wanted, because then they would sign up for more tables.

Yes, Jackie's mind was always working!

As long as she was ordering a clamp-down on liquor, she also put her foot down on the ordering of expensive foods, such as, smoked salmon and sturgeon. She made mention of the fact, too, that the help were ordering huge roasts for themselves at Glen Ora while the children ate hamburgers.

Going one step further, she said that it was necessary for one person to be in charge of all food, from birdseed to banquet. So she told Tish that all menu and wine planning would now be taken over by the Housekeeper's Office. She admitted that in the past she, herself, might have given the impression that everyone could live off pâté de foie gras, without ever thinking of cost.

As the whole household had seen waste going on, and things had been disorganized, Jackie said she couldn't hold it against anyone for following suit. But now, with Anne in charge, she said she wanted all this to change and maintained that she had never wanted the White House to get the reputation of serving Lucullan foods and wines.

As she busied herself with all these instructions, her husband was also busying himself with a note to me! Evelyn typed it up and sent it over—on that very same day, ironically enough—November 28, 1962!

The President, Evelyn noted, had told her to get in touch with me about the monthly bills. He wanted to see them after this, before I wrote out the checks. I was to send them to Evelyn, and she would show them to JKF. Evelyn assured me that she would get them all back to me for my records.

Yes, notes were flying in all directions. For a while, it was hard to imagine that we would ever get back to the normal run of affairs.

It was about two weeks later when Jackie picked up the budget once again! On Tuesday, December 11th, she called me to her bedroom for our first working session of the day. Provi came in to remove her tray, and I settled in the chair next to the bed for what I expected would be a full day, as she would be leaving in a few days for her Christmas holidays in Florida.

Her good mood was quite apparent as she greeted me with a big smile and, "Hello, Little Mary." This was a pet name that she generally used after being away for a spell, and it invariably told me a bit more—such as, get yourself set, we're ready to go! This was definitely one of those times.

She wanted presents for the children, coming in from various admirers, to be scanned to see if they could be used as Christmas gifts for her children and Lee's, instructing Tish to send them down to Florida, where she would look them over. This, in itself, was unusual, because gifts to the White House were ordinarily sent to charitable organizations. I could see that this new practice would lighten her load in the "Miscellaneous" column of her budget. So it was a pretty good thought, in a way.

She wanted Kenny O'Donnell to suggest any kind of liquor as a welcome gift for the President, as that was where the worst bills were. She said he could mention it to Dave Powers, too, and by way of explanation, informed him that Carmine Bellino had entered her life.

Provi, who often bought Jackie's cosmetics, was told to be frugal—and also to order something cheap for Jackie's bubble bath.

Evelyn Lincoln and Pierre Salinger were asked to help cut down on bills. Jackie asked that the kitchen use every bit of food sent as a gift to the White House. And she wanted the mail room not automatically to send food gifts to orphanages any longer. Instead, they were to be sent to Anne Lincoln.

And if the White House received several turkeys, some of them should be put in the freezer.

I don't think I'll ever forget the day I walked into Jackie's bedroom and found her propped up in bed, looking at a picture catalog for trading stamps! She beamed when she saw me. "Oh, Mary, do you know what I've just learned from Anne Lincoln?" she exclaimed. "You know, all the food we buy here at the White House? Well, she told me that with the stamps the stores give us, we can trade them in for these marvelous gifts!"

For the first time I came to see Jackie as an "average American housewife"!

It couldn't be denied that Jackie had racked her brain for every conceivable measure that might, in one way or another, ease the battle of the budget.

Still, to top it all off, for all her wonderful schemes for economy, in which she believed most sincerely, she also proceeded to include a long, descriptive letter to her favorite clothing scout, Mrs. John Mowinckel in Paris.

It took just this one letter, I knew, to undo all the good that could have possibly been accomplished by the other regiment of "scouts" on the home front, on whose shoulders Jackie had so neatly rested the task of saving. The battle of the budget was far from won!

Alas, after I battled with the Annual Statement of Expenses for 1962, I was forced to report to the President that Jackie's spending had not lessened over the previous year. Her total expenditures for 1962 came to $121,461.61—against $105,446.14 for her first year at the White House.

It always amazed me that Jackie spent more in a year on family expenses than the President's salary of $100,000!

23 ∾ NO DETAIL TOO SMALL

NO DETAIL WAS TOO SMALL TO MERIT Jackie's attention. She once noticed a small broken plate used as an ashtray in Anne Lincoln's office, recognized it immediately, and pointed out that it was from the Red Room. She insisted that it be mended and returned to its place for special occasions. She didn't want *best* ashtrays to be used by everybody. Months later, she checked up on it and found that it still hadn't been returned, and sharply insisted on its return.

Jackie had a thing about ashtrays. She detested vulgar-looking modern trays and preferred dainty little china plates in colors to match the room and bearing a fine design.

Concerning an upcoming staff party, she once ordered all good ashtrays removed and modern ones substituted.

Ashtrays were forever coming up in Jackie's conversation. I note by my diary that on March 30, 1962, Jackie was interested in getting opaline cigarette boxes in pink, green, or blue. "The cigarette boxes in this house that have wild ducks drive me craziest of all," she said. It seemed we were always searching for the perfect ashtrays and cigarette boxes.

One of the first things Jackie took to the weekend home at Middleburg was her own ashtrays. She mentioned them in the same breath with her prized photographs wanting "ashtrays and pictures" to be packed in paper and sent to Glen Ora. The third thing she asked for was a straw basket to keep flowers in.

In 1962, there were endless instructions concerning small details. She wanted an "Empire inkwell" for the Red Toile

Bedroom on the third floor as a finishing touch and was determined to find it. She sent a note to someone on her various White House Committees to start hunting. And she wanted some more little red-and-white plates, similar to one that was already there, as additional ashtrays.

And she had found a washbasin in the Red Bedroom that she felt didn't go with that room, so she suggested it be changed for something else. But she remarked that the washbasin was so beautiful she wanted to do a whole room around it.

Even the fixtures in the bathroom and dressing room off the White House swimming pool had to be changed to be more in keeping with the growing elegance.

Though Jackie may have complained to the Fine Arts Commission about the bright colors of the rooms in the public sector of the White House, the ironic thing was that her favorite room was the Red Room.

She worried about every little detail in the Red Room after it was redecorated—especially the Red Room rug. She was forever trying to protect it, and she gave instructions that people be kept out of there as much as possible, during White House entertainments. She told Anne Lincoln to instruct the aides and butlers to really be on their guard in that room to see that people did not drop ashes or cigarettes on the red rug.

As for what they were supposed to do about it, Jackie suggested that the butlers should carry around ashtrays to hold out to any guests smoking in the middle of the room. She said that eventually the guests would get the idea that coming to the White House should be quite formal.

Every time Jackie went on trips abroad, she came back with new decorating ideas. She would have the carpenters, painters, and upholsterers, scurrying in all directions, carrying out the latest re-arrangement of furniture and paintings.

George, the President's valet, was finally moved to comment, after seeing Jackie return all enthusiastic and full of ideas from India. He watched the activity from a good safe distance, and smiled. "Well, Miz Gallagher, the whole house is at it again. Sure does look like Miz Kennedy's had herself another good trip!"

Jackie could be just as enthusiastic over a historic manuscript as she was about antique furniture. I remember how ecstatic she was over a folder of music that George Washington had had, which came to her as a gift from band leader, Meyer Davis.

Jackie was astonishingly interested in flower arrangements. They were almost a fetish with her. One of the first things she did was to direct that the Housekeeper keep a photo record of every flower arrangement used for State or other formal affairs, with a description of the arrangement and kinds of flowers used for each occasion. Cecil Stoughton, the White House photographer, would be busy before every formal party photographing the bouquets for the flower books. As each book was filled, another would be added. Anytime the flower books had not been kept up, Jackie soon found out and sent a note to the housekeeping department.

Jackie was always surrounded by bouquets of fresh flowers in the living quarters, and she preferred to have them placed in a vase with a seemingly casual look, as if they had just been picked in a field. She liked little flowers of the field mixed in among the more cultivated blooms. Bouquets of roses and ferns were out.

The same look of perfection was achieved outdoors. People wondered how the lawn could look so lovely when so many people tramped on it. The secret was that the grass was sprayed with green paint for special occasions to make sure no brown patches appeared on the lawn. Not a hint of bare earth showed.

It didn't help that Caroline's pony Macaroni was tramping around on the grass. This never worried Jackie, because she loved animals. What bothered her was that people were feeding him through the fence, as the Ushers' Office reported. Jackie's solution left me puzzled. She directed that chicken wire be put up, high enough so people couldn't feed him, or that a gardener should chase people away.

Jackie was adamant that Macaroni not be tied up. Nor did she want the pony sent away.

About this time, in the spring of 1962, Jackie was watching with great enjoyment the planting and flowering of the President's garden, right outside his office. It had been designed by Mrs. Paul Mellon of Upperville, Virginia, a friend of the family, whom Jackie called "Bunny." The President would report to Jackie whenever he had seen "Bunny" in his garden that day.

In this way, Jackie kept track of her friend.

When Grand Duchess Charlotte of Luxembourg came, I was amused that the President wanted to walk her through the garden after dinner. So Jackie called for indirect lights to be installed and requested a list of "what is in the garden now, and where"—so the President would be able to identify a few things.

Jackie kept track of things that were to arrive, and was great on follow-ups.

On June 13, 1962, I was sending a wire to Paris inquiring about a small fragile statue that Minister Malraux had informed her he was sending. The answer I received was that the statue was being hand-carried by a General's Aide all the way to the White House and that it would arrive on the 16th, and would be delivered directly to Mrs. Kennedy.

Incidentally, Jackie had asked her stepfather, "Uncle Hughie," to give Malraux two of his 19th-century political caricature books. Later she learned their value—about $2,000 —with some consternation.

But Jackie hoped he could at least get a tax deduction.

Even the title of a book that Mrs. Parrish had been approached to do about the White House was not too small a detail to take up Jackie's time and attention. She wanted something like *America's Hundred Most Beautiful Rooms*. Also she did not like the thought that Mrs. Parrish would be called the "Decorator" of the White House. Jackie told her the word seemed an unfortunate one.

As for the pictures for the book, Jackie was willing to give permission to have the rooms photographed under the condition that the publisher guarantee that the photographers not be mentioned. Otherwise, she preferred that the pictures be taken by the *National Geographic*, which she knew would be discreet and would not demand a credit line.

Jackie gave the same detailed and meticulous attention to her personal grooming. I'll never forget the first time she wanted me to make an appointment for her with her New York hairdresser, Kenneth, for a hair straightening, shampoo, and set. The "hair straightening" part took me by complete surprise. I wasn't quite sure that I had understood correctly.

Yet, these two words were clearly in my notes—so surely I hadn't *imagined* them. Jackie, I had always thought, had a lovely natural line to her hair. Why would she be asking to have it straightened? Accepting her instruction without question, I proceeded to place the call to New York. In the next few minutes, the receptionist not only confirmed the appointment, but clarified the question—Mrs. Kennedy was, indeed, going to have her hair *straightened!*

Beauty was important to Jackie. She had the little dark hairs on her arms bleached. She used Sardo bath oil and a medicinal-type liquid cleanser, Phiso-Hex. Many of her cosmetics came from the Erno Laszlo Institute in New York, where I would order various kinds of creams, lotions, and a delicate pink cream rouge. Actually, Jackie's complexion was flawless, but she enjoyed using these cosmetics. She also liked experimenting with little hairpieces, wigs, and wiglets, but she didn't need them, either—and most of the female population started imitating her, building up their own hairdos with back combing—teasing—or wiglets to copy her bouffant effect.

Besides Kenneth Batelle (Lilly Daché, New York), who became famous as Jackie's hairdresser, there were others who played a less prominent role in the matter of her daily coiffure.

Jean Louis, of Washington, D.C., nearly forfeited his thriving clientele on Connecticut Avenue due to the long delays he invariably experienced when he came to the White House to do Jackie's hair.

At times, to his complete dismay, both he and his woman assistant would wait for hours before Jackie would be ready for them, causing them frantic concern over regular clients who were patiently waiting it out at their beauty salon.

In utter frustration, Jean Louis would pace the floor of the West Sitting Room, mumbling words of helplessness. With his reputation at stake, he eventually bowed out of personal appointments at the White House. His successor, fortunately, was spared this "occupational hazard." Appointments thereafter were made for Jackie to go directly to the shop of Jean Paul-Norbert in Georgetown.

Meanwhile, as the "mistress of all trades," Provi was eventually drafted into taking hairdressing lessons—to be able to cope with any emergency that might arise.

Dieting was very important to Jackie, and she practiced rigorous control, eating the gourmet foods she loved only at night. The greatest trick in her dieting came in her spartan lunch. Sometimes when we were at work and she wanted to keep dictating, she would ask if I would like to have lunch with her. Usually, I declined and had a heartier lunch a little later. She would continue dictating as she usually had a little broth and a light sandwich. Later she would have a glass of milk and after her nap a tiny snack of honey and English muffin and a pot of tea.

Jackie's attention to detail reached its extreme when it came to the way her clothes were handled by Provi. I think one incident sums it up. I found Provi in Jackie's bedroom one afternoon, ironing Jackie's stockings with a lukewarm iron!

"Provi, I don't believe it!" I said.

"Oh, yes, Mees Gallaga," said Provi, as if ironing hosiery were the most natural thing in the world. "Mees Kennedee likes to find her stockings in nice, neat pile in her closet." With that, Provi carefully folded each pair of stockings and carried a neat stack of almost a dozen pairs to the closet.

24 ∾ WAR OF THE WAGES

*A*LMOST FROM THE BEGINNING, IT WAS EVIdent that my salary at the White House was ridiculous—$4,830. When it had been arrived at, it seemed logical enough, of course, because I was to work only part-time—three days a week.

Now I was working full-time, whether at the office or at home, and long hours at night.

I was available by special phone at any hour, seven days a week. A direct line from the White House was installed in my kitchen. I was honored, of course, to have the responsibility of working for the First Lady, but surely a salary to fit the job had to be granted.

The bookkeeping part of my job alone, I felt, was now worth at least my present "part-time" salary.

By August, 1961, I started checking into the possibility of a salary adjustment. I sent a memo to Kenny O'Donnell, who I understood was "proper channels" and explained that my hours were now full-time, not what had been anticipated when I went on Government payroll as a "Secretarial Assistant" in the White House. This ridiculous title, rather than Personal Secretary to the Wife of the President, had been the only one available. I had to take it in order to be put on the rolls at the part-time rate Jackie and I agreed upon, $400 a month.

My weekly net income was averaging less than $75, while my expenses amounted to $32 per week (transportation and baby-sitting). I requested a proper adjustment that would place me at a minimum level of between $8,000 and $9,000 annually.

Nothing happened. Jackie returned from the Cape on September 18th, and the weeks ahead passed, busier and busier. So did the months, with no word at all—September, October, November, December.

On January 10, 1962, Jackie returned from her Christmas holiday in Florida. After her first few weeks back, I began receiving frantic calls from Provi, asking me to come to the office every day. "Mees Kennedee keeps asking for you all the time," she'd say.

So, after the first few such calls, I resigned myself to nothing short of full-time—five days at the White House, plus nights at home. I completely relinquished any further hope of operating at home on Tuesdays and Thursdays.

It was to cut no ice so far as my salary was concerned.

At the end of January, I briefly mentioned the situation to Jackie, hoping she might take positive action.

"Speak to Mrs. Lincoln about it," she said, implying that this would get the matter squared away. I arranged an appointment with Evelyn. She listened attentively. She was, actually, one of the very few who understood my overall duties and realized the amount of my time devoted to them. Still, the month of February passed, and the month of March. Evelyn assured me that the matter was "in the works." Eventually, she reported that to "get things started" for my reclassification I should prepare a complete list of all the duties I performed each day for Mrs. Kennedy. "*Everything*," she emphasized.

This nearly bowled me over. I was beginning all over again! I prepared the list of duties, then submitted the copies.

Next came word that Mrs. Kennedy "will have to submit something in writing." By now, Jackie was vacationing in Florida for the Easter holiday. This had all gone too far already. I was discouraged beyond words.

It became clear that to continue working as I was, my hourly rate of pay would average close to $1, sometimes $2, a situation beyond the ridiculous. It was almost a year since I had first spoken to Jackie about it.

Evelyn was kind enough to send a note to Jackie in Palm Beach, and included the memo for Jackie to sign. One of Jackie's first questions upon returning from Florida was whether anything had been done about my salary.

I said no, and she again suggested that I go back through channels to Kenny O'Donnell and ask that the raise be made retroactive from the first of the year.

I did. Nothing happened.

April, May, and part of June, 1962, passed the same way. Meanwhile, I checked and found that in 1945 Mrs. Truman's secretary had been rated a GS-12, a rating which currently would pay about $10,000. And here I was now, all of seventeen years later, with my GS-6 ($4,830.00)! My eyes were opened a bit more to full reality about people as well as "proper channels." I wondered bitterly if I was in a "right channel."

Preparations were underway for Jackie's trip to Mexico with the President and after that, her summer vacation at Cape Cod. This would be followed by another trip abroad.

In March the Indian trip had already nearly sent me into a tailspin with work. This stepped-up activity was simply the norm, and I continued to devote myself completely to Jackie's every need, days, nights and, when she asked, on Saturdays.

The overnight case in my White House closet received its fair share of use, yet for over nine months after my official request, I was still stalled on salary. By this time Jackie must have felt a little sorry for me. Noticing mail on my desk that did not pertain strictly to her personal affairs, she quickly exercised her authority. She asked that I write a memo to Tish Baldrige and sign my name. It read:

Tish

Mrs. Kennedy asked me to send you all this mail I am getting as she thinks it confuses things to have people writing me—and that all that should go to your office.

I told her I felt guilty about adding my mail to your burdens, but she said, "No, this is the best way."

Mary B. Gallagher

But I was not content. On June 28th, I reminded Jackie again that no action had been taken. This time, she said she would look into the matter personally.

In mid-afternoon, I received a visit by Mr. West, the Chief Usher, which was most unusual in itself. The message he came to convey surprised me even more. As Mrs. Kennedy's emissary, apparently, he politely informed me that Mrs. Kennedy was arranging for me to get a raise in salary—to GS-8 (about $6,000)!

Now I could guess why Jackie chose to have Mr. West carry her message.

"Mr. West," I said, "I'm sorry—but tell Mrs. Kennedy for me that I'm not settling for any Grade 8. I feel I'm entitled to a Grade 12, and that's what I'll accept—nothing less."

I didn't like the idea of putting Mr. West in the position of liaison man between me and Jackie. But since she sent him to me, I followed suit.

He left, agreeing to carry back my message. No more than a minute passed before my phone rang. It was Jackie, wanting to see me right away. She was alone in the Sitting Room, smoking a cigarette at her desk. I took my usual place in the chair beside hers.

She immediately began discussing my salary, trying to convince me that it wouldn't be possible for the White House to pay me anything higher than a GS-8 salary.

It would be difficult to relate our conversation verbatim. However, during the next twenty mintues or so, I was to see Jackie as I'd never seen her before. She worked herself into a frenzy over what my compensation should be.

Her temper gradually flared, and she spoke in loud, angry words while newly lit cigarettes were being stubbed out in the ashtray on her desk, one after the other.

She actually stamped the floor with her foot, trying to persuade me to accept the GS-8 offer. But I wasn't to be swayed; I had suffered too many months of frustration. I calmly came back in my own defense. As she carried on, I could see her not as a First Lady of the United States, but rather, as a child raising a fuss when she was deprived of having her own way.

She intimated that I should accept what the girls in the Correspondence Section were earning, ignoring the duties I performed as her personal secretary.

It didn't seem necessary to remind her of the bookkeeping. She had invariably commented on the "fantastic" job I was doing to keep her financial records in order.

Now she boldly brought out a clincher. "Just look at Tish. She puts in long hours every day till seven or eight o'clock."

It seemed incredible that Jackie should raise the issue of long hours. I, myself, wasn't staying late at the White House because of my home and family responsibilities. But, just when would my bookkeeping chores get done if I didn't do them at home—evenings and weekends?

I finally said, "I could go out anywhere right now and easily get a job that paid me three times as much."

Jackie's quick retort to this was, "Well, Mary, if it's the money you want!"

"No, Jackie," I replied, "right now, it isn't the money alone that bothers me any more—it's the principle of this whole thing." I wasn't about to relent in my position.

With a completely new twist, Jackie leaped to her feet, announcing that, inasmuch as I handled her strictly personal affairs, the Government couldn't be expected to pay me for *that*.

I simply said, "Well, Jackie, if that's the case, and if it'll make things any simpler, I'll agree to staying on the Government payroll now at GS-6, if you'll agree to pay me the difference between that and GS-12 by putting me on your New York office payroll."

I hardly had these words out when she retorted rather petulantly, "But then the money will be coming out of *our* pockets."

I agreed with her.

"Yes, Jackie," I said, "that's right—it would—but it would

still be the same as when you were personally paying me before. You could afford to pay me *then*."

This apparently was about all that Jackie herself could take now. Her mood quickly changed, and she resigned herself to one last move. It was time for her to leave for her tennis game. I arose from my chair to walk to the elevator with her.

As I did, she put her arm around me and said, just as softly and sweetly as she could, "Oh, Mary, I know how hard you work for me. You're the only one who *really* knows how to take care of all my things, and I don't know *what* I'd do without you. But please, just go to Mr. West and tell him you'll settle for a Grade 8."

I was completely disheartened. I couldn't prolong this subject. I simply told Jackie that I never intended for her to become so upset and that, as she was leaving for Mexico, she should just think about her trip now and have a good time.

Within the next week she was back from Mexico and settled at the Cape for the summer.

She probably basked in the happy thought that my salary was satisfactorily resolved. If so, she was partly right. I would not approach her again. After much pondering, I finally decided to place my case before JFK himself. The President was scheduled to leave on the morning of July 4th to spend the long holiday weekend at Cape Cod, so my appointment with him was arranged for July 3rd, at 3:45 P.M.

"Miz Gallagher," came George's husky voice, "the President will see you in his bedroom."

Just as in my first interview with him in Boston back in 1952, my knees quivered as I approached the door.

Yet again, just as before, once he welcomed me into the room, every nerve suddenly relaxed with the magic of his voice and smile.

"Oh, hi there, Mary," he said, "how are you? Did you want to see me?"

Our session was brief. I apologized right at the start for taking up his time with my personal problem.

He quickly said, "Not at all. What can I do for you?" and

appeared most interested. I quickly outlined my attempts to get a salary raise, beginning with my memo to Kenny O'Donnell nearly a year before, and told him I was still getting $4,830 a year. I mentioned how Jackie had approved my original request for a raise, how I had sent the necessary job-sheet to Kenny, and how absolutely nothing had yet been done.

"Are you still working just part-time for Jackie?" he asked.

"No, Mr. President," I replied, "if that were still the case, I wouldn't be here right now, taking your time. The part-time arrangement lasted for the first few months, that's all."

"Well, what about during the summer?" he asked further. "When Jackie's at the Cape—what do you do then?"

"There, again, Mr. President," I said, "whether Jackie's at the Cape or right here, it makes no difference at all. She keeps in daily touch with me by mail or phone." I described the work at the White House and at my home.

These were his only questions, and he seemed to understand, nodding his head as I explained.

He assured me that he would "definitely look into it" and, with this, I expressed my thanks and left.

This was about as far as I could go. Only time would tell the results of such a last desperate effort.

July ... August ... September ... Jackie was away. There was no let-up in the daily courier mail to me. It increased.

Before leaving Washington for a 10-day vacation in Boston, I arranged to receive my White House mail and phone calls at my sister's home. This would spare me the horrors of facing a 10-day backlog on my return.

After several days, my sister, Eleanor Tarallo, remarked incredulously, "Mary, I thought you came home for a *vacation!*"

The matter of my salary continued to fester. But the deep faith I had in the President was entirely unchanged. His assurance that he would "definitely look into it" left me with no doubts. However, when three more months passed without word, I could only *assume* what might have happened since our talk—that during his stay at the Cape over the Fourth, he must have mentioned our discussion to Jackie and Jackie, in turn, must have assured him—as she apparently believed herself—that the crisis was passed.

By October it seemed high time to make a last attempt with Kenny O'Donnell. I had to find out what the score was, and I sent him a "final" memo.

His response—after two weeks—was a note from his secretary, Helen Lempart, saying it wasn't in Kenny's bailiwick, and he suggested I discuss it with Evelyn Lincoln.

The very end of the proverbial rope—this was it!

I was making no more walks to the Executive Offices now. I called Evelyn. She was sitting by my desk within minutes.

"Evelyn," I said, "unless definite action is taken by the end of this year, I'll just leave it to you and Kenny to explain to Mrs. Kennedy why I am *not* here when she returns from Florida in January."

On the 19th, two days later, I received word from the Payroll Office that "action is now being taken to adjust your salary."

It was November 11, 1962, fifteen months after my initial formal request for a raise, that I received the official "Notification of Personnel Action," covering title and salary.

Position Title and Number	Grade or Level	Salary
From—Secretarial Assistant	Unclassified (equiv. GS-6)	$4,830.00
To—Secretary to the Wife of the President	(GS-11)	$8,045.00

I learned later that the only reason I did not receive my full GS-12 was that "it would raise too many questions with the Civil Service Commission."

25 ∽ "YOU'RE MY ONLY FRIEND IN THIS IMPERSONAL WHITE HOUSE."

*A*s the autumn chill nipped the air that second year in the White House, Jackie was talking about "fur" just as enthusiastically as she had talked about "jewels" in the spring. She was, as a matter of fact, inquiring whether a batch of skins—I can't recall the kind—could be made into two jackets or a coat by Madame Potok of Maximilian.

As I recall, from the sketches sent down, Jackie decided to have a full-length coat made. And the President made a big fuss over it, saying that it was beautiful, in fact, "terrific."

Jackie's exuberance over this particular fur piece did not dim her enthusiasm for yet another fur creation—a little black vest—a Christmas present from furrier Ted Kahn of New York. She was so delighted with it that she decided it could be used for more than just lounging—she would wear it over evening dresses and under suits.

She said that she had always considered little fur evening wraps as dull, but that Ted had broken her phobia against them.

In October, Jackie turned her attention to auctions and I see that on October 16, 1962, she had some bad news. She had asked her New York art scout to get a certain watercolor by Boldini, which was going to be sold at auction at Parke-Bernet. It was estimated by them at $1,250 to $1,500, but she evidently thought this over-priced and expected to get it for less. On the 16th came the bad news from Roy Davis that

238 ಆ

she had lost out, and that it had gone to an antique dealer for $1,700.

During the Cuban missile crisis, when the world held its breath while President Kennedy out-faced Premier Khrushchev, I did not notice her taking any unusual interest. On Tuesday, October 23rd, the atmosphere in the White House was hushed and suspenseful.

The next diary entry paints the picture.

Wednesday, October 24, 1962:
    9:00 A.M.—At White House
    9:30 A.M.—News broadcasts each ¼ hour today with regard to the Cuban blockade. Everyone upstairs speaking in whispers.
    1:00 P.M.—Had few minutes in Queen's Bedroom with Lee Radziwill.
    2:00 P.M.—Sad to learn from Provi, John, Jr. suffering with 104° temperature.

That afternoon, Jackie left the Mansion to play tennis, probably working off nervous energy.

A month or so later, Jackie gave a speech in Spanish to the Cuban Invasion Brigade in Miami, to take part in some ceremonies with the President.

The President's firm hand was seen every once in a while in the things she would do if he insisted.

My entry for November 8, 1962 reads: "JBK does not wish to attend the funeral of Mrs. Eleanor Roosevelt..." But then my next day's entry says, "JBK *will* attend funeral!"

It was the same way with people—sometimes Jackie avoided meeting them, and other times, she went out of her way to see people. On November 19, 1962, I sent a hurried note down to her from my office:

"Jackie: Evelyn Lincoln called. Said you asked her to let you know when Indian Ambassador was here so you could nonchalantly bump into him—NOW IN FISH ROOM—Mary G."

In November, Jackie was in full swing finding the perfect Christmas presents for all members of her family. But I had to smile when she tried to explain to the Housekeeper the thing that she wanted to get for Ethel: "Could you give me the name of that big hot thing with compartments that the President uses in the summer, that we used a few days ago, that you could stick dishes to be warmed up in?"

In spite of Jackie's lack of familiarity with such things as food warmers, she did know foods and saved magazine recipes to be tried out. Some time in November, 1962, the President was put on a special diet of bland foods by his doctor because of a slight stomach disorder. Jackie was much concerned and gave strict instructions to the Housekeeper and chef René about what the doctor said the President could eat.

She ordered that he be served soups that were consommé or chicken broth or puréed vegetables or fish chowder. She ordered his meats broiled or roasted—steaks, chops, chicken, roast beef, or leg of lamb, and without thickened gravies or sauces. Jackie ordered that no wine or other seasoning than salt be used in preparing his meats. For vegetables: potatoes, rice, macaroni or noodles, but without onion or butter.

The President's desserts were a variety of puddings—tapioca, snow pudding, custards, floating island, vanilla soufflé.

The only cheeses he was permitted for appetizers or in cooking were to be Gruyère, Swiss, and cream cheese.

Jackie took great pains in checking the menu when guests were dining with them, to make sure that the President's diet was adhered to without having to embarrass him by serving two separate menus.

It was Bob Luddington, interior decorator for the Jordan Marsh Company in Boston, who usually arranged to have the Kennedys' house at the Cape opened, ready for their arrival there before Thanksgiving. Jackie wanted me to notify him that she would arrive on Wednesday, November 21st, and ask that he arrange to have the beds made and heaters put in the children's rooms.

They were to stay there through the weekend, leaving on Sunday, the 25th. This time, the Ambassador was in a wheelchair.

At this particular time, too, Jackie's planning about houses extended even to the following summer. She asked that I call her real estate agent at the Cape, Bill O'Neil, to give him the message that "we might be interested in renting the Thun house next summer. Will there be anyone in it over Thanksgiving? Could you possibly show it to the President then?"

She wanted Bill to sound out the owners on the rental. If they didn't raise the price, he could discuss it with the President when he was up there. But Jackie warned that she didn't want to be around herself when rental was being discussed with the President.

When they returned from the Cape, Jackie was delving into the details of a party at the White House for Caroline and John, whose birthdays fell within two days of each other —John's, the 25th of November, and Caroline's, the 27th— so a joint celebration was to be held in the private dining room of the family quarters.

On the morning of her birthday, Caroline came in with Miss Shaw to visit with me for a minute and said, "Even though you're not on the list, you can come to my party— you and Miss Shaw!" I thanked her and felt rather privileged at the personal invitation!

In fact, before the day was out, she must have invited me at least a half-dozen times, finally ending up with, "If you can't get away from your desk, I'll be having a *little* party on the 28th. You can come to that!"

As it turned out, I never did get to the party, but I saw the many pictures of the gay, colorful affair taken by the White House photographer. The two "his and her" birthday cakes, whipped up by René and his staff and beautifully decorated, were photographed endlessly. I eventually pasted each and every shot into the children's picture albums.

Two round tables were set up in the dining room with John-John's little friends seated around him, and Caroline's around her. Jackie, Mrs. Auchincloss, and all the other mothers milled happily about, and the President took a few minutes from his busy schedule to join them.

A few days later, Miss Shaw told me that, "of all the birthday cards Caroline received, the only ones she insisted on keeping in her room were the ones given her by Christopher and Gregory." They had made them themselves.

As Christmas approached, Ted Kahn was sending a little pink fur muff as a present to Caroline, but it failed to arrive. I talked with the Mail Room men, who quickly checked their records and did verify that the muff had been received. Also, that they did not see any "code" on the package and therefore automatically sent it over to the Social Office in the East Wing. I followed the thread over there, only to discover the muff had been given to one of the White House employees as a Christmas gift to his daughter.

I decided not to mention it to Jackie. Instead, I called and explained to Ted on the phone that it had inadvertently been given away, and that I knew he would understand the situation. I described the heavy volume of mail at the White House and explained that since the "code" had not appeared on the package, it had gone through regular channels and not directly to me for delivery to Mrs. Kennedy.

Ted generously offered to let the other little girl keep that particular muff and said that he would make up another one instantly for Caroline. This time, of course, he did not forget to apply the code: "Attention—Mary B. Gallagher—Special."

Still in the midst of the Christmas rush, it was time for Jackie to leave for Palm Beach for the holidays. Many of her instructions concerned gifts to be sent there, as well as those to be delivered locally in Washington in her absence.

At one moment I detected Jackie's mischievous smile as she reached for a prettily wrapped box. Handing it to me, she gave me strict orders that "it's not to be opened before Christmas!"

In spite of Jackie's smile and my warm acceptance, there

was a little sadness in her attitude as she prepared to leave, and I responded to that mood. I did feel sorry for Jackie's problems—her continuing battle of the budget, and also the hint, concerning the possibility of Tish's leaving next year, which she had dropped into a day's work session.

In the hour that remained before her take-off that December 14th, I could feel the strain. It was now 3 P.M. I made a final check to see that Jackie's briefcase was all in order, and wanted to tackle the things on my desk. I went into the dressing room, where she was applying the usual finishing touches to her make-up, and announced that all was in order.

If it was all right with her, I would quickly say goodbye and get back to my desk. But somehow, I could sense that she preferred my not leaving her—not at the moment, anyway. I asked her if there was anything more I might do.

The nature of her slight request convinced me that for some reason she was trying to detain me.

"Oh, yes, Mary," she said in a rather meditative way, "would you ask Miss Shaw if she and the children are ready? Tell her we'll be leaving in just a few minutes."

In the children's rooms, I found that Miss Shaw, of course, had her hands full. Snapping shut suitcases and promising that she and the children would be with Mrs. Kennedy shortly, she reached for their little coats and began the buttoning-up process.

I left them to assure Jackie that there would be no delay. By now, she too was completely ready, waiting beside the front table in the Center Hall.

"Miss Shaw will be right with you, Jackie," I said. "She's buttoning up the children's coats right now..."

As I bade her farewell with best wishes for the holidays, she embraced me gently in her arms. In a most sincere way, she said, "Thanks so much, Mary...I hope you, Ray, and the boys have a Merry Christmas, too."

And though I had hardly expected anything like this, she continued with traces of tears in her eyes, "You know, you're my only friend in this impersonal White House. What would I ever do without you? Jack has Ted Reardon, Evelyn Lincoln, and the others . . . But you work so hard upstairs in that office—always messy with my clothes . . ."

Her emotions truly touched my heart. I was afraid if I let her say any more, I'd be in tears, too.

"Now, now," I broke in, pretending to be all business, "none of that . . . I do appreciate it, and I hope you'll always feel this way. But Jackie, the only time I ever want you to feel that you *should* say something to me is when I've *stopped* being useful to you. Because then, I wouldn't want to be around. Meanwhile, as long as you do need me, I'll do just anything for you."

And I meant it!

PART THREE

THE UNFORGETTABLE YEAR

26 ∽ HOUSES, HOUSES, HOUSES

*H*OW CAN I FORGET MY FLYING TRIP TO help Jackie in Florida?

How good I felt. Behind me was Christmas, and it had been most satisfactory. I had opened the big box from Jackie finally and was thrilled to find a lovely evening dress of pink-and-gold brocade made by Oleg Cassini. It was two-piece, an underdress with low-cut back and a matching jacket.

Also, there had been two presents for our house. An antiqued gold-framed etching of the White House, autographed:

> For Mary—with love and appreciation
> Jackie
> John F. Kennedy

The other was a beautiful watercolor of the Red Room, autographed:

> With our appreciation and best wishes for
> a happy Christmas—1962
> John F. Kennedy   Jacqueline Kennedy

Jackie, herself, had received some exciting art, too, a Renoir and a Prendergast from the President. One, she felt, was not shown to best advantage, and she immediately sent it back for reframing in a Louis XVI frame.

One of her favorite gifts, I recall, had been some pajamas from Princess Irene Medici of Rome, to whom she wrote humorously from Palm Beach. Every evening, she said, found her wearing it like a uniform, and she wished Irene could see her and Lee there—it was like a convent.

Before Jackie left for Florida, she had made my joining her sound almost like a vacation, extending the invitation to my husband, too.

After several "alert calls" from Florida over the Christmas-New Year holidays, Ray and I arrived in Palm Beach on the morning of January 2nd. My mother-in-law was left in charge of the home front. A lovely suite of rooms had been reserved for us at the Palm Beach Towers.

The beautiful residence of Colonel C. M. Paul, where the Kennedys were staying, had a swimming pool just a few steps outside the bedroom Jackie occupied.

The spacious house provided Secret Service quarters, as well as an office for me, on the ground floor. My working hours were long ones, as usual, including Saturday and Sunday sessions. And, as Jackie delved through her accumulated business, she invariably remarked with surprise that I could "keep up" with her!

By the third day, Jackie announced cheerfully, "Mary, you'll just have to stay here through Tuesday, when I return!"

That would be January 8th, barely a week to catch up on the three-week backlog!

I hardly saw Ray. I remained closeted with Jackie, and the thought of any fun on the beach soon left me.

Even so, Ray and I managed to squeeze in a little social life of our own, by meeting for an enjoyable evening with our friends the Frank Lambs, just about a mile or so further up the road from the home of Ambassador Kennedy.

After dinner at Maurice's, Mrs. Lamb entertained us at her home with some relaxing music on the organ. At this point I appreciated every soothing chord.

We departed from Palm Beach January 8th on Air Force One, and once in the sky, it was as though I were still sitting in the office with Jackie. She summoned me to the plane's private compartment and dictated throughout the entire flight back! But we weren't really alone there. Lee Radziwill and Peter Lawford sat opposite us, chatting away. Caroline and John-John, in their usual good spirits, romped freely about. And the pet dogs, Charlie and Clipper, nestled obediently at our feet, taking the flight like two old pros.

A visit from France's André Malraux was involving Jackie at this point, and she was concerned with what wines to serve him at dinner. The more serious problem of too many chefs at the White House also troubled the First Lady. She wanted Anne Lincoln to take care of releasing one of the assistant chefs but to do it in "a friendly fashion." Jackie wanted me to caution Anne to go out of her way to be nice to him. When giving him notice, the reason was to be that the President could not continue to pay so many chefs out of his own pocket. Anne was to assure him that he would be given excellent references and adequate severance pay—and tell him how much Jackie and the President regretted his leaving.

For Jackie, if it wasn't little decisions, it was big decisions. By February, it was nothing but houses, houses, houses.

Jackie could measure time by the house she was in, almost year by year.

For their first year the Kennedys rented the Blair Childs house on Dent Place.

The next year, during Jack's long convalescence, they were at the Ambassador's in Palm Beach.

"Hickory Hill" came during the third year.

Joe Pyne's house on P Street marked the fourth year.

Then came Caroline and the Georgetown house on N Street, which lasted three years.

And then the White House.

As a fringe benefit, there was Camp David, the official Presidential hideaway in the Catoctin Mountains of Maryland with its swimming pool, skeet-shooting facility, bowling alley, and tiny golf course.

And the weekend retreat from the White House—Glen Ora in Middleburg.

But Jackie was not content with merely renting, or using

the Government-provided retreat. She suddenly decided to buy a piece of land, on Rattlesnake Mountain in Virginia, with just a little "prefabricated" house thrown up.

It was in June, 1962, that she had repainted and redecorated the Glen Ora house—and seemed to have it the way she wanted it. Then came the idea, the challenge of having her own place.

Actually, it was I who eventually notified Tom Walsh in the Kennedys' New York office that Jackie was thinking of putting up a house in Virginia.

I went on to tell him in a note that she would like him to "send plans and costs for a one-floor prefabricated house ... should have about 5–6 bedrooms, living room, dining room, kitchen, possibly 3 single maids' rooms, and carport. Send down plans and price ranges as soon as possible. Send to me. MBG."

I'm sure the President knew it wasn't going to be an *economy* move, but he wanted Jackie to be happy.

And, now, for the first time, Jackie was going to have a house that had been designed and built just for her—her own *real* home at last!

I was very happy for her.

But January ended on a bit of a sour note.

When the Kennedys did not renew the Glen Ora lease, the owner of Glen Ora discovered that Jackie had redecorated the place, so that now the owner's furnishings were at war with Jackie's walls. A little restoration was called for.

This was a shock to Jackie, who was trying to budget. Especially since her major interest now was the furnishing of the new house, Atoka, for the move planned for April.

Jackie sadly told Mrs. Parrish, her decorator, to check the cost of painting several rooms, plus the cost of curtains, and said she hoped that it wouldn't cost "a million."

I will never forget January 11, 1963. As Jackie was dictating to me in her White House sitting room, she casually asked, "Mary, would you say I've done enough till now as First Lady?"

It was, of course, a leading question. I realized she must have asked it for a reason—perhaps, as her maid Provi and I had privately suspected, she might be pregnant.

"Yes, Jackie," I replied, "I think you have—even more than your share. Except for what the President feels you *should* do, I don't really think you should worry about doing anything else."

She seemed pleased with what was, obviously, a confirmation of her own thoughts, and immediately informed her social secretary, Tish Baldrige, "I am taking the veil!" Jackie told Tish to cut off *all* outside activity—whether it was having a glass of sherry with a poet, seeing the wife of some president, dedicating an art gallery, or that sort of thing. Only the most important matters should merit her time from now on, she said. She gave as her reason, however, that she did not see enough of her children and that she had done enough as First Lady.

But Jackie and her sister, Lee Radziwill, did go to Congress on January 14, 1963, to watch JFK deliver his State of the Union message. The event gave me further insight into the relationship between Jackie and her sister. The morning of the 14th, Lee was readying herself in the Queen's Room, the room she usually occupied on her visits to the White House. Later, as she waited by my desk for Jackie, I commented on how pretty she looked. "Oh, I don't feel it," she said, "Jackie is the one in her mink coat."

She then observed her handbag more closely, and expressed the wish for a better one. I tried again to assure her that she couldn't look nicer, but she sighed, "Oh, well, no one's ever going to notice . . ." I really felt sorry for her. It was tough to compete with Jackie.

January in the White House started so gently. My diary shows me huddled over my "Black Book," again with year-end balancing of books. And involved in Jackie's newest concern—what the children were eating; she had complained that Caroline and John-John had been getting the "same thing" to eat day after day. She wanted Miss Shaw to work out the children's menus carefully so that the same meal was never to be served twice in the same week. They ran for a three-week period and included 6 different kinds of soups, 10 different kinds of meats, 10 different kinds of vegetables, 17 types of desserts.

At the Staff Mess, Pierre Salinger was taking a lot of ribbing. The President was on a health kick after someone sent him Teddy Roosevelt's letter of 1908 to the Marine Commandant saying any Marine officer worth his salt should be able to hike fifty miles. JFK volunteered his rotund Press Secretary to lead a fifty-mile hike. Everyone was bringing Pierre little gifts of corn plasters and liniment.

Pierre said he'd go—but only as an ambulance driver. Eventually, Bobby Kennedy led the hike.

For January 16th my diary records: JBK dictated from bed and seemed rather despondent. Foreign Minister Fanfani was to be greeted by the President, and he had phoned upstairs to find out whether Jackie would like to go down. "Tell him I'm not up to coming downstairs," she said.

A few days later Jackie asked that I call Evelyn Lincoln to tell her that the President had lots of little airplanes in his closet to give John-John every morning, but nothing for Caroline. "He suggested that you get some little horse figures so that he will have something to give Caroline each day, too," I said.

Among the things that drew Jackie's attention as the year began was the service at one of her dinner parties. On January 22nd she was issuing a blast to the housekeeping department. She pointed out that the wine was not passed until everyone had finished his fish. Next time, she said, there should be a battery of waiters to pass the wine before the fish, even if they did nothing else.

She also complained about the Brie cheese, saying it was hard as rubber, even though it was a very good cheese. In the future, she wanted the chef to leave the cheese OUT of the refrigerator all day.

Her observations had not *all* been so one-sided. Jackie was pleased that at least the red wine and champagne were served properly with the courses they accompanied.

She ended her blast by pointing out that a word used to describe the dessert had been misspelled—"Surprise . . . not Suprise." She said perhaps not all cards were misspelled, but the ones at her table certainly were.

On the restoration front, Jackie said she was discouraged that "absolutely no progress" was being made on Jefferson's idea for a proper library for the White House. She wanted some rare books for it, but she didn't want to have to put up locked grilles that would make the room look like "a prison."

She said she didn't think it should be used as a working library, because she was afraid that the rare books would gradually disappear. It was her feeling that if the books were not loaned out, their appearance wouldn't have to be marred with numbers on the backs.

Anyway, she was tossing the problem in Arthur Schlesinger's lap, asking him to work it out for her.

Living on the President's bland diet which the doctors had ordered seemed to be chafing to Jackie. She said she was tired of bland foods and ordered chef René to try out some new dishes from the *Au Bon Gout* cookbook for herself and guests, while feeding the President something that was on his own diet. Some of her suggestions from the book were Zucchini Mousseline, Artichokes Mousseline, and Eggplant Shoreacres.

Even the new city plans for handling increased Washington traffic concerned Jackie, and she got in touch with a high official of the General Service Administration asking if there was any way to stop the Three Sisters Bridge. She suggested that Key Bridge be widened, instead, to handle the traffic, leaving the park near fashionable Foxhall Road alone. The fact that it was one of the few places left where children could take nature walks with rangers was the basis of her stand.

The White House guest list also took her attention now. Jackie asked Tish to come up with some new names of amusing people to be invited to a party for Eugene Black, the president of the World Bank, explaining that the present list looked like a tired meeting of the same old club.

February was Jackie's season for adding to her collection of paintings. She spent a week at the Kennedys' Carlyle Hotel apartment, in New York City—probably making the rounds of the little galleries. For me, it was an ideal time for catching up on the backlog of mail, personal bills, bookkeeping, "Monthly Statement of Expenses" for January, and ordering of things she wanted. I also took on an extracurricular chore, typing up pages and pages of individual menus that Miss Shaw had made out, covering a three-week span. The kitchen help would now be guided in preparing meals for the children to avoid "duplications."

It seemed the cooks were still taking Caroline and John-John down the Hamburger Trail. "I gave the order once before, but it was never carried out," Jackie had fumed when she gave me the menus to type.

While she was at it, Jackie wanted her daiquiri to be properly made and told Miss Bowen, the assistant housekeeper, to Scotch-tape her recipe to the wall: "2 parts rum, 3 parts frozen limeade, and 1 part fresh lime juice. Add a few drops of Falernum as sweetener." I was to explain to Miss Bowen that the "daiquiri should not be too sweet"—she should use too little rather than too much Falernum.

Jackie was completely exhausted but happy upon her return from New York, exclaiming, "I just bought a charming Judith Lewis." After a late breakfast, she slept away the whole day.

A few days afterward, while I was talking on the phone with the assistant housekeeper, my line was suddenly disconnected. The operator in a formal tone announced, "Mrs. Gallagher, the President would like to speak with you!" In a sharp and clear voice, he asked about the status of JBK's

January bills. I gave him a quick report on the phone. He asked a few questions, then said that he would call me later in the week to discuss them further.

At noon, at the Staff Mess, a call came from Jackie to "meet me in the Treaty Room." My lunch had just been served, but I left it behind and dashed off to the Mansion. Instinct told me that bills might be uppermost in *her* mind, too—and so they were. But she had a solution.

Jackie wanted to approach Eunice Shriver again about renting the house in the compound. She and the President had rented the Thun house on Squaw Island for the whole summer. She asked Eunice if she and Pat wanted to rent the JFK house in the compound again from July 4th through September 15th.

Why she needed the Thun house somehow escaped me.

Jackie left for Palm Beach on the 21st, but dictation continued via long distance! She was in the thick of preparations for the move to Atoka. Every day, it seemed, she had new plans for me, new things to shop for in Washington.

There were the curtains for the bedrooms of the children, Miss Shaw, and the two maids. These I purchased at The Hecht Company in Washington, charging them to my personal account, to be reimbursed from the "Mary B. Gallagher—Special" account. This way, we conveniently avoided any excitement at the store over purchases made by the First Lady.

Jackie wanted a straw rug for one room, which involved one-foot squares being sewn together to fit the room wall-to-wall. I had no choice about revealing who the order was for. The salesman personally went out to Atoka to take proper measurements; but, angel that he was, he did his job without any fanfare.

I got in touch with Adele Murphy of Residential Services, asking her to put aside some time the last week in March to work on the inventory at Glen Ora before the move to Atoka. Jackie wanted to be sure that Mrs. Murphy knew exactly which things at Glen Ora belonged to her and which belonged to the owner. "If there is any question," Jackie said, "tell her to come down early in March, and I'll show her."

Suddenly it was March. Any March wind could have blown me over! I was back in the doctor's office. After a blood test, Dr. Donnally administered a B_{12} shot and told me to try to get some rest. Later, he called to report that my blood count was very low; I needed iron.

Tired as I was, it felt good to be seeing Dr. Donnally— Reamur Donnally—who was almost part of the Kennedy family. He had been JFK's old doctor in the Senate days, and the Chief had recommended him to me when I was just a newcomer to his Senate office.

That first weekend, I had to prepare the February "Monthly Statement of Expenses" for JBK. It was a real push, but I knew JFK would be looking for his copy the first thing Monday morning. It was on Evelyn Lincoln's desk by 11:30 A.M.

Jackie arrived back from Florida the first week of March, and we worked the first day until 7:30 P.M.

We were back at art. I was contacting the London art scout, Bier, to find another 18th-century Hunting scene like the Judith Lewis Jackie had mentioned to him.

Jackie was also pleased that Roy Davis had made a fine picture frame for the President's own painting, a seascape he had painted while recuperating after his back operation. "It would make the painter feel as though he were Utrillo," Jackie said, applauding the frame.

Jackie had apparently spent much of her time in Florida just jotting notes to herself. She wasted no time in dictating a million messages on things to be done at Atoka. Then she switched to a newer subject—the hiring of her new social secretary. Tish would not leave till May, but the person Jackie had chosen was Nancy Tuckerman, an old classmate from Miss Porter's at Farmington, Connecticut.

One thing on Jackie's mind was that she wanted to offer some reassurance about the new job and asked "Tucky" not to get worked up over it. By now, I must say, Jackie was no longer in terror of her job as First Lady, either. She herself said, "Sometimes, I get furious with myself, thinking about all the energy I wasted, worrying about what life would be like in the White House."

But though her own life was easier, life for everyone else around her was getting busier and busier ... I see that even Caroline was getting impressed with speed:

> March 31, 1963: Another late evening session. As we walked into the Treaty Room for the last lap, Caroline followed us. Apparently, JBK hadn't been stepping ahead quite fast enough for her daughter, who wedged her way into the room with "Slow poke, Mommy ..." John-John also joined us but had more exciting things on his mind than dictation. He soon left, calling back, " 'Bye, Ma-wee ... 'Bye, Ma-wee ..."

On March 25 I met JFK in the elevator. He again inquired about the status of Jackie's bills, and as we parted, I heard the familiar request. "Tomorrow, please send me figures for the first two months of this year as compared with the first two months of last year."

It was another evening of frantic homework! The totals for January and February, 1963, indicated *some* improvement over the first two months of 1962. For example, in January, 1962, Jackie's clothing purchases had added up to around $5,000, whereas in January, 1963, they only approached $2,000. (But, of course, Jackie was pregnant in early '63 and not buying many clothes.) As for the food and liquor expenses, January, 1962, showed purchases of $7,000, which had been reduced to a little more than $5,000 in January, 1963. Beauty salon, however, had remained about the same—January, 1962: $340; January, 1963: $300. Art in January, 1962, totaled $1,600, but in January, 1963, there were no art costs at all because, even though Jackie had received two new paintings, the President had paid for them—they were his Christmas gift to her.

Jackie's personal expenses for the first two months of 1963 had come down by more than $12,000—to a total of about $16,000.

The President obviously felt there was still room for improvement. When he looked at my report, he said, "Mary,
I want you to show Jackie the latest clothing figures!"

When Jackie awakened from her nap, I carried out the
President's order. She listened without comment, then proceeded to go over the books thoroughly. That little chore
over, she left at 7:30 P.M. for another quick jaunt to New
York. I knew it wouldn't be long before we'd be re-enacting
this little scene again.

27 ～ ART, ANTIQUES, ATOKA

*A*S APRIL BEGAN, THE PRESIDENT WAS PLAN-
ning his life—his life even after the White House. And Jackie,
who always planned ahead, decided to help.

She approached the Chief Usher, Mr. West, to ask if he
could find a wonderful wood-carver. She went on to tell how
the President, like President Truman, wanted a replica of
his office. She added that she knew she had picked the worst
possible desk to duplicate.

Jackie was referring to the magnificent, intricately carved
antique desk that had been made of the timber of the H.M.S.
Resolute and presented to America by Queen Victoria. It
was, in fact, the desk she had found stored away in the basement of the White House. Jackie's plan was to have a stucco
or wax impression made of the whole desk. But, as was her
way, even in this she wanted secrecy, suggesting that Mr. West
tell the craftsmen that some museum in England wanted a
duplicate of the desk.

But the desk was only one small issue.

Jackie was also busy collecting paintings. She wanted Bier,

of London, to find her some 18th-century paintings of the Spanish Riding School of Vienna. Lipizzaner Stallions fascinated her.

Jackie was also ordering a "War of 1812" print for the President's birthday, May 29th. She told the dealer to watch for more naval engravings the President might like, as well as paintings of ships. She told him her budget was small, and she couldn't ever go over a couple thousand dollars, so it would be best if he didn't even let her know about superb pictures. At least, I thought, she wasn't getting him more scrimshaw! It became a standing joke around the White House that whenever Jackie didn't know what to get the President, she got him another piece of scrimshaw. The President liked the large whales' teeth, and he would keep them on his desk. Jackie had some of them embellished with the Presidential seal.

As spring approached, Jackie was thinking houses—not only about the building of Atoka, which now was going ahead full speed and was making Rattlesnake Mountain in Virginia a livelier place than it had ever been before, but of the Thun House at Cape Cod, where she looked forward to spending the summer.

One afternoon in April, while Jackie was dictating, JFK came into the room barefooted and wearing a terry-cloth robe. He said, "There they are—the most efficient couple in the White House!"

As he walked over to us, Jackie handed him the letter she was reading. It had to do with their summer rental of the Thun House, and she sweetly asked his approval for the times she wanted to spend there. He agreed and, as even more of a favor, was about to dictate a reply to confirm the specific dates.

"Mary, would you take a letter?" he began.

But Jackie retrieved the letter from his hands and said, "Oh, Jack, *I'll* dictate the letter!"

He left the room looking just a bit less chipper than when he first arrived; I felt rather sorry for him.

That same month, Jackie had discovered that the President's custom-made shirts were being mistreated by the laundry to which they were being sent. She ordered that an Oriental who knew something about laundry be hired to come to the White House to do them, or perhaps the wife of one of the Filipinos who worked in the kitchen.

Another scene occurred when Jackie discovered that a cigarette company was using the Presidential Seal on package wrappers of the cigarette it was supplying to the White House. She issued a blast, ordering that stopped—both the supplying of free cigarettes and the use of the Seal in this way. She resented their plastering the Presidential Seal, which she said should be treated like the flag, all over their cigarettes.

Then it was clothes again—Jackie's clothes. In a letter to her clothes scout in Paris, Jackie wrote that she was really going to economize, even though a new designer the scout had found sounded fabulous. Jackie added that she was sick of going to all the old ones. She suggested that if the designer was that divine, the scout could let Lee buy a suit so Jackie could borrow it anytime.

On April 5th, Jackie was looking for me at 8:45 A.M. She was leaving late in the day for Palm Beach—the rush was on.

I spent the whole day at her side. She wanted me near even as she dressed for the trip, suggesting that I take a few moments to lie down on the bed as I waited for her.

I appreciated her thoughtfulness, but there were too many little details to be attended to. Finally, as I helped her to zipper her dress and get into her coat, she thanked me for all my help. "That's just great, Mary. You've done so much. Get a good rest while I'm gone. If you like, bring your boys over to play at school or picnic on the lawn."

It was three days later that I received my call:

> April 13, 1963: Saturday—2:00 P.M. JBK's S.S. Agent Paul Landis called from Palm Beach. Jackie wants me down in Palm Beach next Wednesday (17th) ... bring along the flowered box, marked Clothes.

And on the 15th, Paul Landis called again with three pages of instructions from JBK, followed by "she also said you could have 3 or 4 days of rest in the sun when you get here."

On the 17th, Ray and I were flown to Florida aboard one of the Presidential planes. Provi was the only other passenger.

My diary tells the rest of the story:

> April 18, 1963: Formal announcement of the expected birth of Jackie's new baby made from Palm Beach. When I saw JBK today I offered my congratulations, and smiling, she said: "Oh, Mary, you knew it for ages but were so cute not to say anything."
>
> April 19, 1963: Remained at the Palm Beach Towers all day working at the typewriter till midnight. Room service lunch.
>
> April 21, 1963: Sunday—Returned from Mass for some relaxation by the pool. As I lay stretched out on a chaise-lounge, I was paged. Within seconds, the telephone was in my hand and I was scribbling into my notebook on my lap. The poolside no refuge.
>
> April 22, 1963: JBK called at the hotel at 9:00 A.M. To work!

My week was fast up and as usual Jackie's offer for "3 or 4 days in the sun" had indeed proved but a mirage.

I had hardly settled back into the White House routine again when I ran into JFK one morning as he was on his way to his office. Just as if I'd never been away, he immediately wanted to know, "What's the situation on the bills, Mary?"

"Well, Mr. President, I think we're in much better shape now than we were a year ago . . ."

He didn't let it go at that. "Send me a comparative report for the first quarter of this year and last!"

I was sorry I had used the regular elevator. Hereafter, I promised myself when I heard the elevator's three buzzes I would run the other way or use the waiter's elevator.

So my entire weekend was spent on that report, as well as on drawing up the regular itemized monthly statement for April. I planned to drop off both of them with Evelyn as I passed her office, on my way to the Staff Mess on Monday afternoon. As luck would have it, I ran into the President before the reports reached him. "Oh, Mary," he called out, "I'll be waiting for your report today."

"Yes, sir!" I practically saluted him. "They'll be in your hands shortly!" I was glad to be finished with them. I had too much "house" work to do—Atoka house, that is.

And the rest of that whole month was spent getting ready for the new house. In fact, on that final day, April 30th, so much had to be done that Ray and I forfeited the celebration of our eighth wedding anniversay so that I could supervise the big move.

At 7:30 that morning, I rushed to the White House to oversee all phases of the operation—inventory lists, truckloads of furniture, and handling delicate items. In my office were dozens of small things, each carefully marked for its appropriate spot.

At 7:30 that evening, I was still typing away when I should have been in a restaurant with Ray over a candlelight dinner.

Before leaving for home, I stopped in to say good night to Provi, and was surprised to find her laboring over an alteration to the gown Jackie had decided at the last minute to wear to that evening's reception for Grand Duchess Charlotte of Luxembourg.

"You mean that with all the gowns in Mrs. Kennedy's closet, you have to end up fixing *this* one?" I asked.

Shrugging her shoulders, Provi agreed, "Yes, Mees Gallaga ... t'at's the way eet ees," and kept right on with her race against the clock.

The next day I was on my way to Atoka to oversee the unloading. A gorgeous day for the ride through the countryside. After the truck shipments of the past two days, I was to oversee the placement of furniture in the rooms, etc. The private roadway to the house was not completely finished, and heavy pieces of equipment moved to one side so we could pass.

Gardeners were busy with landscaping. Considerable

thought had been given to making Atoka as lovely on the outside as on the inside. Along the back of the yellow stucco house, overlooking the beautiful green pastures, was a brick patio. And, in front, lovely shrubbery enhanced the entrance to the house. Huge holes were being dug for planting the mammoth-size boxwoods that came from Mrs. Auchincloss's estate. After the planting, the boxwood looked as if it had been growing there for years.

It was easy to imagine how lovely Atoka would eventually be. But when I went in, I could see the amount of work in store for all hands.

With three other women—Mrs. Murphy and Mrs. Jessup of Residential Services, and Lucinda Morman, the White House seamstress—and a White House carpenter, we immediately set to our tasks.

A few days later, Sunday, the 5th, Jackie called me at home asking that I arrange to go to Rattlesnake Mountain on Monday: "Pack a little overnight case." I was to share Jackie's first night at Atoka.

I smile as I see the day's diary entry:

> May 7, 1963: Started right in again at 9:00 A.M. after a quick breakfast. JBK breakfasted from a tray in bed. By 11:00, notebook in hand, JBK giving one instruction after another. Rooms beginning to shape up.

Looking chipper in her slacks, Jackie walked through the rooms, checking off items written on her yellow pad.

There were curtains to go up, pictures to be placed on the walls, pieces of furniture to be moved from one spot to another. "Let's take this chair from here and put it here," or "Put this lamp on the table in Jack's room," or any of a thousand and one similar details.

Grouping the pictures on the dining-room wall was of paramount importance to Jackie. She was putting up her collection of Indian Mogul miniatures and asked, as she held certain ones in place, "What do you think, Mary, do they look better as a group, or spaced apart like this?"

Frankly, I wondered a little about those pictures in a dining room at all. To me, somehow, they seemed more appropriate for a boudoir, because they were rather erotic.

I was touched that Jackie kept referring to the guestroom I had slept in as "Mary's room" or "your room." Whenever she wanted something carried there, she said to me, "Take this to *your* room." *My* room was most unusual—really rather stunning—with red paisley wallpaper that continued up across the ceiling. Even the window blinds were custom-made in the same red paisley pattern. As usual, Jackie had neglected no detail.

It was time to leave. My diary shows:

> 5:00 P.M.: Helicopter settled down just a short walk from Atoka. JBK asked that I sit in seat facing her. At our feet, Clipper curled up in his usual fashion. JBK dictated until the "chopper" touched its pad! Before we parted for the evening, she said, "Don't come in tomorrow—just rest up."

How I wished I *could* rest. But there was too much to do, and I worked at the White House the next day as usual. But Jackie followed the advice she had given me—she stayed in bed that day.

Evidently, she was too exhausted to get up even for one of her favorite people. Her father-in-law, Ambassador Kennedy, was at the White House, accompanied by his devoted companion, his niece, Ann Gargan, who pushed him from room to room in his wheelchair.

I was in the West Sitting Room that afternoon, sorting some mail at Jackie's desk, when Ann wheeled the Ambassador in.

This was the first I'd seen him since his stroke and, to my surprise, he looked quite well. I felt that he had been making more progress than had been reported in the press.

He acknowledged my greeting with a nod and made a vocal sound, trying to say "Hello." His eyes were bright and alert.

Both he and Ann waited some time for Jackie to come out from her bedroom, but it became apparent that the wait

264 ॐ

would be longer than they anticipated. Mrs. Rose Kennedy was not along. But, besides Ann Gargan, the Ambassador traveled with Fritz, his male companion and masseur. As I recall, their visit was cut short because the Kennedys were expecting some State visitors, and the guestrooms were needed. Neither Jackie nor anyone else got to see much of the Ambassador during his short stay.

28 ∽ CAUGHT BETWEEN BLASTS

*M*AY WAS A STRANGE MONTH, FULL OF HU-mor, excitement, and changes around the White House—and even a few good "blasts."

In May, Jackie was ordering books—Kipling's *Kim* and *Coronettes Among the Wind*. In fact, it was now her season for books.

The White House Library was a great concern. Jackie's great triumph in the month of May was the "Lincoln Record Book," the gift of Vice President Lyndon Johnson to the White House Library.

Jackie wrote the Vice President, how proud she was to have it and how grateful she was to receive it.

But it was not all that simple.

As I got the picture, the Kennedys had paid for the book, and Vice President Johnson wanted to reimburse them for it to the tune of $3,960. The President, however, refused to allow the Vice President to pay for it.

So the Vice President had another solution. He then insisted that he be permitted to buy back the cows that he had given to Jackie as a gift for Glen Ora. Now that Atoka was built, Jackie no longer wanted to keep the cows and was returning them. She told the Vice President most graciously that she couldn't let him buy back the cows that he had given them.

That should have ended it. But it didn't.

A few weeks later, Liz Carpenter, who was working for the Johnsons at their home, was calling the Social Office to find out to whom the check for $3,960 for the Lincoln Record Book should be made out.

Jackie sternly instructed the Social Office that the Vice President was not to pay for the Record Book.

In answer to Liz Carpenter's question, Jackie said it would be an honor to give it in the name of Lyndon B. Johnson.

That ended the "book and cow incident."

During May, my working schedule was running exceptionally tight. But one evening I had received a phone call from two visiting friends, Mrs. Raymond Casale and Mrs. Clement Lazarovich, who were campaigners for Senator Edward Kennedy in Massachusetts and a visit to the White House seemed the least I could do on the Kennedys' behalf. They arrived an hour or so before the morning's working session and were delighted to join me for a cup of coffee upstairs.

I poured the coffee, and it was piping hot. So, allowing it to cool, I took them for a quick look at Caroline's playschool. When we returned to my office we raised the cups to our lips, and in chain reaction, returned the cups to their saucers. Our mouths were full of such a thick, lumpy, liquid substance, we nearly choked.

For the first few seconds, I was at a loss, until the sugar bowl caught my eye. Its silver gleamed on the inside, as well as on the outside!

"Looks like John-John's been here," I told the ladies, "having a gay time loading our cups with sugar cubes. They're *all* gone!"

Sugar cubes were a great favorite of John-John's. Usually, on his morning visits to my office with Miss Shaw, I would "treat" him to one or two (Miss Shaw's limit), which he quickly popped into his little mouth and chewed with joy. I could imagine that her little charge had wandered into my office alone and found the full bowl of sugar cubes just too much to resist. John-John's skillful maneuver had proved a highlight of the ladies' visit.

But it wasn't the only one.

As the ladies and I passed Evelyn's office, after lunch, she, the President, and Dave Powers were watching Astronaut Gordon Cooper's TV address to Congress. The President caught a glimpse of us at the doorway, waved, and called out, "Come on in and join us!"

I could never have *arranged* a more eventful, exciting visit for my old Massachusetts friends.

The following day Jackie suggested that I send a White House driver to pick up Chris and Greg and bring them to the White House for supper and a movie with Caroline. Before I left, she asked, "Would you keep watch over Caroline and John? You know, you be their mother and see that they behave."

For me, taking over Miss Shaw's duties for a few hours on her day off came as a welcome change—away from the typewriter.

The children behaved commendably both at dinner, which was served in the family's private dining room, and at the theater in the East Wing where, after a few cartoons, they became engrossed in the movie PT-109. The audience also comprised several other children, including Ethel's and Bobby's, too. Ethel and I were pretty much in charge of escorting the little ones at necessary intervals to the restroom down the hall.

The President and Jackie joined us in their lounging clothes to watch for a while. Caroline, who had been sitting on my lap when her father walked in, jumped down to curl up on a cot with him. Jackie sat next to me with a cheerful greeting for Gregory, who took Caroline's place on my lap. I was rather surprised that the Chief didn't stay to see the finish—it was about his own life, and apparently this was the first time it was being shown. He quietly left before the movie was completely over.

On JFK's birthday, May 29th, a surprise birthday party was held at the Staff Mess, with Pierre Salinger and Jack McNally officiating, in turn, as emcees. But before the festivities began Jackie had thoughtfully arranged for a photograph of her husband to be taken with the two members of their household staff who had served them the longest—George Thomas and Provi.

A long table had been set up with food, and in its center was a huge, gaily decorated birthday cake. The President was provided with his own rocking chair to sit in, with Jackie seated next to him.

Ceremonies began with a champagne toast by the President, who beamed broadly and said, "From now on, we should have a party just like this for everyone here who has a birthday coming up." His admiring audience agreed in loud applause. Then came the gifts, each carefully thought and wryly humorous. Each gift proved more clever and humorous than the one before. The President laughed at the replica of himself sitting in a miniature "JFK rocking chair."

Then came boxing gloves "to deal with Congress," and finally an exaggerated replica of his Rose Garden was carried in, in triumph as an achievement of his Administration.

The emcees "ordered" the President to the podium to read aloud a speech, supposedly prepared by himself; he obeyed rather sheepishly and suspiciously. As he stood there, quickly scanning the first few lines of the script, his hands busied themselves with his coat buttons and even his pocket flaps. His face took on his broadest smile and laughing, he began to read, "Two score and six years ago, my father brought forth on this continent a new Kennedy..." By the time he had finished the complete rewrite of Lincoln's Gettysburg Address, the whole room was rocking.

At the party, I noticed that the President's hair had taken on reddish highlights, which gave him a new youthfulness, and I commented to myself that he was going to stay young in spite of birthdays—as long as he had a good barber. Yes, he looked young, he looked happy and so carefree, especially as he left the room shaking hands in the crowd—while everyone joined in and sang, "When Irish Eyes Are Smiling!"

That last week in May marked Tish's departure from the White House as social secretary. Before she left, however, Jackie became very upset to learn that Tish had thrown away many memos Jackie had written to her.

Jackie said that it was unbelievable that Tish would destroy the things she had written. She was visibly annoyed. Expressing her dismay over the loss of the historically valuable correspondence, Jackie said that she had never written one memo that the public couldn't see. She immediately ordered the Social Office to save every scrap of paper from her from then on.

Jackie said she was distressed that gone were her memos on the Mount Vernon party, the State visit interchanges, and things she had said to Tish about different people.

Jackie told Tish that the worst thing she, Jackie, had ever said was about the Archbishop of Canterbury's wife. What that was, I never found out.

Jackie and I were working in her bedroom when one of the doormen delivered a little round table that had been made in the carpenter shop as a going-away gift for Tish. On the white parchment top, handwritten signatures could be applied. Jackie was to be the first to sign in the center, and around hers would be the signatures of all of those who had worked with Tish.

After Jackie signed, she asked that I have it sent to Mr. West for the rest of the signatures to be included.

It was a smooth transition, with Nancy Tuckerman taking over the duties of social secretary. I had, of course, known about Nancy. Jackie and she had been corresponding for some time, and her letters came to me marked with "code" for Jackie.

I was glad that Jackie had someone who had known her for

a long time and who understood her. Best of all, she shared the same sense of humor. In their old school yearbook, Jackie had been quoted as wanting in the future to be found "laughing with Tucky."

She arranged for Nancy to have a discussion with Anne Lincoln, the housekeeper, who had been Tish's secretary and knew everything about the Social Office. It was amusing the way Jackie assured her friend that the job was not at all superhuman, telling her that if she should suddenly get chicken pox, the office could run in the same familiar routine.

Although at the beginning I wondered why Jackie appointed Pam Turnure as her press secretary, as time went on, I could easily see why. Jackie once expressed how Pam felt the same way about the press as she herself did—be nice, but don't blurt out every last, intimate thing they want to know.

When Nancy was hired, Jackie warned her that when anyone was new, they fell upon you like wolves. Even though Pam tried to keep the press away from Jackie as much as possible—except at the State parties where it could not be avoided—Jackie was still dissatisfied. She said that having the press come in after dinner at a State function and mingle with the guests always made her feel like some social-climbing hostess, who invites a columnist to every party.

According to Jackie, it was, among other things, the notebooks that the press ladies carried that bothered her, and she wondered if they should be permitted to keep them. She decided they should, however, because then, at least, the guests would know who they were. But she felt that they should be kept together as a group and not be permitted to mingle with the guests. In fact, with her lively wit, she suggested to Pam that a couple of aides with bayonets should stand near them at the next dinner.

But then she decided that the problem was too hot for Pam to handle and turned the matter of keeping the press separate from the guests over to Mac Kilduff, of the President's Press Office. She explained that a man should do it because it wouldn't be fair to pit Pam against the "harpies"

270 ॐ

and that the press would accept her new ultimatum better from a man.

The plan she outlined to Mac Kilduff was that the women of the press could come in for only five or ten minutes before she and the President arrived. They could look over the dining room and the flowers and walk through the reception rooms, but not mingle with the guests.

As I recall, news stories in 1963 reported that the press was kept "behind the potted palms" and that they had to peep out at the guests to see who was there.

This arrangement lasted for only one party before the press came back again—notebooks or no notebooks.

On Monday, June 3, 1963, after completing Jackie's May financial statements over the weekend, I stopped at Evelyn Lincoln's office, to leave a copy for JFK. Scarcely fifteen minutes later, the President phoned me at the Staff Mess to question the "high expenses last month!"

With the figures still fresh in my mind, I quickly suggested that he refer to the Atoka column—pointing out the extra furnishings and equipment for the new house. Then, trying to soothe him, because I realized he was rather upset, I volunteered, "But, Mr. President, if you'll compare these with *last* May's figures, you'll see we've actually done better by about $700!"

He said, "Well, now, take this memo to Jackie . . . 'Jackie: The President feels that these accounts are still too high, and would like to have you go over them again. He says we really have to do better than saving only $700 per month.' Show her the comparison figures . . . and, Mary, *you* sign the memo."

"My" memo was placed on Jackie's desk that afternoon.

Two days later, Jackie faced the bills situation. With my memo in hand, she remarked rather guiltily, "Gosh, I guess Jack was real-l-ly upset, wasn't he?"

I could only agree, adding: "Well, Jackie, I don't mind so much his being upset. It's just that I'm always in the middle."

She apologized; then, studying the figures a bit more intently, she poined out that the figures didn't even include the salaries for me, Provi, and George Thomas.

I hadn't grasped the significance of her remark, and asked what she meant. "Oh, you know, like afterward . . . when we move up to Boston, I *hope* you'll still be with us."

Surprised, I said I would be happy to think about it but that it seemed such a long way off. My dream at the moment was not Boston five years hence, but some change in spending habits for the next few months, at least—for all our sakes.

Then I was suddenly embroiled in a new situation. It started with a certain Dr. X phoning me about Jackie's choice of color in the Presidential rooms being prepared for her at Walter Reed Hospital for the time when the baby arrived. I asked her about her preference the next morning.

"White, and I hope I don't have to have the painting done by General Eisenhower staring at me at the foot of my bed!" was her quick reply.

Soon after, Evelyn Lincoln called. "The President wants Jackie to send over the picture for Mike DiSalle right away." I knew she had an appointment with Dr. Travell, so I rushed downstairs to her office and almost bumped into Jackie, who was on her way out. She looked startled at seeing me.

"Oh, Mary," she said, "you're not sick, are you?"

"Oh, no, Jackie, nothing like that. Evelyn just called. The President needs the picture for Mike DiSalle and wants you to send it right over to him."

"Well, let that wait for just a minute," Jackie said. "First, come in the Map Room with me and take a blast to Dr. X." She mentioned the name of a military doctor.

For once, she caught me off guard, without my notebook. Fortunately, I spied a large manila envelope on the Secret Service Agents' desk and grabbed it. By the time Jackie finished up her little "blast," the envelope was well covered with shorthand scribbles. During her session with Dr. Travell, the matter of decorating her hospital suite had somehow come to a head and gotten Jackie all steamed up.

She quickly let the inquiring doctor know that she didn't want him involved in her affairs, telling him that he had no responsibility for her, her children, or Provi, George, Miss Shaw or me, Mary Gallagher.

She said she could not care less if the walls were bright purple, and that there was one kind of headline the President could do without: "MRS. KENNEDY DOES OVER ENTIRE SUITE—THROWS OUT EISENHOWER PAINTINGS."

Right on the heels of this incident, a second query aroused Jackie's ire. The President was planning a trip soon to Europe, and someone phoned one of his physicians concerning the President's diet during his trip.

It was the President's English host, Prime Minister Macmillan, who had started the inquiry into the diet, and Jackie learned that a bunch of menus had been sent to Lady Macmillan.

Jackie immediately began "Round 2" with a series of blasts, demanding to know who had procured the menus. When she found it was a Secret Service man, she told him to get his information next time by going to me or Anne Lincoln and we would check directly with her. She told him that when she was in India, planeloads of bread were being flown in from Beirut because someone told her hosts she liked creamed-cheese sandwiches for lunch.

She then instructed the housekeeper that on future Presidential visits she should not be too specific if asked; she should just say no fried foods, no strong seasonings, nothing ice-cold, etc.

In June, the President's mother had sent him some Johnson's mustard plasters for his back. The President had his doctors at the White House to prescribe for him—Dr. Travell and Rear Admiral George Burkley, to name but two—but like a dutiful son, the President did use the plasters and liked them. Jackie told Dr. Burkley that they weren't a cure, of course, but they made the sore spot feel warm, which provided some comfort, at least.

Jackie was not going along on the European trip due to the approaching birth of her baby.

As her final gesture, before the President took off, she instructed Dr. Burkley to stock up on the plasters for her husband's trip, asking further that he give George, the valet, some mineral oil and talcum powder to use when a plaster was removed.

In Germany, facing a vast multitude, the President spoke the famous phrase: "*Ich bin ein Berliner—*I am a Berliner." On the way home, he made the little side trip to the town of Dunganstown where with high good humor he visited his Irish relatives.

As I followed his trip in the newspapers, my mind kept coming back to those mustard plasters. No, Jackie couldn't go along, but she did manage to make her presence felt *in absentia.*

29 ∾ CHRISTMAS IN JULY

*J*ULY WAS THE MONTH OF BRIGHT PROMISE. Everything seemed so secure, so full of good omens for the future. Jackie was hinting that I would be taking many trips with her from now on. And a new phase of traveling started with a trip to the Cape.

One afternoon early in June, as we worked by her desk in the West Sitting Room, Jackie interrupted her dictation to ask, "Do you suppose you could arrange to come up to the Cape with me this summer? Do you think Ray would let you?"

I told her I felt sure he wouldn't mind, but that we'd have to consider what to do about Chris and Greg. I explained that it might be a bit too strenuous for my mother-in-law to spend full time at our house while I was gone. The only way I thought I might go was if she could agree to my bringing the boys along, too.

"We could solve the baby-sitting problem," I suggested, "by having various members of my family in Boston come over to stay with the boys a week at a time, if you think that's a good idea."

She readily agreed. "Oh, yes, Mary, that would be great. Just arrange it to your convenience. I know that with the baby due, I'll really be needing you."

In less than a minute, the issue was settled.

Yet, looking back to that year, there was something prophetic about how death would creep into the conversation almost lightly, kiddingly.

The morning of July 1st was filled with excitement for Chris and Greg, enjoying their maiden flight on the Presidential jet and accompanied by their neighborhood friend, young Raymond Walsh. Raymond's parents had originally planned this week's vacation with their son at the Cape, anyway, and in a neighborly way consented to stay with Chris and Greg until after the weekend of the Fourth.

A beautiful cottage at West Yarmouth, called "Dun-Roamin'," was rented for us by Mrs. Kennedy for the month of July at $1,000. It was absolutely ideal—clean, attractive, spacious, well-equipped—and located "just a stone's throw" from the water!

One of the White House chauffeurs had been assigned to me for the daily runs to Squaw Island, about a half-hour's drive from the cottage. But after I had familiarized myself sufficiently with the route, I accepted the offer of a car. A white Ford Galaxie was rented and placed at my disposal!

Each day I drove beyond the Kennedy compound at Hyannisport over a long, narrow stretch of road, leading to Squaw Island and the Thun house.

During this first week there, Jackie jovially quipped, "Oh, I could shoot the people who own this house . . . I'd love to buy it, but I know they will never sell it!" And then in her usual way of tending to formalities, she wrote a nice note to the owners, the Louis Thuns of Sinking Springs, Pennsylvania, telling how happily settled she and her family were, and thanking them for the condition in which the house had been left.

Personally, I did not understand Jackie's deep attachment to this house. It was extremely large, lovely, and well furnished, true. But it was located at the very end of the road— a sort of jumping-off place, facing the huge expanse of the ocean.

Jackie apparently thrived on the privacy and seclusion it offered. Yet, as the days went on, I found it stranger and stranger that such a young woman could enjoy such a remote and lonely spot. Her days, for the most part, were spent in her bedroom upstairs and the adjoining closed-in porch, which served as her office. From here, as she dictated, we could feel the strong breezes and hear the lashing of the waves against the rocks.

Surely, I would think to myself as I sat there, the wind and noise must be much more discernible during the stillness of the night. How could she possibly stand it? Almost completely alone she remained in these rooms so far away. At the farther end of the hall, the children and Miss Shaw, bristling with life and activity, were a relief to the stillness. But still she thoroughly enjoyed it.

With the birth of her baby due around the end of August, Jackie rested, dictated, painted, and read. On weekends the President arrived from D.C., bringing his usual air of excitement. Surrounded by aides, friends, and Secret Service Agents, he brought all of Squaw Island "alive."

Stationed at the end of the gravel road, bordering the marshes, was a long trailer that served as the Secret Service Agents' headquarters. And at the opposite end of their working area was an office for Evelyn Lincoln and me. Evelyn would use it on the weekends when she arrived with the President. I, of course, used it the rest of the week.

The steady flow of mail from the White House came by daily courier planes.

Jackie was looking ahead to her social schedule, advising Nancy that she had spoken to someone about commissioning Jerome Robbins to do a special ballet and about having Menotti compose something for the White House.

She requested Nancy to find out what she could about the dates of next winter's State visits, and she suggested as possible entertainers: Fonteyn and Nureyev, Callas and/or Leontyne Price, Lunt and Fontanne.

She followed up a little later telling Nancy that if she hadn't sent Callas a letter, to forget it and ask Price.

Two days later, Nancy called me to say that it was all straightened out. Maria Callas could not come.

In September she and the President would celebrate their tenth wedding anniversary; Jackie was already searching for something unusual as an anniversary present for her husband.

Enlisting the help of General Ted Clifton, Jackie told him that the President had once mentioned he would like some buttons of the Irish Brigade for his blazer. She asked if the regiment called "The Wild Geese" still existed. If it didn't, the General could just get Irish Army buttons.

Two weeks after my arrival, Jackie expressed sheer delight at my being at the Cape to help her. By the end of this first month, she happily announced, "Gosh, Mary, I'll have to have you come every summer with me! I don't know how I've ever managed without you!"

Into these few weeks she also squeezed another matter, which she apparently hoped to settle before entering the hospital. Christmas lists and presents! In July!

One morning, as I entered her cool bedroom with a sweater draped over my shoulders, Jackie asked admiringly, "Mary, where did you buy that pretty sweater?"

"At the Sweater Bar, right here on Route 28," I answered, proudly adding, "... only $8.95!"

"You don't *mean* it!" she gasped.

"It's a wholesale house," I explained. "They have all kinds of sweaters there at discount prices."

"Oh, that's just great!" she exclaimed. "Everyone will get a sweater from me this Christmas!" And she rattled off a list, finishing with the request that I find something in yellow and beige for Caroline.

There were to be a few, however, whom she excluded from the sweater category. For Nurse Maud Shaw, a spacious handbag; for Pam Turnure, a velvet pullover blouse; and for Mr. West, the Chief Usher, a pillow—white with embroidered handwriting on it: "You don't have to be crazy to live here, but it helps!"

Jackie did not fail to put in a bid for herself. She told Evelyn Lincoln and Tom Walsh in the Kennedys' New York office that the only thing she really wanted was so expensive, no one would ever give it to her. A fur bedspread!

She explained that perhaps some members of the family might want to join in to buy it and she was willing to settle for white or grayish-white sheared rabbit or squirrel. But she confessed that what she would really love was fox or chinchilla.

I checked a furrier and relayed cost estimates to Evelyn to show to the President in all these furs—in size 80 by 80 inches:

Rabbit: $350
Squirrel: $750
Blue Fox: $1150
White Fox: $1500
Chinchilla: $4,000
Chinchilla-Dyed Rabbit: $1,000

As the third week in July rolled in, Jackie casually announced that "Caroline would like to have a birthday party for her and her cousins some time around *my* birthday!"

So, planning the occasion for Wednesday, the 24th, I had all of two days for the invitations, refreshments, decorations, entertainment, and presents.

My list was endless:

Call all the mothers—Joan, Ethel, Jean, Eunice, and Pat.

Tell Della Cruz (in the kitchen) to prepare hot dogs and hamburgers for around twenty children.

Ice cream and cake—with lots of surprises in the cake and "Happy Birthday" on it. The movie Caroline wanted most to see was *My Friend Flicka*.

Besides seeing about the movie, I was to pick out dozens of little presents for the children and wrap each one in colored tissue. There were to be two groups of children—those under three years and those over—so appropriate presents were to be bought for each age group.

Jackie made up the list of children's names in categories— those over three years in Caroline's age group, those under three, in John-John's.

(*The Robert Kennedys*)	(*The Stephen Smiths*)	(*The Peter Lawfords*)	(*The Sargent Shrivers*)	(*The Teddy Kennedys*)	(*The John Kennedys*)
Kathleen	Stevie	Christopher	Bobby		Caroline
Joe		Sydney	Maria		
Bobby					
David					

Under 3

Michael	William	Victoria	Timmy	Kara	John
Courtney		Robin		Eddie	
Kerry					

I was to ask the Secret Service Agents to find two large wooden barrels and long bamboo sticks, which were to be used as "fishing poles." Strings were to be attached to the ends of each. And after I'd wrapped the gifts, they were to carry individual name tags and be tied to the ends of the strings.

The "fishing poles" were to go inside the wooden barrels, with the presents hanging over the sides so each child could find his own.

It took much leg work around Hyannis, but the agents finally succeeded in getting the large barrels from some lumber yard.

As I worked on party things in the trailer, I was suddenly

struck with apprehension. Glancing out of the window, I saw Jackie standing in a canoe in the inlet nearby, paddling first on one side and then the other as Caroline and John-John sat enjoying the little ride.

I gasped. "Will one of you men please go out there and get Mrs. Kennedy off that canoe? If she ever tips over, it'll be just too bad ..."

The words were hardly out when Agent Meredith rushed out to make the quick rescue. During these few moments, Jackie had gotten stuck in the mud, and it was obvious she needed some help. Throwing off his shoes, he waded out and soon had Jackie and the children back on dry land.

Caroline and John-John loved this little adventure with their mother, of course, mud and all. In a few minutes, I was completely absorbed again in my world of balloons, barrels, and sea breezes.

Up at the house in that last hour of doing the outdoor decorations, the Secret Service men and I would no sooner have the streamers and balloons prettily fastened in place than a new gust would come along and we'd turn around and find our efforts gone with the wind! So back up again on the stool it was, with more tacks and Scotch tape!

Yet, as wild and frantic as things were, one of the little cousins, with obvious concern, beckoned me to one of the decorated barrels. "Mrs. Gallagher," she said, pointing to the name-card on one of the fishing poles, "you spelled Sydney's name wrong ... it should be 'S-y-d-n-e-y' instead of 'S-i-d-n-e-y.'"

I tried hard to force a smile. "Oh, yes," I agreed, "but you *do* know that it *is* Sydney's fishing pole, right?"

"Oh, yes, ma'am," she smiled back.

"Well, then, I think that's all that *really* matters right now," I managed, leaving her to study my error more closely. There was another drooping streamer to be tended to, so I quickly grabbed the roll of Scotch tape and hurried to it!

I left the children to enjoy their birthday party and returned to the trailer. But not for long. Within minutes, the phone rang. Jackie asked if I would get hold of the local ice cream vendor. "It would be nice if they could have their truck come up to the house, ringing the bells for the children so they could choose their own ice cream."

I proceeded with the two calls involved—one to the vendor and one to the guard at the entrance post to allow the truck to come through. And at 6 o'clock I sighed as the bells cling-clanged merrily away! It had been such an exhausting nine hours I could hardly wait to put my feet up at good ol' "Dun Roamin'." I grabbed my brief case and ran.

For Jackie's birthday on Sunday, July 28th, it was hard to think of some little appropriate gift. After spending the better part of an evening shopping through the Hyannis gift shops, I finally accomplished my mission at "The Little Fan Shop." On a shelf, I spotted a lovely ceramic pitcher—"Parian Ware" —with its figurine designs expressing the love between mother and child. Since Jackie's "big event" was soon due, I knew I needn't look further.

I arranged with Provi to carry the gift in to Jackie on her breakfast tray that Sunday morning, and when I saw Jackie on Monday, she expressed great delight over it. A few mornings later, as she sat up in bed, browsing through one of her art magazines, *The Collectors' Guide*, she spotted the exact replica of the pitcher on the page before her, which delighted her even more.

30 ∾ TRAGEDY IN AUGUST

*J*ACKIE WAS PLEASED WITH ALL HER PLAN-
ning. "We're so caught up, we're even ahead of ourselves,"
she declared happily. She was still busy. She had never been
more concerned with the way things were going at the White
House than during those days before the birth.

Jackie wanted Anne Lincoln to send her the menu for the
Afghanistan dinner before she went to the hospital; she
wanted to start out this year with all menus written so they
could be understood, not in garbled French. She felt that one
should be able to know from reading the menu what each
course was, even if the guest couldn't speak a word of French.
So she decreed that henceforth there would be one key word
in English mixed in with the French—Potatoes Purée; Filet
of Beef; Eggs Clamart; etc. And she told Anne not to let
René talk her out of it. Anne should just invent names if she
had to.

Jackie was still on the warpath concerning the menus for
the children. She wanted copies of them posted on the
kitchen wall in each of the houses they frequented—the
White House, Atoka, Camp David, Palm Beach, Hyannis,
etc. She was annoyed that the various cooks were ignoring
the menus that Miss Shaw had worked out so carefully. What
she wanted most was for the children's menus to work like
clockwork.

And she was on the warpath about something else. She
was distressed that the rugs in the Blue and Green Rooms

were being destroyed by the tourists. She wanted the proper person to be "hawk-eyed" from now on in guarding things. After all, she commented, if the life of the beautiful furnishings was only six months, there really was not much point in restoring the White House.

Jackie's preoccupation with small details helped to keep her busy. Now an ashtray "plate" was bothering her. She wanted the Curator of the White House to know where *every* ashtray was in the rooms where she had placed them.

She turned to personal matters. Jackie was making an appointment for the middle of the month to have her hair straightened by Rose Mary. Then, thinking about her figure after the baby, she wanted me to call Morton Downey and ask him about the reducing machine in his basement, describing it as a vibrator with a big strap. "It was so wonderful last summer," she said. "Tell me the brand name and where he got it." She was interested in getting one like it for the White House gym and asked that I arrange for it through Dr. Travell.

Fall clothes were uppermost in Jackie's mind, and she was working out her post-natal wardrobe with Cassini. She was also having Pam Turnure ask quietly whether Tassell had anything she might like—especially something that she could wear to the baby's christening. She was thinking of a dress-and-jacket theater suit as a first choice.

And then it happened . . .

It was a lovely morning at Squaw Island, the 7th of August. The weather man had predicted another hot day. As I showered, I seriously considered the comforts of a cool slack outfit and Keds as opposed to a dress and heels. A whole day in the trailer, I knew, would certainly be more relaxing and comfortable in slacks. Yet, as if by some kind of feminine intuition, I reached into the closet for a dress—the coolest one at that. Clutching my briefcase, off I went—heels and all!

At 11 o'clock August 7, 1963, Ensign George Dalton received the alarm call at the trailer from Jackie's Secret Service Agent at the Kennedy compound.

He was to sound the alert for the helicopter to take Jackie to Otis Air Force Base. Her baby was arriving ahead of schedule.

George swung into motion with complete precision, well prepared for this moment by the automatic routine of all his advance drills.

His face was almost white. This had come several weeks ahead of schedule! Would everyone at Otis be on duty? I was in the trailer, taking it all in, and I felt there must be something I could do—certainly not sit here, working at figures.

With one quick shuffle, I scooped my ledgers, bills, and pads into a big heap and shoved them into my briefcase, leaving it there for the moment. Then, grabbing my shorthand notebook and pencil, I ran from the trailer, calling to the men, "There just might be some little thing I can do for Mrs. Kennedy before she leaves."

Agent Landis was at the driver's seat in the open convertible, waiting for Mrs. Kennedy and Dr. Walsh to emerge from the house. I went inside and stood in the hallway. Soon Jackie was descending the stairs—very slowly, with Dr. Walsh lending careful support.

She smiled when she saw me; I tried my best to seem calm. "Hi, Jackie," I said, "if there's anything you need, or that I might do . . ."

"Oh, no, thanks, Mary," she said weakly.

Dr. Walsh helped her into the front seat of the car. The motor was running. I couldn't stand to see her going off alone; impulsively I asked, "Would you like me to come along?" Her eyes brightened at the idea, as she said, "Yes, hop in the car!"

I jumped into the back seat with Dr. Walsh and slammed the door—only to find that I couldn't sit down because my skirt had caught in the door jamb. The car was in motion. There was nothing to do but yank at my skirt, which came away with a good tear.

Someone was shouting. It was Dr. Janet Travell, JFK's

physician. Standing at the doorway, she called out, "Mrs. Kennedy, would you like me to call the President?"

"No!" Jackie shouted back firmly.

We arrived at the helicopter grounds about a minute before the craft had touched ground. As we waited in the car, Jackie voiced her first bit of concern. "Dr. Walsh, you've just *got* to get me to the hospital on time! I don't want anything to happen to this baby," she said.

Dr. Walsh literally leaped out of the car and ran around to her side. He stood, patting her hand and assuring her, "We'll have you there in plenty of time."

"This baby mustn't be born dead," Jackie continued to plead.

We boarded the helicopter and took off without delay. When we touched down at nearby Otis Air Force Base, we all got in the waiting ambulance. At the hospital, attendants were on hand at the emergency entrance. Jackie was gently raised onto a rolling cot. She did not lie down, but sat on the edge, smiling bravely. They rolled her through the corridors and within minutes, she was out of sight, on the way directly to the delivery room.

The next hour was excruciatingly long. Several nurses had introduced themselves and proceeded to show me and Agent Landis the layout of the new wing prepared especially for Jackie's use in an event such as this, if there was no time to reach Walter Reed Hospital in Washington.

There was a bedroom for Jackie, as well as a bedroom for the President, should he decide to sleep over. Off each one was a large sitting room.

Off the lounge room on Jackie's side was another bedroom assigned to me, and a "station," at the entrance to the wing, for the Secret Service Agents. There were more bedrooms beyond the President's sitting room, with several offices set up for the President's agents.

A nurse was preparing Mrs. Kennedy's room, and an orderly, filled with rare excitement, washed down the hallway.

I offered to help the nurse make up Jackie's bed. Then I

went out to the orderly, to have him show me the little kitchen conveniently located, between the President's lounge room and the outer offices where I hoped I could find a coffee pot. In case the President did arrive, he'd surely be ready for some.

Then, phoning the agents at the trailer, I asked them to bring the briefcase from my trailer office to the hospital. I kept watching the clock and posted myself beside the phone. In Jackie's sitting room, calls from the family were starting to come through, and I knew they would increase. Close to 1 P.M., the head nurse, Major Waters, came in to tell me the good news.

"Mrs. Kennedy has given birth to a baby boy! Born at 12:52." As far as she knew, they were both doing well, but, she said, it would be a little while before Mrs. Kennedy would be brought down to the bedroom. We double-checked the room.

We were all excited and happy.

Despite Jackie's shout to Dr. Travell about not notifying her husband, word had reached him. The President appeared at the hospital shortly after 1:30 P.M. I was in the outer lounge and suddenly saw him standing at the doorway with his agent, Jerry Behn, directly behind him.

His eyes were wide, eager for information.

I greeted him, shook his hand and said, "Congratulations, Mr. President. I'm happy to announce that you are the father of a new baby boy!"

With a rather wan smile, he said, "Oh, great! Thanks, Mary," and in the next breath, "How's the baby?"

He startled me by not asking for his wife first. "Oh, the last report was that he and Jackie are both doing well," I said. "I'm sure he's just fine."

Then he asked, "Where's Jackie right now?" I told him that she hadn't come back from the delivery room yet. At that, he took off like a flash for someone to lead him to her.

I wondered why he was so worried about the baby. I tried to erase the President's fearful expression from my mind. It was just too much to have such worrisome thoughts. After all, he *is* the President, I thought, and the very best medical care was certainly available to *him*.

Later, as Jackie lay in her room, the President waited in the adjoining sitting room until she should awaken and he would be permitted to see her. His sister, Jean Smith, had arrived at the hospital by this time and waited with him.

They talked casually, touching on their family's history in childbirth—problems, and complications that the various women had experienced during their pregnancies and deliveries. Almost as though they were trying to pinpoint and understand Jackie's troublesome births.

I did not participate in the discussion, but neither could I avoid their conversation completely. As I completed another phone call, the President called out to me, "Say, there, Mary, you've had some babies. You must know something about all this. What do you think? Did you have any problems?"

"Well, Mr. President," I replied, "I'm not sure that I can really tell you anything. If you'll think back, you might remember that you kept me so busy when I was expecting my first I didn't have time to think about anything but getting to the hospital in time. And then, before I knew it, I was right back on my feet again, taking care of the baby."

This, I'm sure, hadn't offered him any information, but at least I had made him smile a little.

As the afternoon wore on, it became apparent that the baby Patrick Bouvier Kennedy was suffering from a serious respiratory problem, involving the hyaline membrane.

The President conferred with Dr. Walsh and the other doctors at the hospital. Calls were placed to the Children's Hospital in Boston.

One of the messages I took on the phone for the President was that "Dr. Clement Smith is presently in South America, but he never leaves his department uncovered. He trained all these people all over the country in the care of newborn. Dr. James E. Drorbaugh is an excellent man."

Soon, arrangements were made for Patrick's transfer to

the Children's Hospital at Boston. I watched as he was wheeled along the hallway in an enclosed incubator. He lay on his back, almost motionless. I could see how tiny he was, the name circlet on his wrist barely holding on. His hair was dark, his features well formed.

It was a very sad, shocking moment for all of us at the hospital to know how sick the baby was, and from that moment our cheerfulness was forced. Telegrams began to pour in. The phones continued to ring. My briefcase had arrived, and I was completely occupied, a blessing in itself.

In the evening, nurse Louella Hennessey arrived to be with Jackie—the very best start, I felt, for Jackie's recuperation.

At 6 P.M., Louella informed me that Jackie wanted to see me. I was happy to see her looking so well and, with a warm hug, congratulated her on their new son. She seemed unaware how ill the baby was, and I didn't mention it.

She had a few things on her mind, mostly little items for Provi to get together at the house to be sent over when the President came to visit.

I slept at the hospital. By 10 A.M. JBK was again ready for me. She still seemed to know nothing about the situation, and was already delving into a small variety of things in normal fashion!

She wanted the previous night's *Journal-American, World Telegram, Newsweek, Evening Star*. She wanted a hair appointment with Kenneth. "Leave open Tuesday, 13th—will let him know Monday." She wanted me to pick up Revlon lipsticks—Nearly Peach, Strawberry White Pale.

She asked that I check whether Nancy had received her message of the day before that she wanted ballet for the night they entertained Haile Selassie at the White House.

Further, regarding the Afghanistan dinner, she wanted me to tell Nancy that the President did not think the fireworks and military parade were a good idea.

It was a terribly long day. The President had visited Patrick in Boston in the morning, returned to Jackie's side during the day, then flown back to Boston at night.

He stayed at the Ritz-Carlton Hotel to be near the baby, whose condition still remained uncertain. I returned to the cottage for the night and packed a suitcase to stay the rest of Jackie's time in the hospital right there with her.

I had been in the same torn yellow dress for two days and suddenly thought how fortunate my choice had been the day before when, for those few moments, I had pondered over a "cool, slack outfit" for the day.

On August 9th, my phone rang at 5:30 A.M. It was Secret Service Agent Wells informing me of Patrick's death. It was just too unbelievable.

By 7 o'clock, I was back at the hospital, going through the back door to avoid the press out front.

Jackie had been told the sad news by Dr. Walsh that morning. When word reached us that the President was on his way from Boston (he had been at the Children's Hospital during Patrick's last crucial hours that morning), Miss Hennessey and I helped to prepare Jackie for his visit.

She had been crying but, with some freshening up and some encouraging words, she was propped up comfortably with pillows and looked as presentable as possible under such trying circumstances.

The President arrived with his brother Robert. Other members of the family were arriving—the Kennedys and the Auchinclosses, as well as Evelyn, Nancy, Pam, and Dr. Travell. By evening, a very depressed group filled the sitting room.

There was very little conversation. I recall that Jamie Auchincloss, Jackie's young half-brother, speaking to his father, kept wondering why such a terrible thing had to happen to Jackie. Mr. Auchincloss in his usual quiet and reserved manner tried to console him. It was obvious that Jamie was simply voicing the question that everyone pondered: *Why* did it have to happen?

August 12, 1963: JBK pulling herself together. Thinking of an anniversary present for JFK, she told me: "Get in touch with Tiffany's. If they don't have it, either Cartier or Charles Ernest."

She wanted a St. Christopher medal that could be used as a money clip. It was to be about the size of a silver dollar, gold-dipped, with a plain back for engraving (she drew a picture of what she meant). And she wanted price estimates.

I was also to arrange to have sent to the hospital from the White House 25 Guide Books, 10 White House etchings with mats, 10 photos taken of her and the President during their trip to Mexico. Jackie asked that I obtain a list of names of the doctors and nurses who had helped her. The mementoes were to be given by her and the President before her release from the hospital on Wednesday, and I was asked to do the gift-wrapping.

> August 13, 1963: When I went into her bedroom at noon, Jackie greeted me with: "Sweet Mary . . . you've been staying right here with me every minute! Dr. Travell has told me all about you. She just worships you!"

Later in the day, I checked with Jackie about my return to Washington. Only two weeks remained now for getting the boys prepared for school, and I needed time for shopping. But she quickly responded, "Oh, no, Mary, please stay as *long* as you can." I promised her another week.

I stayed but sent the boys home on the White House shuttle plane with Evelyn Lincoln and Mrs. Frank White, a friend who had taken care of them over the past week. At Jackie's suggestion, I was happy to have Louella Hennessey share the cottage with me.

Jackie left the hospital for Squaw Island on the 14th.

When I saw that she was comfortably settled in the spacious sunroom and I was sure she no longer needed me, I hurried down to the trailer to straighten up the desk that I had left in such disarray.

I awoke the next morning sick from exhaustion and got up to answer a telephone call from Dr. Travell. When I told her

I felt faint, she ordered me right back to bed. In less than ten minutes, Dr. Walsh stopped by on his way to see Jackie.

Suddenly I broke down with the tears that had been pent up inside since the tragedy struck. Dr. Walsh was most comforting and handed me a little red pill, saying it would relieve the nervous tension.

Later Jackie called, very concerned over my not feeling well, and insisted I just rest and not worry about anything. "You've lost so much weight, you'll be able to slide through the eye of a needle!" she said, adding that she was sending Miss Hennessey to me. And by afternoon, Dr. Travell had also come by and given me a thorough massage over my shoulders, neck, and back. When I awoke, I was a new person!

I reported to Squaw Island after a restful weekend and was happy to find Jackie making excellent progress.

She expressed further concern over my health and said, "Everyone is entitled to be sick. But, Mary, if anything ever happened to you, I would be sunk! Take vitamins, B$_{12}$ shots, Equanol, and nap every day at the White House. Go to one of the guestrooms."

Meanwhile, there was the weekend's accumulation of notes jotted to herself, from which she soon poured forth a stream of dictation.

Everything was back to normal!

31 ～ THE GRECIAN ISLES

*J*ACKIE CAME UP WITH A NEW IDEA—THE building of just one more home! It was to be a summer home on Squaw Island, built along the lines of the Thun house, her favorite of them all. The President was to find out for her who owned the marshlands near the Thun property. Meanwhile she was having measurements taken of all the Thun house rooms, from sun porch to movie projection room. Captain Stoughton was requested to photograph the house from the driveway, from the sea, from each side, and to get shots of the wings that sloped back.

It was while the Atoka house in Virginia was being built that Jackie became interested in the land deal at Squaw Island. The President and his brother Edward Kennedy and Morton Downey planned to buy the property and divide the price three ways. There was an old windmill that she particularly liked and wanted to be close to.

As I recall, the asking price for the Squaw Island property was something like $100,000. Jackie said it was absurd, considering the additional cost of landscaping. Eventually the deal fell through.

Jackie was also now showing great concern for the comfort of the President. She asked Dr. Travell to do something about the President's reading lights in his bedrooms at Atoka and at the White House, his chair in the West Sitting Room, his chairs in his office, both by the desk and the rocker by his sofa, and the Cabinet Room and his bathroom. She said that the President read just about everywhere, and his eyes were "giving out."

Jackie called for a complete revamping of the lighting facilities, with the stipulation that there be no goose-necked "monstrosities" in the living rooms. Jackie said she cared about having pretty lamps there and suggested that Dr. Travell confine herself to the proper height of the lamps.

By Labor Day weekend I felt the need of a few days in the mountains. Ray, Chris, Greg, and I enjoyed our favorite resort at Orkney Springs, Virginia. While there, we discussed the boys' return to school the following Tuesday. Greg piped up with: "If I'm the smartest boy in school in every grade, can I be President of the United States when I grow up?" The Presidency seemed entirely familiar to him even though he was just entering the first grade!

During the following weeks, Jackie continued to call from the Cape, then from Newport, with daily messages and dictation.

September 12th was Jackie's and the President's tenth wedding anniversary, and I sent a note of congratulations by courier mail.

Dear Jackie:

Just a little note on this important day to express my most sincere good wishes to you and the President for A Very Happy Anniversary!

Would like to add, too, that the same "lucky feeling" is with me today as it was ten years ago—when I attended the most beautiful feeling in my lifetime!

Today, however, in retrospect, I realize that this feeling is so much stronger only because you both have given me the greatest treasure of a lifetime—my association with you—for which, I humbly express my deepest gratitude.

God Bless you and your precious family, always.

Mary G.

September 12, 1963

Several days later, Jackie returned a large envelope, containing all congratulatory messages, including mine, for filing. She had written on the outside of my letter that it was the best letter she ever had!

I spent most of September 21st wrapping Christmas presents for Jackie—for family, friends, and White House staff—with gift cards that I wrote for her.

Two days later, she arrived back in Washington, coming up to my office and greeting me with a big smile and warm embrace. I braced myself for the new onslaught of work—a combination of matters she had brought back with her, as well as the inevitable details in connection with her trip to Greece the following week.

To help her recuperate after the loss of her baby, the President was sending her on a Mediterranean cruise with Lee and Stash aboard the *Christina*, Aristotle Onassis's yacht. Also aboard the luxurious yacht would be Mr. and Mrs. Franklin D. Roosevelt, Jr.

When the word got out that Jackie was making this trip, our table at the Staff Mess was rife with rumor that I was going with her. I kept assuring everyone that Jackie had not said a word to me about my going, but Dr. Travell and Homer Gruenther insisted that she must be planning for me to go. Before I knew it, arrangements were made for me to be at the Main Navy Dispensary for a yellow fever shot, to be followed by a vaccination for smallpox.

> September 24, 1963: Treaty Room table just heaped with work! At 12:00 noon, JBK and I settled down to it. Caroline joined us, coming in on all fours, like a horse, John-John, marching in like a soldier!

As his mother dictated, John-John continued to parade around, shouting out "Hi, Mary" over and over! When Jackie reached over to grab him for a hug, he struggled to get away, his little feet drumming to his own rhythm.

Jackie asked, "Do your boys like to be kissed?" I told her I thought all boys were pretty much alike, but that I managed quite successfully "at night when they're fast asleep. I kiss them under the neck where it's nice and warm!"

294 ठॐ

October started with a little family incident that showed who was boss of the family. It was the day of her departure for Greece. Mr. Kenneth arrived from New York to do Jackie's hair. At noon, she was to accompany JFK to Union Station to greet Haile Selassie, the Emperor of Ethiopia. Just before leaving the White House, the President came up to the living quarters from his office to see if Jackie was ready. By this time, Kenneth had finished with her hairdo and was in the sitting room on the third floor.

Soon my phone was ringing. "Mees Gallaga," Provi cried, "ees Meestaire Kenneth up there?" When I said he was, Provi asked that he return to the second floor, "right away!"

What was up, I wondered?

A half-hour later, Provi came upstairs, breathing a sigh of relief that her "Lady" had left. "Oh, Mees Gallaga," she said, rather amused, "you should 'ave been downstairs when the Presiden' see Mees Kennedee's hair..." Apparently the President had taken one look at Jackie's new hairstyle and decided that it was too sophisticated for the occasion. He asked Kenneth to change it—with what sounded like one of his natural quips, "What are you trying to do...ruin my career?"

The hat, apparently, was also not quite right either, and he asked Provi to go upstairs and find another.

That night Jackie left for the Mediterranean. As guests were arriving at the White House for the evening's reception, she slipped out by the "back door."

Little did I realize that three nights later, while she was somewhere across the Atlantic, I would be in bed with a severe reaction from that smallpox vaccination. Dr. Travell later said it was an "accelerated take."

October 4, 1963: 6:00 P.M.—My car was waiting on the South Grounds. Before getting in, I wished a nice week to Miss Shaw and the children, who were getting ready to leave for Camp David.

Seating myself in the car, I was giving a last wave to the

children when John-John called out: "I want to give you a `kiss!" I asked the driver to hold up for just a minute . . . John-John was making his run over to the car, took a little spill to the ground, got up, brushed himself off, finishing up with not only a kiss, but a big, tight hug, too!

Caroline was standing back rather shyly, looking as though she might have wanted to come over too . . . but, not wishing to press her, I simply "blew a smiling kiss" to her—she waved and blew a kiss back to me.

It was on October 10th, during the Rose Garden ceremonies for astronauts, that Mr. Gruenther introduced me as Jackie's secretary to John Glenn. He quickly asked, "Why aren't you in Greece with Mrs. Kennedy?"

I smiled back, saying, "Oh, I doubt Mrs. Kennedy will be needing me *this* trip—it's strictly pleasure, you know." There was no need to tell him that my left arm was still throbbing from my vaccination.

October 15, 1963: 11:30 A.M.—Watched Welcoming Ceremonies on South Grounds for President of Ireland, De Valera, from Treaty Room window.

I noticed once more, as I had on his birthday, that there were new vibrant reddish highlights in the Chief's hair.

That's what was going on at the White House. But, in my mind's eye, I followed Jackie as she went aboard the fabulous ship *Christina* while all the ships in the harbor raised their flags in her honor.

It was, from all I could gather, a fantastic experience for Jackie, who not only loved the sea with a passion, but loved ancient artifacts. This trip combined both. She went "barefoot and windblown" in a speedboat to take a closer look at the coastline of the island of Lesbos. I was not surprised to read that even though she seemed as carefree as a beachcomber, there were not one but *two* hairdressers on board ship to take care of the ladies' hairdos.

296 ह▪ॐ

Of course I was interested when I read in a UPI account that Jackie "was accompanied by Onassis, one Secret Service man and two women who were not identified," when she went down the gangplank and into a car waiting to take them to the Palace of Minos. The story went on to say that her particular interest there was "the Queen's apartment, where she admired the ruins of the ancient boudoir, bathroom, bedroom and vials in which the Queen used to keep her perfume."

I could believe, too, that her interest was genuine when she admired some 3,000-year-old jewelry—bracelets, necklaces and earrings. And she was impressed with a wine jug shaped like a bull's head.

I know that the Greek influence was felt in the jewelry that she became interested in after her previous Greek visit. She had taken a liking to things with figures on them, such as serpents and rams' heads.

I recall that when she got back, she asked me to record Onassis's winter address in my address book—on avenue Foch in Paris—and also his address in Athens on Vasileous Georgious-Glyfada. I mailed a letter to his Athens address.

Among my bits and pieces of notes to myself from White House days, I see one dated "10/18/63" that says, "Big cigarette box—Mr. Onassis," and under it is the name, "Nomikos." (But what the latter name means, I do not know.) There were so many letters and thank-you notes after every trip. In fact, the same slip also lists King of Morocco—box, baby son—goblet, baby daughter—picture frame.

Knowing how important lovely cigarette boxes were to Jackie, I assume that she gave a cigarette box as a thank-you present to Onassis and the other gifts to the King's family.

The following month, I gave Provi a message to send to Atoka, one Greek rug for the President's room as well as two other large rugs that had also come from Greece.

But even before the trip to Greece, Jackie wanted Evelyn Lincoln to tell the President to bring up with him the model whaling ships given to him by Onassis. We were up at the Cape at the time, and the President was coming for the weekend. I was also to tell Evelyn to remind the President to write Onassis and thank him for the models.

As fate would have it, I did see Onassis once at the White House. He was among the many Kennedy friends who stopped by to comfort Jackie during the weekend of John F. Kennedy's funeral. I was in the sitting room of the family quarters, talking with Provi, when I looked up and saw Mrs. Kennedy walking down the Center Hall on the arm of a gentleman whom I did not recognize at the time.

I asked Provi, "Who is that?"

Provi seemed rather surprised that I didn't already know. "Oh, Mees Gallaga, that's Onassee, the millionaire," she said softly. "You mean you don't *know* Meester Onassee?"

To me, he was just a name. With two addresses.

On Jackie's return, I remember, I called Nancy at Jackie's request to get a list of all the people to whom thank-you notes should be written in Morocco. I told Nancy, "She will write to the Ambassador, to the members of the Royal Family and others, including the Minister of Education, Bel Abbes, and other government officials—the Governor of Marrakech, police, and so forth. Mrs. Kennedy wants you to see that those letters go out soon."

I recall being so impressed with Jackie's wonderfully clever expressions she could dream up in a thank-you note—this one to the American Ambassador Ferguson in Morocco, enclosing pictures of an evening at the home of Moulay Abdullah, the younger brother of King Hassan II.

After thanking the Ambassador for all he had done to make her visit to Morocco such a fascinating trip, Jackie paid him a supreme compliment by saying that he was the only Ambassador able to maintain great dignity as he danced the Berber dances.

I see by my diary that an important foreign visitor arrived on the same day that Jackie returned.

October 17, 1963: President Tito of Yugoslavia receives welcoming ceremonies on South Grounds. John-John was out on the Truman Balcony.

I recall, upon hearing his chatter out there as I passed through the Center Hall, how I thought I'd better try to hush him up a bit to avoid his attracting attention from down below and having his parents find his picture, along with his antics, in print that evening! Again, he was in his "marching mood," accompanying himself with vocal sounds as he pranced along. He obediently settled down when I whispered into his ear.

That evening Jackie returned from Greece and was soon planning a fun weekend for the children.

She wanted me to check whether Paul Fout had stocked the pond at Atoka with fish—big fish. She asked that he have someone get three fishing rods.

About a week before Hallowe'en, Pat Haas, a Georgetown friend of Jackie's, called, wondering if Jackie and the children would like to go trick-or-treating.

The last entry for our last happy month reads:

October 30, 1963: As JBK dictated in Treaty Room this A.M., John-John busied himself at table, scooping out the insides of a pumpkin on a tray, eating plain slice of bread as he worked away! VERY BUSY DAY!
 Oh, to be young again ... TRICK OR TREAT!

32 ~ THOSE LAST NOVEMBER DAYS

NOVEMBER, 1963, STARTED OUT ON A BAD note. There was talk around the White House about the President's not liking Atoka. When he finally spent his first weekend there, he found a few flaws in the house—lack of closet space, and especially, he had minded the inconvenience of giving up his bedroom to overnight guests.

The help was also muttering about Jackie's bad mood at Atoka that weekend. I wondered a little whether those exotic Mogul miniatures, hanging on the dining-room wall, had anything to do with the President's displeasure. Perhaps they did because Jackie described her dining room in the country humorously as looking something like a harem. She said it seemed to make the President a little uncomfortable but that after all everyone had his own way of showing his collection.

Soon there was some talk of enlarging the house. I groaned as I thought of the work it would involve.

Mary Kosak, my best friend, was lunching with me at the Staff Mess the day Jackie was due back from her weekend at Atoka with the President, early in November. The telephone was carried to my table. It was Jackie.

Before leaving Atoka, she wanted to "get several things off of my mind" and rattled off twenty minutes of dictation. Mary watched with fascination as I scribbled the hieroglyphics in the pages of my notebook. When I finished, she expressed surprise that Jackie hadn't waited to do all this when she returned that afternoon.

"Well," I explained, "when Mrs. Kennedy has something on her mind she calls."

As these November days passed, I noted that Jackie was giving me more and more of the duties previously handled by the Social Office. Among other things, she asked, "Would you arrange for both birthday parties for the children? John's at the White House, November 26th, and Caroline's at the Cape, November 29th."

In November also, the safety of the President at Atoka was causing a problem.

> November 7, 1963: General Clifton's office concerned re small aircraft for Atoka. Cannot get appropriate one for this week-end, but will definitely have something available for next week-end.
>
> Also, about safety in landing . . . location of a certain tree in the pasture, which he feels should be removed.

In November, too, Jackie asked Evelyn to remind the President that he wanted to give citations to Leonard Carmichael, retiring from the Smithsonian, and to David Findley, retiring as head of her Fine Arts Commission. She suggested that the President give one also to Conrad Wirth, head of the Park Service, who she felt had made possible the redoing of the White House grounds. And she suggested that he ought to do it all before the end of the year, if possible.

Around this time, another incident occurred. Jackie became a bit upset because a "dreary plate" of petit fours was served when she was having a few friends to the White House for tea. So Jackie had called the kitchen for some sandwiches to be served and was mortified when they turned out to be big, beefy ones—with pickles. From now on, she said, she wanted a tea table set with tablecloth and tea service. And a variety of dainty things to eat.

Innocent words spoken then seemed eerie afterwards.

It is eerie now, as I look back, to remember Jackie's admonition then—that the staff in the future "when we are no longer here" should be trained to serve as nice a tea at the White House as they did State dinners.

Again, there was another incident, which also seems eerie on looking back. It concerned Jackie's interest in finding additional quarters to serve as guestrooms for White House guests. She had been shown through nearby Blair House with Mrs. Duke, wife of the Chief of Protocol, and had been told by someone from General Services that no funds were available at the time to fix up the needed corner house next to Blair House, explaining that it would have to wait until a nearby office building was built.

My diary records her words, "I am sure we will probably all be dead by then."

Then November brought a thrill of a lifetime:

November 9, 1963: Ray and I received today our very first invitation to a Social Function at W.H.—Judicial Reception —Nov. 20, 1963!

And after dictation, several days later, Jackie concluded with, "Mary, I hope you'll stay to see the Black Watch! Why don't you arrange to have Ray and your boys come over so they can see it, too." We sat in the bleachers on the South Lawn with a perfect view of the stirring performance of bagpipers.

In November, there were plans for a different kind of animal stable. On the 12th Paul Fout was promising that he could have a deer paddock finished by the weekend, if he went to work immediately on it.

November was also the month John-John learned a rhyme and was fascinated with it. One diary entry touches me deeply, telling about John-John's morning visit to my office on the 14th. At 9 o'clock, he began his little performance with a rather staunch "march—like a soldier!"

302 ॐ

Then he posted himself by my desk, reciting the poem I had been teaching him for the past week. He knew the opening line, "There was a little turtle," enough to tell me that he was ready with his emphatic one-word responses after each line.

I took my cue:

There was a little	TUR-TLE
And he lived in a	BOX
He swam in the	PUD-DOWS (puddles)
And he climbed on the	WOCKS (rocks)
He snapped at the	MO-KEE-TO (mosquito)
He snapped at the	FWEE (flea)
He snapped at the	MIN-NOW
And he snapped at	ME!
He caught the	MO-KEE-TO
He caught the	FWEE
He caught the	MIN-NOW
But he *didn't* catch	ME-E-E-E-E!

Always, all the excitement within him would burst forth with his last shriek of "ME!" And, as usual, his next request was for "One more time!"

That same afternoon, as I clicked madly away on the typewriter, Jackie asked me to go to Texas with her.

November 14, 1963: 2:15 P.M.—JBK called me on phone from family quarters, asking out of the blue, "How would you like to go to Texas with me?" Explained it would "just be for two days—please check with Ray and let me know..."

I made a mental note to talk it over with Ray that evening and continued with the business at hand.

Jackie was busy with so many details on this particular day! She ordered two more lamps—little green ones—the same model as a yellow one she had bought the previous spring at the Little Fan Shop in New York.

She asked me to send Caroline's baby pillows to Atoka.

She said she didn't want the new chandelier installed in the dining room at Atoka and asked for a $350 refund. But if she couldn't get the refund, she said she would keep the chandelier.

She turned down an invitation from a museum head to look at his art collection on Thanksgiving weekend, as it conflicted with their family gathering.

And, in this never-to-be-forgotten month, Jackie was finally getting around to redecorating the President's office. She was going to surprise her husband with how beautiful and colorful his office could be. She was getting rid of his "tired" green rug and the green walls that had not been changed since the Eisenhower Administration. In their place would be Jackie's favorite white walls and a bright red "cheerful" rug. Then, there would be a comfortable grouping of chairs and sofas at the fireplace, where the President loved to sit with his guests.

The upholsterers, painters, and houseboys were going to work furiously while the President was in Texas and have it ready for his return.

The days before any of Jackie's trips inevitably turned out to be hectic and tiring for all of us—with the minutest details to cope with! I rather enjoyed the busy moments of this particular day because of the adventure that lay ahead.

As Provi was not going to Dallas, I watched her pack the various ensembles Jackie would wear those two days and proceeded to type lists of what would be worn at various functions.

Scotch-taped to each piece of luggage was the list of costumes inside and the itinerary of events involved. The carbon copies of these lists I kept tucked into my handbag for quick reference on arriving at various destinations.

Provi was always most methodicial in her packing, but, as she kept adding to each suitcase, I was finally compelled to remind her that Mrs. Kennedy expected to be away for only two days—not two weeks.

Provi, however, had learned from past experience that to pack too much was better than to pack too little. Despite my pleas, she went right on, explaining she was "playing it safe."

All day I was concerned—would Jackie appear at the Judicial Reception that night? I had waited so long for the chance to see her descend the grand staircase, as I had imagined it so many times. But, just a few hours earlier, she had seemed out of sorts, not at all excited by the prospect of the evening ahead, for which I had built up such great enthusiasm.

I wondered, as I dressed, what special dress Jackie might wear if, in the end, she did decide to go. I was, of course, wearing my most special evening dress—black sequined bodice, white satin bell-shaped skirt with red velvet sash.

By 6:30 P.M., Ray and I were back at the White House, parking our car on East Executive Avenue. As we hurried through the East Gate, invitation in hand, Ray made a prophetic statement that did not hit us until later.

"We'd better frame this invitation," he said. "It might be the first and last we'll ever get."

I was surprised, as we handed our wraps to the attendants, to notice that the white maids' uniforms worn in the daytime for regular duties had now been exchanged for black, more formal, uniforms—black with a perky white apron.

With other guests, we walked up the stairs to the official entertainment rooms, first to the East Room, stopping to talk with friends along the way.

The butlers were stationed by the buffet table; the Marine orchestra played background music. Among the guests, we talked with Postmaster General John Gronouski. I introduced Ray to General Ted Clifton and General Godfrey McHugh, two of the President's military aides.

As the time for the President's appearance drew near, there was a noticeable air of expectation. We soon made our way into the hallway to await the arrival of the President and— I hoped—Jackie.

Suddenly, there he was. And just as suddenly, the first strains of "Hail to the Chief." Jackie was directly behind him. They made such a beautiful picture as they came down the stairway.

If there was any disappointment on my part, it was that, of all the lovely dresses Jackie owned, she did not appear in any I would have expected. Instead, she had chosen a suit—a burgundy red velvet, over a little blouse, with a strand of pearls.

At this moment, we were standing with Evelyn Lincoln, who had come directly to the reception from her office in the West Wing, and with Jackie's doctor and his wife, Dr. and Mrs. John Walsh. We watched as the President and First Lady slowly made their way to the East Room, shaking hands and mingling with the guests.

Ray and I were satisfied now; we had seen the grand entrance. We proceeded to the State Dining Room where cocktails and refreshments were served. The rooms were very crowded, but the President and Mrs. Kennedy made their way from one to another—the Green, the Blue, the Red, shaking hands, and, suddenly, they were beside us.

The President held out his hand to Ray and held it for a few seconds while he groped for the name that went with the face. He hadn't seen Ray since Georgetown. For once, his fantastic memory for names suffered a slight lapse. But only for seconds. Seeing me standing beside Ray, he grinned even more broadly and immediately came through: "How are you, Ray? Nice to see you again . . ."

Jackie was shaking so many hands in the other direction that we never did meet face to face that night.

The President and Jackie were soon on their way out of the dining room and into the elevator to go upstairs.

A cherished memento I have of this occasion is the picture taken by Cecil Stoughton, which shows the President shaking hands with U.S. Marshal Jim McShane, with Ray and me in the group of onlookers.

Now the mood changed. The orchestra struck up, playing dance music in the East Room. Since the President had gone, there was a sudden relaxation, though many hoped that he and the First Lady had stayed to dance, too.

We danced and danced in the beautiful room—and somehow, I don't know why, a little thought kept creeping in. Will they play the President's favorite, "Bill Bailey"?

But they didn't...

PART FOUR

FAREWELL TO THE CHIEF

33 ∽ WE ALL VISIT DALLAS

*T*HIS WAS MY FIRST "CAMPAIGN TRIP" WITH the Kennedys. Though it was a new experience for me, I did not lack confidence—as long as I kept a shorthand notebook and pencil close at hand.

The White House chauffeur, the morning of November 21st, had me out to Andrews Air Force Base with minutes to spare before the President's and Jackie's arrival by helicopter from the White House. Take-off time was 11 A.M. sharp. I was still in a happy glow over the Judicial Reception at the White House the night before.

When I boarded Air Force One, I caught sight of Evelyn Lincoln, and sat beside her. Instinctively, I found myself carrying out the order Jackie had given me that I "stick close to Mrs. Lincoln as though you are going along as her assistant. If anyone asks you your name, you can say, 'Mrs. Barelli.'"

To ask me to use my maiden name did not, of course, strike me as a strange request, coming as it did from Jackie, who still preferred that I remain incognito. After the entourage had boarded, JFK and Jackie boarded. She went to the private compartment, while the President mingled with the group.

As we climbed rapidly toward the sky, I felt a sense of well-being. Here I was, sitting next to one of my dearest friends, who was just as delighted to have me for company on the trip as I was her—Evelyn, of course. We had known each other so long, and it was our first trip together, she for JFK and I for Jackie, and we relished these first few hours when we could enjoy relaxing away from our desks and telephones.

At 1:30 P.M. we were scheduled to arrive in San Antonio, where the President would dedicate the Aero Space Medical Health Center. Shortly before landing, the steward approached me with the message that Jackie would like to see me in her private compartment at the rear of the plane. I went quickly, clutching my notebook. But, as it turned out, her call was not for dictation. Rather, she asked that I "help fasten the back of my dress" and, as I did, she expressed concern about the weather, which now appeared to have turned much warmer than earlier predictions. Jackie asked, "Do you think I will need a coat?" I thought she would be comfortable just as she was—without a coat—and she seemed grateful to have this little problem resolved.

We also concluded that her mink hat would be much too warm. So she asked if I would please remove the grip-comb from it and transfer it to the band of another hat, which she felt would be more suitable. Fortunately, the plane was equipped with even the tiniest conveniences—and, in a matter of seconds, I was furnished a navy blue sewing kit. The job was soon done.

Later, I was in Jackie's bedroom with her when there was a knock at the door, and she asked me to see who was there. As I reached the door, it was opened by JFK, who poked his head through the opening as he held onto the knob. Jackie was in the adjoining alcove, brushing away at her hair and, when I told her that it was the President, she called out, "Yes, Jack, what is it?"

He stood where he was, calling back, "Oh, Jackie, just thought I'd check to see if you were all right."

Pressed for time, her hairbrush in mid-air, she answered impatiently, "Yes, Jack, I'm just fine. Now will you just go 'way?" He closed the door and left.

We were only minutes away from landing now—with just enough time for me to get back to my seat and get strapped

312

in. When we touched ground, President and Mrs. Kennedy were the first to descend the stairs.

Months afterward, the little sewing kit managed to reappear among my personal effects—and only then did I realize that, in the rush of things, I had carried it off the plane with me. It remains with me as a reminder of those hectic and historic moments.

With great precision, a motorcade was soon formed. The first four or five cars were filled with the Presidential party, aides, Secret Service Agents, and the press. Evelyn and I and others were assigned to the "VIP bus," which followed.

It was a lovely afternoon, and as we waved from the open windows in acknowledgment to the waves and cheers of people along the way, we were greatly heartened by their boundless enthusiasm. There was no doubt in our minds that the Texans were happy and proud to have the Kennedys visiting their state.

After the dedication of the Aero Space Medical Health Center, which the President performed with his usual ease and grace, the motorcade departed for Kelly Air Force Base, where we re-boarded for the 45-minute flight to the Houston International Airport.

In Houston, a motorcade took us through the city to the Rice Hotel, arriving around 5 P.M. Because of the huge crowds here, it took much maneuvering before Evelyn and I could make our way inside and up to our rooms. At this point, I was thinking of a quick shower, change of clothes, and something to eat—I was beginning to feel the strain of activity and excitement.

But, instead, my first obligation was to tend to Jackie. She was scheduled to join the President at a dinner at the Coliseum in honor of Congressman Albert Thomas, and I was to see that her clothes were ready. "See to it that I'm ready about fifteen to twenty minutes ahead of time," she had told me before we left.

I inquired about the Presidential Suite, and there I found

George Thomas carrying on with his duties. The President and Jackie had already retired to their adjoining bedrooms, and George relayed a message to me to call Mrs. Kennedy from her nap at 7:15 P.M.

The door to the President's bedroom remained open, and I saw that he was still busy, talking with Kenny O'Donnell and taking phone calls. He appeared to be in general good humor.

At the appointed time, I awakened Jackie with a few quiet words, put out her clothing and jewelry for the evening, and told her about the telephone messages that had come in for her.

Pam had several questions from the press. And there were other questions, concerning Jackie's speech, which was to be in Spanish.

The hotel's hairdresser also called, offering to come up to fix her hair. But Jackie declined the offer with thanks, saying that she felt she could manage it herself. She dictated answers to Pam and continued with a few fresh notes to me. As she looked into the mirror, combing her hair, she happily exclaimed, "Gosh, Mary, you've been such a great help. You'll just have to plan to do a lot of campaigning next year!" This I found wonderfully reassuring—I had passed the first day's test!

Soon, Jackie was completely ready, looking lovely in her black velvet dress, pearls, diamond bracelet and earrings, and black satin shoes and evening bag. As I checked her from head to toe, I glanced at my watch and had reason to be even more proud. She was ready ahead of time!

President Kennedy came in to join her. In what turned out to be the last piece of business for the day, she asked him what he would like to have for lunch on Sunday, when Ambassador Lodge would be up at the Cape with them.

The President said he would like "some nice quail," and Jackie immediately came up with a menu built around it, which she asked me to pass on to Anne Lincoln.

Crab Meat Mousse—in a ring—with sauce
Casserole of Quail
Wild Rice
Green Vegetable—purée of peas—or other
Currant Jelly
Something light for dessert—can't think of anything, but
  have something nice

She went on further to say there would be five people for lunch, asking that the Secret Service Agent, Mr. Rodham, on duty at their Virginia home "get enough quail in Virginia."

Before leaving the hotel for the Coliseum, the President called Vice President and Mrs. Johnson to invite them to the suite for a few moments. Knowing I wouldn't be needed, and to give the two couples a little privacy, I stepped out into the outside corridor and joined the Secret Service Agents who were posted there.

From the elevator came the Vice President, followed by Mrs. Johnson—and, as they walked by me, I found myself trying to imagine their feelings at being in the Number 2 spot, following the commands and wishes of a much younger President and First Lady.

From where I stood in the hall, it was quite obvious that excitement had spread throughout the hotel. In the corridor now, almost as if on cue, a group of maids and other employees suddenly appeared and lined the walls, waiting for a glimpse of the Presidential party.

Their hopes were more than fulfilled, too, when, finally, as President Kennedy came forward, he graciously responded to their smiles with a warm and friendly handshake for each! Jackie followed, smiling.

With a last-minute check now into Jackie's bedroom to see that nothing was being left behind, I secured her luggage for transport to the plane. Then I traced Evelyn to her room down the hall for our next move. Observing her room with its lovely décor, flowers, and fruit. I couldn't help commenting how lucky she was!

She said my room was just as lovely, but I hadn't seen it

yet, having spent the entire time here in the Presidential suite. Before leaving, I couldn't resist a peek, at least. Sure enough, there it was—Room 526—looking so inviting! How I wished for the chance to use it for just five minutes and to sample some of the appealing fruit, heaped in a bowl on the dresser. I left it untouched.

We were to get ourselves out to the airport without delay. The President and First Lady would be returning by 10 P.M. for the last lap of the day's trip—on to Fort Worth.

We arrived at the Texas Hotel, in Fort Worth, shortly after 11 P.M. The crowds were so thickly gathered by the entrance doors that it seemed only a pair of wings would get us inside. We desperately tried using our elbows but were still getting nowhere fast! Luckily, we spotted one of the President's aides, and with his strong arms and convincing pleas, he managed to cut a narrow path so that we could get one foot in front of the other. We finally made it to the lobby elevator.

When the elevator doors opened on the eighth floor, there was no doubt I was being loudly paged by the familiar voice of Dave Powers. When we caught sight of each other, he excitedly ushered me to the Presidential suite with: "The President wants to see you!" The anxiety in his voice told me something was up. With all the composure I could muster, I soon stood before the President and asked, "Yes, Mr. President?"

He looked quite disturbed, and his message came out in concerned tones. "Mary," he began, "Jackie's in the bedroom waiting for you. She's upset over your delay in getting here. You'll just have to make arrangements to get to the hotels before we arrive. Speak to Muggsy about riding in the luggage car; it takes a different route from the motorcade and reaches the hotel first..."

I told him I'd be happy to do that, and I went in to Jackie's room. She was sitting on the bed, and I began to apologize, explaining about the crowds. She smiled sweetly. "That's okay, Mary," she said.

What she wanted seemed rather trivial now—unlatching her suitcases for her nightclothes and putting out things she would be wearing in the morning—considering the President's agitation of a few minutes before.

I assumed that her first feeling of ire had unfortunately been taken out on the President—and for this, I felt even worse!

Before long, we all exchanged pleasant goodnights, and I retired to my room next door. On the dresser was a complimentary fifth of bourbon from the management. I was rather tempted to break the seal for a little nightcap, but I really didn't need it at all. I was so exhausted at this point that I collapsed into bed and was immediately asleep.

I was suddenly awakened by noises outside. The rain was pouring down, and murmuring voices were rising from the street below. It was still quite dark, and I glanced at my watch—only 5 A.M.! Curious, I peered from the window to gaze down on a huge mass of opened umbrellas, miniature in size eight floors below. I was groggy, but I realized that people had *already* come to find their places for President Kennedy's morning appearance! How could I help but marvel at their obvious idolatry!

It was impossible to catch any more sleep. After a quick shower, I dressed, snapped shut my suitcases, and found my way to the coffee shop. Evelyn would not be joining me, since she was breakfasting in her room with relatives. I was hardly finished when I received word that Mrs. Kennedy was ready for me.

Before entering the Presidential suite, I was urged by the men in charge of the luggage to get Jackie's bags into the hall as quickly as possible. The President's orders of the night before flashed into my mind; I would have to be ready to go along at the same time!

With a cheerful "Good morning" to the President and to George, his valet, I proceeded to Jackie's bedroom, exchanged the morning's greetings, and went into fast action with the luggage. Jackie was in her robe, breakfasting alone in the sitting room, glancing through the newspapers at the same time.

President Kennedy, meanwhile, was getting dressed for his 8:45 A.M. breakfast appointment at the hotel being sponsored by the Fort Worth Chamber of Commerce. Buttoning up his shirt, he walked over to the window, curious about the noises outside. The crowds were far greater now than when I had my first look three hours earlier.

In an almost unbelieving tone, he exclaimed, "Gosh, just look at the crowds down there! Isn't that terrific?" He was obviously happy and inspired by what he saw—and, to acknowledge his comment, I said, "Yes, Mr. President . . . and you'd better get yourself dressed and out there. They've been waiting in the rain for you since five o'clock this morning!"

Jackie continued with her breakfast and newspaper. I proceeded with my chores. Within minutes, the President made a cheerful departure, calling to his wife, "I'll meet you here later, Jackie . . . try to be ready . . ."

In Jackie's bathroom, a general state of disarray met my eyes. It was incredible that all these jars of cream, bottles of lotion, various cosmetics could be put into use for just an overnight stay!

The words from the men in the hall outside kept flashing through my mind to get Jackie's bags out to them. Quickly scooping up various clothes and towels, I began packing up. I was concerned for the poor maid who would be unpacking that evening at the LBJ Ranch. As scheduled, the entire entourage was to return to Washington while the President and Jackie flew on to Austin to visit the Vice President's ranch nearby.

The last case, though comparatively smaller in size, was the most important. Used for holding Jackie's cosmetics, it had been uniquely designed—with many separate little compartments—bottom, top, and sides; a tricky folding pattern opened and closed it. I quickly removed from the sink and cabinet

318 ❧

shelves all her items, drying them off and tight-fastening the tops. After shifting and re-shifting, I was proud of solving the puzzle of where everything went. It had been an almost impossible task.

But luck was not with me all the way!

Finishing up her breakfast, Jackie went into the bathroom and, after a few seconds, came out again, asking rather dejectedly, "Mary . . . where's my make-up?" I stared blankly at her.

"Oh, Jackie . . . I've packed it away . . . I thought you had it on already!"

She smiled and said, "Thanks, anyway . . . but I haven't!"

I resignedly reached for the case.

At, perhaps, the precise moment that President Kennedy amused his audience with the remark: "Jackie and Lady Bird may take a little longer to dress but, then, they always look much better than Lyndon and me," Mrs. Kennedy was winding up in the bedroom with her last finishing touches.

Dressed in her shocking-pink and navy-blue Chanel suit, with navy accessories, she seemed pleased with her appearance. But upon closer observation in the mirror, she evidently detected a wrinkle or blemish of some sort around her eyes. She remarked rather matter-of-factly, "One day in a campaign can age a person thirty years."

To me, of course, she looked just fine—with one last item remaining to complete her handsome outfit.

From the neat selection of gloves laid out on the dresser, she asked that I choose "something appropriate" for her suit. I handed her a pair of short, spotlessly white kid, with tiny wrist button, which I happily noted met with her immediate approval.

Now she was all set, ready for the President. I felt that if Provi could have witnessed this, she would have rated my first morning's job "well done."

Evelyn was waiting in the hotel corridor for me, and I told her of the President's edict, which meant that we were now to split up. I was to dash along with Muggsy and his helpers, the White House drivers Joe Giordano and "Bootsie" Miller, who were already moving the luggage from the hotel to the cars.

Pondering only a minute, Evelyn chose to come along with us. We arrived at Carswell Air Force Base well in advance of the Presidential party. At 11 A.M., the plane took off as scheduled for the next short flight to Love Field, at Dallas.

By the time we touched ground, the weather had cleared considerably, and a vast, cheering crowd—straining within a roped-off area—waited to greet the President and Mrs. Kennedy.

My spirits were slightly dampened at the thought of not joining the motorcade to the Trade Mart, where the President was scheduled to address a luncheon group.

Since Muggsy would be staying at the airport, I would have to remain with him. Evelyn, however, was most reluctant to go without me and prodded me to come along.

She suggested that we could slip away from the Trade Mart immediately after the luncheon—before the President delivered his speech—and that way, be back at the airfield at least a half-hour or more before the Presidential motorcade returned. This seemed logical—but I could hardly conceive of disobeying the President!

Jackie and the President were the first to alight from the plane and were greeted by the official delegation. A bouquet of red roses was presented to Jackie. They made their way along the roped-off crowd and, for the next several minutes, the President happily shook many of the outstretched hands before they got into their open convertible.

With the rest of the motorcade quickly forming, I finally gave in to Evelyn's constant prodding and decided to leave it to Muggsy as to whether I dared go along with her.

Without hesitation, Muggsy agreed. "Oh, sure, *paisan*," he said, "go ahead! The Boss won't mind." Evelyn and I scurried over to the VIP bus. . . .

As we made our way over to the bus, Evelyn spoke with some concern, saying, "They're expecting demonstrations to-

320 ⧉

day." I didn't question her statement; I naturally assumed that she meant *happy* demonstrations, such as we had been enjoying so far.

It would be impossible to calculate the number of people that had turned out to see the Kennedys along the motorcade route. It was obvious that most businesses had temporarily ceased operation for this great occasion. Employees were thickly clustered at the windows of their buildings, and others also lined themselves along the roof-tops. Children had formed in orderly groups in front of their schools, holding welcoming banners. There were housewives with babies and youngsters in tow. There were businessmen on their lunch-hour, who obviously couldn't have cared less about eating right now. There were storekeepers who had no customers to worry about anyway. The sidewalks were all filled!

The largest crowd jam-packed the city's downtown shopping district, causing the motorcade to travel at a snail's pace. Here, for the first time, I caught sight of the world-famous Neiman-Marcus store and recalled the gay and attractive "Kennedy Girl" campaign outfit they had made up and sent to Jackie in 1960. She later gave it to me, and I still have it.

In all my life, I had never seen anything to equal the sight before us today! With just a short stretch to go now before reaching the Trade Mart, we all had every reason to believe that this welcoming reception had been nothing short of a resounding success. With soaring spirits that matched the momentum of this great event, Evelyn and I couldn't possibly have been more proud to be part of it—a trip with the nation's most popular and inspiring couple—President and Mrs. John F. Kennedy!

From the open windows of the bus, we waved back to the happy, cheering people outside—but, little did we know, for the very last time. Within seconds, the crowds were running wildly, scattering in all directions. A bit farther along, a policeman was struggling to reach the top of a steep, grassy embankment. His gun was drawn—as if in pursuit of someone.

It was quite obvious that something was wrong and, instinctively, I shifted my gaze from the side to the front window of the bus for a view ahead.

I said, "Eve!" turning to Evelyn. "I have the feeling that something terrible must have happened. I can't see the President's car up ahead any more. And that policeman with the gun in his hand ... I'm sure it *must* be something serious."

Yet the bus rolled on, the driver seeming composed.

So we simply assumed that the President's chauffeur had sped ahead of the motorcade to stay clear of the trouble area —whatever it was. Reaching the Trade Mart, we were still completely unaware of what was going on. With the others— Pam Turnure and Elizabeth Carpenter, Mrs. Johnson's press secretary—we were about to enter the building in the midst of all the confusion.

Suddenly, then, a man rushed by, crying out, "The President's been shot!"

We were stunned—nothing such as this had entered our minds.

For the next minute or so, we just remained speechless— standing in the crowd—and again these striking words reached us.

During these most bewildering moments, it seemed too much to expect that we could place faith in the words offered by Elizabeth Carpenter, "Don't believe it ... it's all just a rumor ..."

My thoughts were jumbled: in the first place, who would *dare* conceive such a rumor? Then, just as quickly, the still too-fresh sight of the policeman with his gun in hand went through my mind. I could not dispel *this* thought. Perhaps we had heard the truth, after all! And what about Jackie?

Desperate for further information, Evelyn, Pam, and I— noticing an officer who was standing by his parked cruiser not too far away—held onto each other and dashed madly over to him. Presenting our credentials, we asked him to tell us whatever he knew.

Jack Valenti and Marie Fehmer, of the Vice President's

staff, had also made their way to the officer with us—and together we listened to his words confirming the fact that the President had been shot and that he had been taken to the Parkland Hospital. He was kind enough to listen to our pleas to get us there, and then sped us all the way, siren blaring.

For the first few minutes, after we had all scrambled wildly into the car, I found myself worrying about the man who was left behind! This was a Mr. Baines (if I recall his name correctly), a stranger to the rest of us, who was inconspicuously aboard Air Force One coaching Jackie on her Spanish speech.

I turned to look out of the back window at all the confusion and excitement behind us, and there he stood—among those who were running and screaming about—motionless, looking so alone... I wondered: How would he manage to get back to Washington unless he would find us later at the airport? Why hadn't we seen him sooner; he could have come along with us. I find myself still wondering about him at times. Whatever happened to him?

We raced toward the hospital; nothing was ever more important than what we would learn when we reached there. Feeling so completely helpless during these tense, excruciating moments, I reached into my handbag for my rosary beads. We rode in silence, and I prayed harder than I ever had.

Once inside the hospital, we could not at first find out just where the President had been taken, and what his condition was. The hospital personnel knew nothing; there was confusion here, too.

With mounting anxiety and determination, Evelyn, Pam, and I went from office to office along the corridors—until we came upon the group of faces, all so familiar, but now completely enshrouded in sadness.

It became clear that the President's fate was not yet known. The appearance of everyone along our way was that of tense and eager anticipation. We were immediately shown into one of the glass-enclosed offices and, from here, I could see Jackie, who stood in the opposite waiting room.

In trancelike form, she stood by the closed door of the

operating room for word of her husband, whose blood had just been shed into her lap, staining her suit, legs, and shoes.

We could only imagine the experience she had been through, and could easily see how tormenting the uncertainty of her husband's condition was for her. The waiting moments seemed endless, and only sheer hope remained. We clung to this.

The door of the operating room finally opened—and Dr. Burkley came out, making his way directly to our little cubicle.

Addressing General McHugh, the Air Force aide, he whispered softly that arrangements must be made immediately for our flight back to Washington "while I arrange for a coffin." Direct and to the point, I overheard the word and it stunned me!

"Dr. Burkley . . . did you say 'coffin'?" I gasped. "Yes," he said, "and please try not to change your expression . . . but I'd like it now if you would go over and stay with Mrs. Kennedy."

Nothing had ever been so difficult for me. I knew I had to do it, and somehow I did. Evelyn and Pam followed.

While standing there, I was handed Jackie's pillbox hat and couldn't help noticing the strands of her hair beneath the hatpin. I could almost visualize her yanking it from her head. I was also given her handbag.

She was now sitting straight and motionless in a little chair by the door until someone escorted her into the operating room. My heart sank at the news she was about to receive.

When she emerged, she was walking beside the long table that carried the sheet-covered body of her husband, which was being rolled into the opposite room. The door was closed and, within minutes, we were instructed to prepare to return to the airport. The ride still remains totally blank in my mind.

I was the first to board the plane after Jackie, and I can still see her now as she sat in the little compartment, facing the coffin directly in front of her. There were no words to be found at this moment, but with a gentle embrace, I could

324 ঙ

only hope that she understood the imparted message that, should she need me, I would be right there.

As I turned from her, I looked down at the coffin and felt the strong desire to bend down and kiss it. But I refrained. I was afraid that it might upset Jackie. And since I led the others, I thought they might feel compelled to do the same ... I just couldn't be sure.

Within those few seconds, however, I did know that I *must* manage my way to my seat. The stark reality of the coffin had overwhelmed me, and I felt faint. I reached for the tall backs of the rows of seats before me—until I finally settled into the one I thought was mine. The one, all too incredibly, so happily occupied only a few short hours earlier.

All hope was gone now. And this grim realization also seemed to be reflected by Air Force One itself. With all its curtains drawn, it remained in complete darkness—preparing to carry its most renowned figure for the last time.

The silence was broken by the Vice President's voice as he stood in the doorway between the two compartments, announcing that the swearing-in ceremonies would soon be taking place in the front compartment. He invited us to join him—and despite the emotional upset, we respectfully obliged.

As the people congregated, I happened to glance out into the narrow corridor and saw Kenny O'Donnell pacing back and forth with his hands holding his head as if unable to believe the terrible thing that had happened. But when the swearing-in ceremony was about to take place, he came in and joined the group.

The area here was most confining and was quickly crowded to capacity. It also presented problems for Captain Stoughton, the White House photographer, whose job was to capture these historical moments, no matter how he might be suffering himself.

Wedging himself into a corner and standing on a chair, he did remarkably well to get any pictures at all.

Evelyn and I were standing directly behind Vice President

and Mrs. Johnson and saw Jackie as she came forward from the adjoining compartment.

Her face was pathetically taut, and her body moved as though it required all her energy to cover the short distance to the Vice President's side.

I thought how cruel it was that she should be required to fulfill this official role. But, dutifully, she stood—with her head bent low, as Lyndon B. Johnson became the 36th President of the United States.

And the name of her husband, John F. Kennedy, was taking another place in the annals of history. Evelyn, Pam, and I shook President Johnson's hand and returned to our seats.

We left Love Field at approximately 2:30 P.M., and without delay, President Johnson and his staff settled down to the tasks of their new office.

During the entire three-hour flight to Andrews Air Force Base, Jackie remained in the private compartment with the late President's aides, Dave Powers and Kenny O'Donnell.

As I sat next to Evelyn, there were few words to be spoken. Perhaps one question—that still remains—occupied both our minds. Why? There was no answer then, and there is no answer now.

At one point, we were being offered a bowl of soup by Marie Fehmer, President Johnson's secretary, but we declined and thanked her. We were simply without any appetite at all. I believe she understood.

As my thoughts turned again to Mrs. Kennedy, I became aware that perhaps there was something I might do to help her. She might like some help in getting washed up and changed, ready to meet Caroline and John-John, who I assumed would be waiting for her at the White House. The thought carried me to the door of her compartment; it was an hour or so before landing.

Upon knocking softly, I was met by Kenny and I asked if he would please give my message to Mrs. Kennedy. But he preferred not to ask her about it. He said, "If she wants to

326 ᣟᣟ

stay this way for five days, it'll show the world what's been done to Jack."

Rather impulsively, I expressed further concern for the children. I hated to think that they would see their mother in her blood-stained condition. But, then, I was somewhat relieved when Kenny said that it hadn't yet been definitely decided whether we would go directly to the White House or to the Bethesda Naval Hospital. This gave me some hope that the children might be spared, and I pressed no further.

Returning to my seat, then, there seemed one more way to help. Again, as if by instinct, I stepped into Jackie's bedroom compartment to make a last check for any personal items that might be left behind. I felt a chill at the sight before me.

There, on the bed, lay one of Jackie's gloves. No longer spotlessly white and soft as it was that morning; but now completely blackened by her husband's blood, dried and stiffened to the actual shape of her hand as she had removed it, finger by finger.

It rested on a newspaper, which carried the large, bold, headline: "DALLAS WELCOMES JFK."

Picking it up as gently as possible, I carefully wrapped it between several layers of clean tissues and carried it as discreetly as possible to Secret Service Agent Clint Hill, asking that he see that it was put in a safe place until he could turn it over to Mrs. Kennedy. He assured me that he would give it his special care. Confidently, I left it in his good hands.

When we landed at Andrews, Evelyn and I were asked by Dave and Kenny to escort Jackie from the plane after the lowering of the coffin. We were positioned to either side of her—Evelyn to the left and I to the right.

However, in the next instant, there came from behind us a startling voice: "Jackie . . ."

The voice and the accent were so much like those of the late President, I quivered. Then I suddenly realized that it was his brother, the Attorney General. He had boarded the plane at the other end as it touched ground.

Quickly he made his way toward us, and Jackie cried out, "Oh, Bobby..."

Immediately I could sense that she would much prefer now to have Bobby escort her from the plane. Evelyn and I stepped backward as he took her arm.

A hydraulic platform had been hoisted to the plane's doorway. The coffin was placed on it and lowered and, within minutes, carried into the waiting ambulance.

Following Bobby and Jackie off the plane, Evelyn and I watched as they, too, climbed inside the ambulance. Then we took our places in one of the cars that followed to Bethesda Naval Hospital.

Beyond the room where the late President's body was taken was a large sitting room, where several relatives and close friends had already gathered.

As I sat there and looked around, I was overcome by the poignant memory of this same group which, only three months earlier, had filled the sitting room at Otis Air Force Base Hospital in Massachusetts when the late President and Jackie had lost their newborn baby, Patrick.

That, I knew, was one of the saddest and most heartbreaking experiences the late President had ever known. And now, I thought after his desperate fight to save the life of his baby son, he would be joined with him forever in heaven.

As the hours passed, Jackie remained remarkably composed, talking softly with those present. I spoke with her stepfather, Mr. Auchincloss, and we marveled at her bravery.

Sandwiches and coffee were being passed on a tray. But, despite my having gone through this entire day on the early morning's coffee and toast, I could only reach for some black coffee. I was still completely without appetite for any food at all.

Close to midnight I prepared to leave, since I knew my family would be waiting up for me. Stopping on the way out to say "Goodnight" to Jackie, I asked, too, that she please try to get some rest. She expressed her thanks, then quietly made one last request for the morning. "Please pick up several pairs of black stockings for me and a long black mourning veil for the funeral on Monday."

I was surprised at her usual sense of organization. But, fortunately, my notebook and pencil were still in my hand. Quite automatically, I recorded her last wishes of the day.

As we parted, she said, "Goodnight, Mary . . . and please stay strong for just a few more days . . . I need you now more than ever."

34 ～ WOULD THE GHASTLY DAY NEVER END?

WOULD THE GHASTLY DAY NEVER END? THE ride home seemed endless. The White House chauffeur and I exchanged just a few words—"I still can't believe it." "No, I can't get used to it," and "To think that such a thing can happen in the United States."

One thing kept haunting me. It was my one regret about that plane ride back in Air Force One—and I still think of it, though it was a little thing.

As the staff prepared to leave the plane, on arriving at Andrews AFB, I recall passing Mrs. Johnson, who was seated with Liz Carpenter next to her, and I felt the strongest impulse to shake her hand and wish her well in her new duties as First Lady.

However, I refrained, mostly because neither Evelyn nor Pam had. Both of them had walked ahead of me and, I noticed, did not offer any such gesture. So I hesitated, and of course the moment passed. But the feeling of not having done the right thing has remained with me. I can still see the rather expectant expression in Mrs. Johnson's eyes as we filed past her.

What a strange feeling it was, to drive up in front of my house. The driver held open the door. Did Jackie still need me back there?

Ray and my mother-in-law were waiting up for me. They had hot food ready, but my appetite had not yet returned. I was, in fact, too depressed and exhausted even to talk. The boys were fast asleep.

Ray said that Secret Service Agent James Jeffries had been the first to call. Jeff didn't know that I had gone on the Texas trip and had informed Ray of the first news bulletin on the assassination. Ray had already known. General C. J. Mara, our next-door neighbor, heard the first report and came over to tell Ray. At 2:40 P.M. in Washington, the President's condition still remained uncertain. Many of our relatives and friends were phoning.

When Chris and Greg had come home from school at 3:15 P.M., their first question to their daddy was: "Have you heard the President was shot in Dallas?" As first- and second-graders, they may not have been fully aware of the horror that embraced the entire nation. They were not too young, of course, to know that something very big and terrible had happened.

Ray said they, too, had watched TV intently. Then, to prepare them for my return, he had told them, "Mummy's going to be sick when she gets home . . ."

Chris had asked, "Why? Because the President's been shot?"

Ray drove into Alexandria with the boys in the afternoon and noted that a quiet, hushed atmosphere prevailed everywhere.

Watching TV later, they saw Air Force One with JFK's body taking off from Dallas, and at 6:08 saw the plane land and the casket unloaded. Ray said that after Jackie was helped down from the hydraulic lift, they saw me aided to the ground. They assumed that I accompanied Jackie to

Bethesda Naval Hospital with the casket. Chris asked, "If I die and go to heaven, will I see President Kennedy there?"

The next morning I hurried to the White House to be with Jackie.

I was able to continue my diary that day.

November 23, 1963: 10:30 A.M. JBK in family quarters with members of family. Evelyn Lincoln was on my mind—I hadn't seen her since she left the hospital last night. Wondered how she was feeling this morning; thought I'd pay call at her office.

Stepping from elevator on ground floor, saw Jerry Behn [JFK's S.S. Agent] standing alone in the hall. There was no point in saying "Good Morning." I approached him with: "Jerry, the one time we really needed you, you weren't there." (But I knew, of course, the assignment had not been in his hands for that trip.)

He, too, seemed to have a lump in his throat; remained speechless.

I embraced Evelyn. We both tried hard to restrain tears. She was, I was amazed to see, in the process of clearing JFK's belongings from office.

"What's the big rush about?" I asked—said she had been asked by President Johnson to have the office cleared out as soon as possible. It was heartbreaking, to say the least, to watch her helpers, Joe Giordano, and Bootsie Miller, packing the cartons.

That afternoon, my sister Louise arrived from Boston—not only to spend these few trying days with me but even more, I know, as our family's "representative" from Massachusetts, to express personal condolences to Jackie. She was met at National Airport by a White House chauffeur and taken directly to the White House.

Once she was upstairs at the mansion, I explained that Mrs. Kennedy was receiving dignitaries on the first floor. I hoped at some point through the day to have her accomplish the purpose of her mission.

Yet, as the hours went on, my hesitancy to interrupt Jackie

resulted, I'm sure, in a big disappointment for Louise. As it turned out, the opportune moment never seemed to arrive.

Thinking back, there was perhaps one explanation for my not having given Louise just a moment or two with her—my natural feeling of "over-protectiveness" in behalf of Jackie. It had become a habit with me. I regret that I didn't just put Louise in the line of dignitaries filing past Jackie or take her to the second floor and introduce her to the First Lady.

November 23, 1963: 10:45 P.M. JBK called me at home.
Attorney General has found a place in Executive Office Building (next to the White House), where all the President's most private papers are to go.
Move out by next week all private papers and files . . .
Check with Mr. Bundy about a room for my things there.
Books, etc., to storage . . .

November 24, 1963: After 9:30 A.M. Mass at St. Mary's, Alex., went to W.H. to accompany official party to the Capitol where coffin placed for public viewing. As Miss Hennessey and I stood by the elevator on the first floor, just outside the Ushers' Office, we saw Tish Baldrige making her way down the steps from the second floor, where she had, apparently, been working on some funeral arrangement with the family.

We saw Jackie and Bobby as they approached the elevator to return to the second floor. They had just come from the East Room where the coffin was. Just a quick glimpse of Jackie convinced me that she had now experienced the worst, the hardest part—looking at her husband in the coffin. She was very pale and seemed extremely weak, holding onto Bobby's arm for support. I had never seen her looking so wan and desolate; she seemed on the verge of fainting. Bobby, too, was ashen as he helped her into the elevator. This must surely have been the most unbearable moment for both of them since the terrible tragedy of two days ago . . .

Just a short time later, as Miss Hennessey and I waited in
332 ཚ

the Diplomatic Room while the line-up of cars assembled on the South Grounds to take passengers to the Capitol, Mr. Rex Scouten from the Ushers' Office came to find me. He said that Mrs. Kennedy was asking for me upstairs. I had hoped the motorcade of cars would not take off without me; I told Louella that I'd be right back.

Upstairs, Jackie was in the West Sitting Room, talking with Lee, Peter Lawford, and a few others. She was composed and asked calmly if I had procured her mourning veil for the funeral tomorrow.

I was rather surprised that this was on her mind at all, as I was under the impression it had all been taken care of the previous day.

When I had given Provi the black stockings, I mentioned that I would go shopping for the veil. But Provi said there was no need to get one, as Mrs. Kennedy already had two that she had evidently "forgotten about." Provi then showed me two long black mantillas, assuring me that Jackie would use one or the other and that she would ask her to decide later in the day.

Still I was rather skeptical, questioning Provi again: "Are you *sure?* It seemed to me that when Mrs. Kennedy asked for it, she described it as the kind that falls over her face."

Provi stressed her certainty again, saying that Mrs. Kennedy didn't realize she had these two already. As far as I was concerned, there was no reason to doubt Provi. So I felt safe in answering Jackie now with "Provi has two of them in the dressing room. Hasn't she shown them to you yet?"

It seemed she had, and a mantilla was not what Jackie wanted. She now explained more definitely: "A long veil that's worn over the face." With an understanding smile, she said: "Just as long as I have one by tomorrow."

November 24, 1963: At 8:45 P.M., JBK called at home again—
"John's party is put off from Tuesday . . . will be at the W.H. some time before move out—possibly Friday . . . Could all bring present for Caroline; everything for her, give to me . . . Call all mothers tomorrow."

Thanks to Ray, I have an account of that saddest of days—November 25th. For once I was too bewildered and busy even to think of my diary—and too sad. As for the veil, Lucinda Morman, the White House seamstress, finally procured it from Mrs. Joseph Kennedy, attaching it to Jackie's hat in plenty of time.

Ray's account of the funeral:

"This was a very full day for Mary and me. We had received the invitation to the President's Funeral Mass at St. Matthews and were asked to be at the White House at 10:30 A.M. We were driven in a new Cadillac owned by Dr. Burkley, loaned to the White House by him. The demand for cars was tremendous. We arrived at South Lawn Entrance at 10:30, entered the Diplomatic Reception Room on the ground floor and signed Guest Book. The Prince of Luxembourg had signed just before us.

"We immediately went upstairs to the State Dining Room on first floor, west, where we saw Evelyn Lincoln. She was crying. Her husband, "Abe," joined us. This large room was the gathering place for many of the notables of the U.S. I shook hands with Senator Everett Dirksen of Illinois, Dean Sayre, and recognized many others—Speaker of the House John McCormack, Pierre Salinger, Professor Galbraith, Lem Billings, Kenny O'Donnell, Lord Harlech, and many others. Louella Hennessey joined us also.

"An announcement was made that the Walking Group would form in that room, with officials of the Congress going first; then Governors; Office Staff of White House; and, last, friends of the family. We proceeded out to the main front portico where I stood next to Peter Lawford. The entourage walked toward Pennsylvania Ave. It was six blocks to St. Matthews; the curbs were crowded with thousands of predominantly younger people. We were almost the last ones in the Church, and were seated in Pew #34 on main aisle. When the Mass was over, all the key figures came past; we could

334 ॐ

have touched them at arm's length . . . JBK and Caroline with Bobby beside her. She was crying under her veil. A long, shiny line marked where a tear had rolled down one cheek. Then came Ted Kennedy, Peter Lawford, many Kennedy girls and wives. Then Presidents Eisenhower and Truman; Prince Philip; Haile Selassie; Chancellor of Germany Erhard; President de Gaulle; Mikoyan of USSR; King of Belgium; and many more. Stevenson, Nixon, and Rockefeller passed by also.

"Mass lasted about fifty minutes with Cardinal Cushing presiding, then the reading by Bishop Hannan with JFK's own words. We left the church, and had to run to catch car #12—the last W.H. car before the Diplomatic Group. We learned later that Dr. Burkley and Dr. Weisner were left behind in the rush. We saw a longtime friend, Jack Lynch, a Security Officer for the State Department, when we entered the church and, again, at Arlington Cemetery.

"We were driven slowly to Arlington down 17th St., and among the thousands of faces at the south end of the Memorial Bridge, I spotted a neighbor, George Colgan, a stockbroker. Near grave site, there was little to be seen because of the huge crowd. After the burial, we saw Jackie again closely as she embraced the flag and returned to her car with Bobby. We went back to our car for drive to the White House. Remained only for an hour or so before returning home."

Later, I resumed my own diary, with my impressions of the interment and of Jackie's valiant conduct during those days of torment.

Of all the people around us at the grave site, I felt the greatest sympathy for Congressman Torbert MacDonald of Massachusetts—a lifetime friend of JFK. The Congressman stood throughout the entire service with tears streaming down his cheeks.

How I wished I could let some of the hurt within me spill out just a tiny bit. For Jackie's sake, I controlled myself. Whenever I weakened, I remembered her words at the hospital on Friday night: "Please stay strong for just a few more days. I need you now more than ever."

November 27, 1963: Mr. Bundy's office advises that Room #302 at Executive Office Bldg. available for JBK—next door to Evelyn Lincoln in Room 300 . . . Immediately set to packing and moving JBK's personal papers, files, etc.

November 28: 1963: Thanksgiving Day—worked at White House today . . . and through entire weekend on packing of JBK's personal belongings.

There was no time for turkey or for tears.

35 ⟋ LAST DAYS IN THE WHITE HOUSE

*I*T WAS THE BEGINNING OF DECEMBER, AND WE were still in the White House. We were all stricken with sympathy for Jackie, and did whatever we could to ease her burden. And the children—how my heart ached for them.

John-John paid a morning visit on December 2nd, calling out, "Mary Gallagher . . . do you have some gum for me?" He was disappointed to hear that I didn't have any.

"But I'll bet I have something else that you'll like even more!" I told him. Now he looked happier, and came close to my desk to see just what I did have.

"Oh, not here," I said. "It's something that doesn't even *fit* into my desk drawers." He was enjoying the little game immensely. He looked around the room, on the bed, under the table behind me. When he reached the closet door, I coached: "You're getting warm . . ." He took the cue, turned the doorknob cautiously, and within seconds let out one of his wild shrieks! He had spotted his treasure on the floor immediately. He scooped it up and with happy shouts circled around the room with the toy airplane, waving it through the air!

He exclaimed, "Look, Miss Shaw, I have a new airplane!"

I now had a new job to do. Jackie couldn't possibly write all the cards of appreciation to those who served her and the President in the White House. I was to write hundreds of notes edged in black for her.

Jackie carried on as normally as she could, giving me instructions:

Ask Mr. Luddington to close the house at the Cape.

A message to Provi, regarding things to be unpacked over at the Harrimans' house in Georgetown, where Jackie was to move for a temporary stay when she left the White House.

Get a copy of JFK's speech made at Aero Space Medical Center the day before he died.

Start a new file under JACK.

Ask Mrs. Lincoln for any letters Jackie wrote to JFK, from Greece, etc.

Arrange an appointment with Dr. Walsh.

There were a great many such items to cover.

Among the celebrities who arrived after the funeral was Princess Grace of Monaco, who came the first week in December. She tried to visit Jackie, but Jackie did not see her and remained in bed. The Princess visited the grave site and placed a spray of white carnations on the President's grave.

My diary notations for December 3 stand out:

John-John visits again this morning. "Some gum!" This time I had some candy to offer, which he happily accepted.

At 11:00 A.M., Clint Hill—JBK's SS Agent, who leaped to her aid in the car when JFK was assassinated—was to receive citation for his bravery in Dallas. . . . Ceremony held at U.S. Treasury Bldg. across the street from W.H. . . . JBK scheduled to attend. Evelyn Lincoln and I had arranged to walk over together, and we met on the ground floor of the Mansion. As we passed the Diplomatic Reception Room, we saw JBK and Lee sitting down, waiting for the car to drive them across the street . . .

The next day was especially exhausting.

Everything was in a jumbled state as we were packing up for the move. The third floor was the busiest those days, fairly buzzing with activity. All the storage rooms had been opened and the things brought out to be packed. That moved smoothly enough. But the complication was Jackie's clothes: special tall cartons had to be made to hold the closets full of gowns.

Then came the late President's clothing; all his personal effects were brought up to the third floor and put on racks and couches. Jackie looked them all over and decided what to keep and what to give away. I will never forget how sad and lost I felt seeing JFK's things go. How considerate Jackie was, even to think of those around her, at a time like this.

On the fifth, I worked with her all day on distribution of gifts to JFK's closest aides and others. His ties went to "The Irish Mafia"—T. J. Reardon, Jr., Kenny O'Donnell, Larry O'Brien, Muggsy O'Leary, Dave Powers, and others. Golf shirt to Carol Rosenbloom. Cigar case to Pierre Salinger. At one point, Jackie said to me, "Oh, Mary, I'll see to it that you get something of Jack's, too. But first I want to take care of the people in the White House before we leave.

"And your Christmas gift," she continued, "I'll give you that, too . . . it's already gone to storage . . . that's what I get for being so secretive!"

I was happy to see that Jackie had shown such thought for George Thomas, JFK's personal valet. She asked that I arrange to have a plaque made for him, to be put on the rocking chair in the President's bedroom. She drew the shape of it for me and said it was to be bronze, with the inscription, "For George Thomas—The Rocking Chair of John Fitzgerald Kennedy—35th President of the United States. It was always

in his bedroom—I know he would want you to have it. JBK."
I knew George would be happy and proud with his gift.

Miss Shaw, the children's nurse, approached Jackie directly
and asked for something to remember the President by ...

"But of all things," she told me later, expressing some disappointment over the gift she received, "she handed me one
of the President's shirts. I wanted some little trinket like cuff
links or tie clip that could be a keepsake ..."

I hardly knew what to say, and commented: "Oh, Miss
Shaw, so far I haven't anything."

Friday was moving day from the White House. Jackie went
to the Harrimans' house at 3036 N Street, NW, Georgetown.
I moved into her new office at the Executive Office Building.
The past two weeks had been simply a nightmare—the funeral,
the long days and nights of hard work, supervision of the
move from the White House, my move to the office across
the street, the endless handwritten notes filling my late-hour
evenings. Before the weekend set in, I stopped in to say
goodbye to Dr. Travell. She checked my blood count and
found it down to 65!

On Monday, the 9th, I see by my diary that I had a rather
strange feeling this first morning to be reporting to the Executive Office Building rather than the White House. Now, I
would be working out of two places—here, where I had access
to Jackie's files, and Georgetown, where I would take daily
dictation. At 11 A.M., I was in her bedroom at the Harriman
house and found her in a lonely, depressed mood. We chatted
for about twenty minutes. She wept, saying how very lonely
she was.

"Why did Jack have to die so young? Even when you're
sixty, you like to know your husband is there. It's so hard for
the children. Please, Mary, don't ever leave. Get yourself
fixed for salary on my Government appropriation—just don't
leave me!"

I kept wondering what would happen to Jackie, what she
would do. I hoped she would use her great talents in so many

fields. Others realized her abilities, too. Representative Martha Griffiths of Michigan told reporters that she had had a tremendous response through the mail when she suggested that Mrs. Kennedy be named Ambassador to France.

I knew how much the position of First Lady had meant to Jackie when she ordered a little plaque placed over the fireplace in the Presidential bedroom. The plaque said, "In this room lived John Fitzgerald Kennedy with his wife Jacqueline —during the two years, 10 months and two days he was President of the United States—January 20, 1961–November 22, 1963."

Jackie placed her plaque below the one already there which read, "In this room Abraham Lincoln slept during his occupancy at the White House: as President of the United States —March 4, 1861–April 13, 1864."

36 ∽ BACK TO GEORGETOWN

*I*T WAS NOW THE MONTH OF CHRISTMAS, BUT there was no Christmas spirit. I reconstruct it all now through my diary, with memories flooding back as if it were yesterday.

At the Harriman house on N Street, Jackie's bedroom was on the second floor and she seldom left it. During those weeks I was constantly aware of her suffering. After the busy days moving from the White House, her depression set in. All activity was confined to the first floor.

One of the Navy men, loaned from the Staff Mess at the White House, was busy preparing the meals. Secret Service Agents were posted by the phones. The Harrimans' housekeeper was on hand to answer household questions. Provi, as usual, rushed up and down the steps and in and out of Jackie's room, delivering messages to the people below. And, like clockwork, Dave Powers would arrive at 12 noon to lunch with John-John and to "drill" around the rooms.

Lee stayed at the Harriman house with Jackie for a while, occupying a guestroom on the second floor, and the third floor was given over to Miss Shaw and the children. Two flights of stairs without an elevator had, in itself, presented a noticeable change in exercise from the White House days, taking some getting used to.

During those difficult days, I was in charge of all of Jackie's correspondence and through my hands passed all the notes from family, friends, and relatives.

The ones that amazed me most were Lyndon Johnson's handwritten notes to Caroline and John-John, which the new President had written on that night of their father's assassination. I marveled that he had had the presence of mind to do such a generous thing under such trying circumstances.

After taking Jackie's dictation at the Harriman house, I would return to my office at the E.O.B.—Executive Office Building—for the remainder of the day.

My driver that first day was waiting out front to drive me back to my office at the Executive Office Building and, difficult though it was, I tried to act somewhat composed as I left the house saying goodbye to those milling about—Bobby, Dave Powers, and Lee, among them.

The first memo I was to type for Jackie that day was a long one, showing her great consideration for the Kennedys' Secret Service men.

It was to be forwarded to the Secretary of the Treasury, Douglas Dillon, telling how the President had always said that before he left office, he was going to see that the highest possible recommendation was left in the file of each of them, with the suggestion that each of them be given a chance to advance.

One line stood out and brought back memories. She told how before they had come to the White House, the thing she dreaded most was the Secret Service, but that she had been wrong, and that they had made it possible for the President and herself to have the happy close life that they did.

Jackie went on to recall how she had ordered them to be firm with the children so they would not get spoiled and yet be unobtrusive so that their presence would not affect the children's friends and make them treat John and Caroline as anyone different or special. As Jackie recalled her own childhood in New York when she had played in the park with Kate Roosevelt, President Roosevelt's granddaughter, she remarked how the presence of a Secret Service man close by made the children around Kate nervous. So it was no fun for them, she said, and Kate had been made to feel lonely and unusual.

It was a great tribute, going on about how fine all the men had been in protecting the President and her and the children. She added a typically-Jackie imaginative touch—that they should all be put into the Diplomatic Corps and made Ambassadors because they had been so tactful.

I was deeply touched. But a few days later she expressed other feelings about a few of the Secret Service men—touching on the subject of the assassination and expressing her mixed feelings. She mentioned one S.S. man who had not acted during the crucial moment, and said bitterly to me, "He might just as well have been Miss Shaw!"

I had tried to offer something consoling. "Well, Jackie," I said, "I really think that the one time the Secret Service should be allowed to overrule a President's wish is when it concerns his safety. You know, like insisting on the bubble-top of the car being left up."

She broke in with, "Well, what can I do now? Send a blast . . ."

I answered, "No, Jackie, I didn't mean that. I just meant as a future precaution. I think they should have the right to overrule the President on something like this."

She seemed to understand my point and, with a relenting attitude, said, "Oh, well, I guess Jack would only have gotten more reckless as time went on, anyway . . ."

I felt worried about Jackie when she made her first nationwide telecast after the tragedy to thank the hundreds of thousands of persons. Over 800,000 sent condolences. The telecast was made from Bobby's office at the Justice Department, and I was afraid that she would break down. Her voice was so low, and now and then there would be a catch in it.

"The knowledge of the affection in which my husband was held by all of you has sustained me, and the warmth of these tributes is something that I shall never forget."

She went on to say, "Whenever I can bear to, I read them. All his bright light gone from the world. All of you who have written to me know how much we all loved him and that he returned that love in full measure."

Jackie promised that all the letters would be answered, though it would take a long time. "Every message is to be treasured," she said, "not only for my children, but so that future generations will know how much our country and peoples in other nations thought of him. Your letters will be placed with his papers in the library to be erected in his memory on the Charles River in Boston, Massachusetts. I hope in years to come many of you and your children will come to visit the Kennedy Library."

We would soon be moving again.

Jackie had bought the house of the James McMillan Gibson's just across the street from the Harrimans', for $175,000.

About the middle of December, 1963, decorator William Baldwin began making trips from New York to Georgetown to discuss decorating plans for the new home, at 3017 N Street. The first time he arrived, at around 9:45 A.M. on December 18th, Jackie's departure for Florida to spend the Christmas holidays was delayed a few hours.

Before she left, she had given me two gifts, both framed etchings of different views of the White House. One, especially, gave me a haunted feeling and brought fresh tears. It had been signed by the President himself before his assassination and was one of the last things he took care of:

For Mary—with greatest appreciation and affection
                                    Jackie—
Christmas 1963   John Kennedy

The other etching was from Jackie alone:

For Mary—who did so much to help me and the
President and helped to make our years here such
happy ones
December 1963   Jacqueline Kennedy

At Palm Beach, Jackie and her sister, Lee, stayed at Colonel
C. M. Paul's house. Jackie remained in seclusion, and a
private Christmas Mass was held at the Ambassador's house.

Jackie broke her seclusion, however, to receive Princess
Lala Aicha of Morocco, who came on behalf of her brother,
King Hassan of Morocco. The Princess brought word of her
brother's gift to Jackie: a century-old house in Marrakesh,
Morocco. They visited together for several hours. I thought
it did Jackie good to see other people, especially someone as
concerned as the Princess. It was strange to realize that just
about two months before, Jackie had been briefly in Morocco
during her Mediterranean cruise and was entertained by the
royal family. As I recall, Jackie later declined the gift house,
with thanks.

When Jackie returned to Georgetown on Monday, January
6th, someone counted over four hundred spectators standing
watch outside the Harriman house. Teddy Kennedy arrived
with her.

The Christmas gifts that Jackie and the children had received in Palm Beach arrived separately that same day: it
took a large van and a little truck to hold them all.

I reflected that we would certainly need that new large
house if the gifts continued in this volume. The house Jackie
had bought had an interesting past. It had been used as the
setting for a mystery novel, *The Simple Way of Poison*, by
Zenish Brown, whose pen name was Leslie Ford. The house
had originally been built by one of the first mayors of George-

town, Thomas Beall, when N Street was still called "Gay Street."

When a special Memorial Mass was held January 18th, Jackie flew to Boston aboard the *Caroline*. Rose Kennedy flew up from her winter home in Palm Beach, but the Ambassador was not well enough to make the trip. Bobby Kennedy was not there, either, because he was out of the country on a Far East mission for President Johnson.

It was about that time that the drive was launched for funds for the planned John F. Kennedy Library. It was to be built in Cambridge on land already donated by Harvard University. Bobby and Teddy made a joint announcement about the million dollars the Joseph P. Kennedy, Jr., Foundation was giving. Another million had been received from various sources, but eight million dollars more were needed.

Eugene Black, the retired president of the World Bank, would be the chairman of the library's trustees. The other trustees would be Chief Justice Earl Warren, former Secretary of State Dean Acheson, Richard Cardinal Cushing, composer Samuel Barber, AFL-CIO President George Meany, General Douglas MacArthur, and novelists John Hersey and John Steinbeck.

Their aim for the library was "to give future generations insight into the issues, mood and accomplishments of John F. Kennedy's life."

In January, too, the Senate approved a bill to establish the John F. Kennedy Center for the Performing Arts, as a national memorial to be built in Washington, renamed from the National Cultural Center. Congress authorized $15.5 million in Federal funds to match the same amount in private donations.

The Board of Trustees for the Center for the Performing Arts was headed by another Kennedy family friend, Roger Stevens.

January ended on a frustrating note for Jackie when she tried to be social in just a small way. It backfired and caused a furor. She had gone to a fashionable restaurant in Georgetown with her sister Lee, Marlon Brando, and movie producer George H. Englund, who had directed Brando in *The Ugly American*. They sat in a secluded corner, but Jackie's presence did not go unnoticed.

When the newspapers said that Brando had escorted Jackie, he pretended he hadn't been with her, hadn't even seen her, and that he was in Washington only to do research for a documentary on American Indians. But unfortunately a photographer had taken a picture in the restaurant. Pam Turnure finally confirmed that Marlon Brando had been there, and had dined with Jackie, and was a close friend of the Kennedy family.

January 15th was moving day to the new house. By 9:30 A.M., the first of the huge vans was parked in front of 3017 N Street, with a number of movers lugging pieces inside.

I was on hand to supervise the deliveries and instruct the men in the placement of furniture. Mrs. Murphy and Mrs. Jessup of Residential Services were also there, checking inventory lists.

Jackie was scheduled to remain at the Harriman house for the next ten days or so, while I was overseeing arrangements at the new house.

By early noon I reported back to the Harrimans' for Jackie's final dictation of the day.

I was to call Mrs. Auchincloss's secretary and ask her for the name of the man she bought rugs from . . .

I was to call Captain Shephard—and ask if Jackie could see Mr. Dueldon, the sculptor, on Friday morning around eleven or twelve . . .

I was to call Mr. West and ask how I could order wineglasses like those at the White House—white wine, red wine, champagne, and water. Jackie wanted them soon, 18 of each, in time for her move into the new house . . .

I was to check on Jackie's needlepoint rugs: she wanted to know if they were at the White House or in storage.

Then Jackie began to dictate various letters of thanks for her gifts:

To Irene Galitzine in Rome—for some pictures.

To Mr. and Mrs. Klejman, New York City—for the gift of a beautiful little bronze horse that the President had seen, and which he had planned to get for Jackie for Christmas.

To The Honorable Randolph Churchill, saying she was touched to receive his book.

After disposing of various other matters, Jackie wound up with a letter to Walter Heller, JFK's economic adviser, thanking him for sending her the notes on his last meetings with the President when Caroline and John-John were present. Jackie said she was putting them away for the children to read years from now, because it showed so much about their father.

The following morning, I greeted the team of workers who were to be assigned their tasks: Mr. Nazarian on custom-made rugs; Mr. Kay on the painting of various rooms; Mr. Beacon, the electrician, on the wiring; Mr. Jake Williams, the handyman, on household and garden chores.

There wasn't a room that wasn't to be tackled in one way or another. For the next week or so, all hands moved full speed ahead, including Mr. Crabtree at Merchants Transfer and Storage, who was besieged with phone calls to find this or that.

Some items were returned to him in accordance with Jackie's changing orders. He would replace, re-catalog—then some of these same items were ordered returned to the house *again!*

Larry Arata, the White House upholsterer, was also finishing some chairs for Jackie—a gold upholstered one, and a wing chair, white, upholstered with a red welt. For curtains and draperies to dress the windows, there was the very capable seamstress, Mary Pescatello of Westerly, Rhode Island. Arrangements had been made for her to come to Washington.

Efficient and conscientious, she put in long hours that in no way affected her easy-going, pleasant manner.

By Monday, January 27th, the house was somewhat livable, and Jackie and the children moved in.

I'll never forget seeing Jackie smiling at last, as she made various trips across the street carrying things for the new house that day. One time it was with her half-sister, Janet Auchincloss, and Caroline and the little dog, Shannon, on a leash. Jackie had the leash, and she was dressed in high boots and slacks. Another time it was with an armful of books.

There still remained much to be done, however, including personal shopping. I chose the morning of the 30th to pursue a bit of this extracurricular activity. On my return, I was greeted by Secret Service Agent Dolan with, "Am I happy to see you! Everybody's looking for Mary Gallagher!"

I quickly found out that he wasn't exaggerating. From every corner of the house came workmen—each asking a slew of questions.

In self-defense, I said, "Okay, fellas, just one at a time now . . ." Good-naturedly, they took their turns. And before long, all questions were answered and we were all settling down once again to our individual chores.

Two Navy men had been loaned from the White House Staff Mess to cook for Mrs. Kennedy at her home. They were also asked to stock the shelves, check supplies, and list additional pots and pans needed.

They were to arrange their hours so that one or the other would be on duty in the evenings when Jackie might have guests, as well as arrange to be with her on the weekends at Atoka.

At first, the Secret Service Agents had established their working quarters in the laundry room, directly off the kitchen, but that became so congested they were eventually moved to the basement.

My office on the second floor was next to Jackie's bedroom, overlooking the street. On the other side was the library; next to that, the guest bedroom and bath. The third floor consisted of a room for each of the children, as well as another for Miss Shaw.

After one week in her new home, Jackie decided that the shade of paint in the front hallway, including the walls leading up to the second floor and the second floor hall area, should be changed to a somewhat "flatter" white. She asked that I instruct the head painter, Mr. Kay. I did, and from the helpless shrug of his shoulders I could sense that he was almost prepared for her change of mind.

"Now," he said in a resigned way, "this is what Mrs. Kennedy said she wanted. If she wants us to do it over, we'll be more than happy to do it. But I'm sure she realizes I'll have to charge her for the extra job."

"You just let us have your bill," I said, "I'll explain it to Mrs. Kennedy."

It was all so familiar—I remembered those times at the White House. The main difference was that, now, there really would be a bill.

For all of us, these first few weeks at the house were the most difficult. As Jackie would dig into cartons containing photographs, books, phonograph records, and scrapbooks, she was faced with the stark, haunting memories of the years gone by.

The atmosphere in the new house was completely different from that of the Harriman house across the street. There, on the first floor, had been all the activity of family, staff, and Kennedy politicians.

But the new house was silent and lonely. During the hours I was there, I saw few people; few guests were invited, and reporters were not allowed. I remember that one news photographer managed to catch a shot of Jackie looking out of the window.

For a while, there wasn't a photograph of the President in sight. Many of the albums and folders of personal pictures remained unpacked. Jackie didn't seem to be able to muster the strength to face this task. Then, one morning, as she sat in my office going through a large envelope of material on JFK that we had ordered by mail, she asked that I remain in the room with her. She said, "It's so much easier doing it while you're here than at night when I'm alone. I just drown my sorrows in vodka."

37 ∽ THE MOST DIFFICULT MOMENTS

*M*Y MOST DIFFICULT MOMENTS CAME WHEN the children were around.

They could not fully comprehend the great void in their lives. Yet it was unmistakable that they missed their "Silly Daddy." To refrain from referring to him in our little conversations proved at times an almost unbearable test of the emotions.

Caroline, of course, was off at school a good part of the day. But on those days when I was at the house when she returned in the afternoon, her shy little "Hello" to Provi, me, or anyone else would grip me with the thought that there would be no more happy exchanges with her daddy. No more clap of his hands and loud call for "Buttons!" No more wild, excited runs into his arms.

John-John, who occupied himself during the day as three-year-olds do, continued to receive noontime visits from Dave Powers. They would lunch together, tell stories, march through the rooms, or do just anything to occupy the time happily.

Jackie's own strength and guidance now came from her brother-in-law, Robert, and he spent a great deal of time with her, coming immediately if she phoned him, or stopping by in the evening to see if she was all right. In order to avoid attention, he parked his car a little distance from the house, on another street.

One morning in early February, another heavy snow had fallen. As I went up the steps at the new Georgetown house, I could see Miss Shaw emerging from the house with the children at what seemed an unusually early hour—around 9 A.M.!

As we met, I greeted her with a cheerful "Good morning, Miss Shaw," adding, "be careful now that you don't fall. The steps are pretty slippery."

She was neither her chipper self nor the least bit receptive to my words of caution. "Hummmph," she snorted. "At least, if I fall down and break my ankle I might enjoy some peace and quiet in the hospital."

During these early weeks the children had been spending more and more time at the home of the Robert Kennedys in McLean. As we passed each other on the steps, Miss Shaw said, "You know, it just wouldn't surprise me at all if their little cousins might soon tire of our going out there so often."

Upon entering the house, I headed for my office upstairs, as usual. The Secret Service Agents, the maids, the kitchen help, and the houseman were tending to their regular duties, but the general atmosphere was quiet.

Soon, with her breakfast and the newspaper out of the way, Jackie called me into her bedroom for the start of another day. First came the folders of mail. Then she began to reminisce about the "JFK days."

She remarked that Mrs. Lincoln and I had been "the first two with him—and the last." She told me how invaluable we both were for the Kennedy Library and the Archives, cautioning that we should "be careful" about our transportation in cars. "You should get yourselves a good driver," she said, "so that nothing ever happens to you."

That rather puzzled me, but I quickly assured her that we did have two whom we considered tops—Joe Giordano and Bootsie Miller. Then, she went on to suggest that Evelyn and I arrange to talk into a tape recorder. "You can call Arthur

Schlesinger...he'll get one for you. Then just talk away about all the good things you remember about Jack."

"That wouldn't be difficult," I told her. "You know, I think I can recite from memory every single word the President ever said to me. Somehow, they've just been reserved in a special place in my mind."

She looked rather expectant. And it seemed now that I should offer just a little something that might make her smile. I related how, when I worked for JFK during his days as a Senator, he had seemed so surprised about my having to quit my job to have my first baby—how I had to remind him "First things first."

Jackie smiled. "That sounds so much like Jack," she said. "I don't think he ever really understood what went with having babies."

Jackie then went on to explain that, since Evelyn and I would be entitled to our offices at the E.O.B. for just a few months longer, she wanted us to plan on moving to the Archives. "Tell them to give you the nicest offices they have. Then, for an hour or so each morning, you and Mrs. Lincoln just sit and reminisce. Have sandwiches and coffee sent up."

February 12, 1964: JBK left for a few days in NYC. Mrs. Lincoln hadn't yet seen the new house, so I asked her to join me there after lunch tomorrow for a little tour.

We talked for a while with Miss Shaw, who was just recovering from a hectic morning. John-John had almost drowned Shannon, the cocker spaniel given to JFK on his trip to Ireland—trying to bathe him in the bathtub. When she went to fetch him, she discovered him, with water overflowing onto the floor. Sighing as though she didn't know quite what to expect of him next, Miss Shaw said, "You know, he's a boy and a half!"

Before leaving, I asked Caroline for a hug for Valentine's Day—the following day. She readily consented. Then, rather mischievously, she asked, "Have you ever had chicken pox?"

When I said no, she threw her arms around me again, saying, "Well, then, I'll give you *another* hug so you can get my chicken pox!"

> February 15, 1964: JBK was back at Atoka for the weekend.
> She called me at home to ask if I would contact Mr.
> Nazarian and tell him that, if he couldn't have her living
> room rug installed by the 26th, to cancel the order—and
> for me to go ahead and place the order with Billy Baldwin
> in New York.

She was setting this deadline "because I'll be having about twenty people to the house and want it down by then."

The phone call to Mr. Nazarian was one I simply dreaded to make, realizing that the wall-to-wall order—involving almost $5,000—for the huge room was actually in the works.

I wasn't at all surprised, either, at Mr. Nazarian's reaction when I relayed the message to him. Initially, I'm sure, my words must have caused him some slight shock. But he rebounded commendably in a rather patient, businesslike way.

"Well, Mrs. Gallagher," he said, "all I can say is that we originally gave Mrs. Kennedy a delivery date of the end of February, which was about as near as we could come when we first estimated."

The question was raised as to whether canceling the order would be an unethical thing to do, and I told him that I would pass his message on to Mrs. Kennedy. She accepted it and let it go at that.

Whether or not the job was completed in time for the arrival of her guests on the 26th, I could only wonder. As it turned out, I wasn't on hand to find out and had other worries.

For the next ten days or so, I was forced to divide my attention between Jackie's household affairs and serious matters on my own home front. On the 19th, Chris had undergone delicate surgery at the Johns Hopkins University Hospital in Baltimore, where Ray and I remained for the first few crucial days. Then it was Greg's turn—he had suddenly come down with chicken pox!

It was a rather anguishing ordeal—spending alternate days with each of them, when they both craved full-time attention. Somehow, it was all made slightly easier to bear by the boys' understanding attitude over the split shifts.

Although I never intended Jackie to know about Greg's chicken pox, she had apparently been told by Caroline of the "Valentine's Day hug" I had received! When she called me at home on the morning of the 24th, she began her conversation with, "I understand you're next in line for chicken pox," going on to suggest that I "get a shot of gammaglobulin from Dr. Travell." I assured her that I would take care of it the first thing the following morning.

Fortunately, life was back to normal within a few weeks—with only a minor problem, involving Caroline and John-John, cropping up on a Wednesday afternoon. Ordinarily, Miss Shaw's day off at mid-week presented no real problems because Provi would automatically take over. However, on this particular afternoon, Provi needed an extra pair of hands herself, as she was packing Jackie's suitcases for her Easter trip to Florida.

When Jackie and I finished up our day's work, I suggested to Jackie that the children could come along with me to the E.O.B. for a few minutes—and, from there, out to our house to play with the boys, have dinner, and return again about 7 o'clock.

She welcomed the idea and asked, "Would it be too much trouble for you if Caroline's little friend, Agatha, came along, too?"

"Oh, no," I answered, "the more the merrier." And we were soon off.

At the E.O. B., I suggested to the children that they visit with Mrs. Lincoln in her office; a visit, I knew, would delight her and the children, too. When I went in a little later, Evelyn was entertaining them at her desk, drawing pictures with them and allowing them to use her paper hole-puncher!

When we arrived at our house, the children darted directly to the back yard to visit Tom Kitten's little grave. After play-

354 ಶಿ

ing outside, and supper, they went up to the playroom. John-John occupied himself with wads of "Play-Dough" and Caroline busied herself with pad and pencil for "a note to Mommy."

Before long, she called me to ask, "Mary, how do you spell the word 'guess'?" She showed me her note, describing her visit with us, and after starting out with "Dear Mommy," she was closing off with, "Guess Who!"

I spelled it out for her, and she seemed quite pleased with herself over the little secret that was in store for her mommy.

The evening ended with our favorite session at the piano, with Agent Lynn Meredith playing. John-John and I gave a little performance, dancing to the merry tunes as Caroline, Chris, and Greg looked on slightly bewildered.

A *busy* mother they could understand, but a *dancing* mother was a puzzlement.

The moment that touched me most deeply happened one morning in the spring. As I was preparing to leave Miss Shaw and John-John at Georgetown to return to my office, it became obvious that this brave tyke was once again searching for the one hopeful answer to the question that lingered in his mind.

"Where's Mrs. Lincoln?" he asked.

When I told him that she was at the office, his next question automatically followed.

"Who's with her?"

How I wished—more than anything I'd ever wished in my life—that I could give him the *one* answer I knew he longed for . . .

38 ∽ AT LOOSE ENDS

*I*T WAS NOT UNTIL FEBRUARY 10, 1964, THAT
Jackie decided to visit her office at the Executive Office Building.

She arrived around 11 A.M. accompanied by her uncle from Connecticut, Wilmarth Lewis, whom she called "Uncle Lefty." He was a fine historian, I understood. First they went into Evelyn's office to go through some of the President's papers; then they came into my office.

When Jackie introduced me to her uncle, he looked puzzled. By way of explanation Jackie added, "Mary Gallagher is *my* Mrs. Lincoln!"

One of the things Jackie was interested in at this time was the suggestion that awards be presented every year in the name of John F. Kennedy. Jackie wrote Dick Goodwin, one of the Presidential aides, saying that they should be certain the awards would rank in stature with the Nobel Prize. Otherwise, they shouldn't be undertaken. She had wanted Goodwin's thinking concerning the fields of endeavor for which the Kennedy Prize should be awarded, and who would be suitable judges.

Among Jackie's thank-you letters was one to Morton Downey, thanking him for the stereo installation that had been his gift to the President and her at Atoka, but which the President had not lived to see completed, telling how excited he had been when she had told him that soon he would just press a button and have his music pouring into bedroom, bath, or any other room.

356 ह⋙

And she sent a thank-you note for the Morgantown glasses which she had ordered but which had arrived as a gift for her new house. The glasses were just like those she had used at the White House, bearing the words "The President's House." Whenever she used them, she said, she would recall those brief, wonderful days—all the official dinners and brilliant toasts her husband made so well as he used these glasses in "The President's House."

In February, too, Lady Bird Johnson paid a courtesy call to Jackie's office. She had phoned the day before to let Jackie know that she was interested in seeing the office. Jackie did not appear in person, but sent Nancy Tuckerman in her place to show Mrs. Johnson through the offices and the mail room where 1,000 pieces of mail arrived daily and were sorted. She was also shown the room full of barrels and bins of various gifts for Jackie and the children, sent by the general public.

There were, as I recall, 10,000 gifts, but the ones that stand out in my mind were the many touching paintings of little John-John saluting like a soldier at his father's funeral.

The day after Lady Bird's visit, President Johnson and his wife paid a call on Jackie at home in Georgetown. They brought along members of the Cabinet and other Government officials, including Central Intelligence Director John McCone, and Mr. and Mrs. McGeorge Bundy.

The President had a gift for Jackie: the four pens with which he had signed the tax cut bill that President Kennedy had been fighting for before he was assassinated. One pen was for the Memorial Library, one was for Jackie, one was for Caroline, and one for John-John.

After Jackie's visit, James Sasser, who had been in charge of her official appropriations, suggested that her office be redecorated. He said that it was the least that could be done for the former First Lady. I explained that the office was really just temporary. "As for Mrs. Kennedy's visits," I said, "they may be few and far between."

But Mr. Sasser felt strongly that the redecoration should be done for Mrs. Kennedy's sake. He asked if I would help choose the paint color, curtains, and carpeting, which I did.

Knowing Jackie's preference for off-white walls, we had chosen this color. For carpeting, I suggested something bright and cheerful—perhaps in red. In choosing the curtains, we decided on off-white nylon mesh, to give the room a light and airy appearance.

Mr. Sasser tended to the details in a most precise, thoughtful manner. When the job was completed, we were both satisfied that it would meet with Mrs. Kennedy's approval on her next visit.

Within Mr. Sasser's province had also fallen the responsibility for JBK's employees under the G.S.A. appropriations. By the month's end, he had become quite concerned over the number of "vacations" that one of the staff had thus far been taking.

As his official duty, he made some inquiries, asking if I knew whether or not she had been granted permission by Mrs. Kennedy for the time off. I told him I knew nothing about that problem. All I knew with any certainty were my own salary problems! I was once more engaged in a "salary marathon," though, on a smaller scale than my long, frustrating experience at the White House.

Back in December, Jackie had suggested I fit my salary into her $50,000 Federal appropriation. I approached Nancy Tuckerman, who I was told might be in charge of arrangements.

Nancy informed me that Dave Hackett—Robert Kennedy's close friend—was handling this. I told Nancy that I wanted to clarify two points. First, that my position with Mrs. Kennedy was that of personal secretary; and second, that I felt my working *full* time justified a fair annual salary of $12,000.

Nancy explained that she and Dave were to have a meeting on the subject within the next day or so. I asked to be included in the meeting or, if that wasn't possible, that I at least be consulted by them if they had any questions at all relating to the salary I was asking, and Nancy assured me this would be done.

A week later, I was taking the morning's dictation from Jackie. Propped up in her bed, she delved into one matter after another with ease and in her typical, methodical manner. All was normal and smooth. Then, casually slipping her feet from the bed to the floor, Jackie walked to the bathroom and reached into the medicine cabinet for a jar of cold cream. As she applied it to her face, she began a conversation that hit me like a small bombshell!

"Oh, Mary," she said, "I understand you've asked for $12,000 on my Government appropriation . . ."

I froze, waiting to hear the rest. Well over a year before, we had had a real spat when I asked for a salary increase.

"Gosh," she went on, "you know I really can't *afford* to pay all my help from the $50,000—what with having to pay for the new house, and Provi, and all the other expenses."

I remained rigid, wondering first of all how she could bring herself to worry about the matter of my salary at a time when she was too upset and grief-stricken to think about it, and wondering next, why I hadn't heard first from Nancy or Dave. I couldn't believe my ears. Nor did I interrupt her. I couldn't. I felt slightly ill.

Jackie continued, suggesting, "Couldn't it be the way it was before? You know, like when you came to the house in Georgetown and worked two or three days each week doing only my personal things?"

At this stage, handling only "her personal things" would certainly add up to more than just "two or three days," but I couldn't bring myself to argue.

Instead, as Jackie came over to the bed again, facing me, I could only say, "Jackie, I'm sorry you had to be troubled by all this. When you suggested that I get myself fixed for salary on your appropriation, I thought you meant just that, and I asked for what I thought would be fair."

She readily agreed, "Oh, yes, Mary, you've just been great! I don't know what I'd do without you . . ."

"Well, Jackie," I said, "I don't have the heart now to sit

here and discuss my salary any more. Let's just leave things as they are for now."

I scooped up the armload of papers and folders from the bed and headed for the door to make my way downstairs. My mind was muddled, and a feeling of helplessness swept over me.

As I passed a little desk in the downstairs library, I sat down. I felt I couldn't go on and pondered writing a letter of resignation. I scribbled a few lines, brief and to the point. But, suddenly, I could see my father's face before me, remembering the devotion with which he had stuck to his job. I sat and thought about him.

He was for forty years a track foreman with the New York, New Haven & Hartford Railroad Company, and his unblemished record of service was something to be most proud of. Even on the worst winter nights, when he was called to work, it took him less time to get dressed and be on his way than it would for us to stir up the courage to wake him.

He wore the heaviest clothing, and often worked through the night, even when he had worked all that same day, and he would come into the house early the following morning almost glowing with satisfaction in doing his job.

He refused to retire at sixty-five, continuing on till he was seventy. He was proud, after forty faithful years, to receive the company's little gold Service Pin in recognition of his services. It meant so very much to him. When he died in 1954, the pin was the one thing I chose as a keepsake, cherishing it ever since as a reminder of his character.

I read the lines I had written and knew that I couldn't possibly do this to Jackie at such a time. I tore the note up.

Then, in January I was ready to try again. I had decided to discuss with Dave Hackett the possibility of reaching for the "happy medium" of $10,000.

When I called his office, his secretary told me that he wasn't in but that she would have him return my call. Several hours later, he called back to say that he was preparing to leave for a trip to Boston, and would come to see me at my office when he got back—"on Thursday."

At 5 o'clock Friday evening, he called—promising he would see me "on Monday."

On Monday, in spite of heavy snow, I decided to brave the weather to keep my "promised appointment."

Joe Giordano was in front of my house at the usual time, and as we rode into Washington, I began to wonder how he managed at all! Cars along Memorial Boulevard were bogged down or abandoned completely.

I waited throughout the long day to hear from Dave. But the snow had long disappeared before I finally did! Two weeks later, his brief phone call came. My diary quotes him: "Nothing I can do about it at this time, but I'll try to do something later!"

"Something later" never came.

On February 25th, Jackie arrived back in Washington after a weekend on the Georgia plantation of the John Hay Whitneys—"Greenwood." Jackie wasn't the only guest. Also there were Lord and Lady Harlech and their daughter, Alice, and Mr. and Mrs. J. E. Sheffield of Camden, South Carolina, and New York. (Lady Harlech died soon after, and it was with Lord Harlech that stories of romance for Jackie arose the following year.)

There were some happy times with the children. On March 1st, Jackie took John-John and Caroline to the Coliseum in Washington to see the circus that had come to town. Little John came home triumphant carrying a turtle in a box—just what he'd always wanted.

On March 4th, Jackie went with her brother-in-law Bobby to the Pan American Union Building to a luncheon hosted by Ambassador Jose Mora, at which it was announced that Puerto Rico had pledged $100,000 and Venezuela another $100,000 for the Kennedy Library. It also was announced that 149 persons would record their memories of the President for the Library Archives.

It was at this time that Jackie told how the words from the musical *Camelot* kept running through her mind: "Don't let it be forgot . . . that once there was a Camelot." And she said whatever she did from now on would be to help people *remember* that Camelot of which her husband had been a part.

I see by my diary that I wasn't the only one of the household with troubles during this transition period. The President's loyal valet, George, was having a worse problem. Early in April, Dave Powers called me at the office and said that neither he nor Kenny O'Donnell had been successful in finding a new position for George Thomas. Effective April 11th, George would be without salary and position.

And there were other things, Dave Powers mentioned in his quick, broad Bostonian accent. It was time to think of discontinuing Provi's salary on the White House payroll and placing her on the Kennedys' New York office payroll.

His final piece of business concerned the two White House stewards at the Georgetown home. He asked that I handle with the New York office a "$100 per month increase for each," ending with his familiar "Thanks, pal—see ya later."

By the following morning, I heard from Dave again. Jackie, he informed me, "wasn't up to discussing Provi's salary. She asked that I talk it over with you and do whatever the two of us decide."

To me, this had come as a rather ticklish responsibility, since past experience had taught me how Jackie felt about salaries. I thought the best thing for me to do was to discuss the matter with Tom Walsh in the New York office; he and I both agreed on the phone that we would not be out of line in arranging for Provi to receive a take-home salary of $100 per week. Since Mrs. Kennedy was so dependent on Provi, every precaution should be taken to avoid dissatisfaction on Provi's part. So the matter was settled between us—quite satisfactorily so we thought.

My office at the E.O.B. was located at the very end of a

hallway, and I could see passengers emerge from the elevators. One morning, as I looked up from my desk, I saw George approaching, and went out to greet him. How strange it seemed to be seeing him here, away from the White House. He seemed a bit forlorn, and asked where Mrs. Lincoln's office was. When I showed him into Evelyn's office, I was asked to sit in on their discussion. As yet, he had no job. More than anything, Evelyn and I wanted to be of some help. It seemed the one thing we could do right now was compose a letter of recommendation, signed by Mrs. Lincoln, that George could use in applying for a position at a good hotel. That was what he had in mind for the moment.

Later, we heard that George had a guardian angel after all —Ted Reardon, who offered George a position, working directly for him at the Federal Deposit Insurance Corporation, located across the street from the Executive Office Building. I didn't realize it at the moment, but that was one down and two to go.

At 6 o'clock on the 10th, I heard from another of the "inner circle"—Provi.

She called me at home, giving me a résumé of the day's events at Georgetown and, from the way she spoke, it was apparent that she was exhausted and depressed.

"Mees Gallaga," she said, "I am verree upset and hurt—I canno' work for Mees Kennedee any more. I would like to geev her notice today an' leave as soon as possible!"

I urged her not to do anything until we could discuss it further. I suggested that she have lunch with me the following week—Jackie was going to be in New York.

She did, but on April 20th, as soon as Jackie was back from New York, Provi called again, this time with the plea to "Pleez come over, Mees Gallaga, and speak to Mees Kennedee fo' me . . ."

Provi was feeling the pressures of her own household responsibilities and needed some time off on weekends. Her mother was not well. Also, because her sons were not getting proper help and attention in their homework, they were not doing as well as they should at school.

Provi stated the facts clearly. She had been carrying quite a heavy load all along. She needed an assistant to take over on weekends. I promised her I would do what I could to help.

At 10:45 a.m., I related Provi's story to Jackie in the privacy of her bedroom. Jackie sighed, "I guess Provi needs to be cheered up!" She agreed to get someone in to help, and said, "Call Mrs. Pauwels. Have her get someone who speaks English. Provi will train her."

It was more than just the feelings of dissatisfaction among the household help, however—an atmosphere of gloom had settled on the house.

With each new day, there were constant heartbreaking reminders of JFK, despairing moods of those left behind, who were trying so hard to carry on without him. Without enthusiasm, the days seemed long and empty.

Evelyn Lincoln began to have hints of trouble.

One day, the dictation done, Jackie talked about the matter of Evelyn's office and mine at the E.O.B. "You know, you won't be able to stay there forever."

I agreed, explaining that we realized this—and adding that we were ready to move at any time we were given the word. She mentioned further that "Mrs. Lincoln will just *have* to start working with Archives this spring," and intimated that she did not feel anything was being done yet on the President's papers.

I assured Jackie that Mrs. Lincoln was spending endless hours on the President's papers and, at the same time, preparing the "JFK Traveling Exhibit." Still, Jackie directed me to give Mrs. Lincoln her message.

When I told Evelyn of the conversation, she said, "Why, I wonder, would Jackie ask about something like that?"

I could offer no explanation—and agreed it was a good idea

364 ૐ

when Evelyn came back with "Well, I suppose I'll just have to submit a written report to let her know exactly what I *am* doing here."

I thought of Evelyn at work. She was the only person who could dare attempt—and successfully—the deciphering of JFK's innumerable notes and jottings.

She would sit for hours, leaning over the papers, sometimes with a magnifying glass until eventually she established the reputation of being "The Female Sherlock Holmes"! For this alone, archivists and historians will have reason to be grateful to her.

She was also, as much as was humanly possible, faithfully acknowledging letters from JFK's many admirers and granting their wishes for photos. She got hundreds of letters a day.

Some people even came to her office and wept openly while relating some memorable incident about JFK.

Within her spacious office, Evelyn had tastefully displayed the ever-popular rocking chair, the PT-boat model, many photos of JFK and his family, which lined the walls. And to add even a warmer touch, the soft sound of JFK's favorite songs coming from his record player.

It was here, in Room 300, that one could nostalgically feel the closest sense of JFK's presence . . . and it was from here that one could leave, knowing that his memory was being cherished. How could Evelyn possibly put all this in a memo?

Her report turned out to be just two pages long! But before it even reached Jackie, Evelyn received a call from Bobby—with whom Jackie had apparently been discussing the subject later that same day. He thanked her for all she was doing, and also told her to keep right on as she was.

From time to time, Caroline and John-John would pick up their phone at home and place their little calls to Mrs. Lincoln. On the next afternoon, one came to her from John-John. After a little chit-chat, he announced that he would be coming over to the office on Thursday to see her—and wanted to know, "Is Daddy there?"

Evelyn was doing superbly, sometimes through her own tears.

Since the President's assassination, Jackie had remained pretty much to herself—venturing outdoors, for the most part, only on her occasional trips to New York. However, as the month of April neared its end, it began to appear a bit more hopeful that she might be thinking in wiser terms of getting out more and occupying her time in some active diversion.

The first signal came when she called me at home on Saturday morning, the 25th, asking that I arrange to get her reducing machine out of storage. The next one came the following Monday morning, when she asked that I order her several pairs of shorts for playing tennis—medium length—size 12. The reducing machine was like one she had seen and admired at Morton Downey's house.

On Wednesday, April 29th, Jackie took off for New York again for several days. While she was gone, the final touches were to be added to my office at the Executive Office Building in order to have it in as presentable shape as possible for her next visit.

In New York, Jackie took the children to see the World's Fair. She had asked the Fair officials not to announce her visit, so that a minimum of people would notice them. And they had had a marvelous time, hustling from one pavilion to another.

By May 1st, a new "distress signal" had come to me. The two Navy stewards called. They said they had been serving as butlers, waiters, and moving men, both in Georgetown and at Atoka. What discouraged them most of all was that they had not been able to devote any time to their studies for Navy examinations and, therefore, might miss possible promotions. They wanted to return to the White House Mess, where they could put in regular hours, spend more time with their families, and above all, work toward promotions. They both confessed that they had put in requests for transfer and hoped that I might do them the favor of making the appropriate explanation to Jackie. I assured them that I would.

Jackie was back from her trip on May 5th, and I was once again by her bedside, taking up the problem of the two Navy men in the kitchen.

I broke the news as gently as I could. Jackie was not the least bit pleased with what she heard. Her quick response to the complaint of working "long hours and weekends" was, "But they have every other day off!"

"That's just the point, Jackie," I said. "What they prefer instead is to have their two days off run *together*. And over the weekends, rather than one day at a time during the course of the week."

I tried to make her understand the situation as they saw it, but she didn't seem to catch it. This time, she remarked, "Well, what do they want? Do they want to go to Texas and work for the Johnsons from six in the morning till six at night?"

Again I tried as best I could, and ended by saying that they had put in their papers for transfer.

Jackie showed no signs of recognizing that her small staff did not like being called on to provide all the services, accommodations, conveniences, and comforts that she had grown so used to receiving from a much larger staff during her years at the White House. Her staff's attitude, as far as I could see, puzzled her.

As the day continued, I could only hope that it would end on a happier note. And it did.

At 5 P.M., Jackie cast aside the cares and woes of her unhappy household for a more enjoyable pastime—the viewing of a new fashion collection from Italy. She met privately—via back-door entrance—with Princess Irene Galitzine at the Shoreham Hotel, and the collection of clothing apparently thrilled Jackie no end.

Upon receiving the bill for the items purchased, I was relieved to see that even though we were all at loose ends, at least her shopping was back to normal.

39 ～ THE SUMMER OF
OUR DISCONTENT

*J*ACKIE'S NEXT VISIT TO HER OFFICE WAS ON May 7th. She came escorted by Jim Sasser and Secret Service Agent Clint Hill, as well as Nancy Tuckerman and White House photographer Captain Stoughton.

Mr. Sasser was proud of the redecoration of Jackie's office, and her immediate expression of approval delighted him.

She didn't stay long, however. She had come to get certain papers from the files, so her visit was rather brief. As we stood talking by the files, I observed Captain Stoughton, at the open doorway with his ever-ready camera. He looked as though he were waiting for a signal from Jackie to take a picture of the two of us. But it didn't happen.

From my office, Jackie went into the anteroom occupied by Ensign George Dalton, assigned to assist Evelyn Lincoln with her work on the Presidential papers and records. When Jackie reached his desk, she greeted him warmly. Then, standing at George's side, she looked toward Captain Stoughton and asked him to snap their picture.

Jackie then went to see Evelyn in the office next to mine. Again the same procedure: Jackie stood at Evelyn's side near the desk and asked that Captain Stoughton take *their* picture together.

Jackie's visit with Evelyn that morning ran well into our regular lunch hour. The minutes ticked by . . .

Finally, Jackie emerged from Evelyn's office and gave her

farewells. Her Secret Service Agent followed with her coat draped over his arm—making a last-minute rush back to my office to retrieve her handbag and gloves.

Within a minute or two, Evelyn was standing in my doorway. She was extremely pale, and I asked if she felt all right. Her reply seemed to come from somewhere far away. We walked in silence.

I could arouse no enthusiasm from her at all over lunch. And, this, too, was most unusual. Finally, when we had finished, Evelyn seemed to have come to a decision, and she told me what had happened.

Jackie had cried, "Oh, Mrs. Lincoln, all this shouldn't be so hard for you, because you still have your husband . . . what do I have now? Just the library . . ."

Evelyn hesitated a moment and continued, "She wanted to know why I needed such a large office. And I told her that since all the people loved the President so much, I felt his things *should* be displayed in a nice office for them to see. Then she burst out with, 'But these things are all mine!' and told me what she wants done with them, not to give them to this one and that one."

Jackie had also questioned her then about what had obviously been bothering her for the past few weeks—what Mrs. Lincoln was actually doing. Evelyn did her best to explain, but Jackie said, according to Evelyn, "Why, Mrs. Lincoln, I could sit down and in a half-day index all these items on cards myself!"

The more I heard, the more my heart ached for Evelyn, but it did seem that getting it all off her chest was what she needed at this point.

To try to make Evelyn laugh, I said, "Did you offer her a chair?" That managed to arouse at least a little smile from Evelyn.

Since she and I had gone through all the past years together devoting them so completely to both JFK and JBK, I suffered with her.

As we prepared to leave the Staff Mess, we ran into Mr.

Gruenther, who introduced us to two celebrities: Ed Sullivan and Mickey "Toy Bulldog" Walker, the former world boxing champion. Thinking of my sons, I requested their autographs. On a fresh page in my notebook, Ed Sullivan wrote:

> "To Christopher and Gregory—
> And all the Clan Gallagher—
> Ed Sullivan"

He then asked, with feeling, that I give a "special hello to Mrs. Kennedy from all the Sullivans."

Mickey Walker drew a bulldog—as part of his signature. I looked at the bulldog and I thought, Evelyn will be like a bulldog, too, hanging on and doing her best for the "Chief" —no matter what.

And so would I.

The next few days were rough ones for Evelyn Lincoln, surrounded as she was by every reminder of JFK and now smarting from the fresh wound.

> May 8, 1964: Mrs. Lincoln still appears quite depressed today over yesterday's blast by JBK. Evelyn openly admitted, "I've just lost so much interest in working." The whole thing was apparently too hard to forget in such a short time.

By the next week, Evelyn was a bit happier. More of JFK's personal office items were being displayed in the Traveling Exhibit. Evelyn told me she practically had to *fight* to have the President's historic H.M.S. *Resolute* desk included. Yet, in later newspaper stories, it was interesting to note Jackie's reference to the desk as "one of the obvious items" chosen for the exhibit.

Life with Jackie demanded that I turn my attention back to my own work. One rare night I attended PTA, and when I came home found a message Ray had left me.

May 18, 1964:
Maria—
Jackie called at 8:50—Wants you at Georgetown at 3 P.M.
tomorrow "with the book of bills"—Says she has to face
the situation sometime. She may contact you in the A.M.
Seemed jolly.

Ray

It was about this time that Jackie turned down the plan
of a friend in France to set up, as she put it, an "enormous
project of scholarships," saying that this was not needed to
make people remember her husband. She said it seemed much
too "sad" to bother people about the scholarship project at
this particular time.

I see by my diary:

May 19, 1964: Arrived at appointed time of 3:00 P.M. but
JBK was engaged in the Living Room with Mayor Willy
Brandt...who was paying her a call. I went directly to
the office upstairs and prepared the books.

When Mayor Brandt of West Berlin left, she and Bobby
Kennedy, who was also there, returned to the living room for
about a half-hour. Then, at 4 P.M., Jackie joined me upstairs,
and we started to face the financial situation—the first time
since JFK's assassination.

As she reviewed the "Food & Liquor" expenses, she found
some reason to wonder why the figures were running so high.
She inquired whether the kitchen help were following the
recommendation she had asked me to pass on to them. Her
recommendation had resulted from one of our discussions
during pre-White House days when she had asked how I managed my meals at home. At that time, I had told her of the
"Consumer Foods Freezer Plan," to which we belonged, and
how it served our needs ideally. I explained that it enabled
us to stock up on choice meats and other foods. Its discount
prices had resulted in great savings to us. Having remembered

this, she suggested that I arrange for the same outfit to furnish her meat requirements.

I assured her now that this plan was still being followed and that expenses were being kept to a minimum in this area. But the meat orders represented only a part of expenditures in the "Food & Liquor" category. Dairy products were being delivered by local stores. I could agree with Jackie that these expenses might be more closely watched. But I could *not* agree at all with her next comment—that the help might be "taking food *home* with them."

I was more than taken aback by this, but assured her as well as I could that she should have no fear of this. But she wasn't quite satisfied. "Well, speak to them about the food bills, anyway . . ."

Quickly turning the pages, she questioned several other entries. To complicate matters, receipts had already been forwarded to the New York office, accompanying the original copies of the monthly financial reports. But to settle any doubts, I promised to call back the receipts and submit a written report to her for the specific items they covered.

Her eye spotted a check for "Petty Cash" to a S.S. Agent. Usually they received $300 a month to cover miscellaneous expenditures while traveling with Jackie. This item was for $1,000, which appeared incredible to her.

"What're they doing," she asked rather hotly, "using my money for *their* accommodations?"

Again, I came to the defense. "No, Jackie, I'm sure not," I replied quickly. "If you'd like, I'll ask for an itemized account. I'm sure he has the receipts, too, for you to look at."

I knew this was the way S.S. Agents operated, and when I approached him in the matter he obliged willingly and accounted for every expenditure right down to the final penny.

As she glanced further over the statements, another check for "Cash" caught her eye. This one, in the amount of $90, had gone to Provi. I told her it covered "overtime" that Provi had put in at the house.

"Overtime?" Jackie asked. "Do you mean to say that for

every little thing extra someone does around here, I have to pay them?"

"Yes, Jackie," I said. "That's usually the way it works. Provi's been working till late in the evenings and weekends. I felt it was justified ..."

"Oh, Mary," Jackie continued, "about Provi's salary ... I just think $100 is too high ... I can't pay her that while I'm away for the summer months." Jackie suggested that I call Mrs. Pauwels of the employment agency to ask "what Provi could get if she worked in Washington as a top maid, free-lancing around for parties and things during the summer ..."

Then, with the subject of Provi's pay still fresh in her mind, Jackie came to my salary. "And *you*," she said, "demanding $12,000 salary. Why, I just can't ..." I couldn't believe she was back to my salary again!

"Jackie," I interrupted, "please don't say that I've *demanded* anything. What I asked for was what I felt I deserved—nothing more. And so far I haven't gotten it ... Now if you'd like to discuss my salary ..."

"Oh, no, Mary," Jackie said quickly, "that's okay." She then repeated that I should get in touch with Mrs. Pauwels about making other arrangements for Provi.

We finally closed the books at 6 P.M., and I now had the unpleasant task of having to speak to the kitchen help about the food bills, of checking with the Secret Service Agent about disbursement of Petty Cash funds, of having to contact Mrs. Pauwels about Provi, and, of course, preparing further statements to clarify the items that had still remained questionable in her mind.

That same evening, I heard from Mrs. Pauwels regarding the maid, Maria Silva, who had been hired to help with general household chores. Mrs. Pauwels was calling to report that Maria was in her office "nervous and upset," feeling she could no longer work for Mrs. Kennedy. As it turned out, Mrs. Pauwels was able to persuade Maria to remain a while longer.

On the 25th of May, Jackie went to New York for the

opening of the Library Exhibit. Nancy Tuckerman and Pam Turnure were also in New York for the occasion.

A few days later, Clint Hill called from New York, saying that Mrs. Kennedy was planning to spend the Memorial Day weekend at the Cape with the children. "She'll need one maid and two kitchen boys."

The advice I received from the White House Naval Office, however, was that Mrs. Kennedy "should hire her own help at the Cape, as it would raise a problem in sending up the Navy boys from the White House." I relayed the message.

I got in touch with Mr. Robert Luddington in Boston as in the old days, asking him to hire the help there, open the house and get the rooms ready for Mrs. Kennedy's arrival on Friday.

On May 29th, the late President's birthday, Jackie and Robert Kennedy flew to Hyannisport for a television broadcast in memory of JFK. Jackie and the children stayed in their own home in the family compound.

On June 1st, I see by my diary, that Jackie called me at home around 6:30 in the evening, asking that I spend the next day at the house "to type poetry, for the fund-raising dinner in New York on the 16th, to be recited by Fredric March." So I typed for a good many hours, copying poetry dealing with death and sadness and leaders fallen on the battlefield—"I Have a Rendezvous with Death," "Ulysses," "John Brown's Body," and many others. Every poem reminded me more of the *one* thing I was trying to forget— the emptiness of the days without JFK, who, until just six months ago, had given such purpose and joy to our White House days.

Jackie had everyone scouting for appropriate poems. I recall she wanted Nancy to find a poem about what was said of the Irish Brigade at the Battle of Fredericksburg, and the answer had been something about "War battered dogs— knawing a naked bone. Fighters in every war and clime for every cause 'their' or 'our' own."

And she asked Arthur Schlesinger for quotes from Shakespeare: "Now is the winter of our discontent..." from *Richard III*, Act I, Scene I. And "Death of Kings..." from *Richard II*, Act II, Scene II. And on and on...

I think her favorite was Robert Frost's "On Stopping by Woods on a Snowy Evening." She wrote out three lines of it for me.

The amount of literature—especially poetry—that had been written concerning death and fallen leaders was staggering. My fingers flew over the typewriter keys endlessly as Jackie added another book and another and another.

June 2, 1964: Arrived at the house a little before 9:00 A.M., to find a few stacks of books next to my typewriter—with paper markers, designating the poems to be copied; just a quick glance told me that it would be, at least, a few days' project! And, I immediately set to typing.

At 10:00 A.M., JBK came into the office, announcing: "Mary, it'll be wonderful when you get yourself set up here—it seems so far away at E.O.B. that I don't want to call." Again, she seemed to have in mind some plan that hadn't yet been spelled out to me. However, I was here —and, knew I would be for a while, as my work was clearly cut out! I asked no questions.

On my third or fourth full day of typing nothing but lamentations and elegys, I was offered a little break by Caroline, who came in to ask if I "would like to play a game" with her. As far as I was concerned, any little game was welcome at this point. We sat together drawing windmills. Windmills! I felt like one too—a human windmill...

40 ∽ JACKIE LEAVES WASHINGTON

IN THE DAYS AFTER THE TRAGEDY, A NEW PHE-
nomenon developed. Crowds of people lined the sidewalks
in front of Jackie's house each day. Busloads of tourists
flashed their cameras as they rode by. Curiosity seekers
strained for even the slightest glimpse of the late President's
family.

It was obvious that many people, total strangers, had felt
such a genuine personal loss that they could not resist the opportunity to be as close as possible to his family.

There were a few humorous moments. Whenever my husband stopped by to bring me something, the tourists assumed
he was one of the Kennedy's VIPs and clicked away to record the "historic" event.

Inside, everyone tried to ignore the crowds for the children's sake, attempting to carry on as usual. I visited with
Miss Shaw and John-John in the dining room one morning
when they were having breakfast, and John-John noticed a
pin on my sweater. He was totally absorbed in it for a moment. "Is that a lobster, or a crab?" he demanded to know.

It was small in design and, for the most part, red. "A
rooster," I said. He was from Missouri and took a closer look.
Only then was his curiosity satisfied. I complimented him on
how nicely he was eating his breakfast. He announced matter-
of-factly, "I'm a lit'tle gen'tle'man!" much to Miss Shaw's
delight.

In June, after Jackie's fund-raising dinner in New York,
she was scheduled to go directly to the Cape. The children

were to remain in Georgetown a few days without her and join her at the Cape on the 18th. They were not happy about this arrangement.

As Jackie said her goodbyes to the children, John-John could not restrain his feelings of wanting to go along, and began to cry. But Miss Shaw quickly won him over and within minutes he was his normal, happy self once more. But I could see that Caroline was trying her hardest to suppress the same urge—and did so admirably. After the final wave to her mother, I could not resist scooping her up into my arms to hug her and tell her how "grown-up" I thought she was! She was delighted with the attention and said, "You must be stronger than Mummy. She can't even lift me off the floor!"

As it was time to get upstairs to my desk, and though I never waited for the elevator, I accepted John-John's invitation to ride up in the little elevator with him. We were followed by his constant companion, Shannon. Inside, and the door closed, we were standing there in pitch darkness. I suddenly realized that I didn't even know where the push-buttons were—for either some light or some motion! But I needn't have worried at all. John-John, at least, knew which button moved us up—this was his usual mode of travel. He was fearless in the dark. When the door finally opened again, he beamed as happily as an "old pro" and scampered off with Shannon.

Evelyn Lincoln and I hurried to Georgetown the morning of the 18th to see Caroline, John-John, and Miss Shaw off for the Cape. We were at the house by 9:15 A.M. For John-John, with his love for the water, I brought along a sailor hat that he could wear up North; and, for Caroline, because of all the happy times we had known with Tom Kitten, I brought along a hat adorned with a striped kitten. The little beach hats were soon plunked on their heads.

We spent a few minutes chatting with Miss Shaw and the children in the living room. Caroline came over to perch on my lap, putting her arm around my shoulder, and asked, "Mary, will you be coming up to the Cape this summer?"

I replied, "Well, Caroline, that all depends ... If Mummy needs me, I will."

She questioned further, "Do you want my mother to need you?"

"Oh, yes," I answered, "... know why?"

She shook her head from side to side.

"Well, because I know I would just feel terrible if she didn't need me!"

Her happy chuckle revealed her great satisfaction—she obviously enjoyed the "quiz game" we oftentimes played together. I found myself reflecting on the past summer at the Cape with Jackie, feeling certain that, before too long, I could expect a call from her to start packing my suitcases. But at the time, the uncertainty of when I would see Caroline and John-John again made our farewells more difficult than ever before. They had come to mean as much to me over the past years as my own children, and I knew I would miss them greatly.

Yet, with hugs and kisses and all the happy words I could muster, I left with Evelyn for the office—waving to them all. Caroline sat atop one of the lion statues in front of the house, John-John atop the other. Smiling and waving, they were a picture of youth and happiness. This will always be the picture that remains vividly in my mind. I had no way of knowing, or even suspecting, that this little visit was our last time together.

The car pulled away from the curb—and the years have since passed between us.

At 8 P.M. on July 2nd, as Ray and I sat in the kitchen enjoying a cup of coffee with our friends, Mary and Peter Kosak, the White House phone rang. I reached for the pad and pencil expecting, as usual, to take a few quick notes from Jackie.

But this was a message that was to engrave itself on my mind instead.

After greeting me with the usual "Hi, Mary, this is Jackie," her message began, "You may have already guessed, but I want you and Mrs. Lincoln to be among the first to know that I am planning to move to New York..."

I was rather surprised at hearing this although Provi and I had privately speculated on all her recent trips to New York. I tried to remain cheerful.

"Well, Jackie," I said, "I'm sure you've thought it over, and if you think life will be easier and happier for you there, then that's where you should be. I want to wish you every happiness."

She thanked me and mentioned that all the announcements would be appearing in the papers next week.

From this, I assumed she would soon tell me more about her future plans for the rest of her staff and me. I did not press her for details. When she finally mentioned the work that would be involved in her move, I immediately assured her, "Well, you know me. I'll be right there as long as you need me."

Jackie sounded relieved, expressing her confidence and gratefulness. Then, she said, "Oh, just a minute, Mary... Caroline wants to speak with you."

Caroline came on, sounding very chipper and asking, "What're the boys doing?"

After a brief report, which brought a happy giggle from her, I inquired about her wrist, which she had sprained in a recent fall from her horse. She answered that it was fine— after which we each hoped the other would have a happy summer and said goodbye. This, as it turned out, was the last time Caroline and I spoke together. Jackie took the phone again, and we concluded the call.

Ray and the Kosaks were, of course, a bit curious. As I told them the news, I commented, "But, you know, there's something about that call that bothers me—something that Jackie has left unsaid."

I couldn't pinpoint it—there was just a strange feeling I had.

Still, I was sure that my job with Jackie would continue in

Washington. There was a great volume of mail coming in, and it seemed logical to assume that Jackie would need me in her Washington office for a long time.

We had realized the eventual necessity to terminate such an office—the ultimate need to break the close, happy, and memorable ties. But I decided to cross that bridge when we got to it.

The announcement of Jackie's move to New York appeared in the newspapers on July 7th. The stories offered no enlightenment concerning my position. Nancy Tuckerman and Pam Turnure were mentioned as remaining with Jackie.

I felt hurt and puzzled. As the day progressed, calls began to pour in from family and friends, whose curiosity had also been aroused by the articles. I was in the difficult and embarrassing position of trying to make appropriate explanations about what I would be doing now. But I didn't know myself . . .

The next morning, Jackie called early from the Cape and dictated with normal fluency. Then she paused, and I waited for her words. As usual, I began to record automatically as she spoke—until I suddenly realized that the message was for me!

"I suppose by now you've read the newspapers about my move to New York," she said.

"Yes, Jackie," I answered, "I have, but . . ."

"Well," she announced, "since my life is all changed now and my staff will be located in New York, I guess I really won't be needing you any more after September first."

I was speechless!

"Mary, are you there?" she asked.

I could hear her, but I could make no response. After a few seconds, I replied weakly, "Oh, yes . . . yes, Jackie, I'm here, but would you mind repeating that again, please? I'm not sure I understood . . ."

She repeated what I *thought* I'd heard. I was weak, and for the moment I believe I was actually in a slight state of shock. I groped for some kind of an answer. Finally, I mustered, "Well, Jackie, if that's your decision . . ." I could go on no further.

"Oh, now, Mary," she came back, "don't get huffy . . ."

Afterward I realized that Jackie couldn't tell the difference between huffy and hurt. I explained that I didn't mean to be "huffy" at all. It was just that, after my long, close association with the Kennedys, I'd never expected this kind of announcement when it came time to let me go—that I just didn't know, really, what else I could possibly say.

"Yes, I know," she said a bit more understandingly, "it's all very sad. But it would be just too impractical to try to operate between New York and Washington, dictating over long distance. And the New York office can handle my bills and bookkeeping, since they do it for all the other Kennedys . . ."

And that was it. I could only remain silent, listening almost in a stupor.

"We'll still be close," she continued, "and, if ever I can do anything for you, just let me know." From that, she went on to mention that Provi wouldn't be going to New York, either.

Actually, moving to New York had been the very least of my desires and expectations. But I had hoped and expected that, when the time would come for Jackie to announce she no longer needed me, it would be in a warm, face-to-face manner. Obviously, I had expected too much.

Then, in the final touch, Jackie asked whether I would be in Washington for the summer to help with her move.

"Have you had your vacation yet?" she wanted to know.

"No," I answered, "there's been so much work to do, I haven't had time to even think about a vacation."

"Oh, great!" she exclaimed, "could you plan to take it later, then? I'll let you know when to start moving my things . . . but I really think you should be all finished by September first."

"Jackie," I offered resignedly, "as I've always told you, I'll be here just as long as you need me . . . to the very last day."

Replacing the receiver of the phone, I stared blankly at

the stacks of papers covering my desk. Until this morning, they had seemed so important. Now, they appeared meaningless.

Glancing over the fresh notes in my book, I was vaguely aware of the transciption. I sat motionless, wondering how I would manage to get through it. I felt sick—one thing in my mind, with room for nothing more—Jackie's words, "I guess I really won't be needing you any more after September first."

There was just one person I could turn to now—and that, of course, was Evelyn Lincoln. I wandered into her office. The minute she saw me, she gasped, "What's the matter? Are you all right?"

I repeated Jackie's message just as I had received it. Evelyn expressed her disbelief, but soon she realized that it was true.

Evelyn and I had devoted ourselves to the Kennedys over the past twelve years, and it had seemed that we were destined to continue to work for them to the very end. Until now, there had been every reason to believe that we would do so together. Jackie had just recently asked that Evelyn and I plan our next move, to the Archives, where we were to occupy offices side by side. Wayne Grover, in charge of Jackie's space there, had asked us to look over the suite of rooms allocated to us on the fourth floor. The final details of the color scheme for walls and carpeting had been decided. The rooms were soon to be ready for us. Now, we had to face the unpleasant realization that Evelyn would be moving to the Archives alone.

Never before had one single day proved more difficult for me. That night, I prepared for bed hoping that sleep would blot out the thoughts that had held me so tautly all day. And with each passing hour, sleep became more and more impossible. In the early morning, I was still standing at the bedroom window, staring out.

July 9, 1964: 9:00 A.M.—Dave Hackett calling me with message from JBK . . .

"Mrs. Kennedy's great intent is that you let us know if

there is any way we can help. Nothing personal involved ... just that since everything is being moved to New York, she said the office there can handle her bills and book-keeping like they do for the rest of the Kennedys..."

Thanking Dave for his call and assuring him that I could manage, I explained that I understood the situation, but that I felt it could have been handled a lot better. Dave was well aware of the many years I had been with the Kennedys and seemed to understand my shock at having received the unexpected news so abruptly.

His phone call had served the purpose of assuring me of one thing—that Jackie herself had, apparently, some second thoughts about her phone call to me of the day before.

Looking ahead to the weeks that were left, there was no doubt that I would need every minute to cope with every detail. Automatically, I began to reach for one thing, then another. To my own amazement, I began to feel some of my old spirit returning. By late afternoon, when my powers of concentration had returned somewhat to normal, I phoned Tom Walsh in the New York office to notify him to terminate the "Mary B. Gallagher—Special" account at the Riggs National Bank. I felt the bank should be given a month's notice, at least.

Tom Walsh was almost speechless. Expressing surprise that I would no longer be working for Mrs. Kennedy, he said that this was the very first he'd heard of it. He finally said, "Well, Mary dear, I plan to be in Washington the early part of August. Let's discuss it further at that time. But don't take any steps yet with the bank account."

I accepted his answer and let it go at that.

At 9:30 A.M. on July 20th, Jackie called from the Cape and, among other things, reminded me to get in touch with Mrs. Pauwels to find out about free-lance jobs for Provi's summer schedule.

Mrs. Pauwels invited me to have lunch with her. Though the invitation in itself was not unusual—she had extended it many times before—it was unusual that, for the first time, I felt free to accept.

I was reluctant to go to one of the downtown restaurants Mrs. Pauwels suggested, because Jackie frequently called me around lunchtime. So I invited Mrs. Pauwels to join me at the White House Staff Mess. I felt that this little courtesy for Mrs. Pauwels would serve as a small gesture of appreciation in Jackie's behalf for furnishing her and her mother with so many recruits for domestic help.

She offered to take a cab, but I told her one of the White House drivers would pick her up.

Noontime found us comfortably seated, enjoying lunch and carrying on our discussion. So far, all was very normal and very pleasant. During lunch, a Navy steward brought a telephone to our table. Mrs. Kennedy was calling.

"Mary," Jackie began, "are you at the Staff Mess?"

"Yes, Jackie, I am," I replied.

"And do you happen to have Mrs. Pauwels there with you?" she asked next, in what I quickly sensed was a disturbed, angry mood.

"Yes, Jackie, I do."

This was precisely where my conversation ended as hers took over for the next several minutes ... I could only listen in disbelief.

In angry tones, she proceeded to voice her displeasure.

"You do not have the right to take Mrs. Pauwels to the Staff Mess with you. All you were expected to do was simply handle the discussion by telephone. That was *all* you were supposed to do. And, Mary, I just don't like the idea of your sending a Government car for Mrs. Pauwels." (It was beyond me at the moment how she had learned of this in just the past hour!)

"It's okay if you want to keep Mrs. Lincoln company at the Staff Mess," she declared, "but that's for President Johnson's people."

Then, apparently feeling the need to substantiate further, she continued, "Don't you know the Johnsons despise us?

They won't even allow the Secret Service Agents to wear their PT-boat tie clips any more."

I was aware that anything I said might cause Mrs. Pauwels to suspect what this conversation was all about.

Jackie kept after me, ". . . and, Mary, getting your office all painted up," she remonstrated. "You know, I just don't like the way you're throwing your weight around!"

I was stunned. My mind was absorbed in trying to figure out the reasoning behind this angry monologue.

Having said all this and more, Jackie told me to let her speak to Mrs. Pauwels. When their conversation ended, Mrs. Pauwels—who realized the humiliating experience to which I had just been subjected—expressed her regrets and apologies.

"Do not be embarrassed for my sake," she reassured me.

When I got back to my office, I immediately got in touch with the switchboard operators. "Should Mrs. Kennedy call me at any time this afternoon," I instructed, "will you please tell her that I'm not available?" And for the next few hours I tried to work. It was hopeless, so at 4 o'clock, I called the operators again to notify them that I was leaving for the day.

As soon as I entered the house, my mother-in-law told me that the White House operator had just called, leaving word that I call Mrs. Kennedy as soon as I got in.

I walked into Ray's office instead and asked if he would take us all out for an early dinner—and then for a nice, long ride somewhere. Anywhere. Just as long as we were back home around 9 o'clock or so, in time to put the boys to bed. Both he and my mother-in-law spared me questions.

It was 9:30 P.M. when we returned. And if there were at least two happy people in our house that night, they were Chris and Greg, who were delighted over staying up beyond their regular bedtime.

We had started upstairs when the White House phone in the kitchen began to ring.

Feeling reasonably sure that the operator would announce Mrs. Kennedy's call before putting her directly on the line, I reached for the receiver and heard: "Oh, Mrs. Gallagher,

Mrs. Kennedy's been trying to reach you all evening . . . shall I put her on the line now?"

"No, thank you," I replied. "Will you please tell Mrs. Kennedy she can reach me tomorrow if she'd like? I'm busy getting the children ready for bed."

By this time, even the telephone operators must have become a bit curious.

It was another toss-and-turn night for me. I still couldn't make myself understand the sharp, sudden change in Jackie this afternoon.

The next morning, the phone calls continued—and I continued to evade them. Twenty-four hours had passed when I felt I could relent.

I was at Jackie's house in Georgetown, and I notified the operator that this was where I'd be for the next half-hour or so; she could put Mrs. Kennedy through if she tried to reach me again. Sure enough, Jackie was on the line in minutes!

In her sweetest, softest voice she began offering her apologies for "yesterday's blast."

"Oh, Mary, I'm so sorry. I didn't mean to blast at you," she said, going on to explain that she had been under a terrible strain, that her "nerves had been on edge," and she really hadn't meant it at all.

When she finished, I thanked her very much, telling her how much it meant to me to have her apology. My own thoughts were sufficiently composed now—and I knew that the only way I could possibly achieve peace of mind was by making them known to her.

"And, Jackie," I added, "the one thing I'd like to ask now is that you never speak to me that way again. I was never more hurt or humiliated."

She apologized again, asking that we just forget the whole thing.

"No, Jackie," I answered, "I'm afraid I can't let it go at that. I have to explain my side of the story." I insisted on getting everything off my chest, against her will or not.

I told her about my original intention of discussing her

business with Mrs. Pauwels by telephone, and the rest of it.

"My membership at the Staff Mess," I explained, "remains exactly the same under the Johnsons as it did before—guests included. They've been kind enough to extend these privileges to me and Mrs. Lincoln from the very beginning, and we've been using them right along.

"And, Jackie," I went on, "I asked Mrs. Pauwels there in the first place with *your* best interests in mind—not mine. I wanted to be handy to the phone for your sake . . ."

"Oh, yes, Mary," she interrupted, "but it's just that when I tried reaching Mrs. Pauwels at her office, some clerk there said that she'd just left in a Government car. Well, that's really what bothered me."

"You know that I'd never have made an arrangement like that if I thought it would cause any problems," I assured her.

I was particularly anxious to explain about the repainting of my office—to help dispel the idea that I was throwing my weight around.

"Jackie," I said, "I wasn't the one responsible for having my office painted, at all. It was arranged by Mr. Sasser, and he did it strictly for you—not *me*. When he first approached me on it, I made it clear that we'd be there temporarily and that it didn't matter one way or the other to me. But he felt something should be done to make it more presentable for you."

By the time we finished, we were both in much better spirits. Jackie seemed to understand more clearly how things stood, and I was greatly relieved to get the tormenting thoughts off my mind.

Now that things were back to normal, Jackie had a favor to ask. She wanted me to delay my vacation a bit further and stay on until October, when her move would be all completed. "Reserve the last two weeks in September."

I sighed. As usual, I left her with the promise that I'd be there just as long as she felt she needed me.

41 ✐ THE MANCHESTER STORY

I SEE BY MY DIARY THAT WILLIAM MAN-
chester came into my life in April, 1964. I didn't know that
his embroilment with Jackie would one day strike such sparks.

> April 2, 1964: Met William Manchester in the office this
> morning ... has been assigned the project of writing the
> book, covering the Dallas trip, by JBK and RFK ...
> Mrs. Lincoln introduced us—and, upon learning I was
> Mrs. K's Personal Secretary, Mr. Manchester frankly ad-
> mitted that he had never heard of me, adding: "I must
> say, you are the most well-kept secret of the whole Admin-
> istration!"

His reaction was understandable; two years earlier, he had
written his previous book about JFK, *Portrait of a President,*
without ever realizing that Jackie even had a personal secretary.

We sat together for the first time in my office at the
E.O.B., where we immediately began the first of our interviews for his projected work, *The Death of a President.*

This first session I found was the most difficult of all, as I
felt the shock effects of the four-month-old tragedy again.
But, as we talked, Bill Manchester's easy manner helped me
through the rough spots, making it possible to go on talking ... We continued for nearly two hours.

He listened attentively, but never once jotted down a written note. It was remarkable, I thought, that he should be
able to remember so much. Our succeeding interviews, about

a half-dozen over the next several months, proved less difficult for me emotionally and in a way offered some therapeutic relief when they were finally over.

I see an interesting item:

> May 2, 1964: Mr. Manchester accepted my invitation to visit with Ray and me at our home this Saturday evening, and we were honored to have him. He gave me a paperback edition of his book, *Portrait of a President*, with an inscription for which I was most grateful.

> "For Mary—
> Who has served the Kennedys—and therefore our country—
> so well.
> > With warmest regards—
> > Bill Manchester"

Just a month before Jackie decided to have Manchester interview me, she had been checking up on whether Evelyn and I were recording our memoirs of John Fitzgerald Kennedy for the Kennedy Library. We told her that we hadn't been able to get around to it, and she suggested once more that we ask Arthur Schlesinger about a tape recorder and how to proceed.

Evelyn and I soon, however, became most fascinated by Manchester and his project. He worked so diligently and conscientiously, one interview after another, that there were days when he had no time even for lunch.

We sympathized with him—he had such a big job ahead—and such great responsibilities in fulfilling his commitments to Jackie and Bobby.

Often, of course, we reminisced about "the Chief" as we knew him, with each other, especially at the White House Staff Mess. These brief periods offered the most relieving moments of every day. We would, in fact, hash and rehash the endless memories of JFK and his regime to the point of total absorption. Often, on returning to my desk at the E.O.B., I would find myself wondering what I had actually eaten for lunch.

Even as late as August, it was difficult to look ahead to the day when my ties with the Kennedys would be completely severed.

Deep inside, I continued to feel a strong desire to continue to serve in some way JFK's cause. One last hope was harbored in my mind for these next few days. In August, William Manchester had been summoned to move to Washington by Jackie and Bobby, and I thought that he might possibly be able to use me as his secretary in writing what he described as his "book on the President's assassination."

Ironically enough, the office at the Archives, which had been prepared and intended for my use there, was now to be used by Bill Manchester. It seemed that the arrangement might work out conveniently and advantageously, for both of us.

When he visited me on Wednesday morning, August 5th, I approached him with the idea. He appeared quite interested and said that he knew I could prove "invaluable" to him. But, he explained, the matter of finances was to be considered. His arrangement with the Kennedys was that he would be operating on an advance payment from his publisher and from his own personal savings. No secretarial allowances had been provided. On the strength of the Kennedy assignment, he had moved his whole family from Connecticut in order to be near the members of the Kennedy family, and now, the major figure, Jackie, was moving to New York. He left my office saying that he would like to think it over.

Considering the vast undertaking to which Mr. Manchester had committed himself, I thought his working arrangement a most stringent one. But Manchester said that in his first talk with the Attorney General, the remark was made: "We do not expect anyone to make a windfall out of the President's assassination."

When the break came between the Kennedys and him, I took it almost personally, so in sympathy was I with him. I couldn't see that he had done anything wrong. After his appearance on *Meet the Press*, when it seemed painful for him to talk of his troubles with the Kennedys, I sent him a telegram expressing my faith and confidence in him.

His Christmas card to me in 1966, showing his lovely family, reads, "Bless you for your letter, Mary—it made a desperate time less desperate. Bill Manchester."

I never thought I would be challenging points in Manchester's acclaimed account of the President's last days.

When the book came out, I found numerous mentions of me, but I took strong exception to some of the things he had written.

First, it was I who found Jackie's blood-stiffened glove on top of the Dallas newspaper, not Dr. Burkley.

Second, and quite important, I saw no division of JFK and LBJ people. I was certainly not angry at any time, as described by Manchester, using such words as "wrath," "blazing thoughts," "stiffened," "scowls," and "searing." Also, Evelyn Lincoln, Pam Turnure, and I did not decline something to eat from Marie Fehmer, Mrs. Johnson's secretary, because we were "angry" at her—we were just too numb to eat. Regarding the feelings of Kennedy men—and I consider this of utmost importance—Kenny O'Donnell did not cover his ears to shut out the sound of the swearing-in ceremony of President Johnson. I saw him when he did this, and it was *before* the ceremony. My story here is no different now than in my early interviews with Bill Manchester back in 1964.

I am happy now to know I have set the record straight in recalling my last moments with JFK—those moments at the window with the crowds roaring below, that broad smile on his face as I told him, "They've been waiting out in the rain for you since five o'clock this morning."

42 ⌐∽ FAREWELL TO A FIRST LADY

*T*HE MONTH OF AUGUST HAD SET IN. JACKIE was back from the Cape for a last race against the clock. Inventories . . . Packing . . . Notes . . . Memos . . . Lists . . . Messages . . . And even a moment for Jackie to drop something heavy into my hand. "Here, Mary, why don't you take this?"

It was a lovely gold case—about five inches by seven, but in the rush of those moments, I quickly thanked Jackie and put the case away to open up later.

When I did, I was amazed to see what the case held. Set into a cream-colored velvet backing, meant to stand up like a picture frame, was a solid gold medallion—about two and a half by three and a half inches—from the B'nai B'rith Anti-Defamation League. It had been presented to the President in 1962 for "Contributions to the enrichment of America's Democratic legacy."

On the face was a bas-relief of the Statue of Liberty, holding high her torch, and behind her, a multitude of faces turned toward it. Beside the torch were the words, "America's Democratic Legacy." On the reverse side was an engraved inscription.

Jackie had given me an official memento of the President's. Or perhaps at this time she wanted no more reminders of official ceremonials.

August 3, 1964: First visitor at the office this morning SS Agent Lynn Meredith, who has been with the children from the very beginning of the Kennedy Administration . . . Now

facing the weeks ahead as sadly and nostalgically as I ...
He left with a rather poignant remark: "Well, I've been
in the circle long enough to know that there will be many
an occasion when you will be missed by Mrs. Kennedy."

August 7, 1964: Today, a little Patrick Kennedy would have
been one year old. Mrs. Lincoln and I started the day by
visiting his gravesite at Arlington Cemetery, placing little
bouquets of flowers, and offering some prayers.

During the brief moments of this visit, I thought of Patrick's two-day struggle for life. It was incredible that a full
year had passed, and that the young father who had struggled
so desperately to save his infant son had followed him so soon.
Here, at Arlington Cemetery, they lay side by side. Patrick
had been transferred here several months before from his original resting place in Boston. On the President's other side lay
"Baby Girl" Kennedy, whom Jackie had lost in 1956.

Friday morning, August 14th, was Evelyn Lincoln's last day
at E.O.B. before her move to the Archives. I could already
sense the loneliness that the next few weeks would inevitably
bring without her. In mid-morning I received a telephone call
from Tom Walsh, who caught me completely off guard with
a question.

"Mary, dear, would you be interested in working for Ethel
Kennedy?" he asked. "Her secretary, Diane, is planning to
leave soon." Tom explained that the job was mine if I wanted
it, and waited for my answer.

My answer came quickly. "No, thank you, Tom," I said.
"I appreciate your asking, but I'm afraid I've given just about
all I possibly can to the Kennedys for now."

By now, a pool stenographer from Archives was helping
Manchester in my intended office there. And eventually I
learned that the girl who would take care of Jackie's dictation
in New York would be Helen Lempart, Kenny O'Donnell's
former secretary at the White House.

I felt sad that I would not be running an office for Jackie

in Washington. It had been very nice to share, in part, the Kennedy way of life.

With somewhat renewed spirit, I proceeded during the remaining weeks in August to close out the "Mary B. Gallagher—Special" account at the Riggs National Bank and transferred the bookkeeping records to the New York office. The voluminous files of Jackie's personal correspondence over the past years were locked up, and the keys turned over to Mr. Sasser of G.S.A., who was to arrange their shipment to the New York office.

I will never forget the day it finally happened. My diary records:

> Thursday, September 10, 1964: 4:00 P.M.—JBK called—in town just for day, packing, etc.—"so depressing"—wanted to say "Goodbye"—"Please remember all the happy days. Come up to N.Y., bring your boys up to the Fair, have them see Caroline & John. You and Mrs. Lincoln come up to a play now & then, look me up at the apt. Do keep in touch. "Sending gift to you—will have S.S. Agent bring it over."

She sounded nostalgic. And then the usual reminder that brought me back to the work-a-day world: "If I have any trouble finding things in the files, I'll call you."

Upon replacing the receiver, I suddenly felt the pangs of this final parting. I wished that Jackie could have given me her gift in person. Yet, I was grateful for her thoughtfulness in calling. This, perhaps, was the easiest, least heartbreaking way. I remembered again her words: "This is so sad; but we've had so many happy times together, I do hope you'll remember those and not the sad things."

At 10 A.M. on the 11th, it was Muggsy O'Leary who appeared at my front door to deliver Jackie's gift to me. And because the bearer was one of the Kennedy family's oldest and most trusted friends, I couldn't possibly have been more honored. I opened the box with the greatest care.

394 ৫৯

There, in a small, black velvet case, was a most exquisite round gold brooch with many turquoise chips. It was lovely, and so very precious for what it represented.

The accompanying message, on a white card edged in black, embossed with the Kennedy crest, read:

September 1964

For dear Mary—
  Please accept this with memories of so many happy days
  —and my deepest affection always

Jackie

During these first few weeks in October, I made some discoveries about happiness—would life *always* be as glorious as it was now? I had found that the greatest going-away present Jackie had given me was my family.

In October, too, I received a telephone call from the Social Office of the White House. Barbara Keehn, secretary to Bess Abell, Mrs. Johnson's social secretary was on the wire. "Mrs. Johnson would like very much for you and your husband to be present at the dedication of the Jacqueline Kennedy Rose Garden on Thursday, the twenty-second of October, at two o'clock."

The event had to be postponed. On Wednesday, the 21st, a telegram came from Bess Abell at the White House saying that the President and Mrs. Johnson would be attending the family funeral of former President Hoover that afternoon.

The dedication was then held April 22, 1965, and Ray and I went. The guests looked around hopefully for Mrs. Kennedy, but she never did appear. Mrs. Auchincloss was her stand-in.

I looked at the lovely garden and could have cried. The flowers were in bloom and truly beautiful in their pastel shades. Jackie would have loved them, and JFK himself would have been proud to know what had been done in his wife's honor. The ceremony was brief but impressive. And when it was concluded, the military aide placed me first in line to greet Mrs. Johnson, who was most gracious and charming.

Although I never had a formal picture of myself with Jackie, now one was taken with another First Lady. One of my proudest possessions is the lovely photograph of Mrs. Johnson, standing between me and my dear friend, Dr. Janet Travell.

In my mind, I was hearing the strains of the Chief's favorite song, "Won't you come home, Bill Bailey?" That happy song with its bright promises.

I thought of the Chief.

It was over. It was all over. Bill Bailey had finally gone home.

When I was a child, I never dreamed I would work at the White House, walk with Presidents, and be on a first-name basis with a First Lady of the United States. Jackie Kennedy was like a sister to me and neither time nor distance can erase the memories of the years we shared together. I wish her happiness and all good things. I cannot express how much she has enriched my life by letting me put one foot in Camelot.